ARGENTINE UNIONS, THE STATE,
& THE RISE OF PERON, 1930–1945

RESEARCH SERIES/NUMBER 76

ARGENTINE UNIONS, THE STATE & THE RISE OF PERON, 1930–1945

JOEL HOROWITZ

University of California, Berkeley

Library of Congress Cataloging-in-Publication Data

Horowitz, Joel, 1949–
  Argentine unions, the state & the rise of Perón, 1930–1945.
    p. cm. — (Research series, ISSN 0068-6093 ; no. 76)
    1. Trade-unions—Argentina—Political activity—History—20th century.
    2. Trade-unions—Argentina— History—20th century.
    3. Argentina—Politics and government—1910–1943.
    I. Title. II. Series: Research series (University of California, Berkeley. Institute of International Studies) ; no. 76.
    HD6603.5.H67   1990
    322'.2'098209043—dc20   89-78062
    ISBN 0-87725-176-2   CIP

To

CAROL, SARAH, and RACHEL

With love and gratitude

CONTENTS

List of Tables   viii
Acknowledgments   ix
List of Abbreviations   xi

INTRODUCTION   1

1. ARGENTINE POLITICS, 1930–1945   9
2. THE ECONOMY AND SOCIETY   26
3. CONDITIONS IN FIVE INDUSTRIES   36
4. THE LABOR MOVEMENT PRIOR TO 1930   56
5. THE DIFFICULT YEARS, 1930–1945   68
6. GROWTH AND FRUSTRATION, 1936–1943   96
7. UNION RELATIONS WITH THE GOVERNMENT, 1930–1943   125
8. DECISION-MAKING AND INTERNAL POLITICS, 1930–1943   151
9. PERON'S IMPACT ON THE UNIONS, 1943–1945   180

CONCLUSIONS   216

Notes   229

Index   275

LIST OF TABLES

1-1	PARTY COMPOSITION IN CHAMBER OF DEPUTIES, 1932 & 1934	17
2-1	INDICES OF EMPLOYMENT AND POPULATION IN BUENOS AIRES, 1929–45	30
2-2	INDEX OF REAL WAGES IN BUENOS AIRES, 1929–45	32
2-3	AVERAGE MONTHLY WAGES FOR BLUE-COLLAR WORKERS IN BUENOS AIRES, BY JOB CATEGORY AND INDUSTRY, 1938	33
3-1	TELEPHONES INSTALLED BY THE UT, 1926–45	37
3-2	MONTHLY SALARIES OF UT EMPLOYEES IN 1934	39
3-3	INDEX OF EMPLOYMENT IN COMMERCE, BANKING, OFFICES, AND INSURANCE IN BUENOS AIRES, 1929–45	41
3-4	CARGO AND PASSENGERS ON THE RAILROADS UNDER NATIONAL JURISDICTION, 1928/29–1945/46	47
3-5	MONTHLY SALARIES OF RAILROADERS IN 1941	49
3-6	INDEX OF EMPLOYMENT IN THE TEXTILE INDUSTRY IN BUENOS AIRES, 1929–45	51
3-7	GROWTH OF THE TEXTILE INDUSTRY, 1935–46	52
3-8	MINIMUM MONTHLY WAGES OF TEXTILE WORKERS IN BUENOS AIRES, 1935	54
5-1	STRIKES AND STRIKERS IN BUENOS AIRES, 1931–45	72
5-2	OUTCOME OF STRIKES IN BUENOS AIRES, 1930–45	73
6-1	UNION MEETINGS AND ATTENDANCE IN BUENOS AIRES, 1935–45	98
6-2	AVERAGE NUMBER OF MONTHLY DUES-PAYERS IN THE FOET, 1935–44	105
6-3	MONTHLY AVERAGE OF DUES-PAYERS IN THE UOEM, 1935–43	111
6-4	AVERAGE NUMBER OF MONTHLY DUES-PAYERS IN THE UF, 1935–44	116
6-5	STRIKES AND MONTHLY MEETINGS IN THE TEXTILE INDUSTRY IN BUENOS AIRES, 1935–45	119

ACKNOWLEDGMENTS

During the many years that it took to write this book, I have accumulated a vast number of personal debts. Many people have generously helped me, and I would like to publicly thank them. While they have assisted in improving this work, I alone of course bear the responsibility for the interpretations and any errors.

Juan Carlos Torre generously shared from his vast store of knowledge about Argentine unions and made several key introductions without which this work could never have assumed the shape that it did. The late Luis Gay and the late Jorge Michellón gave generously of their time to discuss their union activities with me and allowed me to read the voluminous union records they had collected. José Aricó kindly lent me two important sources. The staff of the Unión Ferroviaria made my examination of materials in the union library a pleasant experience—especially Orlando Marchini, with whom I spent hours discussing history. In the bleak years of 1975–76 Julia Amanda Vives and Enrique Daniel Zattara served ably as research assistants.

The writing of history is not all documents and interviews. Nora and Ricardo Tegni and Estela and Juan Carlos Korol shared their city of Buenos Aires with me and made research a pleasurable adventure. Ester Gónzalez and Leandro Gutiérrez kindly extended the hospitality of their home to my family and me.

In the United States Robert J. Alexander shared his vast collection of documents and interviews with one who was then an unknown graduate student. The late James F. King provided advice on the dissertation from which this book derives. Peter H. Smith and Paul Spickard read and offered sound suggestions on a later version. Bojana Ristich of the Institute of International Studies has been everything that one dreamed an editor should be and more. David Collier provided advice, counsel, and help of all types over most of the years of this project. Tulio Halperín Donghi inspired me to go into Argentine history, and his continued wisdom and helpfulness still inspires me.

The research was made possible by grants from the Doherty Foundation and the Center for Latin American Studies of the University of California, Berkeley, and I benefited from a Junior Research Fulbright under the Fulbright-Hays Act. I would also like to thank the Instituto Torcuato Di Tella, with which I was affiliated in 1975–76.

Finally, I would like to thank my family, to whom this book is dedicated. My debt to Rachel and Sarah is very large. They did not seem to mind the hours I spent with this book which should have been spent with them. My gratitude to Carol is immeasurable; not only did she offer sage advice and help in other ways, but also she believed it was worth doing.

J. H.

LIST OF ABBREVIATIONS

CA	Comisión Administrativa
CD	Comisión Directiva
CGEC	Confederación General de Empleados de Comercio
CGT	Confederación General del Trabajo
COA	Confederación Obrera Argentina
DNT	Departamento Nacional del Trabajo
FEC	Federación Empleados de Comercio
FOEF	Federación Obreros y Empleados Ferroviarios
FOEM	Federación de Obreros y Empleados Municipales
FOET	Federación Obreros y Empleados Telefónicos
FOF	Federación Obrera Ferrocarrilera
FOIT	Federación Obrera de la Industria Textil
FORA	Federación Obrera Regional Argentina
GOU	Grupo Obra de Unificación
ITT	International Telephone and Telegraph
UF	Unión Ferroviaria
UOEM	Unión Oberos y Empleados Municipales
UOT	Unión Obrera Textil
UOT(SP)	Unión Obrera Textil (Socialist textile union after May 1941)
USA	Unión Sindical Argentina
UT	Unión Telefónica (telephone company)

INTRODUCTION

With an apparent suddenness in October 1945, the Argentine working class appeared on the political stage and helped propel an army colonel, Juan Domingo Perón, to the presidency. The workers and their unions had become a major political force which subsequent governments ignored at their peril.

The unions and workers had been largely invisible during the Neo-Conservative era (1930–43), yet in 1945 they decisively influenced the nature of the political system. Moreover, they did not support a party of the left, but an army colonel. In this book we shall explore how unions adapted to the rapid changes resulting from the worldwide depression of the 1930s and how this adaptation led to support for Perón. The work will focus primarily on unions because these organizations mobilized and legitimized working-class support for Perón. One central theme will be the multifaceted and evolving relations between government and unions; another will be the union decision-making process and how it affected union actions. By focusing on these two areas of analysis, we shall be able to see why and when many unions began to support Perón. In addition, we shall be able to see whether this transformed the unions or whether they retained old characteristics and norms.

The Neo-Conservative era was a time of great flux. Argentina's experiment with democracy, from 1916 to 1930, was followed by governments controlled through fraudulent elections by rural-based economic elites. The depression battered the export-dominated economy, and the elite responded by an intensification of industrialization, markedly increasing the urban working class.

Unions did not react to the challenges and opportunities of the 1930s in a unified way. Some began to shift from craft-based organization to industrial unionism. Attempts were made to establish national confederations. Many unions turned frequently to the government as the only source of leverage against obstinate employers. The Neo-Conservative governments, while not the blindly anti-labor administrations pictured in much of the literature, remained largely indifferent to unions and only dimly aware of their growing power; however, they were politically weak and knew that aiding unions could at times be less costly than ignoring or repressing them. From the unions' perspective the government's responses were capricious and frequently unfriendly.

Many unions also attempted to redefine their relationship with political parties. The anti-party norms established by the Anarchists and Syndicalists had remained strong despite the declining influence of these ideologies, and unions had not become integral parts of the party system. During the Neo-Conservative era union ties to political parties increased, but these organizations could offer little assistance. The Socialist Party's strength was limited to the city of Buenos Aires,* and it rarely gave any power to labor leaders since it was run by a small coterie of middle-class professionals. By 1943 its relations with many labor leaders had frayed badly. While the Communist Party provided important organizational support, its aid to unions was limited by its illegality. Other political parties had little sustained interest in unions. By 1943 many labor leaders were seeking not only new relationships with political parties, but also a change in the political system.

While unions felt isolated from the political system, workers felt excluded from the society as a whole. The dominant mores were those of the middle and upper classes. Laborers carried their work clothes rather than wear them in the street. Photographs of the famous workers' demonstration of 17 October 1945 show that despite the heat most of the participants were wearing ties and jackets. In Argentine society, it was not acceptable to be a worker.[1]

Despite the unions' increasing size and strength, union inability to organize the rapidly expanding potential membership and the lack of integration into the society and political system resulted in an increasing sense of frustration. This led to fierce intra-union struggles that were only partially based on ideological differences and were sharpened by personal struggles for power and difficulties in achieving peaceful changes in leadership. By 1943 the unions seemed ready for a major change.

A military coup in June 1943 swept away the Neo-Conservatives, and opportunities for unions changed dramatically with the rise of Juan Perón in the new regime. Perón recognized the unions' political potential and tried to form an alliance. The government became truly interested in unions, though the forces of attraction were mixed with harsh repression. A few organizations immediately rejected any contact and faced the state's wrath; for others, relations with the regime evolved slowly, as the

*Buenos Aires refers both to a city and a province, and I shall specify throughout the text when referring to the latter.

government made a greater effort to attract support. Some unions did not make a final decision until mid-1945, when tensions in the country made neutrality impossible. Several organizations that had cooperated extensively with the government in 1944 opposed it in 1945.

History, personalities, ideologies, internal opposition, and pressure from the government and its opponents determined union responses to the blandishments of Perón. Also crucial was union desire to have their power recognized and be fully incorporated into the society.* To some, Perón represented an opportunity for fuller participation, while others considered that his regime would lead to government control of unions. In some senses it was the same labor movement as during the Neo-Conservative era, but it headed in directions that would have been unthinkable just a few years before. The new government had altered the unions' potential and activities.

For many years the dominant hypothesis about the rise of Perón, best presented by Gino Germani, was that the labor establishment of the 1930s was overwhelmed by tens of thousands of rural migrants who flocked into the cities between 1935 and 1945 and could not be integrated into the unions.[2] The migrants were seen as politically uncommitted and particularly susceptible to the demagogic appeals of Perón because of their naiveté and their prior experience with paternalism. Germani and earlier authors such as Robert J. Alexander and George I. Blanksten saw a sharp break in the trajectory of the union movement.[3]

In the past two decades the migration hypothesis has been discredited by a series of electoral studies done by (among others) Peter H. Smith, Eldon Kenworthy, and Walter Little. These authors have found it impossible to discern a substantial difference in behavior between urban-born workers and migrants.[4] While migrants supposedly scorned the Europeanized ideologies of traditional unions, the Communists had their greatest success in industries that contained large numbers of recent arrivals to the city.† It is no longer possible to say that the discontinuities are due to migrants.

*A great deal has been written about attempts to incorporate unions into political systems in Latin America, usually from the perspective of cooption by the ruling elites and corporatism. While Argentine unions may ultimately have succumbed to these forces, this is not what the Argentine labor leaders wanted. They wanted to become full participants in the society, and much of the initiative was theirs.

†The Communists were successful in industries such as meat-packing, textiles, and construction. Given existing sources, it is impossible to say where union members were born. I have found no indication that recent migrants behaved differently from other workers.

The new dominant thesis was posited by Miguel Murmis and Juan Carlos Portantiero in a brief and groundbreaking work. They stated that Peronism was an outgrowth of the changes in the society and the unions in the period prior to Perón's rise to power. They argued that Peronism did not create a major change in the union movement, and they make the rise of a Peronist-like labor movement seem almost inevitable. Works by other authors, such as Ricardo Gaudio–Jorge Pilone and Hiroschi Matsushita, have followed, enlarging aspects of the Murmis-Portantiero argument.[5]

While this more recent group of authors has clarified many issues, it does not necessarily follow that Peronism is not a major shift in orientation. Nor is it possible to believe that a Peronist-like labor movement was inevitable. While the labor movement appears to have been teetering on the brink of change by 1943, this does not mean that the direction it took was not surprising. With the exception of Perón, few people (if any) recognized the unions' potential power. Some union leaders wanted to establish labor as an independent political force. Others—a coalition of Communists, Radicals, and some Socialists—had seemed poised to become the dominant force in the labor movement and promised to introduce a very different form of politicization by tying the unions tightly to left-wing parties. The labor movement seemed about to follow the Western European model when the military shifted the realm of the possible.

This study is based on a detailed examination of five unions which in 1936 comprised 39 percent of all union members.[6] These are as follows: the Federación Obreros y Empleados Telefónicos (FOET), the Federación Empleados de Comercio (FEC), the Unión Obreros y Empleados Municipales (UOEM), the Unión Ferroviaria (UF), and the Unión Obrera Textil (UOT). The unions were chosen to include organizations from all major ideological tendencies and from different sectors of the economy. Unions were selected as the level of analysis because looking at the labor movement as a whole hides tremendous differences in approach and success. An examination of unions can show a much more complex and nuanced picture.

By studying individual organizations, I have not ignored the larger picture but rather illuminated it by constructing it out of pieces, much as the pointillist Georges Seurat created paintings out of points of color. In each chapter the unions are examined separately, and generalizations are made from the individual cases. I do not attempt to argue, as Charles Bergquist does in an intriguing study, that workers in one key industry can be used to explicate the fate of all unions in a country. Nor is this a micro study, such as Peter Winn's excellent examination of labor activities within a single company.[7] This work uses equally valid and important techniques. By breaking down the labor movement into its component parts—the unions—examining them, and then drawing conclusions about larger questions, I hope to clarify what more traditional approaches have obscured.

An analysis on the union level permits me to move beyond the recent works that have taken the examination of Peronist unions to a new level, such as those of Matsushita, Hugo del Campo, and David Tamarin. For example, a central element of Matsushita's discussion of labor support for Perón is the rise of nationalism in the late 1930s.[8] An examination of the five unions in my study indicates that as early as 1930 in the two industries with largely foreign employers, labor organizations were making blatantly nationalistic pitches to the government.

We shall see that unions operated in a specific context. Studied within their industry, union actions are more understandable. Despite a rather quick recovery from the world depression, some unions had to survive in sectors that had serious economic problems. Contrary to the assertions of Tamarin and Gaudio and Pilone, unions during the 1930s had very different experiences with the government.[9] Therefore, generalizations about relations with the government are deceiving unless qualified.

The union-level approach has permitted me to modify the accepted wisdom that has grown out of the work of Murmis and Portantiero. Almost all recent major contributions have agreed with their argument that a discontinuity in the labor movement did not occur with the rise of Perón.[10] In 1983 I argued similarly, basing my assessment on a continuity of union leadership and union desires for contact with the government and for the establishment of union-controlled social welfare programs.[11] However, after I examined unions in more depth over the entire 1930–45 period, it became clear that they made a sizable change in direction under the military regime of 1943–45. While they did not completely change, it was by no means the same labor movement. Unions abandoned many of the norms that had controlled their behavior during the past several decades. They became politicized and the focus of government attention. Their role changed and they lost much of their freedom. Earlier writers—Alexander, Alberto Belloni, and Samuel L. Baily, for example—who argue that a new labor movement was formed in that period, were more correct than more recent monographs have suggested.[12] In other words, 1943–45 becomes a major watershed in the labor history of Argentina.

As noted, one focus of the book is the multifaceted relationship between the unions and the government. The semi-authoritarian Neo-Conservatives lacked a coherent policy toward unions, proceeding on an ad hoc and case-by-case basis, with different parts of the state apparatus often working at cross-purposes. Because of the partially closed political system and the unions' lack of strength, government attitudes played a decisive role in determining union fates. An analysis of the variance in government attitudes (ignored by previous studies) enables us to understand some unions' ability to grow and others' failure to do so. By studying unions in this manner, we also learn a great deal about the Neo-Conservative governments and their responses to social problems—subjects that have been greatly neglected. Union attitudes toward the government and politics played a crucial role in their response to opportunities created when Perón began to change the balance between capital and labor.

We shall also look at decision-making, examining how union structures and leaders' personal attributes shaped responses to crisis. As indicated, in many cases internal union struggles that have been labeled ideological can be better explained by personal rivalry and the inability of dissidents to peacefully challenge dominant leaders. I am not aware of other studies in the historiography of Latin American labor that focus at this level. We shall examine how unions responded to a growing economy during a period of limited political participation. Their actions differed radically, and this difference was determined not only by political ideology, but also by union relationships with the government and employers, the state of their industry, and the strength of their leaders.

The period 1930–43 is of interest not only in its own right, but also because it sheds light on the dramatic changes between 1943 and 1945. Indeed these changes can be assessed only if one examines the earlier years. In particular, it was union frustration with past relations with the government and with existing political forces that gave Perón an opportunity to attract union support. By the early 1940s the unions, while much stronger than they had been in 1929, felt dissatisfied with their progress. In our analysis it will become clear what Perón did specifically to attract the support of union leaders and whether the tactics were new or amplifications of older practices. In addition, it will explain why some leaders opposed Perón while others supported him. It will establish—a matter of some debate—when unions began to give serious support to

Perón.¹³ Moreover, it will show that the initiative was not all Perón's; union leaders as well sought to rewrite the relationship with the government. An examination of individual unions' reactions to Perón and a reaggregation of the information makes it possible to draw out the nuances of the period 1943–45, demonstrating that Perón's rise brought a sharp change in union activity.

The five unions that form the heart of this book differed in ideology, in the type of workers they represented, and in their responses to the challenges of both the Neo-Conservative era and the military regime that took power in 1943. However, they were all based in Buenos Aires; provincial unions played only minor roles in the 1930s.

The FOET, a Syndicalist union, represented the telephone workers of Buenos Aires and its suburbs. While never large, it was one of the biggest Syndicalist unions during the 1930s, as well as among the most influential. In 1932 it won one of the most important strikes of the period, but despite this success it failed to grow during the 1930s. The FOET supported Perón in 1945.

The FEC and UOEM were Socialist-dominated. The FEC's affiliates were mostly retail clerks in Buenos Aires, but some employees from a myriad of other types of commercial establishments also joined. While its leaders' ideology resembled that of the UOEM, the FEC had a different trajectory. It mounted a series of spectacularly successful political campaigns, grew rapidly during the 1930s, and supported Perón in 1945. The FEC controlled the national confederation of similar organizations, the Confederación General de Empleados de Comercio (CGEC). The UOEM represented municipal employees of Buenos Aires.* A medium-sized union, it was influential and closely tied to the Socialist Party, but it had limited success in the 1930s, and its traditional leaders opposed Perón.

The UF, which strove to represent all railroad workers except firemen and engineers, was the largest and most powerful union. It dominated the largest labor confederation, the Confederación General del Trabajo (CGT); to an extent, its problems became those of the confederation. The nature of the railroad system made the UF a national organization, contrasting sharply with the vast majority of unions, which operated in limited areas. Earlier than almost all other unions, it developed close relations with the government and maintained them despite regime changes.

*Until the 1940s the UOEM went by the name of Unión Obreros Municipales. I have consistently used UOEM to avoid confusion with the acronym for the metallurgical union founded in 1943.

The UOT in 1930 was a small, Socialist-controlled textile union which had a Communist-dominated rival. The UOT grew rapidly, especially after its Communist counterpart dissolved and had its members enter the UOT. The Communists gained control of the UOT in 1938–39, and it became an important organization with tactics resembling those of other unions controlled by the Communist Party. Because of tensions largely created by World War II, the UOT fragmented into Communist and Socialist organizations in 1941.* Under the military regime after 1943, the Communist fragment was driven underground and failed to recover, while its Socialist competitor initially cooperated with the government and prospered, but it later moved into opposition and proved unable to compete with a government-sponsored union.

The book is divided into four parts. The first (Chapters 1–3) places the unions in context, examining politics, economics, and the living and working conditions of the workers. The second part (Chapters 4–6) is a chronological examination of the unions prior to June 1943. While the unions are discussed separately, a primary concern is to establish a new picture of the 1930–43 period by reaggregating the disparate information presented. The third part (Chapters 7–8) addresses the major motifs. Chapter 7 explores the unions' complex relations with the government during the Neo-Conservative era, indicating how the relationships helped lead to an attraction to Perón. Chapter 8 examines decision-making within the unions and the internal struggles that such a closed process helped engender. By examining the unions' internal dynamics, we can understand the personal and political dimensions of growing union dissatisfaction. The vital importance of leadership will also be shown. The final part (Chapter 9) sets out the unions' varied responses to the government's changing role from the military coup in June 1943 to the labor movement's emergence as a vital force in October 1945.

---

*The nomenclature in textiles is complex. The UOT went by the name Federación Obrera de la Industria Textil until 1934, but I have used the former name throughout because its Communist rival also used the name Federación Obrera de la Industria Textil, and I refer to it as such. Moreover, when the UOT divided into two parts, both retained the name. The Communist-controlled part has been labeled the UOT, while its Socialist-dominated counterpart has been called the UOT(SP).

Chapter 1

ARGENTINE POLITICS, 1930–1945

In all countries the state helps shape the society's unions, not only by setting boundaries, but also by creating the climate in which unions operate. This is particularly true in the so-called Latin nations, in which a tradition of a strongly interventionist state exists.[1] The evolution of Argentine unions between 1930 and 1945 is impossible to understand unless it is viewed in the context of the governments of that period. In part, union strategies reflected workers' understanding of the changes in their governments; in part, government strategies make sense only when it is understood how weak the regimes were.

THE NEO-CONSERVATIVE ERA

Neo-Conservatives dominated Argentine politics from 1930 to 1943. They were a largely land-based elite who assumed the right to rule because of their dominant economic and social positions. While heirs to an older political tradition, they cannot be accurately labeled Conservatives because they saw the state as playing a larger role than did their predecessors; nor were they necessarily members of the Conservative Party, but belonged to any of three parties that supported the regimes of this period. The Neo-Conservatives inherited the government after a coup in September 1930. However, they were decidedly a minority. Forced to govern with a façade of democracy, they turned to electoral fraud to remain in power. The governing elite was never completely free from the challenge of opposing parties nor from competing elements within its own group. To gain the acquiescence of the opposition to the political system, the Neo-Conservatives supplemented fraud and violence with concessions.

The party system of the 1930s emerged from a political crisis in 1890, when the regime of President Miguel Juárez Celman was challenged by a revolt. The rebels failed in their attempt to change political procedures, and Argentina remained in the hands of a conservative oligarchy which depended on electoral fraud and controlled elections. The popular voice was usually not heard.[2]

Participants in the revolt helped found three key parties: the Radical Party, the Progressive Democratic Party (Partido Demócrata Progresista), and the Socialist Party. The most important was the first, a direct descendent of the organization that initiated the revolt and the first popularly based, modern party in Argentina. Although the political system did not permit effective opposition, the Radical Party grew. The Radicals attempted revolts in 1891, 1893, and 1905 and refrained from participating in the political process, thereby escaping the taint of cooperating with a corrupt system. The Radicals' primary articulated goal was the establishment of fair elections. The party appealed mostly to the rapidly growing middle class, and at the same time it had strong working-class support. However, a significant portion of the leadership came from the oligarchy.[3] Behind the growth of the organization was Hipólito Yrigoyen, an unusual man to lead a mass-based party since his major contribution to it was the building of a strong party apparatus. He avoided making speeches and wrote few manifestoes, but he possessed a certain mystique and became extremely popular.[4]

The Progressive Democratic Party was the result of a quarrel on largely personal grounds between Yrigoyen and Lisandro de la Torre, a potential rival. It became mainly a vehicle for de la Torre, a moralistic and combative man, and it appealed to the upper middle class. It achieved its only major successes in the province of Santa Fe.[5]

The dominant figure among the Socialists during his lifetime, Juan B. Justo, participated in the events of 1890 but rapidly became disillusioned. In 1894 Justo and several disciples joined with foreign Socialist groups to create the Socialist Party. The Socialists resembled their moderate European counterparts, especially in Belgium and Spain. They were well organized, puritanical, and tightly controlled by a small group of leaders. While the party directed its propaganda largely at workers, a significant percentage of its members and most of its leaders came from the middle class. As the years passed, the party became more and more concerned with morality in government. The Socialists failed to build a base of support outside of Buenos Aires.[6]

Fair elections came to Argentina after some members of the ruling elite began to fear that the Radicals would oust them by force and they would lose everything. Believing that the Conservatives could organize effectively and win fair elections (as had conservative parties in Europe),

President Roque Sáenz Peña in 1912 pushed through a series of electoral reforms that made electoral fraud difficult.[7] The Conservatives' hopes were dashed by Yrigoyen's triumph in the presidential elections of 1916. However, the Radicals' victory did not bring fundamental changes to the society. Yrigoyen never challenged the economic power of the landed elite. Change came in politics as the Radicals expanded their influence, taking control of many provinces and constructing an elaborate system of political machines.[8]

Presidents could not succeed themselves but could serve more than one term. Thus Yrigoyen picked as his successor Marcelo T. de Alvear, scion of an aristocratic family and loyal Radical; Yrigoyen believed that Alvear would remain faithful to him. As happens in such cases, after winning the election, Alvear began asserting his independence, and a split developed between those loyal to the president and those faithful to the old boss of the party. The opponents of Yrigoyen became known as the Anti-Personalist Radicals. They tended to be from the more conservative and aristocratic wing of the party. While obviously sympathetic to his followers, Alvear never used the full power of the presidency to back them.[9]

Despite the split in the party, Yrigoyen had lost none of his popularity. In 1928 he won a second term by an overwhelming majority, receiving 57.4 percent of the popular vote. However, the honeymoon did not last long. Yrigoyen was not the same person he had been during his previous term. Charges circulated that he was senile.[10]

Yrigoyen's apparent inability to handle the duties of office may have been owing to the seriousness of the crises that arose. Rumors of a coup began directly after the election. The traditional elite felt uneasy with the new government, which had a decided middle class–professional politician air to it.[11] More important, some political elites felt threatened by the government's use of its power of intervention to take over provinces in order to pave the way for further Radical victories.* For the first time, the Radicals were on the verge of achieving a majority in the Senate. The Klan Radical, a strong-armed group, further poisoned the atmosphere, especially by the murder of Carlos Wáshington

---

*In Argentina intervention means the replacement of elected officials with those selected by the executive branch because of the former's purported wrongdoing or inability to maintain peace and stability. When congress is in session, it must pass a resolution authorizing such action, but when it is not, an intervention can be carried out solely by the executive branch. Frequently interventions were for purely political reasons. They were also carried out against unions, which meant that the state took over the running of the organization.

Lencinas, the political boss of the province of Mendoza. An attempt to nationalize the oil industry also aroused anger and anxiety.[12]

The opposition counterattacked vigorously. The anti-Yrigoyenistas were led by the Independent Socialists, a group that had left the Socialist Party in 1927 because of a series of personal quarrels, as well as a desire to break away from the small, dominant leadership group that wanted to impose its moralistic view of society and retain its influence. The young politicians who led the schism were anxious for power and willing to compromise with the political system.[13] All the opposition parties joined the attacks on Yrigoyen, but the Radicals might have retained the presidency if the depression had not struck with such force.

The agricultural depression of 1929 had ruinous consequences for Argentina because the rapid collapse of the export/import sector was a political as well as an economic blow. Government revenues fell. The Radical Party had based its political machine on a distribution of patronage. An increasingly large portion of the middle class and elite of the working class lived on the bounty of the government. This could not continue, and even the payment of salaries was now often delayed.[14]

In the congressional elections of March 1930 the Radicals did not do nearly as well as they had in 1928—especially in politically essential Buenos Aires, where they fell from 55 to only 28 percent of the votes, placing second behind the Independent Socialists and receiving only two hundred votes more than the Socialists. A coup seemed inevitable. Agitation increased; university students organized against the government. There were street demonstrations. The government became paralyzed by intraparty rivalries; everyone wanted to succeed Yrigoyen.[15]

On 6 September 1930 a very small number of cadets from the military academy marched into the capital. This soon turned into a triumphal procession, cheered by the massed populace. There was no serious resistance.[16] The government was thrown out with hardly a protest. A steady accumulation of problems had destroyed the regime's popularity.

The army was divided into two major factions. One was headed by General José F. Uriburu, the leader of the coup. This group, which had support from ultra-right-wing organizations, wanted to profoundly change the political system to make it resemble the corporatist structure of Fascist Italy. The other, more moderate faction looked to General Agustín P. Justo and had the backing of the traditional parties that had supported the coup—the Independent Socialists, the Anti-Personalist Radicals, and most of the Conservatives. Their major goal was the removal of Yrigoyen and the return to what they thought was normality. This group felt that the Radicals had lost popularity during Yrigoyen's second presidency and that the removal of the Radicals from the government would permit more "responsible" parties to elect their supporters.

While initially neither faction could impose its ideas, the Uriburu group had the upper hand because its leader became president. However, the moderates had forced Uriburu to make a major concession in return for supporting the use of military force. They received promises that the constitution would not be summarily altered. This meant that basic institutional change could not be made by decree but would have to follow some type of electoral process.[17]

The minimal commitment to the constitution did not spare the country from severe repression—nine months under both martial law and a state of siege and then eight months under just the latter. The new government acted against those it viewed as a threat—especially Anarchists and Communists—with a harshness that surpassed anything Argentina had yet seen. Foreigners with threatening beliefs were deported. *La Vanguardia*, the Socialist newspaper, counted 158 deportations between 11 October 1930 and 1 February 1932. One hundred and fifty more were deported nine days later.[18] Activists of many types were held on prison ships, jailed, or transported to Tierra del Fuego. Torture was used liberally, and at least five people were executed. The Uriburu regime shut down Anarchist and Communist presses and made it difficult, if not impossible, for unions connected with those ideologies to exist. For the first time the government tried seriously to control the way people thought and acted, creating the infamous Special Section of the police to eliminate communism from the nation. Even the traditional parties, especially the Radicals and Socialists, were harassed.[19]

The government had a sense of bravado about it, which made its deservedly harsh reputation even worse. The CGT had to publicly humiliate itself to prevent the execution of three Anarchists. A good example of the government's bluster is the information given to the U.S. Embassy in October 1930:

> The escape in Montevideo of deported men from ships on which they were being sent to Europe has been reported by the American Legation in that city. The outcome of this method of evading the Argentine Government's intentions does not alarm the local officials who have said privately that a return to Argentina from Uruguay of any of those deportees would result in a trip across another river from which there would be no return.[20]

Repression and the growing impact of the depression restored luster to the Radicals. This became important when Uriburu launched a plan to amend the constitution after a series of elections. The first electoral test was in the province of Buenos Aires, where the Radicals, strengthened by the return of many Anti-Personalists—including Alvear himself—quashed the entire plan by winning a plurality in the election for governor.[21] It had become obvious that the Radicals were still the largest party. The cabinet resigned and the election was annulled. Uriburu had lost prestige and was ill, and it became necessary to call presidential elections.

The obvious government candidate was General Justo. Identified with the Anti-Personalist Radicals, Justo had been Alvear's minister of war and had extensive support in the army. He also possessed a talent for political maneuvering. He had as well the backing of the parties that had supported the coup and wanted to eliminate the Radicals but still desired a relatively open political system.

Justo's election faced one major obstacle: the Radicals were the most popular party. Conveniently, a pro-Radical revolt by Colonel Gregorio Pomar in July 1931 provided an excuse for the government to crack down. The regime prohibited the participation in the elections of anyone who had served in Yrigoyen's government or was accused of taking part in the revolt. Alvear was not allowed to be a candidate, and the Radicals were reduced to their traditional means of combatting electoral fraud, abstention.[22]

Two alliances participated in the November 1931 presidential election: the Concordancia and the Civil Alliance. Justo was supported by the Concordancia, composed of the Independent Socialists, the Anti-Personalist Radicals who had not joined Alvear in returning to the Radical Party, and the Conservatives, newly united in the Partido Demócrata Nacional. The Conservatives had not had a national organization since the early years of the century and had remained a collection of provincial parties. Although the senior partners in this coalition, they never worked out a coherent party structure. The Anti-Personalists' identification with Radical traditions enabled them to create an element of ambiguity in the relationship between the Concordancia and the Radicals, giving the coalition a wider acceptability. The Independent Socialists had a base in Buenos Aires and had brought several talented individuals into the alliance. However, the party had reached its apogee in 1930, when it had been the chief opponent of Yrigoyen, and it declined swiftly thereafter because of its identification with unpopular regimes that opposed the type of measures which the party supposedly supported.[23]

The Civil Alliance was composed of the acceptable opposition, the Socialists and the Progressive Democrats. The former had opposed both the 1930 coup and Yrigoyen. While the latter had initially supported the overthrow, they had withdrawn their approval because of the government's tactics. The Civil Alliance had little chance of winning; it possessed no substantial organization outside of the home bases of its two parties, Buenos Aires and Santa Fe province. The parties entered the election to spread their philosophies and to profit from the abstention of the Radicals by winning congressional seats.[24] Under the Argentine electoral system, the victors in a district received two thirds of the seats, and those who placed second received one third. Even the loser was rewarded.

The government had no intention of losing, and the Civil Alliance carried only its two home districts. The campaign had been conducted under a state of siege; considerable evidence of election fraud exists.[25] Fraud was public. Government supporters seized polling stations, preventing the opposition from voting. Violence often ensued since opposition militants insisted on their rights. However, the Concordancia's victory was due more to the absence of the Radicals than to electoral manipulation.

Despite its later reputation of depending totally on fraud, the Concordancia tried to recruit voters, especially prior to the end of abstention by the Radicals in 1935. It made appeals to special constituencies. For example, in the 1931 congressional elections the Conservatives wooed the large number of railroad workers in the province of Buenos Aires by placing on their list two important members of the UF.[26]

While fraud was a common means of winning elections, it was sometimes not used. The city of Buenos Aires always had free elections, which the Socialists or Radicals won. In the interior, as long as the basic balance of power remained unchanged, opposition parties were allowed to win some elections. In 1935 a Radical, Amadeo Sabattini, captured the governorship of the important province of Córdoba.

The major problem that Justo faced upon taking office was how to run a country with the appearance of democracy when everyone knew that the government did not represent the majority of the voters. Complicating the situation was the attitude of the military. Since the government was civilian, the military wanted to limit its activities to protecting the government from violent overthrow. The officers who had engineered the 1930 coup feared retribution.[27]

The coalition that had carried out the 1930 coup and which at least nominally backed the new government made Justo's job even more difficult. The corporatists, the followers of Uriburu, and the members of armed right-wing groups saw any move toward normal politics as a threat. The leading authority on the Argentine army, Robert A. Potash, has written as follows: "Many of the former associates of the late Provisional President [Uriburu] perpetuated a state of incipient conspiracy."[28]

The challenge from the far right appears to have been strongest in June 1932. The conjunction of demonstrations by armed right-wing nationalists with discontent about government policies among elements in the army created a crisis. The threat dissipated after a demonstration in support of the existing system by parties of the center and left. It appears that Justo used the threat from the right to present himself as the lesser of two evils. The Socialists, the Progressive Democrats, and even the Radicals preferred Justo's firm hand to the mailed fist of the far right.[29]*

Since the parties that composed the Concordancia had different ideas and constituencies, Justo could not always depend on them to vote as a block. Peter Smith, who has analyzed voting in congress, has pointed out that prior to the return of the Radicals the pattern of party voting was unstable. The Independent Socialists had been Socialists; while they had become more conservative, they retained some of the social consciousness of the parent party. The Partido Demócrata Nacional appealed to elites and rural interests.[30]

The Concordancia held a narrow margin in the Chamber of Deputies between 1932 and 1935 (see Table 1-1). The narrow margin plus the lack of unity led to concessions to the opposition. Cooperation between the Socialists and the Conservatives was not new; they had cooperated in the 1920s to oppose the Radicals. On noncontroversial matters which had public support and for which the Socialists sought legislation, the Concordancia helped the Socialists pass relevant laws.[31] The unstated but assumed quid pro quo was that the opposition would not disrupt the legislative process. The vital role of the Socialists gave the unions connected to the Socialist Party a decided edge because the government would at times aid them in order to shore up its left flank.

With the backing of the armed services and Justo's considerable political ability, the government overcame many of its problems. A contributing factor was that upon Justo's assuming office, the tight grip in which Uriburu had held the country loosened; many kinds of freedom returned and tensions lessened.[32]†

---

*The Radicals attempted a number of revolts before they returned to the electoral process.

†Some restrictions were later restored.

Table 1-1

Party Composition in the Chamber of Deputies, 1932 and 1934

Party	1932		1934	
	Number of Deputies	Percent	Number of Deputies	Percent
Conservatives	56	35.4%	60	38.0%
Anti-Personalist Radicals	17	10.8	16	10.1
Independent Socialists	11	7.0	6	3.8
Total Concordancia	84	53.2	82	51.9
Socialists	43	27.2	43	27.2
Progressive Democrats	14	8.9	12	7.6
Others	16	10.1	18	11.4
Subtotal	73	46.2	73	46.2
Not incorporated or vacant	1	0.6	3	1.9
Number of seats	158	100	158	100

Source: Cámara de Diputados, División Archivo, Publicación y Museo, *Composición de la Cámara de Diputados de la Nación: Por partidos políticos y distritos electorales* (Buenos Aires, 1956), 30, 32.

The government was in numerous ways anachronistic. The landed aristocracy regained the political power it had partially lost to the Radicals after 1916. In 1936 eight of the twelve members of Justo's cabinet belonged to the exclusive club Círculo de Armas. Ironically the landed elite had regained political power as the depression forced the government to favor industrialization. Favoring industrialization tended to shift economic power away from traditional elites and toward industrialists. While the Neo-Conservative elite was chipping away at the basis of its own power, it did not abandon self-interest. It sacrificed other sectors of the economy to reserve a portion of the British market for its prize export, chilled beef.[33] Industrialization and public works projects helped fuel a recovery from the depression but did not bring political stability. The Radicals' return to political participation in 1935 made the situation more complex, despite their acceptance of the existing system.[34] If election procedures had remained unchanged, the Concordancia would have been rapidly reduced to a minority, but the Neo-Conservatives intensified the use of electoral fraud.

The increased use of fraud made compromise with the opposition less possible. Moreover, the Radicals immediately became the second largest and then the largest single party in congress. The Concordancia responded by increasing the power of the presidency while reducing the legislature's. In 1937 congress passed only three bills, two of which permitted Justo to go on vacation.[35]

The choice of Justo's successor was therefore vital. Justo wanted an Anti-Personalist Radical as that group was the least unpopular of the Neo-Conservative parties. Because Justo could not succeed himself and hoped to be reelected in six years, he wanted a candidate who was neither too unpalatable nor too strong. He chose his minister of the treasury, Roberto M. Ortiz. Ortiz had been Alvear's minister of public works but (unlike his former boss) had not rejoined the Radical Party. Ortiz had close ties to the large foreign-owned utilities. For many years he had been the legal advisor of a major railroad company, the Ferrocarril Oeste, and had also served as a director of the Unión Telefónica (UT), Argentina's largest telephone company.[36]

To no one's surprise, Ortiz and his running mate, Conservative Ramón S. Castillo, who had been placed on the ticket to ensure support from particular elements of the coalition, scored an easy victory in the 1937 election. Fraud determined the outcome. Federico Pinedo, a former minister of Justo's, noted the following: "The way those elections were conducted . . . makes it impossible to include them among the best or even the average elections the country has experienced."[37] Nonetheless, Ortiz soon emerged as the champion of free elections. He saw his role as similar to that of Roque Sáenz Peña, who had come to the presidency determined to establish fair elections.

During his first year as president Ortiz moved slowly, talking about electoral freedom but doing little. He consolidated his position with the army. In May 1939 he made his first move against voter fraud, intervening in the province of San Juan. He followed with interventions in Catamarca, Castillo's home province, and in the province of Buenos Aires. Virtually fraud-free congressional elections were held in March 1940, and the Radicals did very well.[38]

The intervention in Buenos Aires province was particularly important. Domination of the province was essential for continued Neo-Conservative control of the executive branch. The intervention also effectively ended the career of the province's outgoing governor, Manuel Fresco. An ultra–right-wing nationalist, Fresco had tried to create a conservative populism which in a number of ways foreshadowed the efforts of Perón. Fresco attempted to improve working-class conditions while simultaneously limiting worker autonomy. He backed the establishment of collective contracts for wide sectors of industry, a move which improved the position of the workers, reduced the number of strikes, and favored larger firms that could no longer be undercut by smaller companies paying lower wages. Without much success, he tried to force all unions to register with the province.[39]

It appeared that for the first time since 1931 elections would have meaning, but this was not to be. Ortiz's plans were doomed by his severe diabetes, which affected his vision. Unable to perform his job, he turned over his duties to Castillo in July 1940.[40]

Even if Ortiz had been able to continue, he would have faced serious obstacles. As he had undercut the very system and parties that had selected him, he needed to mobilize support. The Radicals, who would have been the main beneficiaries of the change in policies, and the Socialists welcomed the return to electoral freedom. However, these parties had been severely weakened and could offer little aid. The moral decay and voter fraud so prevalent in the society had penetrated even the opposition. Radicals had participated in major financial scandals. Electoral fraud, which they decried in the outside world, appeared within the party. Alvear, the party's titular leader, could not hold together the competing elements within the organization.[41] Similar problems weakened the Socialists. Possible electoral fraud provoked the left wing and many of the promising younger members to leave the party and form the Partido Socialista Obrero in 1936. Ortiz's attempt to gain labor support by backing a schism in the UF failed completely.[42]

Castillo's assumption of power marked a return to the system as it had been under Justo, but with a more conservative twist. The change occurred slowly as Castillo was acting president, and only those extremely close to Ortiz realized that he had little chance of returning to the presidency. Castillo did not immediately get his own cabinet, and jockeying for power created tremendous uneasiness.

Castillo's position was weakened by his being a Conservative and by intensifying opposition from the Radicals, whom he had no intention of allowing to come to power. Even worse was Argentina's passionate and divided reaction to World War II. The Socialists and important elements in the Radical Party and the Concordancia strongly supported the Allies since ideology meshed with traditional amity toward Britain and France. Neutrality also had supporters. Those favoring it can be divided into two groups: one favored pure neutrality, while the other proclaimed neutrality yet backed the Axis. The latter had considerable strength. While Fascist organizations never had much success in Argentina, some people admired the "achievements" of the Axis, both militarily and in bringing order to disorganized economies. More important, growing nationalism and a resentment of British economic dominance led to support for Britain's enemies. Castillo shifted the balance on this issue. Ortiz had supported neutrality but favored the Allies; the acting president leaned the other way. The differing views split the Concordancia because the nationalists backed the Axis and a form of neutrality while other elements, including those around Ortiz and Justo, supported the Allies.[43]

All contenders sought support among the military. With the threat of a coup always present, in mid-1940 a three-way struggle for control of the government broke out. The ostensible cause was a scandal revolving around the sale of land for use as an air base, but the real cause was an attempt to eliminate Ortiz's power. Ortiz was defended principally by Radicals and Anti-Personalist Radicals, as well as Socialists, organized labor, and Communists. Conservatives, pro-Axis sympathizers, and nationalists favored Castillo. The third force was General Justo, who, while pro-Allied, saw the Ortiz policy of fair elections as a threat to his return to the presidency. By offering his resignation, Ortiz provoked massive demonstrations, and a joint session of congress rejected his stepping down with only one vote in favor.[44] The victory was hollow. At the end of August 1940 Ortiz's cabinet resigned, ending any hope of fair elections. The new pro-Allied cabinet was a concession to Justo, but it did not represent the views of Castillo, who began to consolidate his power in order to follow policies more to his liking.[45]

Election fraud returned. In retaliation the Radicals, who were just a few seats short of a majority in the lower house, prevented the passage of any legislation, even necessary measures such as the budget. The deadlock forced the resignation of the pro-Justo cabinet and permitted Castillo to appoint his own men.[46]

Castillo began to place limits on political activity. In addition, on the grounds that "it has lost the public confidence," he dissolved the city council of Buenos Aires in October 1941, thereby squelching a center of opposition controlled by Socialists and Radicals.[47] The attack on Pearl Harbor provided an opportunity to impose a state of siege and use it against Castillo's opponents, most of whom were, ironically, pro-Allied. The Communists were a favorite target. Despite the authoritarian measures, Castillo did not stand on firm ground. Until Ortiz's almost deathbed resignation on 24 June 1942, Castillo was only acting president. Moreover, since the Concordancia had splintered over the war, all political groups looked to the army to extract Argentina from the quagmire, and coups from various points of view were plotted.[48]

The United States's entry into World War II placed additional stresses on the political system. Backed by many forces in Argentina, the United States demanded that Argentina give unconditional support to the Allies. The nationalists, including Castillo, opposed the demand, and they were joined by a large sector of the army. Many officers sympathized with the Axis, influenced both by the same factors that swayed many civilians and by the German role in training the army. Both sides vociferously pushed their positions and generated political pressure through street demonstrations.[49]

Death itself intervened. Alvear died, leaving an already splintered party leaderless. More important, in January 1943 Justo passed away. He had never given up hope of being reelected, and his death left a large number of officers without firm commitments, thereby freeing them to participate in a coup.[50]

Castillo's regime finally unraveled because he chose the Conservative sugar magnate Robustiano Patrón Costas as his successor. It was known that Patrón Costas would move Argentina from neutrality to a policy favoring the Allies. He was widely disliked for his role in an industry in which the brutal exploitation of workers was common knowledge. The Conservatives lacked popular appeal, but even within the party Patrón Costas had problems. He had been a key member; he had secured the vice-presidency for Castillo. Still Castillo had to force the resignation of the governor of Buenos Aires province before he could impose Patrón Costas on a reluctant party.[51] Meanwhile, the army did not want to help elect a candidate who was unpopular and was going to align the country with the Allies.

The coup, which had become almost inevitable, occurred after some Radicals, looking for a presidential candidate against whom fraud could not be used, approached the minister of war, General Pedro Ramírez. When Castillo tried to remove Ramírez, the coup began. On 4 June 1943 the military took over the government, and the Neo-Conservative era ended.

In sum, between 1932 and 1943 politics had a façade of democracy but was controlled by fraud, corruption, and limited repression. Traditional accounts have assumed that the Neo-Conservatives survived only by means of repression and voter fraud, but they were also forced to compromise and grant concessions. They were like jugglers with many balls in the air—safe as long as they could keep everything going at the same time.

The Neo-Conservative governments were very different from one another. Justo eased the repression that had been so important under

Uriburu. Prior to the return of the Radicals to the political system in 1935, the Justo regime was marked by a desire for compromise, especially with the Socialists. Ortiz tried to restore democracy, while Castillo moved to limit political participation. Unions had more opportunities under Justo and Ortiz than under Uriburu and Castillo. Under all four regimes unions benefited from government weakness.

THE MILITARY GOVERNMENT

The June 1943 coup had no clear purpose other than Castillo's removal. Its participants lacked a uniform view on the problems that confronted Argentina. After a few days of confusion, Ramírez emerged as president, but with a cabinet that was deeply divided over World War II. Political factions that had been disenchanted with the Castillo government, with the partial exception of the Communist Party, greeted the new regime warmly because they saw the military as the only hope for destroying the old system. They hoped that the military would carry out its pledges to eliminate corruption and restore true democracy.[52]

Communists and those close to them were jailed and harassed after the coup; the government's policies seemed at first to be just an intensification of what had occurred under Castillo. However, in a cabinet shakeup in October 1943 Ramírez ousted those who favored a quick return to civilian rule, as well as those who were pro-Allied. The government took on a decidedly ultra-right-wing, nationalist cast. The virulently anti-Semitic novelist Gustavo Martínez Zuviría (who wrote under the name Hugo Wast) was named minister of justice and public instruction. Repression escalated exponentially. The jails were filled from the full spectrum of opposition groups. Communist unions and organizations were driven underground. Political parties were abolished. Severe restrictions were placed on the press; rather than accept them, the Socialist Party closed *La Vanguardia*.[53]

Ramírez lacked a strong personality, and a military lodge, the GOU (Grupo Obra de Unificación), quickly emerged as an important force in the government. Led by a group of colonels, the GOU was formed with the idea of protecting the position of the army, preserving the country from communism, and retaining Argentina's neutrality during World War II.[54] One member, Juan Perón, rapidly outdistanced rivals both within and outside the organization. Perón's initial post in the government, a high position in the ministry of war, allowed him to influence appointments, but his ascendancy was due more to his political astuteness and his influence among his fellow officers than to any official position. He alone among major figures grasped the political potential of the urban working class.[55]*

In late October 1943 Perón had himself appointed to the hitherto unimportant post of president of the Departamento Nacional del Trabajo (DNT). The agency oversaw labor relations only in Buenos Aires and the lesser populated regions controlled directly by the national government; it had no power in the provinces. It lacked the authority to make reluctant employers negotiate or to enforce contracts or labor laws. A month after his appointment, the DNT, at Perón's behest, was transformed into the Secretaría de Trabajo y Previsión, with national scope and increased authority. Through the Secretaría Perón slowly built support among unions and workers. Parallel to Perón's rise was that of his ally, General Edelmiro Farrell, who added the vice presidency to his position as minister of war.[56]

The war remained a major issue, and the United States pressured the government to declare war on the Axis. Unable to procure arms from the Allies, the Ramírez regime unrealistically tried to obtain them from the Germans. The attempt was discovered. This plus alleged Argentine participation in a coup in Bolivia led to intensified Allied pressure for Argentina to break off relations with the Axis governments. When it did, there were two major consequences. The GOU dissolved (probably to avoid breaking its oath to support the president) and, on 24 February 1944, Ramírez was forced to resign from the presidency.[57]

Farrell, as vice president, assumed the top office, while Perón inherited the ministry of war; in July he also became vice president. Perón had bested most of his rivals for power within the army—at least temporarily—but he was too good a politician to be satisfied with support from the military.[58] Perón seems to have felt that power would have to be legitimized through elections. He tried making approaches to the Radicals but with little success. Particularly in the second half of 1944 and in 1945 Perón threw the government's weight behind the unions in their struggles with employers. In addition, he tried to foster accords

---

*For this work Perón's beliefs are less important than what he did, and no attempt will be made to elucidate them. Perón was influenced by the right-wing thought of Italy, France, and Spain. He was anti-Communist. He was a superb politician who wanted power, and this motivated him more than anything else. While he recognized the value of working-class support, the alliance he headed was shaped by necessity.

with employers who were pleased with the government's support for industrialization. Only in late 1944, when working-class conditions began to improve substantially, did the managerial class break with the government.[59]

A growing opposition movement formed, much of it clandestine or based in Montevideo, with support from all of the traditional parties. Despite the unabated repression, the continued progress of the Allied armies in Europe provided hope because it seemed necessarily to doom Argentina's military regime. Much of the opposition considered the regime and the Nazis one and the same and felt their fates were intertwined. Hundreds of thousands of citizens of Buenos Aires celebrated the liberation of Paris in August 1944.[60]

The United States maintained its pressure on the government, and many in the regime, especially Perón, began to realize how isolated Argentina would be after the Allied victory. Slowly the government lifted restrictions on the press and the universities. In March 1945 Argentina declared war on Germany and Japan. The opposition began to organize openly, and even the Communist Party emerged from its clandestine existence.* It seemed that public opinion had shifted away from the government to its opponents. Despite vigorous efforts the regime could win over only a few Radical leaders of the second rank by giving them cabinet posts.[61]

In June 1945 leading business and agricultural organizations issued manifestoes strongly attacking the government's positions. The universities became scenes of constant agitation against the regime. The opposition used the streets for repeated demonstrations, and the government's supporters hardly answered. The regime seemed doomed despite promises of a speedy return to constitutional rule.[62]

Events took an unexpected turn in early October 1945. Many military officers had long resented Perón's prominence and his flouting of social conventions by living openly with a woman to whom he was not married, Eva Duarte. Many also strongly disliked his support of unions. When Perón obtained an important post, the director of mail and telecommunications, for a friend of Eva Duarte's, it was the proverbial straw that broke the camel's back. On 9 October officers of the powerful army base Campo de Mayo forced Perón to resign all his posts. He was subsequently arrested.

No unity of purpose existed. The seeming inheritor of Perón's power, General Eduardo Avalos, hesitated in establishing a new cabinet

---

*The Communists' official journal, *Orientación*, reappeared on 14 August 1945.

and in removing Perón's friends from vital positions. The civilian opposition demanded that the military immediately return to the barracks and give all power to the supreme court.The military found the idea unpalatable, as did labor leaders who saw the supreme court as a bastion of reaction that would undo the social reforms of the past two years.

Into this political vacuum erupted a force that had remained largely quiet while the opposition had ruled the streets—the workers and their unions. Starting on 15 October workers began demonstrating for Perón, not only in greater Buenos Aires, but in the interior as well. Perón had become the living symbol of working-class gains of the last two years. Urged on by elements of the labor movement, the demonstrations reached massive proportions on 17 October, when workers poured into Buenos Aires and peacefully occupied the downtown area, demanding Perón's return. The army, faced with the prospect of massive violence, freed Perón. While he reclaimed none of his offices, the way was clear for him to run for president.[63]

Backed by the Partido Laborista (formed by labor leaders) and splinter groups of Radicals and Conservatives, as well as the church, Perón won a solid victory over a united opposition in fair presidential elections in February 1946. The popularity of the opposition had to some extent been an illusion. The working class, as always, had been largely invisible.

Perón's policy of improving the conditions of the workers through unions tapped a force that had been marginalized by previous political systems. The workers' emergence on center stage allowed Perón to become a pivotal political actor and remain one. In the following chapters we shall analyze why unions played a vital role.

Chapter 2

THE ECONOMY AND SOCIETY

The economy and working conditions helped determine union activity. When faced with severe unemployment, unions could do little except fight to retain existing conditions. When the job market tightened, labor agitation increased, as did the chance of success. Between 1930 and 1945 the size and composition of the work force altered, making the rise of Perón possible. Perón's appeal to the workers is more comprehensible if their conditions before the coup in June 1943 are understood.

THE ECONOMY AND CLASS STRUCTURE

The worldwide depression of 1929 shattered the economic system that had made Argentina the wealthiest country in Latin America and a prosperous nation by any standard. The export of the goods of the fertile pampas no longer could ensure abundance. The depression brought despair and poverty, but it also fostered a quickening of industrialization.

In the 1920s the Argentine economy was outwardly oriented. It was the world's largest exporter of maize, linseed, and meat, and the third largest of wheat. Exports composed nearly 30 percent of gross domestic product (GDP).[1] The wealth produced by the rural sector permitted the existence of a complex and sophisticated urban society. Stores had a wide variety of consumer goods for sale, but many of these were imported, despite opportunities for domestic production. Little attention was paid to fostering industrialization. Manufacturing nonetheless developed because the local market was considerable, and tariff barriers had been set high enough in many cases to make it profitable to produce goods locally.[2] While the industrial sector was not large, it provided a base for later growth.

Buenos Aires was the hub of the nation. It was the capital in a country that was increasingly centralized and therefore the home of an immense bureaucracy. The railroad system funneled goods into the city, making it the principal port. Buenos Aires was also the center of cultural and intellectual life. Greater Buenos Aires became the site of much of Argentina's modern industry, in 1939 producing 60 percent of the value of industrial production with 58 percent of the work force. In addition, a large tertiary sector developed. Greater Buenos Aires grew extremely large. In 1914, 26 percent of the national population lived in the metropolitan area, and by 1947 the figure had reached 30 percent, or roughly 4,722,000.[3]

The complexity of urban life fostered a class structure resembling that of more industrialized countries. According to Germani, 38 percent of the inhabitants of Buenos Aires in 1914 were middle class; in 1936, 46 percent; in 1947, 48 percent. Many were employees and professionals rather than independent entrepreneurs.[4]

Prior to 1930 the working class lived relatively well, their conditions comparable to those of their counterparts in Europe. The best evidence is that hundreds of thousands of immigrants poured into Argentina from southern and eastern Europe from 1880 to 1930. In 1938 it was estimated that almost 20 percent of the national population were foreigners, and in Buenos Aires almost 40 percent.[5]

Argentine prosperity had depended on the free movement of goods and a decent price for Argentine exports. With the onset of the depression countries withdrew behind tariff barriers and conducted "beggar-thy-neighbor" policies. World trade declined sharply.[6] The depression began for Argentina in mid-1929, when a world agricultural crisis caused prices to drop. Roughly at the same time large amounts of foreign capital were withdrawn to seek higher returns at home. The stock market panic of October 1929 deepened the crisis. Exports fell quickly and prices deteriorated even more drastically. Between 1928 and 1933 the value of Argentine exports declined more than 50 percent.[7]

The economic deterioration had repercussions on all aspects of life. In Buenos Aires real wages and the number of employed fell. Unemployment data are unreliable. A 1932 study found that 333,997 people were without jobs—7.2 percent of the economically active population; in Buenos Aires 9.0 percent lacked jobs.[8] These figures are undoubtedly too low. The U.S. Vice Consul reported statistics indicating 500,000 unemployed. For the first time shantytowns appeared. In 1931, unable to find employment, hundreds of immigrants lined up at the police station in Avellaneda, an industrial suburb of Buenos Aires, hoping to be sent home at government expense.[9]

The fall in the value of exports led to a corresponding decline in imports, putting a severe strain on the national budget since a large segment of the government's income came from tariffs. Given the economic structure and the ideology, the natural response was cutbacks in spending. Because the Radicals' political machine depended on patronage, Yrigoyen did little. Some layoffs were attempted, and the government frequently paid its workers late.[10]

The economic goals of the Uriburu regime were similar to those of the preceding government, but the regime lacked the restraints that had bound Yrigoyen. The peso was allowed to depreciate. To stem the outflow of reserves, the government created an exchange commission that determined the use of almost all foreign currency. A list of priorities was established; after the payment of government debts, it favored national industry and worked against "unessential" goods and the payment of commercial debts. The regime trimmed government salaries and created new sources of revenue, including the first income tax. Import duties were imposed on many foodstuffs and on some manufactured goods, and a 10 percent surcharge was placed on all tariffs.[11]

In some ways the economy remained stronger than it seemed. Argentina did not lose all its sizable gold reserves during the first months of the depression. In addition, during the 1920s many manufacturing plants had been built but were underused; the devaluation of the peso, the increased tariffs, and the exchange controls produced a favorable atmosphere for industrial production.[12]

A major change in economic policy occurred only after General Justo came to power—especially after mid-1933, when Justo appointed a new economic team headed by Federico Pinedo and Luis Duhau. Their ideas have been called "incipient Keynesianism," but their pump-priming was combined with measures to protect the traditional sectors of the economy. The core of their strategy was the encouragement of import substitution—i.e., the manufacture of consumer goods within Argentina. The agrarian elite viewed this type of industrialization as a necessity.[13]

The new team increased the government's role in the economy. Commissions were formed to control the marketing of and raise the prices of agricultural commodities. The government began an extensive program of public works, especially road construction, providing needed infrastructure and jobs. The rules governing foreign exchange were amended to allow more careful supervision of the goods permitted into Argentina, as well as to discriminate against countries that did not buy local products. In 1935 the authorities founded a central bank to give them tighter control of the monetary system.[14]

Spurred by these policies, the economy rebounded quickly, helped along by improving agricultural prices after 1933. In 1935 the GDP was higher than it had been in 1929. Unemployment had practically disappeared; the balance of payments was favorable. The motor of the recovery was import substitution. Formerly imported agricultural goods, such as fruit, cooking oil, and tomato products, were being grown and processed in Argentina. Much more important, manufacturing expanded.[15]*

The nature of the economic change is evident in a 55 percent increase in employment between 1929 and 1945 in Buenos Aires, where almost everyone engaged in secondary and tertiary activities (see Table 2-1). In all of Argentina the number of blue-collar industrial workers jumped from 396,303 in 1935 to 899,032 in 1946, while the number of factories grew from 37,362 to 84,895. The value added by manufacturing products increased over six and a half times.[16]

The recovery did not have a clean upward slope; twice world conditions produced downturns. In 1937 a slump in the United States had worldwide repercussions. Bad harvests intensified the problem in Argentina. In 1938 the value of exports fell 44 percent, creating a negative balance of trade for the first time in years. GDP declined between 1937 and 1938. The import/export source of the crisis is demonstrated by a sharp drop of almost 18 percent in the employment of stevedores in Buenos Aires in these years. The amount of cargo carried on the railroads also fell. Other sectors did not escape; between 1937 and 1938 employment in Buenos Aires declined by small but significant amounts in home tailoring, metal work, textiles, and transportation.[17]

The economy recovered toward the end of 1938 and did well for most of 1939. World War II brought a more serious crisis by shifting demands and causing scarcities of certain goods. The rapid Axis victory on the European continent made Argentina almost completely dependent on Great Britain and the United States for commerce. Because of Argentina' relationship with Germany, the Allies husbanded their limited resources and were particularly selective in what they traded with that country.

The war had a quick impact, cutting demand for grains. Beef exports also declined, though unlike grains, in the last years of the war these recovered.[18] In 1940 the decrease in agricultural exports created an unfavorable balance of trade; as in past downturns, those involved in

---

*While some have questioned the notion of the depression as an economic watershed, for a study of the working class the period is striking for the sharp rise in the number of urban workers.

Table 2-1

Indices of Employment and Population in Buenos Aires, 1929-45
(1929 = 100)

Year	Employment Index	Population Index
1929	100	100
1930	100.9	102.7
1931	97.8	104.3
1932	94.2	105.7
1933	98.2	107.0
1934	104.4	108.2
1935	113.2	109.2
1936	119.5	110.2
1937	126.1	111.2
1938	129.5	111.9
1939	132.1	112.7
1940	129.2	114.3
1941	135.0	115.2
1942	140.6	116.2
1943	147.0	117.2
1944	155.2	118.3
1945	155.1	119.5

Source: DNT, División de Estadística, *Investigaciones sociales 1940* (Buenos Aires, 1941), 35; Dirección de Estadística Social, *Investigaciones sociales 1943-1945* (Buenos Aires, 1946), 57.

the import/export trade suffered. In 1939 the index of the average number of men employed per month in the port of Buenos Aires stood at 136.3. It slumped to 100 in 1940 and had sunk to 58.0 by April 1943. While manufacturing suffered less, employment declined in a number of well-paying industries. These losses were partially offset by growth in other portions of the urban economy. However, the sectors that grew had much lower average salaries, in part because many of their employees were women. The overall level of employment in Buenos Aires declined. Underemployment also became a serious problem. The legal maximum monthly workload was 204 hours, but in the capital in 1940 the average number of hours worked was 164.9.[19]

The economy recovered after 1940. The balance of payments improved because the value of exports increased and there was a forced decline in imports. Industry more than compensated for agriculture. The number employed in Buenos Aires jumped sharply upward; manufacturing averaged 235,000 workers in 1940 and 362,000 in the first four months of 1943. Shortages of rubber, fuel, and iron caused serious problems, but temporary solutions could often be found. Linseed and maize were burned instead of oil or coal. Scrap replaced imported steel. Machinery was built by ingenious, if inefficient, means. Output was frequently increased by adding shifts, not by capital improvements. Some shortages could not be overcome, and there was unemployment in industries totally dependent on imported materials, such as rubber manufacturing.[20]

The economy was increasingly inefficient and costs rose. If the index of the cost of living was 100 in 1939, it had reached 115.3 by June 1943. While the average real wage went up, many wage earners suffered because of inflation. The basic trends continued after the 1943 coup. Industrial production expanded rapidly in 1944, but growth slowed in 1945. The regime's efforts to woo the workers had an impact. The cost of living dropped to 109.6 in 1944, because of such measures as rent reductions, before surging to 131.3 the following year. Despite the government's efforts, the inflation was keenly felt by many workers.[21]

The depression, while bringing misery, intensified economic change. Industry became more important. The number of men and women who owed their living to that sector of the economy soared. Greater Buenos Aires had in many ways been transformed.

LIVING AND WORKING CONDITIONS PRIOR TO JUNE 1943

The rapid growth of manufacturing prevented unemployment from being the long-term problem it was in the United States and certain European countries. With the exception of the two periods already mentioned, after 1933-34 urban unemployment largely disappeared from Argentina. In urban areas real wages did not drop significantly except in 1930 (see Table 2-2). Conditions were worse in rural areas, and after 1935 a flood of migrants poured into greater Buenos Aires—an average of 72,000 per year between 1936 and 1943 and 117,000 per year from 1943 to 1947.[22]

In skilled trades, which had strong unions, workers frequently earned high wages. Similar conditions prevailed where political considerations were paramount, such as employment with the national government or the municipality of Buenos Aires. These workers ate well, could perhaps own a house and even a car, and could give their children an education. With an education the children could join the middle

Table 2-2

Index of Real Wages in Buenos Aires, 1929–45
(1929 = 100)

Year	Wage Index	Year	Wage Index
1929	100	1938	96
1930	91	1939	97
1931	98	1940	98
1932	104	1941	98
1933	96	1942	101
1934	99	1943	107
1935	101	1944	118
1936	95	1945	118
1937	96		

Source: DNT, División de Estadística, *Investigactiones sociales 1939* (Buenos Aires, 1940), 38; Dirección de Estadística Social, *Investigaciones sociales 1943–45*, 61.

class.[23] These relatively comfortable conditions had an impact on the labor movement. Important unions, including the two railroad organizations (the UF and La Fraternidad—discussed in detail in Chapter 4 below) and those for the telephone workers and municipal workers, were dominated by men who earned high wages and good fringe benefits. They could not find comparable jobs elsewhere and were reluctant to jeopardize their employment. This may help explain the unions' often cautious attitudes.[24]

The vast majority of workers earned inadequate salaries. In a study of Buenos Aires published in 1937, the DNT stated the following:

> A monthly income of 120 pesos for a family composed of a couple and three children under fourteen [a typical family] . . . does not permit the meeting of all necessities because some indispensable items remain outside of the financial capabilities of that figure, and those that it does permit have to be purchased in very small quantities.[25]

The DNT also indicated that it was hard for such a family to live on 120 to 145 pesos a month.[26] A study in 1938 found that the combined average wage for both blue- and white-collar workers in industry was only 124 pesos, while blue-collar workers averaged just 109 pesos a month (see Table 2-3).

Table 2-3 shows industrial workers only and not those employed in high-paying service activities, but it is a glaring indication of many workers' status. Another study indicated that 34.1 percent of male

Table 2-3

Average Monthly Wages for Blue-Collar Workers in Buenos Aires, by Job Category and Industry, 1938
(*Pesos*)

Industry	Industry Average Wage	Category of Worker				
		Foreman	Skilled and Semi-Skilled	Laborer	Assistant	Apprentice
State and municipal workshops	156	217	175	149	152	56
Electricity	153	274	166	130	151	53
Primary activities	148	209	155	124	143	60
Printing, publishing, and paper	127	263	138	114	121	48
Metals	118	249	122	102	136	53
Foodstuffs	113	218	112	111	122	61
Wood working	113	208	116	93	110	48
Construction and building materials	111	214	123	91	133	58
Chemicals	108	214	105	114	119	48
Various	101	213	101	97	123	42
Clothing	93	224	95	98	111	41
Textiles	84	219	83	92	119	42
Total	109	229	110	107	129	48

Source: DNT, División de Estadística, *Investigaciones sociales 1938* (Buenos Aires, 1939) 19.

industrial workers earned less than 100 pesos a month and 74.3 percent less than 150. In other words, the earnings of approximately three quarters of the male industrial work force fell below the figure the DNT claimed was necessary for the typical family. Women's wages were even lower; 69.8 percent earned less than 75 pesos, while only 10.2 percent earned 100 pesos or more.[27]

According to another survey by the DNT, the head of household in a typical family on average earned 127.26 pesos per month, while expenditures averaged 164.19 pesos. Obviously many families had more than one wage earner. In 1941, 21 percent of the industrial labor force, white and blue collar, were below 18 and/or were women.[28] Given the social conditions and a housing shortage, it is unlikely that a significant number of these workers lived alone or were heads of households.

What did the working class receive for its money? In a 1941 study Torcuato Di Tella compared the buying power of an hour's work by Argentine workers with that of their counterparts in the United States and six European nations.[29] Bread, butter, coffee, and meat were cheapest in the United States and Argentina. Of the food items examined, only potatoes were relatively expensive. A study by the Armour Research Foundation, albeit less optimistic, supports Di Tella's findings.[30] Argentines consumed large quantities of meat, grain products, and fruit, but few vegetables. They ate well, even if they did not eat balanced diets.[31] Di Tella's study also includes some items of clothing. Although the Argentine working class dressed adequately, it did not fare well in the country comparisons. Finally, items such as sewing machines and radios were much more expensive than in the United States.[32]

Workers faced a shortage of inexpensive and decent housing. Twenty percent of income went for rent and purchased very little. In Rosario, of 31,951 people questioned, only 3,392 (or 10.6 percent) lived two or fewer to a room. In 1943 Emilio Lenhardston estimated that to fulfill the need for decent housing in greater Buenos Aires 350,000 units needed to be built. In one survey of the capital 58.1 percent of the working-class families lived in one-room apartments. On the average, these measured 16 by 20 meters, rented for 30.92 pesos a month, and were inhabited by 4.5 people. They were located in the infamous *conventillas*, tenements built around a patio with no windows, and the only ventilation from the door or an opening above the door. The rooms had independent kitchens, while the tenants shared running water, showers, and WCs.[33]

These conditions may have been improving because a new means of transportation, the *colectivos*, small privately owned buses, permitted workers to travel greater distances in less time. Workers could thus build small homes in Buenos Aires's uncrowded outskirts and suburbs, where relatively cheap land was available. While such homes were undoubtedly small and poorly made, once a family had paid the initial costs, it had more money to spend on other items. Moreover, these houses were larger and had better ventilation than the tenement apartments.[34]

A DNT analysis showed that a typical working-class family's budget was extremely tight. Little was available for such items as travel, newspapers, union dues, or medical expenses. Saving was impossible, and any extra expenses would deal a crushing blow to family finances.[35]

Conditions in the work place were very bad, despite modern labor laws. Prior to the 1930 coup, laws mandated a day off on Sunday, controlled working conditions and hours of women and minors, and established an eight-hour day (among other things). During the 1930s new codes limited work on Saturdays to half a day, mandated paid vacations, and prohibited the firing of women when they married.[36] The problem was enforcement. Under Argentina's federal system each province had a department of labor that took responsibility for working conditions; the only consistency among the provinces was their inability or unwillingness to enforce labor codes. In Buenos Aires the DNT was in charge of labor-law enforcement. While it often tried to implement the laws, it lacked the strength to do so, and it failed to get cooperation from the rest of the government. Only in sectors where unions were strong and could give assistance did the DNT carry out its mandate. The DNT and its provincial counterparts performed in a similarly lackluster fashion in their attempts to mediate conflicts between capital and labor.

Most workers had no pension plans, paid vacations, or sick leave. A few industries—those controlled by the state or where the workers had political influence—had pension plans created by the government and controlled by boards elected by employers and workers. These not only provided security upon retirement, but also gave loans for (among other things) the building of houses. They were a crucial source of credit in a society where workers found it extremely difficult to borrow money. Until 1934 vacations and sick leave depended on what employers wanted to give and what the workers could demand, which was usually very little. In that year congress passed a law establishing vacations and sick leave for workers. A struggle for enforcement ensued which lasted into the Perón era.

Chapter 3

CONDITIONS IN FIVE INDUSTRIES

Not only did the depression's impact on individual industries help determine union actions, but so did salary structure, working conditions, and the work force's social composition. Well-paid workers frequently were reluctant to jeopardize their jobs. At the same time, they had leverage because of relative shortages of skilled labor or because the industry was of particular interest to the government. Employers always felt that unskilled workers could be easily replaced.

The work force's social composition is important because, for one thing, unions responded differently to industries with a large percentage of women. Women were considered difficult to organize. In some industries they considered themselves middle class and were afraid of losing this status by joining unions. Management typically encouraged this attitude. Unions frequently ignored issues of primary interest to women, such as equal pay for equal work, and did little to overcome women's fears of entering a rough and tumble world. This is not to say that women did not respond with heroism in many situations, but in others the unions' failure to organize women proved to be their Achilles heel. For another thing, in much of the traditional literature it is argued that the percentage of foreign-born workers determined the nature of union activity. Little hard evidence has been found that this was true.

As might be expected, economic conditions in the five industries that are the focus of this study varied greatly. The depression did not have an equal impact, and it only partially determined conditions. For example, the expansion of the textile industry did not bring high wages. On the other hand, the railroaders escaped many consequences of their industry's decline. Below we shall analyze conditions in the industries in which the members of our five unions worked.

THE TELEPHONE INDUSTRY

In 1886 the British-owned Unión Telefónica del Río de la Plata (UT) was formed, and it grew to become the dominant company in the Argentine telephone industry. In January 1929 it was purchased by the North American holding company International Telephone and Telegraph (ITT).[1] The UT remained based in Britain, but ITT had complete control and pursued a relatively aggressive policy of innovation. Despite problems created by the depression and World War II, the rate of telephone installation overall increased (see Table 3-1). By 1940 automatic exchanges had nearly completely replaced manual ones in urban areas. Automation had a major impact on employees, despite company claims that no operators lost their jobs. In one office subscribers increased from 1,800 to 3,500, while employees declined from 88 to 9. The UT also "rationalized" work procedures and introduced labor-saving devices—a major source of friction with the union. The chaotic long-distance service improved, especially after the passage of a 1934 law requiring changes. (Prior to this law a resident of the Chaco could not call Buenos Aires but could speak to someone in Peking.) By 1940 Argentina was in general well supplied with telephones; per capita it had more than Italy or Japan, and Buenos Aires had more than Vienna, Amsterdam, or Liverpool.[2]

Despite improved service, the UT was and remained unpopular. Newspaper articles and government investigations found its performance

Table 3-1

Telephones Installed by the UT, 1926-45

Year	Number of Telephones Installed	Year	Number of Telephones Installed
1926	15,837	1936	23,844
1927	19,194	1937	31,945
1928	16,684	1938	26,283
1929	21,427	1939	26,046
1930	20,220	1940	25,416
1931	10,190	1941	25,581
1932	3,077	1942	22,934
1933	7,058	1943	16,073
1934	10,280	1944	14,425
1935	12,478	1945	16,591

Source: Dirección General de Correos y Telégrafos, *Antecedentes sobre el estudio de la situación económica, financiera, industrial, etc. de la Compañía Unión Telefónica* (Buenos Aires, 1937), 135; Enrique Wolfenson, *El problema de los teléfonos* (Buenos Aires, 1956), 46.

less than satisfactory, with rates and profits too high. Moreover, the UT was very large, operating in the capital and the provinces and territories of Buenos Aires, Santa Fe, Córdoba, San Luis, La Pampa, and portions of Río Negro. While 42 other companies existed in 1940—some of which were also controlled by ITT—the UT owned almost 90 percent of the telephones. This plus the company's cavalier attitude toward government authorities and its North American ownership made it a target for popular ire.[3]

The UT did not escape the depression. Telephone installations dropped precipitously in 1931 and especially during strike-torn 1932. They did not recover until 1936. The UT reacted by cutting its work force from 12,147 in 1930 to 9,150 in 1932 to 8,800 in 1934. (The shift to automatic exchanges was a contributing factor in reducing the work force.) With the expansion of service, the number of employees increased to 11,062 in 1939 and 12,317 in 1942.[4]

Gross income increased in every year except 1932. The nature of the industry provided a cushion. If payments were not made, service was cut off; since installations continued, it meant that revenues increased. The company cut expenses by laying off workers and changing work rules. Costs declined before rising again, but the increase was less steep than the rise in income. Profit rates cannot be accurately given since there was disagreement on what they were, but the dividends on ordinary shares between 1929 and 1940 did not fall below 3 percent.[5]

In 1934, 70.1 percent of the work force had been born in Argentina. Few were British; nonetheless, Britons held the key positions in the UT. Of the 64 Britons who worked in Buenos Aires, 48 earned more than 400 pesos a month. The UT also employed a large number of women—approximately one third of the work force—mostly as operators. It did everything it could to foster the women's self-image as middle class.[6]

Most UT employees earned relatively good wages, with pay much higher in Buenos Aires than in the provinces. Women earned less than men for similar jobs. In 1934, 17.1 percent of the work force earned 100 pesos per month or less, but 88.4 percent of these were minors, part-time employees, or rural operators. A little more than 30 percent of the males received over 200 pesos a month (see Table 3-2). In 1939 no employee earned under 50 pesos a month, and 87.1 percent received over 150. New hiring had occurred at the higher levels, undoubtedly due to less demand for operators and more for skilled workers to do installations.[7]

Telephone workers participated in a pension plan created by the national government for private utilities. Workers paid in 5 percent of their salaries while employers contributed 8 percent. Workers received

Table 3-2

Monthly Salaries of UT Employees in 1934
(Pesos)

Salary	Male Wage Earners	Percent	Female Wage Earners	Percent	Total	Percent
1–100	759	13.5%	702	23.9%	1,461	17.1%
101–200	3,148	56.2	2,101	71.6	5,249	61.5
201–300	1,280	22.8	110	3.7	1,390	16.3
301–400	224	4.0	16	0.5	240	2.8
401–499	82	1.5	3	0.1	85	1.0
500+	112	2.0	2	0.1	114	1.3
Total	5,605	100	2,934	100	8,359	100

Source: Cámara de Diputados, Comisión Especial de Estudio del Régimen Legal de Telecomunicaciones, *Publicación de antecedentes* (Buenos Aires, 1936), 178.

pensions upon retirement at age 50 or over with at least 30 years of service or if they were incapacitated. The pension fund board also granted low-cost loans for housing construction.[8]

The union helped impose relatively good working conditions. A contract signed in 1929 for greater Buenos Aires established paid vacations of 7, 10, or 14 days according to pay, seniority, and job category. Workers could obtain sick pay for 30 days a year and half pay for an additional 30 days.[9] In 1939 the company conceded that it was covered by a reform of the commercial code—many employers did not—and recognized its responsibility to give up to 30 days of vacation and six months of paid leave in cases of illness or accident.[10]

Conditions within the work place are more difficult to determine. The UT recognized the union's grievance committee but frequently did not heed it. The FOET constantly denounced speedups and unhealthy conditions, but in part this was to keep the company in line. According to the DNT, the telephone company did not frequently violate labor laws, owing in part to "the effective intervention of the labor union . . . and the permanent contact of this organization with the company."[11] Given the laxity of labor code enforcement in the country as a whole, the telephone workers must be considered to have worked in relatively good conditions. This is not surprising. A significant percentage of the workers had some qualifications. Operators had to handle customers and numbers. Skilled workers did installations and repairs. A skilled work force, a strong union, and the government's interest in a vital means of communication combined to ensure attention to working conditions.

COMMERCE

The FEC represented men and women employed in Buenos Aires in establishments that ranged from funeral parlors and small stores to department stores and banks. The organization's strength lay in retail establishments, especially department stores. Retail establishments will be the focus of our discussion.

In 1946 there were 170,333 retail stores in Argentina, and they employed 288,104 people.[12*] The vast numbers owing their livelihood to this sector permitted the FEC in the 1930s to organize political support throughout the country. In Buenos Aires in 1946 the census listed 39,783 retail establishments employing 93,521 people. By far the heaviest concentration of stores—and even more so of employees—was in the downtown area. Most retail establishments averaged between 1 and 4 employees. The principal exception was 33 department stores that employed 14,760 people—almost 450 per store.

The retail sector felt the impact of the depression as demand declined. In the midst of the larger crisis, the small store owners' problems largely escaped public notice, but the larger establishments suffered more visibly. The profits of two prestigious British chains, Harrods and Gath y Chaves (owned by the same corporation), declined. After taking account of exchange rate losses, the former showed a loss in fiscal 1933–34, while the latter reported losses in both 1930–31 and 1933–34.[13]

After the depression began, the FEC vociferously protested a wave of salary cuts and layoffs. Employment fell much more sharply in commerce, banking, offices, and insurance than in the capital's general population. Only after 1935 did it surpass the figure for 1929 (see Table 3-3). In 1932 unemployment among commercial workers was greater than in any other category except construction; a significant portion were retail clerks. Working conditions worsened as well.[14]

Conditions in the retail sector improved along with the general urban economy, but the 1937–38 recession had little impact. Employment continued to grow, and both Harrods and Gath y Chaves prospered. There were some layoffs, but the number was lessened by legislation that called for indemnification of those who were let go. The onset of World War II initially created problems; employment dropped between 1939 and 1940, but the ensuing prosperity created a sharp increase in employment.[15]

*There were 172 department stores in the entire country, employing 17,098 people.

Table 3-3

Index of Employment in Commerce, Banking, Offices, and Insurance in Buenos Aires, 1929–45

(1929 = 100)

Year	Employment Index	Year	Employment Index
1929	100	1938	118.2
1930	98.6	1939	120.8
1931	93.4	1940	116.8
1932	88.2	1941	124.6
1933	89.4	1942	128.5
1934	92.2	1943	134.0
1935	97.5	1944	136.0
1936	101.4	1945	139.0
1937	106.2		

Source: DNT, División de Estadística, *Investigaciones sociales 1940* (Buenos Aires, 1940), 36; Dirección de Estadística Social, *Investigaciones sociales 1943–1945* (Buenos Aires, 1946), 62.

The labor force mirrored the variety of the retail sector. In 1946 out of the 73,965 nonfamily members employed by retail establishments in the capital, 62,527 had white-collar jobs; of these, slightly over 25 percent were women. Females worked fewer years than their male counterparts. Most women employees were from 18 to 30 years old; after age 40 their number dropped sharply, and there were extremely few over 51 years old. Women seem to have worked until they married or had children, but it is unclear whether this was voluntary.[16]

In 1940 a study by the DNT of retail and wholesale establishments (excluding those selling food) and offices (excluding the professions, banks, the stock market, and insurance) found that the average wage for men was 245.90 pesos a month and for women 131.72. This study included some sectors where salaries were much higher than in retail stores, but the DNT did not feel that in commerce jobs could be categorized in any meaningful way, as age and seniority were the only identifiable determinants of salary.[17] However, sex, type of store, and location were important.

In small stores, especially away from downtown, wages tended to be low. In 1930 corner grocery and liquor stores paid between 40 and 100 pesos a month, usually from 60 to 80—and that for extremely long hours. Delicatessens (*rotiserías*) paid from 90 to 180 pesos, but normally from 120 to 150 pesos. In all types of establishments in 1928–29 female cashiers averaged 124.13 pesos per month, saleswomen 117.27, and aides 76.90.[18] The pay in department stores and other downtown establishments tended to be better, but many employees received commissions, making their income difficult to determine. A contract signed by a department store in 1935 raised the salaries of some cashiers from 150 to 160 pesos, while others went from 120 to 135. After raises, other employees earned 70 to 140 pesos a month. Salaries in the provinces were lower. A survey in the city of La Plata, where salaries were relatively good, found that 77 percent of those employed in food stores earned 130 pesos or less a month, while in other types of stores the figure stood at 65 percent.[19]

Working conditions varied more than salaries. Small store employees were referred to as "white slaves." Many younger ones slept in the store. In 1930 the FEC claimed that those employed in the capital away from downtown in wholesale operations worked 12 to 14 hours a day, in men's stores 12.5 hours, in hardware stores 10–11 hours, and in small grocery stores 15 hours. A law enacted in 1933 mandated uniform closing times for stores; it may have reduced the hours worked, but grocery stores were exempt. In any case, the eight-hour day and other statutes were routinely flouted. Many employees tolerated bad conditions because they dreamed that by hard work they could save enough capital to set up their own store. This vision persisted especially in small grocery stores, where many employees were immigrants who worked in establishments owned by their compatriots.[20]

Conditions in department stores and downtown in general were much better. High visibility and pressure from the FEC meant that laws could not easily be ignored. Moreover, because the majority of the stores catered to the upper reaches of society, they made an effort to foster a middle-class self-image among their employees. For example, the English-owned department stores offered their employees lessons in that language. Still, serious status problems existed. The FEC felt compelled to include in a department store contract a clause which specified that the employees could use elevators.[21]

THE MUNICIPAL GOVERNMENT OF BUENOS AIRES

The government of the municipality of Buenos Aires was not a typical employer; its motivations were usually political and not profit, yet it shared many characteristics with private companies. It too felt the impact of the depression and tended to flout labor codes when it could.

The municipal government employed approximately 26,000 people, from doctors to streetsweepers. The city not only maintained streets, parks, hospitals, and an opera house and collected and disposed of garbage, but also had extensive workshops in which vehicles were repaired, benches constructed, and two carts a day built for the sanitation department. The shops employed cabinetmakers, blacksmiths, boilermakers, and other skilled or semi-skilled workers. However, a significant percentage of the city's workers possessed no skills.[22]

The depression reduced city revenues, unbalancing the budgets between 1929 and 1932. Municipal workers shouldered some of the burden created by the shortfall. Late payment of wages, a chronic problem, increased in frequency. Workers had to depend on credit extended by store owners and landlords. Uriburu reduced the minimum wage from 165 pesos per month to 160 and eliminated a system of automatic raises based on seniority.[23]

The restoration of the city council in 1932 led to a temporary return to pre-coup conditions. Further budget problems once again eliminated the automatic raises. Between 1933 and 1935 a percentage of all wages above 200 pesos a month was withheld; if no deficit existed, it was to be returned. After long delays, the employees got their money.[24]

The city paid high wages. The minimum salary for those not classified as apprentices was 165 pesos a month. The vast majority of blue-collar workers earned between 165 and 200 pesos (blue-collar workers in industry averaged 109). In addition to their salary, municipal workers received five pesos a month for each child under 15. Unskilled workers could not earn more money anywhere else; nor could women (slightly over 20 percent of the labor force), employed mainly as maids, office workers, and nurses.[25]

The city's workers had a pension fund established by the municipality; it not only paid money to the retired or disabled, but also loaned money at low interest. From the time of the fund's founding until 1936, 10 percent of the affiliated had borrowed money for house construction. The large sums borrowed indicate that most of the recipients earned high wages. Nonetheless, many workers used the available credit because, one union official claimed, the average worker owed a thousand pesos to the fund.[26]

Appointment to a municipal job was frequently a reward for political service, a practice dating back to at least the Radical era. According to the longtime head of the UOEM, Francisco Pérez Leirós, the only way to get employment with the city was to know someone. He also charged that large sums of money sometimes changed hands.[27] The municipal executive, the *intendente*, an appointee of the president, held most of the power. He appointed workers and drew up the budget, but he needed the support of the popularly elected city council for many matters, including the setting of his own salary. During the Neo-Conservative era the opposition always controlled the council, and the intendentes needed to placate it. One method was to appoint members of opposition parties to jobs. All political parties shared in the spoils, as the following exchange in the city council shows:

> *Vicente Russomano* (Socialist): The upright conduct of the Socialist Party that we represent protects us from any electoral calculations or any accusations of demagoguery.
>
> But each one of those political parties . . . has begun by placing in the administration the largest possible number of friends, if not relatives.
>
> *Reinaldo Elena* (Anti-Personalist Radical): And enemies also.
>
> *Carlos Edo* (Conservative:) And even relatives of Socialist militants.[28]

The careers of several UOEM leaders hint that they received jobs with the municipality because of service to the Socialist Party. Another indication of a political spoils system was the high percentage of the work force who were naturalized Argentines—20.3 percent, twice the rate of the general population in the capital.[29]

The politicization of appointments had its costs. Massive firings of political opponents took place after Yrigoyen's election in 1928 and especially after the coup in 1930. In 1933 in response to outcries from all political sectors, an *escalafón* (system of job classifications), which laid out rigid rules for hiring, promotions, and firings was established. Advancements and appointments became subject to examinations in an attempt to limit political pressures and obtain the most qualified personnel. The measure provided limited protection from arbitrary layoffs and from some types of political harassment.[30]

Both because of a constant searching for votes and because of the spoils system, the city council frequently acted as a grievance committee for the municipal workers. The council could move in three basic ways to help them. First, since the council had no legal authority to concern itself with the administration of the executive branch, when a problem arose, it asked that the executive take action. Almost every year the council requested that sanitation department personnel be granted leave on Christmas and New Year's Day. While invariably granted, this did not mean that workers had the days off.[31]

Second, the council could request information, thereby publicizing problems and applying pressure. For example, in 1932, according to information obtained by council members, appointments had been made which disregarded the rights of the substitutes (*suplentes*—see below). Councilor José Marotta, a Socialist and a UOEM member, called for the council to take part in the enforcement of municipal regulations by requesting information about all recent appointments and the status of all substitutes. The council passed the motion with no debate, and the intendente complied.[32]

Third, in certain cases the council could pass resolutions that required action. After the national government enacted a law establishing a five-and-a-half-day week, the city's blue-collar employees still had to work six days a week. The council passed a resolution requiring the intendente to obey the law.[33]

The council ensured that the workers had good conditions—at least on paper—but the autonomy of the city's executive branch meant that working conditions varied greatly. For example, according to the rules, workers could have twenty days of paid leave a year if conditions permitted. The number of workers who enjoyed this benefit increased over time, yet in some divisions of the city administration not only did employees not have paid vacations, but even holidays were rare. Slaughterhouse and certain other workers lacked the same rights as most employees.[34]

The most pernicious labor practice was the use of substitutes, who went to their department each day hoping that someone would not come and that they would be called on. They were paid only for the days they worked. When full-time jobs became available, substitutes had first priority, ranked according to length of service. In some departments seniority lists were drawn up only during the 1930s, and even then they were frequently ignored. Conditions for substitute nurses were particularly bad. Many worked for free, receiving only tips and the hope that they might be appointed to a permanent position.[35]

THE RAILROAD INDUSTRY

By the late 1930s Argentina had the sixth largest railroad network in the world. The majority of the lines in the rich and fertile pampas was owned by British corporations; a few French-owned lines existed as well.

The State Railroads operated largely in areas where private capital had been reluctant to invest.[36]

Railroads played a strategic role in the economy since they transported good to the ports for export. No government could afford to allow them to malfunction. Very early the state began to try to control them. This was made possible by the public's aversion to the railroad companies. Critics claimed that the railroads lacked the cars to handle harvest-time traffic, charged excessive rates, and had failed to modernize. Many believed that profits were based on watered stock. The mistrust of foreigners controlling such a vital link in the economy added fuel to the fire.[37] This unpopularity permitted the government to defy the companies on many issues when it considered it in its best interest to do so. By the 1930s the state, through the General Railroad Board (Dirección General de Ferrocarriles), played a major role in railroad management, from work rules to rates and schedules. The board's power over the companies varied with the strength of its director, but its presence greatly aided the unions because in many situations the government made the crucial decisions.[38]

The railroads were extremely vulnerable to shifts in demand for exports. During the first year of the depression freight traffic declined over 15 percent, then remained essentially unchanged for the next two years before dropping sharply once again. Recovery was slow, and only in 1936/37 did the railroads again approach pre-depression tonnage. The economic slump in 1937/38 created a sharp downturn. During World War II, after an initial decline, freight traffic increased rapidly because of economic prosperity and because shortages of petroleum and rubber hampered the railroads' competitors. Passenger traffic followed a different pattern. The number of riders declined more slowly, reaching its low point in 1935/36. Ridership then began a steady climb that surpassed the figures for 1929/30 only in 1941/42. In the last years of the war ridership soared as commuters turned to the railroads while problems beset other means of transportation (see Table 3-4).

World War II brought special problems, especially an acute fuel shortage. As early as September 1939, the companies reduced service; by 1941 the government had placed severe restrictions on fuel consumption. Locomotives had to be converted to burn wood or other vegetable matter. The conversion was expensive and inefficient, particularly as the emergency fuel was extremely bulky and needed to move toward the ports along with exports.[39]

Due to the railroads' habit of buying from subsidiaries and the likelihood that their stock was watered, it is impossible to accurately

Table 3-4

Cargo and Passengers on the Railroads under National Jurisdiction, 1928/29–1945/46

Year	Cargo (Millions of metric tons)	Passengers (Millions)
1928/29	53	162
1929/30	44	171
1930/31	45	166
1931/32	44	150
1932/33	39	144
1933/34	40	138
1934/35	43	139
1935/36	42	135
1936/37	51	147
1937/38	42	158
1938/39	45	164
1939/40	43	164
1940/41	40	165
1941/42	46	173
1942/43	51	188
1943/44	53	209
1944/45	53	246
1945/46	53	282

Source: Dirección General de Ferrocarriles, *Estadística de los ferrocarriles en explotación, ejercicio 1942/1943*, LI (Buenos Aires, 1947), 412; Juan Manuel Santa Cruz, *Ferrocarriles argentinos* (Santa Fe, 1966), 30.

tally the companies' profitability. However, it is clear that the 1930s and 1940s were not good times for the railroads. Not only did traffic decline, but also government exchange policies blocked or reduced remittances to Britain. Increased road building favored a competing mode of transportation.[40]

Labor averaged 68.4 percent of costs, so the companies saw layoffs and lower wages as at least a partial solution to their problems.[41] Determined union opposition and government unwillingness to have traffic disrupted prevented the railroads from moving very far in that direction. Instead the companies urged the government to limit competition. In addition, the railroads decapitalized, refusing to invest in maintenance, electrification, or new equipment. Between 1921 and 1930, 1,042 locomotives were imported; in the following decade only 114 were. In 1944 some 60 percent of the rolling stock was between 30 and 40 years old, though some had been modernized. By 1945 the system was on the verge of collapse.[42]

Another solution—acceptable to the unions, the government, and the companies—was for the state to purchase the railroads. This would have permitted the companies to retire with their capital rather than be trapped for the foreseeable future with little chance of large profits. One step was taken in this direction—the purchase of the Central Córdoba, the hardest pressed of the major lines.[43]

Despite the problems, railroad workers considered themselves, and were considered by others, the elite of the working class.[44] Their unions shielded them. One reason for the strength of the unions was the size of the potential membership. Between 1930 and 1946 the number of railroad workers ranged from 124,659 to 148,717. (The lower figure was due to layoffs in 1930–32 and a failure to replace workers who quit or retired. The nadir was in 1937–38, and hiring picked up after that.) Railroaders lived throughout the republic but were heavily concentrated in the politically vital provinces of Santa Fe and Buenos Aires, as well as in the capital.[45]

Many railroaders did not earn high wages. Nearly 50 percent earned 150 pesos or less a month, while 34.3 percent earned 125 pesos or less. On the other hand, a significant percentage earned a good salary (see Table 3-5). The differences in salaries were primarily due to two factors: job category and employer. Skilled jobs paid better, and the British-owned wide-gauge railroads paid better than did narrow-gauge lines. Salaries on the State Railroads were much lower.[46] The wages presented in Table 3-5 are in some ways deceiving. They include estimates of the value of other types of compensation, including tips and the housing (generally poor) that some workers in remote rural areas received. Moreover, while a government-sponsored pension plan (similar to those described above) provided for later benefits, workers contributed between 5 and 8 percent of their wages to the fund. Thus when earning 150 pesos a month, a worker received only between 138 and 142.50 pesos.[47]

Working conditions were generally good by the standards of the day. Almost all railroaders were covered by collective contracts which established grievance procedures that were usually effective. If not, workers slowed traffic or took other job actions to settle problems. The government's extensive and complex rules for railroads also favored decent working conditions, and the government was inclined—at times—to enforce them.[48] Thus the railroader was protected from many

Table 3-5

Monthly Salaries of Railroaders in 1941
(Pesos)

Salary per Month	Number of Earners	Percent	Accumulated Percentage
Up to 50 pesos	594	0.4%	0.4%
51–75	12,810	9.4	9.8
76–100	14,226	10.4	20.2
101–125	19,334	14.1	34.3
126–150	17,569	12.8	47.1
151–175	17,835	13.0	60.1
176–200	18,279	13.4	73.5
201–225	10,754	7.9	81.4
226–250	8,158	6.0	87.4
251–275	3,426	2.5	89.9
276–300	3,412	2.5	92.4
301–325	1,896	1.4	93.8
326–350	2,978	2.2	96.0
351+	5,468	4.0	100
Total	136,739	100	100

Source: Caja Nacional de Jubilaciones y Pensiones de Empleados Ferroviarios, *Memoria correspondiente al año 1941* (Buenos Aires, 1942), 158–59.

of the arbitrary acts that threatened the lives of most workers.

The collective contracts included other important features. Systems of promotion that lessened favoritism and took seniority into account were set up. Workers had vacations of from seven to fifteen days, depending on job category and seniority. Sick leave could also be obtained.[49] Tradition provided railroaders with an additional advantage: their children were the first to be considered for employment—an important benefit in a time of limited job opportunities. This made the railroaders a closely knit group, a major advantage for the unions.[50]

There were exceptions to the good conditions. The government refused to establish for the State Railroad workers the improvements that it had helped force on private companies. As mentioned, salaries for State Railroad workers were lower. The unions were not as strong on the State railroads, and the workers had to face political pressure, paternalism, and generally poorer conditions. When the Central Córdoba was bought by the state, conditions deteriorated to the extent that the UF began to reconsider its long-standing desire for the nationalization of the railroad system.[51]

Road and track maintenance workers were in many ways a subcaste. Before 1930 (when regular job shortages began) these tended to be seasonal employees, leaving to work on the harvests or at other jobs and then drifting back to the railroads. After 1930 they became permanent employees. Only in 1938 was the union able to sign a contract covering these workers. However, wages remained low, and many lived in isolated rural areas in extremely poor housing (provided by the railroad).[52]

THE TEXTILE INDUSTRY

The textile industry was a prime beneficiary of the economic policies put in place because of the depression, and it grew rapidly. Not only was adequate protection provided against much foreign competition, but Argentina produced large quantities of key raw materials, wool and cotton. A small but growing industry had existed even prior to 1929, with woolens developing earlier and more quickly than cotton. As early as 1923 Argentina was supplying approximately one fourth of its own textile needs.[53]

The depression had less of a negative impact on the textile industry than on almost any other sector of the economy. The employment statistics for the capital show that no decline occurred, but this is deceiving as 1929, the benchmark date, had been a very bad year (see Table 3-6). Textile production in 1931 and 1932 was lower than it had been in 1930, and companies laid off numerous workers and trimmed wages.[54]

After the initial dislocations, the industry began a prodigious boom. From 1930 to 1934 the number working in silk-weaving increased from 2,300 to 8,990; in the spinning and weaving of wool, from 7,150 to 11,000; in the spinning and weaving of cotton, from 5,580 to 9,770; in the knitting industry, from 14,000 to 17,000.[55] By 1932 local production covered 90 percent of national needs in knitted goods, 65 percent in spinning and weaving of wool, and 60 percent in silk production. Six years later all demand for silk, knitted goods, and stockings could be met locally and large gains had been made in woolen production. However, 17 percent of cotton yarn was still imported, as was 60 percent of cotton goods.[56]

The textile industry developed unevenly, with some sectors using large modern plants and others depending on inexpensive labor and a protected market. This is well demonstrated by the two segments of artificial silk (rayon) production, spinning and weaving. Two international corporations dominated the former: Rhodiaseta (a French-owned

Table 3-6

Index of Employment in the Textile Industry in Buenos Aires, 1929–45
(1929 = 100)

Year	Employment Index	Year	Employment Index
1929	100	1938	211.5
1930	100.8	1939	218.9
1931	105.2	1940	241.0
1932	117.5	1941	254.1
1933	132.7	1942	276.3
1934	151.6	1943	298.2
1935	181.2	1944	289.2
1936	209.7	1945	290.4
1937	224.5		

Source: DNT, *Investigaciones sociales 1940*, 36; Dirección de Estadística Social, *Investigaciones sociales 1943–1945*, 62.

corporation), with a capital of 1,500,000 pesos and a profit in 1941 of 448,900 pesos, and Ducilo (Anglo–North American—a joint venture of Imperial Chemical and Dupont), with a capital of 34,000,000 pesos and a profit of 3,645,543 pesos in 1939. In sharp contrast, while several large weaving firms existed—Industria Sérica Argentina (capital of 2,800,000 pesos), Sedalana (2,150,000 pesos), and Textilia (1,000,000 pesos)—there were also many small producers with two or three looms—so-called *façonniers*, of which there were as many as 300.[57] These entrepreneurs bought looms at low prices and on easy terms, and they received yarn from larger companies, which also purchased the finished product. The small establishments were almost all run by immigrants (usually Polish Jews) and were family enterprises operating on small profit margins and caring little for the law. They tended to overproduce; when the larger companies slashed the prices that they paid for finished products, the façonniers had to cut wages.[58]

The overall growth of the industry is impressive. The value of textile production jumped over 200 percent between 1935 and 1943 and more than doubled again by 1946 (see Table 3-7). (The later jump is due as much to inflation as to increased production.) Expansion occurred almost exclusively in the city and province of Buenos Aires, with faster growth occurring in the latter.[59] The labor force increased less rapidly than production because new technology permitted costs to be reduced by increasing the number of machines tended by each worker. Between 1929 and 1938 the number of workers needed to maintain a set quantity of machines in cotton spinning had decreased by 46.4 percent; in cotton weaving the decline was 26.7 percent, and in silk weaving 24.1 percent. Other branches of the industry varied less.[60]

The recession of 1937–38 hit the textile industry hard. Production slumped dramatically. Beginning in mid-1937 workers were fired, hours cut, and factories closed. Cotton spinners worked an average of 24 days in December 1937 but only 17.6 in May 1938; similar declines occurred in other branches of the industry. In mid-1938 a Radical deputy estimated—in what was probably an exaggeration—that 40 percent of textile workers were unemployed. According to the executive branch, in Buenos Aires textile employment declined by 9 percent in the first half of 1938.[61]

Employment soared during the first years of the war. The decline shown for the last years in Table 3-6 seems incorrect, as the industry grew to meet expanding demand. Production of cotton yarn increased from 29,016 tons in 1939 to 63,625 tons in 1945. Imports were limited, and a large market for exports existed, though this began to disappear

Table 3-7

Growth of the Textile Industry, 1935–46

Year	Number of Plants	Number of Workers	Value Added by Production (Thousands of pesos)
1935	780	52,576	280,248
1937	1,045	65,040	372,603
1939	1,052	69,075	402,959
1941	1,164	81,397	512,522
1943	1,324	102,643	893,113
1946	2,061	127,161	1,838,970

Source: Dirección Nacional de Estadística y Censos, *Cuarto censo general de la nación*, (Buenos Aires, 1949), III, 26–27.

before the end of the war. Since acquiring new machinery was difficult, factories met demand by using equipment to capacity. During the last three years of the war, cotton spinning machinery ran an average of 19 hours a day. In sectors that depended upon imported materials, some problems existed—for example, Rhodiaseta could not obtain cellulose acetate to produce rayon and had to close. Despite the problems, many firms earned very high profits.[62]

The textile workers were not an elite. The vast majority were unskilled and could easily be replaced. In the capital in 1935 many were women—63.9 percent. According to the data, slightly over 10 percent of the women were minors, as were 3 percent of the males, although the real numbers were undoubtedly higher. Foreigners were not numerous— 60.2 percent of the personnel were Argentines—but a striking differentiation by sex existed. While 58.2 percent of the males had been born abroad, just 29.5 percent of the women had been. The women tended to be young; over half were under 25, and 80 percent were under 45. (At lower ages, in the population as a whole, the percentage of foreigners decreased.) The age distribution of the men was likely to be more even, and many Europeans performed skilled jobs that they had learned on the other side of the Atlantic.

By 1946 the composition of the work force had undergone a major change. Only 21.2 percent of the blue-collar workers were foreigners—a figure in keeping with expanding employment in textiles and the ending of large-scale immigration in 1930. Moreover, the work force had become more male—50.4 percent. The newer, highly capitalized factories tended to hire adult males.[63]

The average textile workers earned very little—84 pesos per month in the capital in 1938. However (unlike in the other industries in our study), wages declined sharply during crises and then rose again. They are difficult to calculate because frequently they were based on a piece rate with a set minimum. In 1935 a majority of the male workers had a minimum monthly wage of under 101 pesos, and slightly over 90 percent made under 151 pesos. The salaries for women were even worse; 92.3 percent received 100 pesos or less (see Table 3-8). A few skilled workers earned good money, as did foremen (who are not included in Table 3-8), averaging 219 pesos a month. The difference in salaries between males and females is due both to the types of jobs held and a policy of paying women less.[64]

Textile workers did not have pensions or paid vacations in 1930. Vacations became possible in 1934 because of a reform of the commercial code that established vacations; however, it was unclear whether industrial workers were included, and the unions fought for vacations on a plant-by-plant basis—usually failing.

Conditions inside factories were generally wretched, though better in the capital than in the province of Buenos Aires. Labor laws had little impact. Factories were kept hot and humid to control flying particles, which hung in the air anyway. Lung disorders, especially tuberculosis,

Table 3-8

Minimum Monthly Wages of Textile Workers in Buenos Aires, 1935
(Pesos)

Wage	Number of Male Wage Earners	Percent	Number of Female Wage Earners	Percent
Up to 50 pesos	1,217	9.6%	11,535	49.2%
51–75	3,859	30.5	8,204	35.0
76–100	2,617	20.7	1,908	8.1
101–125	2,445	19.3	1,116	4.8
126–150	1,293	10.2	407	1.7
151–175	470	3.7	132	0.6
176–200	383	3.0	60	0.3
201–225	181	1.4	70	0.3
226+	192	1.5	16	--
Total	12,657	100	23,448	100

Source: DNT, División de Estadística, *Industria textil: Capacidad normal de trabajo de los obreros, especialmente mujeres y menores* (Buenos Aires, 1939), 9–10.

NOTE: Highly paid foremen and assistants are not included.

ravaged many workers. Employers frequently ignored the workers' dignity and safety. According to the UOT, some plants never hired married women; others announced the need for female workers from 18 to 25 years old and required that they be pretty and of a certain size. In one plant the management kept the humidity at 80 or 90 percent and gave the workers coffee laced with liquor to restore bodily fluids, causing an exceptionally high accident rate. In another, when a woman's hair was caught in a piece of machinery, it was just cut off.[65] Textile companies depended upon the availability of a large pool of labor and the state's indifference to working conditions. However, by 1943 the unions had become stronger and in some plants conditions had improved.

The varied conditions the unions faced helps explain their very different characters. Because telephone workers had high salaries and generally good working conditions, fired workers wanted their jobs back years later. The FEC's major problem was the sheer number of employers and the small size of the average store. That many retail clerks considered themselves middle class and that a large percentage was women were perceived as drawbacks. Yet these drawbacks were also strengths. Not only were retail clerks numerous in all regions, but also they were white-collar workers in a society in which class distinctions were important—a factor which helped them become an important political force. The political aspects of municipal employment both hurt and helped municipal workers. While they received very high salaries, the municipality would not tolerate traditional union behavior, and the spoils system created a work force that was so politicized that it was difficult to unite. The railroad industry never fully recovered from the collapse of 1929, permitting the companies to keep the workers almost continuously on the defensive. Only the power of the unions prevented a serious deterioration of conditions. While the textile industry grew rapidly because of government economic policies, the workers' conditions remained very bad.

Clearly union members had very dissimilar needs and desires. Differences in behavior which have been ascribed to ideology or union leadership can be better explained by the conditions of the industry in which the various organizations functioned.

Chapter 4

THE LABOR MOVEMENT PRIOR TO 1930

Prior to 1916 the labor movement was dominated by immigrants and seemed to concern the governing elites only when it shattered the peace, as it did on numerous occasions after 1900. The tens of thousands of immigrants who poured into Argentina around the turn of the century brought with them the working class ideologies of Europe. Three principal currents competed for support: anarchism, socialism, and syndicalism. Anarchism early emerged as the dominant ideology.[1]

In 1910 severe government repression badly wounded anarchism, however. According to some sources, the movement never fully recovered.[2] Syndicalism began to grow, aided by the coming to power of Yrigoyen and the Radicals. The government became a key player in the relationship between capital and labor, a role that has continued until the present. The regime developed a good relationship with Syndicalist unions, and other unions learned that cultivating the government could be useful. In the 1930s and 1940s they constantly sought government help, setting the tone for much of their activity.

When the Radicals came to power, they did not develop a systematic plan for unions. Yrigoyen was primarily interested in expanding his electoral base among the working class. He also realized that responding to labor unrest with repression would provoke more turmoil, which would be intolerable for any popularly elected government. Yrigoyen courted support by not always using the repressive powers of the state against strikes led by Syndicalists; at times the police took a neutral stance. In industries such as railroads and shipping, in which there were large concentrations of native-born workers—i.e., voters—in important districts, Yrigoyen pressured employers to settle conflicts on terms favorable to the workers.

Yrigoyen's approach dovetailed nicely with the desires of the Syndicalists. Ideologically the Syndicalists believed that the revolution would come from a general strike, and they scorned bourgeois politics. In practice they were willing to negotiate with governments on working conditions, wages, and the like, but preferred to bypass formal structures to deal directly with officials in the executive branch. This had special appeal to the Radicals: they did not want a formal relationship, and Syndicalist ideology precluded one. Moreover, the growth of syndicalism undermined the Socialists, the Radicals' principal rivals in the capital.[3]

Radical policies led to the growth of Syndicalist unions. With direct support from Yrigoyen's government, the Federación Obrera Marítima (for maritime workers) emerged as a powerful force that controlled the port.[4] Yrigoyen also wooed railroaders; he did not set the agenda but reacted to the workers' initiatives. For example, in 1917 a wildcat strike began after the dismissal of two workers from the shops of the Central Argentino. It spread, halting traffic on the entire line. Despite extensive violence, Yrigoyen maintained contact with the unions and refrained from sending troops. When finally deployed, the troops were not used against the strikers. The strike ended after the government pressured the company into rehiring all workers, including those whose dismissals had sparked the action.[5]

The government did not hesitate to use repression if it felt that a strike was to its political disadvantage, however. In 1917–18 Yrigoyen used troops against strikers in meat-packing plants. The strikers were not only mostly foreigners and therefore ineligible to vote, but also they were led by Anarchists. Toleration would have alienated crucial sectors of the society.[6]

The government's attitude was decisive in allowing the Syndicalists to become the largest segment of the labor movement. Most unions had organized only a low percentage of their industry and found it difficult to close down a plant or the industry if they were opposed by the state. Most employers refused to negotiate unless forced to do so, and only the government could apply the necessary leverage. Unions did not have special legal status.* A few began to depend on government intervention. This is not to say they were coopted. Unions were dealing with the societal limits and were trying to improve conditions for their members.

In 1917–21 intense labor agitation was spurred by the Radical regime's attitude, high inflation, and the Russian Revolution. Strike activity rose precipitously, as did union formation and membership. Sympathy strikes and boycotts were common. The bourgeoisie found this unsettling because it feared a Russian-style revolution in Argentina.[7]

A breakdown in the tacit alliance between the Syndicalists and the Radicals began with the "Tragic Week" of January 1919. When police

*A few had *personería jurídica*, which gave them legal standing equal to that of a country club.

ambushed and killed four workers after an officer had been killed during a stoppage at a metallurgical plant, a general strike broke out. Both workers and police escalated the violence. The army and key elements of the Radical coalition threatened to withdraw support from the government. The regime responded with a massive use of force against left-wing organizations. Moreover, the government permitted civilians from the upper and middle classes to attack working-class neighborhoods. Workers and their families were assaulted; Jews and Catalans were primary targets since the former were considered infected by Bolshevism and the latter by anarchism. What in essence was a pogrom took place in Buenos Aires. Deaths were in the hundreds.[8]

The violence did not stop the wave of labor agitation. The number of strikes and strikers increased, surpassing in 1919 and 1920 the figures for 1918. Yet government assistance to unions and workers did not end immediately. In early 1919 telephone workers formed a union and in March struck for twenty days. The stoppage ended after Yrigoyen personally intervened and offered the capital's chief of police as a mediator. Most of the union's demands were met, but in November the organization called another strike. The workers failed to respond and the union collapsed.[9]

The failure of the telephone union was not atypical. Many new unions had inexperienced leaders who tried to go too far too fast, and the organizations disappeared after defeat. Moreover, employers began to harden their positions. Also, in 1921 and 1922 the cost of living dropped and real wages rose, while the industrial sector suffered difficulties created by increased imports. The government abandoned its policy of supporting strikes because politically it was too costly. In 1921 when the Syndicalists called a general strike, the government nipped it in the bud by arresting union leaders. The new attitude contributed to the military's brutal slaughter of hundreds of striking rural workers in Patagonia in 1921 and 1922.[10]

Unrest had threatened to alienate vital elements of the Radical coalition, and between 1919 and 1921 the party changed its tactics. David Rock, in the best book on the Radicals in power, argues that the party preferred to depend on political machines and personal contacts rather than direct government-union relations.[11] This seems to be an oversimplification. The Radical Party did not abandon the Syndicalists. While the Radicals' relationship with labor remained informal, they wooed unions through concessions. To a measured degree, they aided unions that avoided the type of disruptions that had occurred earlier. Their support of the UF was the key to the union's success.

During Alvear's presidency the UF won a number of important victories with government aid. A highly centralized, disciplined organization, its leadership realized the value of government support and knew that it was in both its own and the government's interest to preserve peace on the railroads. The union was reluctant to strike, preferring to use tactics such as slowdowns, which demonstrated strength without completely halting railroad traffic.* It also took over what would have been the government's job—maintaining order on the far-flung rail system. When a local struck, the UF used its power to isolate the action. When the authorities decided to end a stoppage, it was not necessary to send troops because the union leaders took it upon themselves to restore service. The UF was an insurance policy against a crippling national rail strike. In addition, its leadership, composed of both Syndicalists and Socialists, was primarily interested in narrowly construed union activity. The UF grew rapidly into the largest union that Argentina had yet seen, with 18,925 dues-payers in 1923 and 70,793 in 1930.[12]

The UF's relationship with the government was exceptionally positive, but other unions, including those of the maritime workers and the trolley-car workers, attempted to follow in the UF's footsteps. The Radicals tried to expand the number of organizations with which they cooperated. For example, in 1929 after Yrigoyen had returned to the presidency, he helped force the telephone company to sign a contract with a newly established Syndicalist union, the FOET.[13]

For most unions the 1920s were a period of unsettling fluctuations. Many never recovered from the defeats of the early years of the decade. They were further weakened by severe internal divisions. In 1922 a new Syndicalist confederation was created, the Unión Sindical Argentina (USA). While it rhetorically maintained an anti-political attitude, by the end of the decade it had ties to the Radical Party which could not be expressed openly because (as noted) relations with bourgeois parties were frowned upon. It was not a strong organization. The railroad unions never joined. Many of its craft-based unions began to lose members and became less important, while several other organizations, including that of the maritime workers, lost strikes which crippled them.[14]

In 1926, antagonized by the policies of the USA, Socialist-dominated unions withdrew and joined the two railroad organizations in

---

*According to Charles Anderson, "power contenders" in Latin America enter the political system by demonstrating power but using it with restraint (*Politics and Economic Change in Latin America* [New York, 1967], 105ff.).

creating a new confederation, the Confederación Obrera Argentina (COA). While the bulk of the affiliates belonged to the railroad unions, which largely maintained political neutrality, Socialists played a key role in the COA. Two Socialist members of the Chamber of Deputies, Francisco Pérez Leirós (head of the UOEM) and Agustín Muzio, served on the executive committee. When the Socialist Party split in 1927, Muzio backed the Independent Socialists and was soon expelled from the confederation.[15]

The Socialist Party's relationship to the labor movement was complex. In 1918 the party adopted a resolution based on the policies of its French counterpart: it called on its members to join unions but also to keep the labor movement separate from all political parties and ideologies. However, the party had a Comisión Socialista de Información Gremial (Commission on Socialist Union Information) designed to coordinate Socialist participation in the labor movement. Within individual unions Socialists set up caucuses to establish uniform positions and control the organizations. Nonetheless, no formal relationship existed between the party and Socialist unions.[16]

In the 1920s the Communists became an important force in the labor movement. Founded in 1920, the Communist Party attempted to win control of the USA and almost succeeded. As the decade progressed, support for the Communists declined.[17] In 1928 after a shift in Comintern policies, the party took an extremely aggressive stance, rejecting alliances. In 1929 it created its own confederation, the Comité Nacional de Unidad Sindical Clasista, which had few affiliated unions or workers, though pockets of strength existed in such industries as textiles and meat-packing.[18]

Estimates of the size of the other existing confederations vary widely. Because of the membership of the two railroad unions, the largest was the COA. Several sources believe it had over 80,000 members—a likely figure since in 1930 the UF had slightly over 70,000 dues-payers.[19] According to *La Vanguardia*, the USA had 20,008 dues-payers in 1922, but these had shrunk to 15,927 in 1925 and 15,638 by 1929.[20] Opinions on the strength of the Anarchist confederation, the Federación Obrera Regional Argentina (FORA), range from insignificant to 200,000 members. There is little reason to doubt that the FORA had declined since the first decade of the century and had lost almost all importance. It remained strong in Rosario, where it had ties to the Radical Party. In the capital the Anarchists' domain had been reduced to construction, carting, stevedoring, and breadmaking.[21]

In 1928 a new national organization of printing unions urged the establishment of a nonideological confederation. Both the USA and the COA accepted the idea and submitted it to their memberships. In the former, unification was put to assemblies of constituent unions, and a vast majority of participants approved the idea. In the latter, the situation was more complex. While many Socialist union leaders—especially Pérez Leirós—opposed the idea, the party liked the plan. When the COA submitted the proposal to a referendum, it passed easily but with the help of voter fraud.[22] The new confederation, the Confederación General del Trabajo (CGT), was formed after the September 1930 coup.

Except for the UOEM (founded in 1916), the unions in our study were founded during the Radical era. Only the UF and UOEM were noteworthy before 1930. Below we shall explore how these unions developed.

THE FOET

The collapse of the telephone workers' organization in 1919 left the industry without a union until the second Yrigoyen administration. Unhappy with conditions, a group composed largely of young men, many of whom had worked for the UT only a short time, began to meet on payday in a cafe near where they received their salaries. In early 1928 they circulated their first propaganda, and on 26 July 1928 a meeting of approximately forty workers formally established an organization. The new organization began as part of the FEC, but the alliance failed because the leaders of the telephone workers had Syndicalist inclinations while the Socialists dominated the FEC. The FOET was founded in December 1928.[23]

The FOET presented its demands to the UT at a time when the corporation was very vulnerable because it was being purchased by ITT, and the Radical government had a deep-seated fear of Yankee capitalism. Yrigoyen participated in the negotiations with the UT, and an agreement was reached on 4 March 1929 in the Ministry of Interior. The UT claimed that it signed because the government forced it to. The pact established higher and uniform wage rates, improved conditions, and won recognition for the union's grievance committee.[24]

The news of the victory mobilized the interior, and the FOET lent support to a wave of organizing. In Córdoba and Bahía Blanca strikes were won, achieving recognition of the union and better salaries. In La

Plata a settlement including union recognition and better salaries was obtained without a stoppage. The FOET also helped telephone workers in Tucumán and Santiago del Estero who won agreements but could not maintain them. Workers for Standard Electric (the manufacturing arm of ITT) and for the other small telephone company in the capital also formed unions.[25]

Only in Santa Fe province did the workers encounter major problems. In Rosario, where a contract had been signed as early as 1928, the local organization struck in January 1930. The walkout was violent and long. The FOET lent its support and helped obtain the friendly intervention of local authorities. The stoppage ended with pre-strike conditions restored. In addition, the workers received 60 pesos as strike pay, and those who had been arrested were given their jobs back.[26]

In May 1930 in the city of Santa Fe a union was founded; in July a violence-plagued strike began after the company refused union demands. This time the authorities were less cooperative, partly because the union itself was less inclined to use the good offices of the government. To put pressure on the company, the telephone unions in the capital, La Plata, Bahía Blanca, Rosario, and Córdoba staged a twenty-four-hour sympathy strike. According to the FOET, a majority of male workers joined everywhere, but only in Bahía Blanca did large numbers of women operators participate. In the short run only the operators could disrupt service; the failure to obtain their support was to pose a serious problem for the union. The sympathy strike's impact cannot be judged because the September 1930 coup forced an end to the stoppage.[27]

The FOET in the capital and its suburbs grew from an average of 2,490 dues-payers in 1929 to 3,278 during the first eight months of 1930.* However, the UT began to stiffen its resistance, forming a mutual aid society to draw employees away from the union. Union officials were being fired in the provinces, and there was talk of layoffs.[28] The offensive intensified after Yrigoyen fell from office.

THE FEC

In 1919 commercial employees participated in the labor unrest that followed the Tragic Week. Only two feeble unions existed, but in April

---

*Based on an estimate that 10 percent of members paid dues of 50 centavos instead of one peso because they were women or others in special categories (*Federación*, 1929–30).

employees of several large stores struck and won significant victories. Before the end of the month, the retail clerks struck Gath y Chaves, which responded with strikebreakers. For two weeks the employees held out alone and then called for help. Important unions such as those for maritime workers and printers responded by boycotting everything that had to do with the store. Because printers refused to print advertisements for Gath y Chaves, they were locked out of many newspapers. Despite the aid, the walkout collapsed after forty days. In August the two unions merged to form the FEC.[29] The new union could not maintain the gains that had been made.

The strike against Gath y Chaves was the high-water mark until the 1930s. The FEC went through a period of murky ideological upheaval and emerged with a Socialist leadership about 1927. Between 1927 and 1930 the union was little more than a cluster of Socialist militants who met in the party offices and had little impact on working conditions.[30]

THE UOEM

The UOEM became an important organization during the 1920s, as did the UF, but its mode of operation was very different from the UF's. The UOEM had open ties to the Socialist Party. In this lay both its strength and its weakness.

The UOEM was founded with the aid of the Socialist Party in January 1916. Its early base of support lay among the largely Spanish refuse workers. In 1916 the union called three strikes, each increasingly larger, in order to improve pitiful working conditions. With the third stoppage, the organization wrung from the municipal government an agreement to end a system of fines and to rehire those fired during previous strikes. The Conservatives still controlled the city government and were less hostile than might be expected because they hoped to use the Socialists as a counterweight to the Radicals.

The appointment of the first Radical intendente in late 1916 changed conditions because he refused to cooperate with the union. A cut in salaries imposed by the previous administration further exacerbated the union-government relationship. Despite the opposition of the Socialist Party, a fourth stoppage began in March 1917 and met with harsh repression. Five thousand workers were fired. There were jailings and simulated executions. The treatment of the Spanish strikers was so bad that their ambassador intervened. The municipality attenuated its actions only after a reluctant intervention by the Syndicalists, who threatened a general strike when the full extent of the repression became clear. Workers, who had not been replaced, were allowed to return, and gains made in 1916, such as the eight-hour day, were recognized as still in force. The municipal authorities' hostility did not cease immediately, but a series of partial strikes from 1919 through 1921 won the UOEM the right to survive.[31]

In the 1920s the UOEM became an accepted part of the municipal system. Its success came in large part because of the establishment in 1917 of a city council with all members elected at-large and the enfranchisement at the municipal level of male foreigners who met certain qualifications. The council allowed popular pressure and the Socialist Party to play a significant role in the affairs of the city. The spoils system also helped focus the attention of the municipal authorities on its workers. Conditions for municipal workers improved greatly. In 1918 the average municipal worker earned 70 pesos a month, but by 1930 the minimum was 165. Prior to 1926 nurses earned 60 pesos a month, and after 1926, 165. The new conditions included 90 days of sick leave a year, better hygiene, and more job security.[32]

The UOEM had de facto recognition from the municipal authorities, who received its representatives and often acted upon its petitions. The city gave the UOEM the use of some land and a subsidy to develop a recreational facility (see Chapter 5 below). The union expanded its support to the rest of the blue-collar work force; by 1930 it had approximately 5,000 dues-payers, about one quarter of the blue-collar workers.[33]

The UOEM faced serious opposition in part because of its ties to the Socialist Party. In 1927 municipal workers founded a union with connections to the Radical Party, the Asociación Trabajadores de la Comuna. The UOEM failed to win the elections for worker representative to the pension board until after the September 1930 coup.[34] (Pension board elections are the best tool for measuring union popularity because all workers could vote.) Nonetheless, the UOEM had carved out a role for itself in the municipality.

THE UF

The most important union during the 1920s was the UF. It was created to solve the problems of La Fraternidad, a union of railroad engineers and firemen founded in 1887 with the aid of a North American who belonged to a railroad brotherhood in the United States. By 1910 La Fraternidad had become a sizable force. However, in January 1912—at the height of the harvest season and with the hope of disrupting exports—it called a general strike against the railroads but received little help from the average worker. Approximately 11,000 railroaders struck, 8,000 of whom were engineers or firemen. Thus the government was able to follow a dual strategy of negotiating and keeping the trains running. After 52 days a settlement was reached; however, many workers, especially the strike leaders, did not get their jobs back. The reason for defeat was clear: La Fraternidad had not received help from railroaders who did not drive the trains. A major goal for the next decade was to create that support.[35]

The Federación Obrera Ferrocarrilera (FOF) had been founded just prior to the 1912 strike to represent all railroaders not in La Fraternidad.* However, it had been unable to offer more than moral assistance. A mutual suspicion existed between La Fraternidad and the FOF. While the former was legalistic and centralized, the militantly syndicalist FOF believed in direct action and autonomy for its locals. By the end of 1916 the FOF claimed a membership of 9,322 and had signed a pact with La Fraternidad.

The two unions planned a general railroad strike for the end of 1917. However, a series of strikes broke out earlier; afraid of losing control, the unions struck in September. The extremely violent stoppage lasted 24 days. At the behest of the government, the railroad companies made concessions including increased pay, the establishment of work rules, and the rehiring of the 1912 strikers.

It was a Pyrrhic victory because the railroaders' unity shattered. Upset by the violence and the FOF's reluctance to accept a government-assisted solution when it was first offered, La Fraternidad refused to participate in future strikes. Railroaders continued to press their demands. There were 31 strikes with 56,273 participants in 1918 and 73 with 27,863 participants in 1919. Believing that the unrest undermined its political aims, the government became unsympathetic. The stoppages were increasingly less successful and the FOF disintegrated.[36]

Defeat led to the rise of leaders who believed in centralized, disciplined unions. In 1920 such leaders helped create an umbrella organization, the Confraternidad Ferroviaria, composed of La Fraternidad, a union for shop workers, and one for the remaining railroaders. In 1922 the leadership merged the latter two unions and

*The union was later called Federación Obrera Ferroviaria.

created the UF. Immediately after its formation, the UF applied for and received personería jurídica, ensuring that its signature was legally binding.[37]

The new organization was highly centralized and valued government aid. The leadership had participated in the 1917-19 strike wave and had been scarred by the indiscipline and the defeats. From the very beginning it adopted cautious, peaceful, and controlled tactics.

The Confraternidad had immediate success. A few months after its founding, La Fraternidad and the railroads signed the industry's first collective contract.[38] In 1921 in order to obtain a similar pact for other workers, the Confraternidad threatened to "work to regulation": by following all the many intricate rules of the railroads to the point of exaggeration, the unions intended to slow rail traffic to a crawl. The government intervened to expedite agreements covering traffic department personnel.[39]

In the 1920s workers in almost all job categories gained collective contracts that established grievance procedures, set wages, and regulated promotions. Working conditions improved markedly and wages surged upward. For example, a telegraph linesman earned 115 pesos a month in 1918 and 180 in 1930; shunters went from 105 to 165 pesos, while workshop artisans averaged 134 pesos in 1918 and 206 in 1930. By 1930 an elaborate system had been created to settle grievances. Sixty-eight permanent committees annually handled 1,600 cases to which a satisfactory solution could not be found on the local level. If the committees failed, the UF's executive board brought the matter under dispute to the company's directors.[40] The union also won recognition from both the government and the companies as the legitimate representative of the railroaders.

The UF was most effective during 1925-27, when it signed agreements establishing basic conditions which lasted until after Perón began his rise to power. As part of the Alvear administration's attempt to wean popular support from Yrigoyen, the government played a key role in wringing concessions from the railroad companies. A major participant was Minister of Public Works Roberto M. Ortiz; the bonds he forged had tremendous impact on the union when he became president.[41]

After the 1928 election the UF had less success. In the hope of winning a 150-peso per month minimum wage and other improvements, in November 1929 it instituted short work stoppages that tied up traffic but ended at the government's insistence. Shop workers and those in several other job categories received paid vacations. In March 1930 the union again tied up traffic, but again the government stepped in. A special commission was formed to study the conditions of the railroads and their workers, but nothing important came of it.[42]

Not only had the attitudes of the government and the companies hardened, but a dispute erupted between the UF and La Fraternidad. The Confraternidad was dissolved in 1929.[43] On the other hand, the UF had become a powerful organization. By 1930 it had established its style, cautiously demonstrating its power and maintaining a close relationship with the government.

THE UOT

Workers had struck textile plants as early as 1901 and had formed a union by 1905. In 1921 the UOT was founded as the Federación Obrera de la Industria Textil. Between 1921 and 1929 textile workers struck thirty-eight times in the capital. The union claimed over a thousand affiliates in 1926–27. However, ideological conflict weakened the organization. For a short time the UOT was a member of the USA but was then expelled. The Communists gained control of the union but lost it in 1928, and the following year the union split into Communist and Socialist fragments. Neither group had more than several handfuls of militants.[44]

By 1930 most successful unions had adapted to the realities of local politics. Many had developed an orientation to the society and the political system that was to be vital in determining their responses to developments after September 1930. Nonetheless, during the 1930s the labor movement underwent major changes. It grew. Unions connected to political parties and those serving industrial workers expanded the fastest. Those in export-based industries suffered. The situation in services varied, depending on the state of the industry and on the union leadership.

Chapter 5

THE DIFFICULT YEARS, 1930–1935

For unions the early years of Neo-Conservative dominance were extremely difficult. Under Uriburu the depression and political repression permitted employers to fire workers, cut wages, and cripple unions. At best unions could survive. Communist and Anarchist unions were suppressed. During the Justo presidency restrictions were eased, allowing unions to try to recover lost ground, but they had little success until the urban economy improved. The unions that did best were those that developed a good relationship with some branch of government.

Unions offered no resistance to the overthrow of Yrigoyen. Some unions contemplated defending the Radical regime, which is not surprising. Elements in the labor movement openly backed Yrigoyen almost to the end. Some Anarchists and Syndicalists planned a general strike but were foiled by the government.[1] A successful general strike would have been surprising because key unionists championed noninvolvement in bourgeois politics, and it would have been difficult to justify such an action. Furthermore, without the help of the Socialists a general strike would have been futile, and the Socialists' concern for legality, plus their rivalry with the Radicals, made their participation highly unlikely.

Despite their inactivity, unions as disparate as the Syndicalist FOET and the Socialist Unión Obrera Marítima (Union of Maritime Workers) felt compelled to proclaim their noninvolvement in politics. Unions asked their members to remain calm.[2] Nevertheless, the Uriburu regime moved quickly to suppress unions perceived as threatening. On 7 September 1930 (the day following the coup), three hundred leftists were rounded up. As noted in Chapter 1, hundreds of others suffered arrest, torture, and exile. The government shut Anarchist and Communist newspapers and unions, frequently with a great deal of violence. For example, in January 1931 the police assaulted the headquarters of the Communist meatpackers' union in the industrial suburb of Berisso, detaining thirty-six leaders. According to *La Vanguardia*, some of those apprehended were beaten until they vomited blood. Many spent the entire Uriburu regime in jail, while others were deported.[3]

The FORA fought back with general strikes, which failed dismally and led to further arrests.[4] The Anarchists never recovered and their influence lingered in just a few industries. While the decline was directly linked to the persecution, the Anarchist base was in sectors of the economy that were weakening, either because they were archaic (such as carting) or tied to exports (such as stevedoring). Communist unions reemerged after the Uriburu regime in part because their strength lay in modern industrial sectors which expanded with economic recovery. More important, the Communist Party, while small, was disciplined and well financed. In 1931 it sent Rufino Gómez to organize the petroleum fields of Comodoro Rivadavia. He started not by creating a labor organization, but by forming party cells and then a union.[5]

Even for unions that the regime did not try to suppress, martial law and the state of siege made normal activity almost impossible. Strikes in progress when the coup occurred had to be ended. Unions were forbidden to hold meetings. After appealing to the government, they were informed that if they behaved legally, they could carry on normal activities. But restrictions remained. Meetings could be held only after permission had been obtained, but to obtain it was often difficult and time-consuming. The police frequently harassed those distributing propaganda and attempting to organize.[6]

The Uriburu regime was sharply divided about unions. Its labor policies were not simply repressive, as some have claimed.[7] One faction was openly hostile, believing that labor should at best be tolerated. Another, heavily influenced by corporatist ideals, thought the state should play an active role in labor relations in order to lessen social conflict. While the latter group looked with favor upon union activity and tried to mitigate the impact of the depression, it did not tolerate organizations that refused to cooperate with the new political situation.

The major figure in the corporatist-oriented faction was Eduardo F. Maglione, president of the DNT. Soon after the coup the DNT promised all employer and worker organizations that labor laws would be enforced. It also suggested the establishment of labor-management commissions, arbitration to settle disputes, the setting of conditions through contracts—still rare—and the reduction of workers' hours rather than layoffs. The DNT displayed an awareness that employers were making the most of the coup:

> The support which the industrial and commercial institutions have spontaneously offered to the government should be proved by deeds.

This consists in not taking advantage of present circumstances to modify the basic working conditions which existed prior to the Revolution.[8]

If working conditions were to be changed, the DNT wanted it done slowly and rationally. In addition, it informed unions that it would respect the right to assemble, associate, and strike, but would repress boycotts and sabotage.

Maglione claimed that when he took over the DNT, 2,500 fines for violations of labor laws had not been given to the police for collection because the police already had 1,500 which they had not acted upon.[9] Enforcement became a priority; Maglione even invited unions to discuss how it should be done. He also attempted to stretch the powers of his agency by arbitrating disputes and becoming involved in the problems of the textile and telephone industries. The DNT's attitude had little impact since the agency had weak statutory powers and could not force employers to make agreements with unions. When Maglione urged the UT to accept an alternative to layoffs, the company refused to consider the proposal. Other government agencies circumscribed the DNT's limited abilities. When a busdriver protested to his company that he had not been paid, he was fired. The driver then complained to the DNT, which sent the company a citation. The company accused the driver of being an Anarchist and he was arrested. The DNT was powerless to help.

By the time Maglione resigned in May 1931, he had won the respect of *La Vanguardia*.[10] Labor law enforcement was almost a revolutionary step—one that Juan Perón used with great success slightly over a decade later. Maglione was just the most important of the corporatists. For example, in Mendoza the provincial *interventor* (acting governor, selected by the central government) appointed the president of a UF local to head the provincial department of labor.[11] However, the corporatists soon lost ground to the hardliners. Maglione's replacement was a lieutenant colonel in a right-wing paramilitary organization.

More influential than the DNT were the police, who were interested in stopping what they perceived as subversion. Their stance stunted union activity. Workers feared jailings, torture, and the loss of jobs. Intensely nationalistic, the government frequently expelled aliens it considered undesirable, and the many immigrants active in the labor movement were under constant pressure. In the above incident involving the busdriver, a representative of the busdriver's union went to the police to inquire about his detention. The representative, who had been born in Galicia but had an Argentine child and had become a citizen, was told that he should leave if he did not want to be deported because "the country did not need Gallegos."[12] Of the FOET's five principal leaders, two withdrew from active roles in the union—one because he was afraid of the outcome of a lawsuit pending against him, and the other because he was a foreigner and did not want to be deported.[13] While Argentines did not face the threat of deportation to Mussolini's Italy (where they might face a death sentence), they were not spared the other fates that the regime reserved for its opponents.

Unions were unable effectively to counter employers who drastically lowered wages and laid off large numbers of workers. In a few cases employees responded with strikes—forty-seven in the capital between 6 September 1930 and 31 July 1931 and forty-two in all of 1931. These were acts of desperation; in 1931 over three quarters ended in defeat.[14] Victories came through the intervention of the DNT or other government agencies.

Under Uriburu the labor movement had changed. The UF's affiliates composed a high percentage of all union members. Anarchist and Communist unions had been seriously weakened. Many smaller, craft-based unions, such as those in the furniture industry (which had been influential in the USA) had begun to fade away, hurt by the depression and the general atmosphere. The Syndicalists could offer little help.[15]*

With Justo's assumption of power in February 1932, more normal conditions returned. The state of siege was lifted (though it was to be reimposed frequently). Strikes seemed possible, and with the buildup of grievances, a wave of walkouts rolled across Argentina. Workers struck the UT, meatpacking plants, petroleum fields in Patagonia, and shoe factories. There were more strikes and strikers in the capital in 1932 than in any of the subsequent years under study. The strikes were very large (see Table 5-1).[16]†

---

*Of the unions in the USA which the Socialist Party thought important in 1929, only the Federación Obrera Marítima was still important several years later (Partido Socialista, *Anuario Socialista 1930* [Buenos Aires, 1929], 130–40).

†For 1932 there is a major discrepancy between strike figures in DNT, *Boletín informativo*, Apr. 1934, 3919, and DNT, División de Estadística, *Estadística de las huelgas* (Buenos Aires, 1940), 20. The former is more likely accurate since there is more detail. Strike statistics must be used with some skepticism. Strikes not ended by 31 December are sometimes counted twice.

Table 5-1

Strikes and Strikers in Buenos Aires, 1931–45

Year	Number of Strikes	Number of Strikers	Average Number of Strikers per Strike
1931	42	8,442	201
1932	122	165,376	1,355
1933	52	3,321	64
1934	42	25,940	618
1935	69	52,143	756
1936	109	85,439	784
1937	82	49,993	610
1938	44	8,881	202
1939	49	19,718	402
1940	53	12,721	204
1941	54	6,606	122
1942	113	39,865	353
1943	85	6,754	79
1944	27	9,121	338
1945	47	44,186	940

Sources: DNT, *Boletín informativo,* Apr. 1934, 3919; Ministerio de Trabajo y Securidad Social, Dirección General de Estudios e Investigaciones, *Conflictos del trabajo* (Buenos Aires, 1961), 163.

The spasm of strikes ended quickly when the vast majority were lost (see Table 5-2). The economy remained very weak, and after an initial period the government became less tolerant. Strike activity practically disappeared during 1933, to pick up only slightly in 1934. The stoppages of 1932–34 were largely defensive in that they tried to recover lost ground, but in contrast to the Uriburu period, few were spontaneous reactions to the initiatives of management.

Strikes are a deceptive measure of dynamism because many powerful unions did not use them as a principal weapon. The FEC, for example, made large gains through political campaigns. Dynamism is also evident in a wave of creation of national and industrial unions beginning in 1932; the trend peaked after 1935. In 1932 the FEC helped found a national confederation of commercial employees. Industrial unions began to replace craft-based organizations—especially where Communists were important, such as in construction and woodworking. Strikes were used as organizing devices to aid the consolidation rather than simply as tools to deal with bread-and-butter issues. In 1935 the Communists shed their confrontational tactics, adopting a popular front

Table 5-2

Outcome of Strikes in Buenos Aires, 1930–45
(Percent)

Year	Won	Compromised	Lost
1930	33.9%	6.3%	59.8%
1931	9.5	14.3	76.2
1932	18.6	8.9	72.3
1933	14.0	10.0	76.0
1934	13.2	13.2	73.7
1935	17.5	26.3	56.1
1936	31.7	26.0	42.3
1937	43.2	25.9	30.9
1938	30.9	35.7	33.3
1939	40.8	24.5	34.7
1940	35.3	33.3	31.3
1941	34.0	36.0	30.0
1942	40.5	32.4	27.0
1943	38.8	37.6	23.5
1944	77.7	--	22.2
1945	68.1	2.1	29.8

Sources: DNT, *Boletín informativo*, Apr. 1934, 3918; DNT, División de Estadística: *Estadística de las huelgas* (Buenos Aires, 1940), 15, 63–69; *Estadística de las huelgas 1940* (Buenos Aires, 1941), 15; *Investigaciones sociales 1941* (Buenos Aires, 1942), 90; *Investigaciones sociales 1942* (Buenos Aires, 1943), 101; Dirección de Estadística Social, *Investigaciones sociales 1943–1945* (Buenos Aires, 1946), 56–59.

NOTE: The percentages are based on strikes ended during the year. After 1934 the categories' names changed, but they seem to represent the same measures.

policy and dissolving the Comité Nacional de Unidad Sindical Clasista.[17] The change in tactics and an improving economy led to a surge in strike activity in 1935. Almost half the stoppages were at least partially successful—a major change from 1932.

While Justo's government was more tolerant than Uriburu's, it was not friendly. It wanted stability and was willing to make certain concessions. Especially in its first months, it tried to work out a modus vivendi with the unions in the CGT. It succeeded in obtaining a vague understanding with a large portion of the movement: unions did not go beyond certain ill-defined boundaries, and the government did not try to suppress the unions. The regime did not tolerate threats to general peace, and it remained indifferent to workers' desires. Below we shall study in detail how the confederations and unions coped with the difficult years.

THE CGT

Directly after the September 1930 coup the COA and the USA merged to create the CGT. The Uriburu regime permitted its formation, no doubt because it did not consider the CGT threatening. Faced with repression and lacking a clearly defined mission, the CGT limited itself to making special appeals to both the dictatorship and employers. It had far greater access to government officials than most unions because of its size and because it was dominated by the UF, which maintained an ability to talk with the government.

The CGT's most dramatic success came when it prevented the execution of three members of an Anarchist drivers' union. To save them it signed a statement proclaiming that the government retained the state of siege only to maintain peace and that the CGT was willing to help the regime's social program. While the confederation was not in such close accord with the government, it so presented itself in order to save lives. It was not always so successful. In 1931 the CGT adopted a program which called for (among other things) paid vacations, a five-day work week, and a minimum wage, but it could do nothing to achieve these goals.[18]

Although the vast majority of union members belonged to the CGT's constituent organizations, the confederation's role did not increase markedly under Justo. It continued to issue statements which were largely ignored. It did manage to help some unions that lacked access to the state and employers. For example, during a strike at the Narciso Muñoz textile plant, CGT delegations went to the police in the hope of securing less interference, presented the workers' position to the DNT, and advised the UOT.[19] The CGT could not expand its role because it was hamstrung by a struggle between Syndicalists and Socialists—in part a continuation of an old rivalry based on ideology, and in part a fight for control of a confederation whose structure did not permit changes in leadership. The factions did not have deep philosophical differences but differed on the proper relationship between unions and politics. The Syndicalists insisted on strict political neutrality while favoring cooperation with the state. The Socialists preferred a more distant relationship with the state and closer cooperation with the

Socialist Party. In individual cases the differences between the two groups were frequently small.*

In the early years the Syndicalists controlled the CGT. To maintain their position, they stayed close to the government, a tactic which had served them well during the Radical era. Their approach is well demonstrated by a controversy that erupted in November 1933. In a statement dismissing any need to study fascism because the conditions that produced it did not exist in Argentina, the CGT's five-member executive board expressed satisfaction with the regime's stance:

> [President Justo had confirmed to key labor leaders] the democratic orientation of the present government, which would indicate the need to encourage him in his resolved intention of maintaining himself within the law, fighting for the general good, against all attempts to replace the existing order, whether originating from demagogism or from reaction.[20]

The statement's sycophantism angered almost all sectors of the labor movement. The larger central committee, which had ultimate control over the CGT, agreed almost unanimously that the language had been a mistake. However, a heated debate ensued on the interference of political parties in union affairs. The central committee adopted a statement directed more against the Socialists than against fascism. The controversy indicates both the depth of the antagonisms and the Syndicalists' willingness to cooperate with almost any government.[21]

The CGT's approach was unproductive because the Neo-Conservatives were largely indifferent to unions. When the government wanted contact with labor, it frequently found it more profitable to turn to the Socialists, whose support it needed to legitimize the political system. Moreover, while the Syndicalists were eager to cooperate with the government, frequently they were extremely combative with employers. Nonetheless, Alejandro Silvetti and Andrés Cabona, two key Syndicalists who served for a time as pro-secretary and treasurer (respectively) of the CGT, became state employees after losing their jobs in the private sector. While they did not obtain important posts, employment by the state was always political.[22] This type of support was insufficient to help the Syndicalists against attacks from Socialists, who had the backing of a party vital to the working of the political system, nor even from the

---

*Neither the term Socialist nor Syndicalist is very accurate, but this was contemporary terminology. Some Socialists sided with the Syndicalists.

Communists, who had a disciplined organization. By 1935 the Syndicalists controlled only a minority of unions. They had lost control of even the UF.

The Syndicalists' declining power created a crisis because the agreement establishing the CGT did not allow for a reflection of changing strength, and the Syndicalists remained in control. The confederation was paralyzed. However, on 12 December 1935 representatives of Socialist-influenced unions—the UF, La Fraternidad, the UOEM, the CGEC, the trolley-car workers' union, and the state employees' union—met secretly, deposed the CGT's authorities, and reconstituted the confederation.[23]

THE FOET

The UT used the opportunity presented by the repressions of the Uriburu regime to attempt to destroy the FOET. The union survived, but even winning an important strike did not bring major rewards.

The UT greeted the September 1930 coup enthusiastically. It immediately fired the union's secretary general, Luis F. Gay, and began massive layoffs, ignoring seniority and targeting others in the union leadership. As noted in Chapter 3, the work force was reduced by almost one quarter during Uriburu's dictatorship. With the repressive conditions, the strike in Santa Fe collapsed (see Chapter 4).[24]

The FOET's ties to the Radicals had become a liability; the union needed to fight to survive. The garrote kept tightening. As mentioned, several top leaders ceased playing an active role in the union. The UT intensified its efforts to draw workers away from the union and into a company-controlled mutual aid association that provided health and athletic facilities. It had some success, especially with female employees.[25]

The police harassed the FOET. Distributors of the union paper were detained. Police dissolved a meeting of the committee on celebrations at the union's headquarters, claiming that it was an illegal gathering because a permit had not been obtained. Gay was arrested and held in jail for eight days with no charges brought against him. Gay claims that the arrest was intended to induce him to accept the UT's offer of a job in another country.[26] The number of dues-payers began to drop sharply in 1930—from 3,849 in August and 3,170 in September to 2,869 in October, a decline of slightly over 25 percent. The average number of dues-payers for the first quarter of 1932 was less than half the figure for August 1930.[27]

The FOET could not strike since it knew that disruptions of communications would not be tolerated. It turned to the government for help. While the DNT sympathized and attempted to maneuver the UT into a compromise, the company refused to negotiate seriously.

Unable to protect its members, the FOET needed to buoy their spirits. It ceaselessly agitated against violations of labor laws. Its most successful campaign was against extending female operators' hours until 10 P.M., claiming that such an extension violated a law prohibiting night work for women. (If women worked later, the company could lay off better paid part-time male operators.) Under Maglione the DNT agreed with the FOET, and a change was prevented. After Maglione's resignation, the UT again tried to extend women's hours and was granted permission to do so by the minister of interior. However, it was forced to give up because of negative public opinion and resistance from workers and the union. While the FOET usually failed in its endeavors, the protests maintained a union presence while it awaited an opportunity to strike.[28]

The FOET assessed the Justo government with a combination of hope and skepticism and turned once again to the DNT. The agency again attempted to forge a compromise, but the UT refused to negotiate and remained intent on crushing the union.[29] The FOET was not sure of its next move; the twenty-four-hour strike of August 1930 had shown that a simple walkout could not stop service because few female operators would join. The workers would have to depend on sabotage and hope that the government would impose a favorable solution rather than suppress the FOET.

On 23 May 1932 the FOET called a sudden strike everywhere that telephone workers were organized—the capital, Bahía Blanca, Córdoba, Santa Fe, Rosario, and La Plata—but it collapsed quickly except in the first two cities, where sabotage created severe problems with telephone service and newspapers reported daily damage to lines and violence between strikers and strikebreakers. Strikers even cut the cables that served the Casa Rosada (government house) and Campo de Mayo. The police made arrests, but the top union leadership was not jailed.[30]

Many telephones ceased working, and the cost to the UT was very high. The mood is summed up by Amancio Spagnuolo:

I believe that this strike is much graver than it is supposed.
It could signify a terrible modification in the system of strikes known until now. . . .

If this new and surprising system, tried during the telephone strike, spreads, there will not remain even this consolation, the until now constant fact that when there is a taxi strike one does not spend money on taxis; this will only be a memory of better times. If this new method of paying to speak by telephone with telephones through which one cannot speak is implanted, then in the future, during periods of strikes, one will have to pay the bakers for the bread which they do not knead and the trolley companies for the trolleys which do not circulate.

The danger is that since this system will turn out to be much more convenient for them, the entrepreneurs and industrialists will decide to declare, on their own, a general and unending strike.[31]

The strike ended when the government found it too politically costly and demanded that the UT reach a settlement with the FOET. After 52 days a contract was signed which, while not a resounding triumph, permitted the union to survive. It called for the company to rehire 120 laid-off workers in Buenos Aires and 30 in the interior. Future vacancies would be filled from a list of those who had lost their jobs, and they would be ranked by seniority and competency. How the list was to be drawn up was left pending. It was acknowledged that the 1929 contract was still in force, and the strikers returned to work. The future of those who had been arrested would be decided later.[32]

The FOET faced major problems because the UT's attitude remained unchanged and a number of important questions had not been resolved, including the issue of the rehiring of the leadership. The FOET had few options because another strike was virtually impossible. For one thing, it was unlikely that the workers, who had just expended tremendous effort, would respond a short time later without a significant threat. For another, the UT became more sophisticated in its opposition to the union and avoided giving it a major issue around which to mobilize workers. Also, the government was extremely unlikely to tolerate a second strike.

To keep spirits high and to wring concessions, the FOET continued to constantly hound the UT. For example, it complained to the government and the UT that a new law establishing a five-and-a-half-day week had not been implemented. It agitated for the rehiring of both the leaders fired in 1930 and the workers who had been jailed for strike activity. While sometimes successful on the smaller issues, the union failed on the larger ones. The FOET survived because its actions had improved conditions; according to the UT, the average wage had increased 28 percent between 1928 and 1933.[33]

Slowly the FOET recovered its strength. The number of dues-payers rebounded sharply after the strike; in the last three months of 1932 they averaged 2,313—a gain of over 400 from pre-strike figures—but the figure declined to an average of 2,047 in 1933. A slight recovery then occurred, with the monthly average reaching 2,278 in 1934 and 2,373 in 1935. The FOET also began to rebuild its base in the provinces, organizing the rural workers in the province of Buenos Aires and trying to restart the union in Rosario.[34]

In late 1934 the FOET pushed in earnest for fulfillment of the 1932 contract, with a flurry of agitation and a threat of a strike. It charged the UT with failing to give jobs in the interior to the number required by the contract, not rehiring laid-off workers before others, not taking back those jailed during the 1932 strike, and using contract labor to avoid the conditions set in the 1929 and 1932 contracts. In July 1935 an agreement was signed in which the UT promised to rehire forty workers from a list presented by the union. Future vacancies would be filled alternately from a list of laid-off workers drawn up by the UT and a list from the union until 75 percent of one list were employed. The UT agree to discuss other issues.[35]

The overthrow of Yrigoyen had given the UT an opportunity to crush the FOET. The easing of repression under Justo permitted the workers to wage a bitter strike. Ironically, victory did not create a dynamic union, but one that had few options.

THE FEC

The Uriburu era demonstrates well the retail clerks' inability to use traditional tactics. Only when the political system opened up and the FEC acquired new leadership did the union respond effectively to the problems of its industry.

In the aftermath of the September 1930 coup, retail clerks faced a major offensive from employers, but the FEC could not prevent wage reductions and layoffs. Moreover, employers in the central shopping district, confronted with increased competition for scarce customers, abandoned such traditional practices as the five-and-a-half-day week. Small and weak, the FEC could not respond independently. It campaigned for the enforcement of labor laws, trying to enlist the government's help, but it had little success. It proposed that unions be recognized legally to protect legitimate organizations from competition.

This proposal was disregarded. The government did set mandatory closing hours for stores, thereby limiting the number of hours that could be worked. However, the regulation seemed motivated more by a desire to limit night-time activity than to aid workers.[36]

The political system that developed under Justo—prior to the Radicals' return—gave the FEC a unique opportunity to prosper. Ties to the Socialist Party paid dividends because of the party's role in the political system. In addition, the FEC was an atypical union. Its potential members frequently believed themselves to be middle class, were disinclined to strike, and were considered to be more respectable than the average worker by the upper reaches of society. The union leadership converted weaknesses into strengths and built a strong organization through political mobilization. The concentration on politics permitted the FEC to avoid traditional union tactics that would have alienated many of the retail clerks and would have been ineffective because of the great number of stores it would have to reach.

The FEC was able to make the most of its opportunities because of the emergence of an astute leader, Angel G. Borlenghi. The small handful of militant Socialists who ran the union in 1930 had lacked vision and were too tightly tied to the Socialist Party. In 1931 the union went through a period of upheaval set off by an intention to print the pictures of the chief of police and a politician in the union paper, thus violating norms about keeping unions separate from the government. Shortly afterward Borlenghi emerged as the dominant figure.[37]

While a Socialist, Borlenghi never enjoyed the party's trust, perhaps because his name had appeared on a manifesto which led to the formation of the Independent Socialist Party (he claimed it had appeared without his consent). After Borlenghi's initial successes, the party leadership may have distrusted him because he had a large, fervent personal following and could not be controlled. Despite great political skills and ambitions, only once was he placed on the Socialists' electoral lists, and then not high enough to win. His fellow labor leaders were suspicious of him because he broke the code of austerity: he dressed well, had a rug on his office floor, and was a womanizer.[38]

Borlenghi placed distance between the union and the Socialist Party while retaining the ties. For example, when in a general assembly someone proposed a round of applause for the party and a telegram of thanks to its next congress, Borlenghi responded that the union should have nothing to do with the congresses of any party.[39] Such tactics permitted the FEC to widen its appeal.

While vital to the FEC's political victories, the Socialists could not pass legislation without considerable help. For reasons noted above, the retail clerks attracted the interest of other parties (prior to fraud becoming the dominant means of electoral expression). Their appeal and the space opened up between the FEC and the Socialists permitted the union to garner support from every major party. In addition, the "respectable" press, which normally paid little attention to unions, gave more coverage to what was a movement of its readers.[40] As a result, the FEC was able to launch three successful political campaigns in 1932 that transformed working conditions.

The first campaign was for Saturday closings. The stores in downtown Buenos Aires had traditionally closed on Saturday afternoon, but because of competition from outlying areas, where stores remained open, the downtown stores began to stay open as well. If the so-called "English Saturday" was to be restored, it had to be through legislation. The FEC secured the necessary law easily, in part because it had the support of some seven hundred commercial establishments, which preferred to close but feared their competitors. Despite the FEC's efforts to widen the reach of the law, it applied only to the capital and the sparsely populated national territories. Nonetheless, it had a tremendous impact because all workers in the capital had their work week cut by half a day.[41]

Second, the FEC campaigned to limit the hours worked per day. Many retail clerks worked extraordinarily long hours, but neither the DNT nor the FEC had the strength to enforce the legally mandated eight-hour day. The union wanted legislation that established an easily enforceable mandatory closing time which would limit the number of hours that could be worked. The union did not face massive opposition, but the law which was enacted covered only the capital, and the most flagrant violators of the eight-hour day—the small grocery stores—were excluded despite the FEC's vociferous protests.[42]

The third successful campaign resulted in legislation which reformed the commercial code and gave all employees dismissed without cause an indemnification of not less than half their monthly salary for each year of service. Suspensions of more than three months or wage reductions which did not have the permission of the employees were classified as layoffs. Provisions were included for paid vacations and sick pay. (After its passage, the legislation was interpreted to include blue-collar workers, but consistent enforcement for these workers had to wait for the Perón era.) While the campaign for the reform of the commercial code faced more opposition than the FEC's two other campaigns, it closely resembled the other two and therefore will be discussed in detail.

The Socialists played a crucial role in obtaining the reforms in the commercial code. One, Adolfo Dickmann, presented the proposal to the Chamber of Deputies, and another, Silvio Ruggieri, guided the bill through committee. *La Vanguardia* offered strong support.[43] However, the FEC's leadership realized that it needed wider support than just the union and the Socialists because the base was too small and too concentrated in the capital.

A suggestion from the organized retail clerks in the province of Buenos Aires to form a national confederation was quickly taken up and merged with the drive for the reform of the commercial code. The reformed commercial code was one of the few items on the agenda when a constituent congress met in March 1932. The new confederation—what soon became the Confederación General de Empleados de Comercio (CGEC)-was a useful tool for conducting a national political campaign since retail clerks could speak with a single voice even though the organization's twenty-four initial affiliates were scattered across the country.

By helping to create the CGEC, the FEC did not surrender its leadership of the reform campaign: the initial congress was held in its offices, and four of the seven members of the first executive committee represented the FEC.[44] In mid-1932 to further widen support, the FEC joined with other unions—including those for traveling salesmen, tailors, bank clerks, and pharmacy employees—to create a special committee. This organization called the meetings and led the demonstrations for reform, but again the FEC was the key component.[45]

The campaign's success lay in the very large number of employees who demonstrated—and kept doing so—until the reform legislation passed. Every time the Senate and Chamber of Deputies debated the reform, retail clerks gathered outside the congressional building and packed the galleries. When a petition was presented to the legislature, thousands went to support it, pushing their way to the congress's front steps despite the efforts of police to restrain them. This mobilization was made easier by employers, who, afraid that the reform law would pass, laid off workers with high salaries and slashed wages—moves that the reform would block.[46]

The FEC worked to keep the agitation broad-based. The Socialist caucuses within the FEC and related unions attempted to take over the campaign by collecting funds and setting up their own central committee, but they were pushed aside by those more interested in victory than benefits to the party. At rallies orators from all major political parties spoke. For example, the speakers at a demonstration on 1 September 1932 included Borlenghi and national deputies representing the Conservatives, the Independent Socialists, the Progressive Democrats, and the Socialists.[47]

The mobilization was not limited to the capital. Union leaders joined key Socialists and representatives of other parties in extensive speaking tours of the provinces. Special committees were created to coordinate propaganda. In the city of Bahía Blanca the four locals of the UF, the regional unions of the telephone workers, and the retail clerks joined to form such a committee.[48]

In September 1932 the Chamber of Deputies passed the reform, but the Senate adjourned without considering it. When Justo called a special session of congress, the reform's backers tried to induce him to include the bill on the agenda. At the request of the bill's sponsor, Justo consented to receive a delegation from a rally. The demonstration was timed perfectly since it was the first day that the law establishing the English Saturday went into effect. Ten thousand retail clerks used their first legally mandated free afternoon to press for further reform. They were addressed by Justo from a balcony of the Casa Rosada. In an unusual move, the organizing committee included a specially selected group of between fifty and eighty female retail clerks in the delegation which visited the president. Justo was reputed to have a weakness for pretty women, but he did not agree to include the reform bill on the agenda of the special session.

The FEC renewed the reform drive in 1933, and the Senate passed the reform.[49] A hitch developed when Justo vetoed the law because of a clause making it retroactive, but it was unclear whether the veto covered the entire legislation or just the offending part. The committee of unions supporting the reform held a special congress that gave the executive committee the power to do anything it felt necessary to obtain the legislation—including calling a general strike. The veto turned out to be partial, and the agitation continued along normal lines until July and September 1934, when both houses sustained the veto. The unions knew that they lacked the strength to overturn a veto, and they wanted the rest of the legislation.[50]

The three new laws resulting from the FEC's campaigns not only improved conditions for retail clerks, but also benefitted the union. Across the country new unions for retail clerks were established; by 1936 the CGEC subsumed 44 organizations with 26,349 members. The FEC went from an estimated 820 affiliates in 1932 to a claimed 18,489 in 1936.[51]

The FEC used its new strength to make agreements with some major retail establishments. For example, in 1935 it signed a contract with Albión House setting working conditions and raising some wages; however, a few days later the store fired four workers. The union presented four demands: the firing of an accountant who had been harassing employees; the creation of a union shop; reincorporation of the fired workers; and detailed listings for all workers of the component parts of their salaries. The store agreed to the second and fourth demands and took back one worker but claimed that the other three had abused the owner and that their return could result in violence. The FEC found this acceptable.

The FEC even used its new prestige to call a strike. In late 1934 the Tienda San Juan began to pay wages late and not comply with the reforms of the commercial code. When the FEC protested, it got no response. After the union called an employee meeting and received its unanimous support, the store promised to meet the union's demands but did not. The FEC called a one-hour strike. All the employees responded and the store capitulated after forty minutes.[52]* The FEC had become strong enough to act like a more traditional union.

THE UOEM

While the Socialist domination of the UOEM was beneficial to the union during the early 1930s, it was also a major limitation. The union had good relations with the city government but was unable to expand its base among the workers.

During the Uriburu regime the UOEM could do little to help the municipal workers, despite improving its own position. With the city council disbanded and a strike unthinkable, the union could not prevent a serious deterioration in conditions.

The Uriburu authorities purged the work force. According to the government, between 6 September 1930 and 20 February 1932, 2,092 workers lost their jobs. The number was probably higher. Despite government claims of reorganization, the firings were blatantly political. In 1932 an Independent Socialist city councilor (and therefore a member of

---

*Unfortunately for the workers of the Tienda San Juan, soon after their victory the store had to go before a bankruptcy court.

the Concordancia) divided the fired workers into two groups: those whose posts were needed for political appointees and those fired out of political vengeance.* The UOEM could not impede mass political firings. However, in a few individual cases it demonstrated the sheer injustice of a dismissal and got it reversed. For example, in June 1931 a delegation met with a municipal official to ask for the reinstatement of a maid fired from a hospital because she was pregnant. As the union pointed out, it was illegal to fire someone for that reason, and she was reinstated. Aside from individual firings, the union was unable to protect workers from the extraordinary political pressures. Workers were forced to attend meetings of right-wing groups and send petitions to the intendente. Nor could the UOEM prevent reductions in salaries.[53]

The municipality displayed no animus toward the UOEM and even seemed to favor it over its rivals, but unions did not rank high with the government. In December 1930 for the first time the UOEM won the election for the blue-collar representative to the pension board with an overwhelming 67.3 percent of the vote. The margin suggests that the government did not oppose the UOEM, but it had little choice because the principal opposition had ties to the Radicals.[54] Moreover, the city continued to subsidize the UOEM's recreational facility. More important, city officials negotiated with the UOEM about working conditions. The matters discussed were frequently of little importance to the authorities but vital to workers. For example, as early as 10 September 1930 a union delegation visited the head of the department of public works to ask for enforcement of regulations concerning the length of the work day. While rulings were not always favorable, municipal officials received the union deferentially, and such efforts marginally improved working conditions. The UOEM's favored status allowed it to expand from slightly over 5,000 dues-payers to slightly over 6,000.[55]

The return to civilian rule did not greatly aid the UOEM despite the reopening of the city council, which was dominated by allies of the UOEM—Socialists and Concentración Obrera (a small municipal party that had developed out of a split in the Communist Party). The two organizations had a plurality in the thirty-member city legislature. In 1932 the Socialists held twelve seats and Concentración Obrera one, compared to the Concordancia's twelve. The remaining councilors represented minor parties. The next election did not bring major changes.[56]

The UOEM's inability to imitate the FEC's success was partially due to the composition of the municipal work force. The spoils system

*The number of employees actually increased.

led to high politicization and identification with political parties. Since the UOEM had extremely close ties to the Socialists and (until 1935) to Concentración Obrera, it had difficulty attracting workers with other loyalties: there was little room for dissent within the union. Other parties could gain little by supporting the UOEM because the municipal system made it difficult to assess whether gains were owed to the union or to the Socialist Party. Furthermore, while the executive branch did not look with disfavor upon the Socialists (and on some minor measures favored them), the intendentes (who had control over most administrative decisions) would not unbalance the city's budget to favor the UOEM. Neither for that matter would the Socialists, who were extremely proud of their fiscal prudence.

While the UOEM did not conduct extensive propaganda campaigns—perhaps because the leadership realized the futility of such efforts—it tried to obtain reforms. In April 1932 the union presented a petition to the intendente containing 28 goals, including a 44-hour week, a minimum monthly salary of 180 pesos, raises for certain job categories, and an ordinance controlling hiring and firing as well as the promotion of workers. Few were achieved in totality before 1943. Some that were—such as the 44-hour week—owed little to the UOEM's efforts.[57]

The major legislative achievement in which the UOEM had a hand was the escalafón of 1933 (see Chapter 3 above). While the law protected workers from some of the executive branch's arbitrary acts, the intendente retained great leeway in dealing with his employees. The Socialists and the UOEM could not claim full credit for the law. The purges carried out by Yrigoyen and Uriburu convinced all parties, at least theoretically, of the value of separating personnel issues from politics. An extensive campaign was not needed, and the ordinance passed unanimously. The UOEM did not get a chance to rally the municipal workers.[58]

The UOEM maintained its good relations with the municipal executive branch, and it resolved numerous small problems by speaking with the intendente or his subordinates. When speaking with the executive branch failed to solve a problem, the union turned to its allies on the city council. For example, a national law limited work in dangerous places to six hours, and the UOEM included a request in the April 1932 petition that *all* employees at municipal incinerators work a shortened day. On 2 December 1932 the council representative of Concentración Obrera, José Penelón, proposed that the council express its desire that the personnel at the Chacarita incinerator work a six-hour day. The measure passed without major debate. On 13 December the intendente informed the council that steps had been taken to shorten the hours. However, the union and the council were not always so successful.[59]

While unable to make significant progress in improving working conditions, the UOEM succeeded in attracting members and creating a sense of solidarity by means of an extensive social services program. Most Argentine unions wanted to provide such a program but lacked the resources. The UOEM had a steady income from dues, and it did not spend it on strikes. It also received help from the city (as noted). The centerpiece of the social program was the recreational facility. Members could attend dances and barbecues, and the facility had a pool for children, soccer fields, and basketball courts. In addition, the union provided free or low-cost medical and legal consultations. In 1935 the union embarked on the most ambitious social project yet established by an Argentine union—the creation of a vacation resort in the hills of Córdoba.[60]

Despite the seeming stagnation, the UOEM was institutionally successful. It handily won the elections to the pension board for blue-collar workers in 1932 and 1934, though the margin of victory declined between the two elections, and the UOEM bitterly complained about a lack of support from shop workers in the later election.[61] Membership remained stable—approximately 6,000 dues-payers—except in 1932, when it dropped sharply.[62]*

THE UF

The depression hit the railroad industry very hard, but the UF reasserted its power after a period of hesitation that had permitted large layoffs. Both the government and the UF realized the value of maintaining the relationship that had developed between the state and the union.

The day after the September 1930 coup the UF urged its members to remain calm and emphasized its indifference to politics. Shortly thereafter, delegations from the UF, accompanied by those of other unions, began meeting with government officials. In one meeting the unions

*The decline in membership appears to have been due to the city's unusually poor record for paying salaries on time. By the end of June 1932 the city owed its workers four months' salary, and this was not the only time it was late that year (*La Vanguardia*, esp. June 1932).

expressed their willingness to collaborate in the normalization process and their belief in the regime's good will toward labor. In another the UF asked for government help in restarting negotiations for improvements in its contracts.[63]

The UF received no immediate rewards for its cooperative behavior. The railroads began to lay off workers, starting in construction and spreading especially to the shops. How many workers lost their jobs is unclear. There were 18,291 employed in railroad shops in 1929 and 16,998 in 1932. Railroad employment fell 7.8 percent between 1930 and 1931. (These numbers include natural attrition because there was no new hiring.)[64]

The UF fought back within the limitations imposed by the regime. It appealed to the government by claiming that the import of railroad equipment was against the precepts of sane economic nationalism and the regime's stated policies because the equipment could be built more cheaply in Argentina. It also stressed that workers should not be laid off while company officials (whose only distinction was their inability to speak Spanish) received raises of three figures.[65]

The UF's protestations had little impact, and in mid-1931 the railroad companies presented the General Railroad Board with a plan to reduce costs by cutting back the labor force. The board suggested that salaries be lowered in order not to add to the unemployment problem and that the unions be consulted. The two railroad unions, the UF and La Fraternidad, could not decide on a common approach, though they agreed that concessions had to be made and that layoffs were unacceptable. The UF proposed *prorrateo*—i.e., days off for which the workers would not be paid. In this way jobs would be saved, and when the supposedly inevitable upturn in traffic occurred, wages would return to normal. La Fraternidad suggested that workers contribute three to twenty pesos a month to the company (depending on their salary) for as long as conditions warranted. In the initial talks the Ferrocarril Sud and the UF reached a provisional accord which called for most workers to have two days off a month and those in road and track maintenance to have one. In addition, the company agreed to revoke recent raises to management. La Fraternidad could not reach an agreement.[66]

The other railroad companies insisted on wage reductions and the right to consider further layoffs. The UF's leadership was in a difficult position. On the one hand, it believed that concessions had to be made. On the other hand, a growing number of locals resolved that no concessions were acceptable. With the situation deadlocked the companies suggested that the General Railroad Board intervene, a move acceptable to all parties. The government must have worried about the consequences of an unpopular solution because the board's suggestions were very similar to the unions'. Contracts were signed with each company; they called for no layoffs and prorrateo for workers represented by the UF and contributions for those represented by La Fraternidad. Rather than a solution, this was just the first round. The companies were dissatisfied and so were the workers. All the UF's powers of persuasion were needed to convince the workers to accept the agreements. Despite rhetoric to the contrary, the agreements reduced income. Discontent was exacerbated by factions which wanted to seize control of the UF and used the dissatisfaction to rally support.[67]

Justo's ascension had little impact because the UF already had a decent working relationship with the government. However, the lessening of political restrictions made it harder to control grass-roots discontent. It erupted, for example, on the Ferrocarril Oeste in 1932 over the appointment to a vacancy in the principal station in Buenos Aires, a hotbed of dissent. The contracts specified that appointments were to be made according to seniority so long as an applicant was qualified for a given post. In January the railroad chose a candidate who was thirty-seventh in seniority. The union grievance committee complained that workers with more seniority were qualified. No action had been taken by 21 April, so workers in the section directly involved stopped work for fifteen minutes. The next day they did not work for thirty minutes in both the morning and afternoon. The union denied authorizing the stoppages, but the parties agreed to submit the problem to the General Railroad Board. At the board's suggestion, the Oeste repeated the promotion procedure but came up with the same candidate. On 11 May the UF warned that it would not be responsible for the actions of the workers, and on 17 May the tactic of work to regulation began and spread up the lines of the Oeste. Work to regulation was a common weapon because of the detailed and complex rules of the railroads. If a train was supposed to proceed with caution, workers would see that it went at a snail's pace. Conductors would not allow a train to move until it had all the equipment listed in the rules and all the workers were dressed in proper uniforms. Schedules became meaningless, and commuters often rioted, destroying equipment in protest. In the work to regulation begun on 17 May, in order to ensure popular support, the workers did not slow commuter trains, but freight traffic was snarled. The UF began to demand the end of prorrateo. On 6 June the government gave the workers and the company forty-eight hours to normalize service, and they did. On 10 June the parties met with the government and agreed that the minister of public works would interpret the contract.[68]

More serious disruptions threatened when the railroads announced that on 1 August all wages were to be cut by 10 percent. The unions protested and the government insisted on negotiations. During the ensuing meetings the companies demanded not only the wage reductions, but also layoffs and the voiding of existing contracts. Under pressure from the rank-and-file, the UF's position was simple: everything had been solved the previous year. When negotiations appeared fruitless because the companies stood firm, the government suggested opening talks with the Pacífico line. Under considerable pressure from the administrator of the State Railroads, Pablo Nogués (a close advisor to Justo), to compromise or face a government-imposed solution, an agreement was reached which retained the format of the previous pacts but increased the number of days without work for most job categories. Understandings with some other lines followed quickly. However, when the Sud insisted on cutting wages, the UF signed an agreement that reduced wages from 0 to 8 percent (depending on the railroad's income) and in return prevented layoffs.

The Sud contract clearly departed from the mandate of the UF's last congress, which had insisted that prorrateo be retained. To defuse rank-and-file anger, the Comisión Directiva (CD—the executive committee)—called an extraordinary congress—the union's first. After heated debate the delegates rejected the pact and insisted that prorrateo was the only acceptable mechanism for wage reductions. When the Sud and the Oeste lines threatened to lay off workers and cut wages, a majority of the CD voted to press for an agreement based on prorrateo, but if this was impossible, to accept the Sud contract. While CD members agreed that a strike was impossible because the government had announced that one would not be tolerated, the committee split into two factions, Socialist and Syndicalist. The former called for government arbitration because it could not accept the rejected Sud contract. The latter, the dominant group led by Antonio Tramonti, favored negotiations, with the government as mediator. This stance meant accepting the Sud plan since the companies were in no mood to compromise. Despite the victory of the Syndicalist faction, the UF asked the minister of public works to propose a solution. He suggested accepting the Sud contract, and it was signed in January 1933. The UF then signed similar pacts with companies with which it had not yet made agreements.[69] The decision to disregard the congress had political costs; the Socialist faction used it to help take control of the union.

In 1934 the annual congresses of both railroad unions called for ending all wage reductions. They pointed out that the number of railroad workers had fallen sharply; they argued that while conditions for the companies had improved, the railroads' problems were no longer transitory and therefore the government ought to study measures to help the companies so that the workers did not bear the burden.[70] The unions then announced that they would not accept wage reductions after 31 August. Government-convened negotiations made no progress; on 31 August the minister of public works requested that the unions restrain their locals while the government investigated further. No tactic for the next day had been announced; although some type of stoppage would have occurred, it was not specified in order to shield the unions from government wrath. However, new talks began, the companies stood firm, and the unions made concessions. The General Railroad Board then offered arbitration by either a panel or Justo; the unions accepted, choosing the president.[71]*

The UF's leadership believed that a strike could not be won, both because the companies would not compromise and because the government had been pressing strongly for a peaceful solution. Moreover, the UF had been seriously weakened by the internal Socialist-Syndicalist struggle; the Socialist faction had just gained control. The UF could not present a united front, and the leaders feared a stoppage that could not be controlled. They felt that at most a strike could force arbitration and that it would be better to arbitrate without a stoppage.[72]

Justo issued his arbitration award on 23 October. It did not answer all the unions' demands, but it was not unfavorable given the concessions made during negotiations. Except in the shops, where prorrateo was kept, wages were reduced as under the Sud contract, but the money was considered to be retained and would be given back when the companies' financial conditions permitted. The return of wages was to have a higher priority than interest on ordinary shares. The railroads' books were to be examined and their costs relatively well defined, though no attempt was made to determine the companies' real capital.[73]

The rank-and-file disliked Justo's award, thus leading to further internal problems. Yet an analysis indicates that most railroaders did not fare too badly. During long periods—especially immediately after the decision—wages were not withheld or returned on many lines. The

*By 1934 the conflict between the UF and La Fraternidad had been resolved (*El Obrero Ferroviario*, 1/20 June 1932 and 16 Aug. 1933).

railroaders were spared layoffs and could hope that the wage reductions were temporary. However, the award had an unequal impact—for example, those working for companies with severe problems knew that money would be deducted for the foreseeable future—and this unfairness added to the strains upon the UF.[74]

The UF held up remarkably well during the Justo years. Membership fluctuated between a monthly average of 66,450 and 71,081 duespayers—an increase from 1929, when there were 63,485.[75] Nonetheless, it was a bleak period because the UF faced constant pressure to lower benefits and was torn by dissent.

THE TEXTILE UNIONS

In many ways the fate of the textile unions is archetypical. The Communist Federación Obrera de la Industria Textil (FOIT) virtually disappeared after the September 1930 coup, but it again became a vital organization in 1933. Its Socialist counterpart, the UOT, continued to function but not effectively, gaining strength only as the textile economy improved.

The UOT could not respond to the layoffs and wage reductions that followed the 1930 coup. Actions were taken by the skilled stocking workers themselves. The elite of the industry, they conducted desperate strikes. Employees of the firm Casa Pastra struck after their wages were slashed by 30 to 40 percent. In September 1930 at the firm of Muñoz, Sauca y Salzman employees refused to work after an announcement of a large wage reduction. They adjourned to the local Socialist Party headquarters and selected a strike committee, which was to inform the DNT and be advised by the UOT. *La Vanguardia* reported five strikes between 6 September 1930 and the end of the year and two more in 1931.[76] The strikes did not prevent conditions from deteriorating. Gains from the victories could not be sustained. The strike at Muñoz, Sauca y Salzman wrung an agreement from management, but the company ignored it throughout 1931. The workers could do nothing until the government changed in 1932.[77]

The UOT acted primarily as a spokesman to both management and the government. It was a small, Socialist union, so the government was not hostile toward it; in any case, the government considered textile strikes as only minor disruptions because they were isolated occurrences with minimal economic impact. Virtually helpless in the face of determined employers, the police, and a reserve army of the unemployed, the UOT turned regularly to the DNT. Attempting to both keep its name before the workers and ameliorate (or at least control) the horrible working conditions, the UOT regularly denounced violations of the labor codes—usually futilely. It also sought DNT help during conflicts with employers. Especially under Maglione, the DNT was sympathetic, but frequently it could do little. When the firm of Salvio Morley decided to lay off an entire shift, the workers proposed that tasks be divided equally among all employees, but management rejected the proposal and fired those who had presented it. The workers went to the DNT, which suggested that the company accept the workers' proposal. Salvio Morley rejected both the suggestion and an offer of mediation, telling the DNT that the plant was going to be closed. Two weeks later the company hired two new shifts.[78]

The improvement in the political climate in 1932 had little immediate impact. The textile unions were too small to attract favorable government attention. A myriad of competing firms and cut-throat competition made organizing difficult because concessions from one firm gave its rivals an advantage. Workers still reacted to employers' initiatives. However, there were few strikes in the capital—only 4 in 1932 and 6 (with 566 strikers) in 1933.[79] Nonetheless, the UOT had begun to build a base. When the employees of Casa Levy struck because of the firm's failure to pay salaries, the agreement that ended the walkout included the establishment of a grievance committee. In 1933 in Casa Saltzman the union blocked layoffs and established a form of prorrateo without resorting to a strike.[80]

The union could not protect workers even in plants where it was well established, however. In February 1933 the workers of Narciso Muñoz had their wages cut by as much as 50 percent; they struck, staying out for forty-five days. The strike ended with an agreement prohibiting salary reductions and establishing a commission of workers and management chaired by a DNT representative. In December the firm lowered wages by 15 percent. A female worker complained, the UOT intervened, and salaries were returned to their previous level. However, the woman who had made the initial complaint was laid off, supposedly because of a lack of work. A few months later her position was filled by someone else, despite a partial strike on her behalf.[81]

Worker combativeness slowly increased. The number of strikes in the capital rose to 12 in 1934 and 13 in 1935, with 556 and 4,183 participants respectively. Membership also increased. In 1932 the UOT had 140 dues-payers, but it had grown to a monthly average of 1,275 in 1934 and 1,510 during the first half of 1935. The union's strength lay in several large stocking plants in which strikes had occurred between 1930 and 1932. In February 1934 out of a total of 1,663 dues-payers, 681 worked for Salzman. Membership fluctuated wildly; plants would have a large number of affiliates and then dues-paying would drop off suddenly. In one month in 1934 the union had only 883 dues-payers, while in another it had 2,030. The fluctuations were not an indication of union weakness. Because of extremely low salaries and the potential for retribution from employers, union membership was a burden. However, a large number of workers had learned what a union could do, and they were a reservoir of support. As Camilo Almarza (a leader of the CGT after 1935) pointed out, the strength of the UOT lay not in the quantity of dues-payers but in the number of followers.[82]

When the FOIT reemerged in 1933, it lacked a base such as the one the UOT had created among the stocking workers, but it could depend upon the loyalty of Communist Party members. Competition between the two unions posed a barrier to organizing; strikes were at times complicated by rivalry.[83] The problem eased after the Communists shifted to popular front tactics. In June 1935 the FOIT called for unity, but the UOT replied that it was open to all. The FOIT still existed in January 1936, but it finally dissolved and had its members enter the UOT. Despite the UOT's hesitation, cooperation between the two unions began almost immediately.[84] The movement toward unity among textile workers was paralleled by drives to organize plants in the province of Buenos Aires and to go beyond factory-by-factory organization. In 1935 the UOT responded to the tremendous increase in textile production in the capital's suburbs by opening a local there.[85]

A vital step in the direction of sector-wide organizing occurred in the silk industry, where employers had been lowering salaries and provoking strikes at the plant level. The FOIT believed that its only hope of improving conditions lay in unionizing the entire sector. In order to do this, it reached an agreement in July 1935 with the hard-pressed façonniers (the small producers), who were being paid increasingly less by the large manufacturers. The façonniers accepted the union's basic demands—a minimum wage and equal pay for equal work. They also agreed to contribute to a strike fund, set up a joint strike committee, and defend the union during conflicts.*

*Many façonniers had belonged to left-wing organizations in Europe.

On 8 August 1935 a strike in the silk industry began, slowly widening in both the city and province of Buenos Aires; the façonniers joined. While the FOIT controlled the strike apparatus, the stoppage seems to have spread with little direction. The Socialists cooperated; strike meetings were held in the party's local headquarters. In early September settlements were reached in some plants, but in others the strike dragged on to an inconclusive end.[86]

While only partially successful, the strike marked a major shift in strategy: the FOIT began to use sector-wide organizing. Sector-wide contracts eliminated the need to organize individual plants before conditions could be improved. Better conditions were a good recruiting device, and the contracts permitted the union to sidestep the problem that many workers had little exposure to union culture. Many large employers were not averse to sector-wide contracts because they eliminated an area of competition and gave an advantage to those with superior machinery.

The FOIT cannot take all credit for the new tactics: in February 1935 the UOT had led a stoppage in the small knitting shops in the neighborhood of Villa Crespo in an attempt to create uniform conditions. The strike succeeded, but too few workers participated to have a measurable impact.[87]

The textile unions had made perceptible progress during the difficult years. They had changed from unions unable to respond to owners' initiatives to organizations strong enough to undertake sector-wide activities.

Chapter 6

GROWTH AND FRUSTRATION, 1936–1943

In 1936 the labor movement was healthier than it had been at any time since the onset of the depression. The urban economy was growing rapidly and repression had eased. In some cases strong unions had developed from weak ones. Unions had demonstrated an ability to use the political system. Strikes had become organizing devices capable of mobilizing workers whom the unions had difficulty reaching. However, both the government and union politics impeded uninterrupted growth and created frustration. The political system placed strict limits on labor's strategies. Congress and the Socialist Party became less important after the Radicals' return to politics, and it became almost impossible to make gains through the legislative process. In addition, the police would not tolerate too many disturbances. The restrictions on political freedom after Castillo came to power meant that strikes as a tactic to achieve larger ends were no longer practical. In the labor movement change in the Communists' strategy after the onset of World War II was in part responsible for a series of intra-union quarrels that prevented the organizations from extending their scope. The strategies that looked so promising in 1936 could not deliver. Nonetheless, in 1943 unions were more powerful than they had been in 1936.

According to the DNT, in 1936 there were 369,969 union members—11 percent of the economically active nonrural population, a rate comparable to that of Canada and the United States prior to 1936. The figure is somewhat inflated because it is based on information submitted by the unions themselves. There is a considerable gap between dues-payers and claimed members. Also, Catholic workers' organizations probably should not have been included in the statistics since they more resembled mutual aid societies than unions. Their inclusion is partially compensated for by the exclusion of Anarchist and other unions which would not cooperate with the government.[1] Despite the inaccuracies in tabulation, the number of union members had increased markedly from the 1920s.

A shift in the composition of the labor movement had begun. While transportation unions—the UF, La Fraternidad, the Federación Obrera Marítima, and the trolley-car workers' union—still dominated the confederations, dynamic unions operated in industries such as woodworking, construction, and commerce. The Socialists, in alliance with the Communists, had become the dominant force in the labor movement.

By far the largest confederation was the CGT of the Calle Independencia, which comprised the unions that had seized the CGT in December 1935.* It claimed 262,630 workers, or 71 percent of union members. Communist unions had joined those under Socialist influence in the first months of 1936, so the CGT of the Calle Independencia contained almost all the large organizations.² With the exception of the FOET, all the unions that are the focus of this study belonged. Syndicalist unions rejected the seizure of the CGT and regrouped, forming the CGT of the Calle Catamarca, which had just 25,095 members, or 6.8 percent of the total.† Most of the affiliated unions were small, the largest being the Federación Obrera Marítima, with 6,200 members, and the FOET.

The seizure of the CGT created serious problems. The national government employees' union split. The FOET, which had been helping to organize light and power workers, abandoned the effort because the light and power workers decided to back the larger CGT. Still, once the UF had made a definitive move into the camp of the CGT of the Calle Independencia, passions cooled rapidly. The Socialists' victory was too overwhelming to ignore.³

Aggressive tactics dominated the mid-1930s. Strikes were no longer used to improve conditions in just one plant but were aimed at entire industries. Unions were restructured to cover entire industries and to become national in scope. Among the unions transformed were those for brewers, woodworkers, municipal workers, food workers, printers, and construction workers. The leading force behind these changes was the Communists.⁴

Between 1935 and 1937 strikes were numerous and large. In 1936, 109 strikes took place in Buenos Aires and averaged 784 participants. Moreover, workers struck with a growing hope of victory. Strikes lost

---

*The CGT of the Calle Independencia was located in the UF's headquarters on Calle Independencia. The CGT unions which had not joined this confederation formed the CGT of the Calle Catamarca, located on the Calle Catamarca in the FOET's headquarters.

†The remaining union members belonged to autonomous or Catholic organizations.

dipped below 50 percent for the first time in 1936. Worker enthusiasm is evident in the extremely large attendance figures at union meetings. In 1936, 926,398 people went to such gatherings in the capital—i.e., 2.5 times the number of union members in the country (See Table 6-1).[5] Union activity declined in 1937 and especially in 1938. The economic downturn played an important role, but so did fatigue: waves of labor unrest usually last for a short time. The decline in activity was not owing to defeats because the percentage of strikes lost continued to drop.

Table 6-1

Union Meetings and Attendance in Buenos Aires, 1935–45
(1935 = 100)

Year	Number of Meetings	Index	Number Attending Meetings	Index	Average Number at Meetings
1935	5,672	100	1,034,702	100	182
1936	8,034	142	926,398	89	115
1937	7,139	126	466,053	45	65
1938	7,317	129	466,136	45	64
1939	7,089	125	389,588	38	55
1940	6,178	109	308,939	30	50
1941	3,776	67	210,500	20	56
1942	3,610	64	283,147	28	78
1943	2,530	45	117,697	11	46
1944	2,890	51	217,683	21	75
1945	4,079	72	406,645	40	100

Sources: DNT, División de Estadística, *Investigaciones sociales 1940* (Buenos Aires, 1941), 46; Dirección de Estadística Social, *Investigaciones sociales 1943–1945* (Buenos Aires, 1946), 18.

Between 1935 and 1939 a rare unity on the left existed. Attempts to establish a popular front failed, but its spirit was symbolized by a unique May Day rally in 1936 sponsored by Radicals, Communists, Socialists, and the CGT of the Calle Independencia. The Spanish Civil War reinforced the unity. All Argentine unions passionately embraced the loyalist cause and expended large quantities of energy and money to help the Spanish Republic. By December 1936 the FOET had dispatched 2,000 pesos of its own money and 2,750 pesos in contributions to the loyalists.[6]*

---

*The average monthly wage for a blue-collar industrial worker in Buenos Aires in 1938 was 109 pesos (see Table 2-3 above).

Unity disintegrated in the wake of the Hitler-Stalin Pact, World War II, and the shift in Communist tactics from no enemies on the left and anti-fascism to a belligerent stance of neutrality and anti-imperialism. The strongly pro-Allied Socialists accused the Communists of using the labor movement as a vehicle to act out their anti-imperialism. The Communists took a more aggressive attitude against companies with connections to the Allies. In 1940 the Communists and Socialists began to fight openly, and it became difficult to hold union meetings. The CGT's central committee did not meet for more than two years, mostly because of these tensions.[7] The conflict made union activity more difficult and it declined.

Following the Nazi invasion of the Soviet Union in 1941, the Communists again called for a popular front. While cooperation resumed between some Socialists and the Communists, in organizations such as the UF and the UOT the battle continued. Despite the conflict, union activity revived slightly. In 1942 attendance at meetings rose, as did the number of strikes, but these were only plant-level stoppages.[8] Any hope for a strong revival of union activity was stifled by new problems. As noted, since the Radicals' return to the political system, the Socialists no longer carried as much weight in the legislature and could offer little help to the union movement. Moreover, the Communist Party's principal goal (after the invasion of the Soviet Union) became helping the Allies win the war. The party was more worried about inflation and the need to feed Europe than about wages. According to Mario Rapoport, in a letter to the British ambassador, José Peter, the leader of the meatpackers' union, expressed a willingness to end a strike in order to guarantee the flow of meat to the Allies.[9]*

Castillo took a much harder line against unions than had his predecessors. During much of 1941 the DNT refused contact with the UOT or the Communist-controlled construction workers' union. The state of siege imposed in December 1941 led to increased restrictions on union activity and the arrest of many Communist labor leaders. In June 1943 *La Vanguardia* blamed the decline in the number of union meetings on problems with the police.[10]

The government's role regarding unions had expanded. Ortiz had introduced regulations requiring detailed reporting on union affairs. They had little impact, but they indicated the government's increased

*The meatpackers' strike took place after the June 1943 coup, but this timing should not have affected Communist strategy on the issue of meat supplies to Europe.

interest in controlling unions. In the province of Buenos Aires Governor Fresco had instituted tighter control over unions, including mandatory arbitration.[11] As Ricardo Gaudio and Jorge Pilone have pointed out, the government seems to have worked to moderate labor conflicts by encouraging the signing of contracts.[12] From 1937 to 1942 the labor departments in the city and province of Buenos Aires assumed a larger role in the resolution of strikes. However, it does not appear that the national government clearly understood that union power had grown. Employers increasingly had to deal with unions either directly or with the help of a government agency. (Many firms preferred to negotiate with government help.) In 1938 in 54.5 percent of the strikes in the capital, employers dealt directly with their workers, bypassing the unions, while they did so in only 8 percent of the stoppages in 1942. The percentage of strikes lost continued to decline, falling to just 27 percent in 1942.[13] Contracts became more acceptable, and in some cases owners favored them in order to limit competition. Nonetheless, in the capital they were not numerous, and there were fewer than claimed by Gaudio and Pilone.* In the province of Buenos Aires there were many more because of the provincial government's greater powers and because contracts were often of exceedingly short duration and needed to be renewed frequently. In both jurisdictions contracts were much less important than they seemed since they could be flouted with impunity. This clearly differentiates them from contracts signed under Perón.[14] Below we shall examine how the confederations and unions fared just prior to the advent of Perón.

THE CONFEDERATIONS

In mid-1936 the UF decided to support the seizure of the CGT, thus sealing the fate of the Syndicalist CGT of the Calle Catamarca. The rump confederation lost any hope of a steady flow of income. In May 1937 it joined with several autonomous organizations to form a new confederation, the Unión Sindical Argentina (USA). The principal unions to join were the Federación Obrera Marítima, the FOET, and the Asociación

---

*A close examination of Gaudio and Pilone, "El desarrollo de la negociación colectiva," 272, indicates that some of the listed contracts were not really contracts. With the exception of stocking workers, raises in the textile industry in 1942 and 1943 did not involve a union (see below).

Trabajadores de la Comuna, a smaller rival of the UOEM. Pockets of support for the USA existed in the interior, especially in Entre Ríos and in the city of La Plata.[15]

The USA failed to grow. Indeed the number of affiliated unions declined because there was little advantage to belonging. The confederation lacked the size to gain government respect and could do little for its members. It was also hurt by internal conflict. In 1939 a bitter struggle raged between the old-line Syndicalists (who had controlled the first USA, the Syndicalist confederation of the 1920s) and the leadership of the FOET and the Federación Obrera Marítima over the appointment of a delegate to the International Labor Organization. The victory of the FOET and maritime union alienated the older leaders. In addition to the internal problems, the USA failed in attempts to merge with the CGT or independent unions.[16] Rather than aiding its member organizations, the USA depended upon them for survival. After 1939 the FOET permitted the USA to use its headquarters rent-free, and in 1942 it gave the confederation a contribution of 200 pesos despite its own declining revenues.[17]

The CGT had a more substantial role. It had money and manpower, two prerequisites for action. In 1942 it had an income of 6,000 pesos a month and a full-time staff of six, four of them clerical.[18] In addition, it used the staff of the UF. After its ideological problems had been settled, the CGT began to assist with organizing. For example, from 1936 through 1940 a CGT delegate advised the UOT and participated in negotiations, lending the confederation's prestige to a union that employers and the government had not learned to respect. Firms could not lightly dismiss the CGT, partly because it was dominated by the UF, which molded the CGT in its own image. The CGT was cautious but not passive and always moved from a position of strength. It became for many what the *Review of the River Plate* called it: "a legally constituted and entirely respect-worthy entity."[19]

As noted, the war shattered the popular front spirit. The CGT's tutelage of the UOT ended and was replaced by bitter feuding.[20] Once the German invasion of the Soviet Union removed the war as a source of conflict, partisan struggles became even fiercer. Radicals and some of the more politically oriented Socialists joined the Communists in a revolt against the domination of the UF and its former president, José Domenech, in the CGT. Moreover, the dissidents challenged the dominant leadership's control of the UF. Beyond calling demonstrations for the Allies, the CGT could do little.

For a time the CGT held together, but in March 1943, when the central committee met to elect officers, two slates were presented: Slate I was headed by Domenech (the current secretary general) and Slate II by Pérez Leirós of the UOEM. The UF had already purged its delegates to ensure the correct outcome; however, one, Marcos Lestelle, a Radical, voted for Slate II. The meeting was immediately adjourned, Lestelle was replaced, and the voting began again. Slate I won by a single vote. This was too much for the opposition, and the CGT divided again. Each kept the name CGT and bore the number of its slate. CGT I had the support of the UF, the trolley-car workers' union, and the brewers' union (among others), while CGT II included La Fraternidad, the CGEC, the UOEM, and the Communist-dominated unions. The bitterness was extreme. The only organizing during 1943 was for the creation of parallel unions.[21]

THE FOET

The FOET failed to make any major breakthroughs in 1936–43. The UT's hostility remained intense, and the government offered no assistance. Moreover, the union was increasingly torn by internal strife.

With little hope of making major gains, the FOET continued constantly to protest violations of labor laws or contracts. Despite having reached an agreement with the UT in July 1935, by 1936 a new wave of protests had begun. The principal point of contention was that the UT had refused to rehire those laid off between the coup of 1930 and the strike of 1932. Moreover, some had been employed as temporary workers and were therefore not covered by the contracts or the pension fund. The union also objected to the UT's use of contractors, who, like temporary workers, were not covered by contracts or pensions. Other grievances included the working conditions on certain jobs, the UT's lack of compliance with the reformed commercial code of 1933, and the failure of the UT to rehire Luis Gay, the most powerful man in the FOET.

By December 1936 the workers seemed ready to strike, but the negotiations continued. On 23 February 1937 an agreement was reached that was not a contract but a note from the UT replying to the FOET's demands. The UT agreed to use temporary workers for only a specified period during emergencies and to add sixty-five temporary workers to the permanent staff. Several problems concerning work procedures were also settled. However, the union did not accept the company's refusal to rehire Gay, its failure to meet the specifications of the reformed commercial code, and its continued use of contractors. Considerable sentiment existed for rejecting the agreement, but the FOET leadership did not want a strike. General weakness was probably the major reason for accepting the agreement, but the stated justification was a tense situation brewing in Santa Fe.[22]

The FOET had been assisting to organize the interior. In 1936 in La Plata a union that had been crushed in the 1932 strike reemerged. Rural telephone workers were organized in the provinces of Buenos Aires, Santa Fe, and Córdoba.[23] The workers of the Sociedad Telefónica de Santa Fe formed a union in 1935, but in mid-1936 the company was sold to the UT. Prior to surrendering control, the Sociedad Telefónica promised that salaries would be improved, seniority recognized, and the workers' jobs respected, but the UT did not honor these promises. The FOET presented the UT a set of demands to which the firm had fifteen days to respond or face a strike in Santa Fe. With just a few days remaining, the UT asked for more time and was given an extra week. Then the provincial authorities intervened, and again the union agreed to postpone the strike. The UT refused to accept any prior agreements. The FOET accused the UT of forming a company union to lure workers out of the real union and when that failed, using force to drive them out.

For the FOET, the struggle in Santa Fe became fundamental. It offered to fully finance it and warned the UT that the workers considered its attitude a provocation. Delegations traveled to Santa Fe to help rebuild the union, which had collapsed under pressure, its membership falling from 250 to 35.[24]

In 1938 an internal struggle completely paralyzed the union in the capital, but the situation in Santa Fe improved. Both the company union and the organization allied with the FOET had applied to the provincial department of labor for recognition. Under a provincial statute unions had to register and conform to certain rules to use the good offices of the department. The department accepted the application of the FOET ally and denied that of the company union on the following grounds:

> It is evident that the Compañía Unión Telefónica de Santa Fe, by means of its natural agents ... has carried out an intensive campaign among its workers and employees to create a workers' association ... that exists for the purpose and end of preserving the interests of the employer. This maneuver, although it was *a priori* a violation of Article 54 of law 2,426, would not have been such a grave infraction if there had not occurred the circumstance that in Santa Fe there already

existed a workers' organization . . . against which agents of the employing enterprise have used methods of intimidation, pressing on the spirits of the affiliated workers in order to compel them to resign from the union. The proof is clear and evident, because in return for resignations [from the FOET ally], workers and employees are offered improvements in salary and classification.[25]

With the assistance of the department of labor the FOET ally won recognition for its grievance committee. However, the UT continued to fire or transfer workers who refused to resign from the union. Appeals to the department of labor were futile; for some unclear reason, when the agency did intervene, it did so against the union's interests. It attempted to force a merger with the yellow organization. When the idea was rejected, the department dropped the union from the list of registered organizations. It then conducted an election to determine which organization truly represented the workers, and the UT's yellow union won. The FOET charged that the voting was overseen by police and agents of the UT. The UT refused to receive the grievance committee, and pressure on members in the affiliate union increased. The union slowly died.[26]

In the capital the FOET continued its barrage of protests in 1938 and 1939; they had a familiar ring. The UT hired workers not on the lists of those who had been laid off; it continued to employ contractors; work rules had been unfairly changed. The union showed no inclination to strike. Few of the issues were likely to induce workers to walk out and possibly lose a job which others still coveted years after they had been laid off. With the passage of time and the rehiring—at least according to the company—of 80 percent of the laid-off workers, it had become difficult to rally workers even around the issue of rehiring those who had been fired. A few key leaders had not gotten their jobs back, but some within the union no longer cared. The internal conflict in 1938 was in part a battle between leaders who still worked for the UT and those who had not been rehired. The FOET could claim one victory: in August 1939 the UT promised to comply with the reformed commercial code.[27] The FOET began to carry the battle to different fronts. It opposed a proposed reform of the communications system and called for the nationalization of the telephone companies.[28]

In 1941 the union was again consumed by an internal struggle, but in April 1942, in response to rising prices, the leadership decided to seek a 10 percent wage raise. The proposal was presented to the UT on 11 June. On 17 June the UT announced new salaries: workers earning 170 pesos a month or less received an extra 10 pesos, those earning 171–350 pesos got an additional 15, and those in the 351–499 category got an additional 25. The FOET called for a minimum raise of 15 pesos but did not seem eager to press the issue. The UT had taken the wind out of the FOET's sails by moving before the union had fully rallied worker support. Nonetheless, buoyed by its success, the FOET began a campaign to establish an escalafón, which would permit orderly promotions and lessen favoritism.[29] The union achieved its goal in 1945.

The FOET's general lack of success is reflected in its membership figures. The average number of dues-payers declined continually, falling sharply during periods of intense internal crisis. The decline totaled 41 percent between 1935 and 1942 (see Table 6-2). The union was stymied by an unyielding and intelligent employer, and frustration fueled internal struggles.

Table 6-2

Average Number of Monthly Dues-Payers in the FOET, 1935–44

Year	Average of Dues-Payers
1935	2,373
1936	2,144
1937	2,083
1938	2,129
1939	1,827
1940	1,780
1941	1,434
1942	1,393
1943	1,435
1944 (first eleven months)	1,599

Source: Calculated from *Federación*, 1935–44.

NOTE: The figures from 1941 on may be slightly low because in mid-1941 dues were lowered for night operators, and the figures given are based on the formula indicated in Chapter 4 above.

THE FEC

The FEC continued the tactics that had brought it success, but the Radicals' return to the political arena and the ensuing changes in political style made these efforts fruitless. A shift in the union's tone began almost immediately. Between 1936 and 1938 the FEC was on the defensive, protecting the reformed commercial code from employers who for the first time realized its full implications—i.e., that blue-collar workers might be included. Efforts by both employers and the executive branch to change the law reached a peak in 1936, such that in addition to normal tactics, the FEC's membership voted 4,054 to 98 to strike if necessary to protect the law. However, the issue died down until 1938.[30]

In 1938 employers again pressed for changes in the commercial code. The FEC responded with a typical campaign and a promise to strike if employers held a rumored one-day lockout. The CGT appointed a special commission, dominated by the FEC, to organize supportive demonstrations. Among the unions sponsoring rallies were the UOT and those for printers, construction workers, packing-house workers, and woodworkers. The CGEC feared that if an amendment to the reformed code reached the floor of the Chamber of Deputies, it would pass; the amendment had to remain in committee. A surprise committee meeting was called just prior to the adjournment of the Chamber of Deputies. Eight of the nine committee members were split evenly on whether to table the amendment or send it to the Chamber floor; the ninth member leaned in favor of sending it to the floor. Through political pressure this member was induced not to attend the special meeting, and since the unions' supporters on the committee also boycotted the special session, a quorum was lacking. The immediate danger subsided.[31]

The defense of the reformed commercial code did not end in 1938, but it merged almost entirely into a drive to establish a government-organized pension fund for commercial employees. The agitation soon reached the levels of previous years and continued whenever congress was in session until 1943. The propaganda machine functioned as smoothly as ever, but in the Chamber of Deputies the legislation made it out of committee only in 1940 and was not approved until September 1941. The Senate never even considered it. The Radicals, confident that they were the majority party, felt no need to strenuously back the legislation (although they did support it) because the political beneficiaries would have been the Socialists. The Socialists were no longer a major force in the Chamber of Deputies; from 1938 through 1941 they held just five seats. The Neo-Conservatives had abandoned most attempts at broadening their support and depended increasingly on frauds.[32]

Despite the changes in the political system, the CGEC grew rapidly. In 1939, 87 organizations belonged—almost double the number of 1936—

and by 1942 there were 235. Membership grew somewhat more slowly, reaching a claimed 26,349 in 1936, 35,000 in 1941, and 45,000 in 1942.[33] The rapid expansion owed a great deal to the national campaigns, which were replicated on the provincial level. The laws establishing the English Saturday and uniform closing times applied only to the capital and the national territories. The confederation worked to have similar legislation enacted in the provinces. Statutes securing the English Saturday or *el lunes criollo* (creole Monday—a half a day of work on Monday) were enacted in a number of provinces, including Santa Fe, Córdoba, San Juan, Entre Ríos, and Santiago del Estero. Efforts to push through uniform closing laws were less effective.[34]

The half workday and uniform closing campaigns were often arduous and long. For example, agitation for the English Saturday in the province of Buenos Aires began in 1932 and met with intense opposition, especially in the capital's suburbs, where store owners benefited from the closings in the city. The CGEC could not mobilize sufficient Neo-Conservative support until Governor Fresco adopted the idea of the English Saturday as part of his social program in 1938. Despite the effort involved in the campaign, *La Vanguardia* pointed out its advantages:

> This campaign constitutes an important element in strengthening the commercial employee unions of the different localities. With it they will have a great opportunity to work in a practical manner for the total organization of the industry.
>
> In the hypothetical case that the [English Saturday] law is not passed, something that we believe is improbable if the agitation is done well, it is certain in a campaign of this nature that there would be left for the entities composing the provincial federation a substantial gain in the number of members.[35]

Like the CGEC, the FEC made great progress. In 1936 it claimed 18,489 members—four times the number of the previous year. A major breakthrough came in late 1936 with a victory over Gath y Chaves, the firm that had broken the strike in 1919, the year of the previous attempt at organizing retail clerks. When the FEC requested that Gath y Chaves raise salaries, as other establishments had recently done, the company fired two employees, including a member of the union's executive council. The firm also began to lay off old and ill employees, which was illegal under the reformed commercial code. Moreover, it had its lawyer work on having the code declared unconstitutional. The FEC saw that Gath y Chaves had to be stopped if the union was to become a creditable force.

A strike was problematical since the FEC was unsure of the retail clerks' reactions. The union knew that the store feared a loss of clientele, so it requested that the unions composing the CGEC and the CGT send notes to the store expressing solidarity with the FEC. The veiled threat of a boycott was particularly effective because it was December, a period of peak sales. Gath y Chaves quickly admitted defeat, agreeing to the salary demands and promising to continue to obey the commercial code. It claimed that its lawyer had acted on his own. The fired workers were taken back after a brief suspension.[36]

The victory over Gath y Chaves established the FEC as an organization with which stores had to deal. The union depended heavily on its prestige. In a surprising number of cases it achieved its goals without resorting to forceful measures. For example, in September 1940 the waiters of the Confitería Ideal, an elegant café, asked the FEC's assistance in persuading their employer to obey the section of the commercial code governing vacations. The owner and his lawyers insisted that the café could not follow the procedure advocated by the FEC because competitors did not. While the employer and union representatives were negotiating, the Anarchists, the traditional representatives of waiters, advocated direct action; the FEC opposed this, claiming that its methods were more successful. After eleven months of negotiating, the Confitería Ideal gave its employees full vacations and paid them the average of their tips during the time off. In other cases the FEC secured such benefits as closed shops, raises, and the right of the union to approve and inspect booklets showing the hours worked.[37]

Once the FEC established relations with employers, these were frequently amazingly smooth. Store representatives came to the FEC's offices—a practice unheard of in other industries. The positive employer-union relationship is summed up in an FEC executive committee report: "This policy of mutual respect between the Federation and Gath y Chaves has permitted a satisfactory solution of all the issues raised."[38] In a few cases the FEC reluctantly called strikes.[39]

The FEC's new strength is demonstrated by a 1942 agreement with the Chamber of Department Stores and Subsidiaries. The pact covered 38 stores and 5,000 workers, granting a 10 percent raise to all male employees earning less than 225 pesos a month and to all females earning less than 190.[40]

The organized retail clerks became a major force. If the CGEC membership figures for 1942 are accurate, approximately 15 percent of retail clerks in Argentina were organized—a large percentage given the nature of the industry.⁴¹ The clerks had used political mobilization to create an organization that operated in a more traditional union fashion.

THE UOEM

In the second half of the Neo-Conservative era the UOEM's position weakened. After the Radicals returned to the political system, they won every municipal election; after 1938 they held the largest number of seats on the city council of Buenos Aires. In addition, the city council had lost prestige because some members had become involved in a series of sordid scandals.⁴² This loss of leverage plus the increasing lack of political freedom and competition for the allegiance of municipal workers were detrimental to the UOEM, although it managed to perform many of its traditional functions.

The UOEM began to model itself on the FEC. In March 1936 it helped organize a municipal workers' confederation. Seven unions attended the convention, while two others expressed their support.⁴³ The confederation had minimal impact because its members depended on local governments and it was at that level that pressure had to be applied. It could only bring problems to the attention of the press and provide votes for the UOEM in the CGT.

The UOEM also conducted a series of campaigns with petitions, demonstrations, and rallies with speakers from all political sectors. Such tactics had little success. The same demands appeared year after year. Not one of the sixteen goals in a petition presented in 1937 had been fully met by the end of the Neo-Conservative era. The Socialists on the city council, as well as councilors from other parties, introduced the appropriate bills, but the problem lay in securing passage and the support of the intendente. For example, in the 1937 petition the UOEM demanded an increase in the minimum wage to 180 pesos a month and a 10 percent raise for those earning less than 300 pesos. The Socialist city councilors introduced a similar measure but modified the raises to range from 5 to 20 percent. On the motion of a member of the Concordancia, the bill was amended so that the minimum salary for white-collar workers was set at 200 pesos. While the bill easily passed, the power to include raises in the budget lay with the intendente, and he did nothing.⁴⁴

Three newer organizations increased the competition for worker support. The Asociación Trabajadores de la Comuna had ties to the

Radical Party, and with the large number of party members in the work force, this union should have grown after 1936, but it did not. In 1937 the Asociación requested and received land to create a recreational facility—just as the UOEM had done earlier—but it did not get consistent support from the Radicals. Moreover, at least two key members—Alejandro Protti (a former secretary general) and Alejandro Villanuestre, who had been the organization's candidates for the pension board—joined competing unions. The Asociación claimed only 1,500 members in 1936 and 893 in 1941, 589 of whom were dues-payers.[45]

The Conservatives founded their own union, the Asociación Porteña de Trabajadores, at the initiative of Atilio Dell'Oro Maini, one of the municipality's chief administrators and the former head of an employers' association. The membership remained small—820 members and 372 dues-payers in 1941.[46] While the union had little impact on the UOEM's fortunes, it posed a threat because of its ties to the government.

The most serious challenge came from the Federación de Obreros y Empleados Municipales (FOEM), created after members of the party Concentración Obrera withdrew from the UOEM in 1935 because of unhappiness with the leadership. The dissidents formed a Committee for Unity among Municipal Workers that in 1936 easily won the election for blue-collar representation on the pension board. In 1938 the committee became the FOEM, which won the remaining contests for blue-collar representation to the pension board.[47]

The FOEM remained considerably smaller than the UOEM, however. From the dues collected, it is clear that it had less than 2,000 members. Why then was the FOEM able to win the pension board elections? Its extremely close ties to Concentración Obrera (which was a vocal force on the city council) are not sufficient explanation, nor is the popularity of the party's leader, José Penelón. Penelón used his seat on the city council to do everything possible to improve the conditions of municipal workers, but the Socialists performed a similar service, even if in a less flamboyant manner. Furthermore, the UOEM was more successful with the municipal authorities than its rival. As the Communist paper *La Hora* suggested, workers might have been expressing frustration at the failure of the UOEM to significantly improve conditions.[48] Moreover, the UOEM's rigidly Socialist orientation precluded support from workers belonging to other parties. For those who opposed the Socialists little political cost was entailed in aiding the FOEM since Concentración Obrera was a marginal party. It is likely that in the pension board elections the FOEM received support from other parties, especially the Radicals.*

The UOEM continued to meet with the municipal government. In one four-month period in 1941 it made sixty-seven presentations before parts of the city administration. At times it was successful. In August 1941 after the CGT had called a work stoppage and demonstration to show support for the Allies, the UOEM secured pay for participants who failed to show up for work. The Socialists were still a force in Buenos Aires, and the Neo-Conservatives preferred them to the Radicals.[49]

The UOEM lost its basic source of leverage when Castillo closed the city council in October 1941. While it intensified agitation for wage increases, without pressure from the council there was little chance of success. The union could still negotiate with the municipality on small issues, but the board appointed by the government to replace the city council offered no support.[50] The UOEM was less able than ever to achieve its goals.

The increasing problems lowered the average number of dues-payers in the UOEM, though the decline was not drastic (see Table 6-3). With the help of its social programs, it remained by far the largest organization among municipal workers. It represented 17.2 percent of the total work force in 1942.[51]†

Table 6-3

Monthly Average of Dues-Payers in the UOEM, 1935–43

Year	Average of Dues-Payers
1935	5,971
1936	6,329
1937	6,111
1938	5,536
1939	5,542
1940	5,218
1941	5,317
1942	5,403
1943	5,439

Source: *El Obrero Municipal*, 1935–44

*A fifth union—a Catholic organization—was founded in 1935, but it remained small (Federación de Asociaciones Católicas de Empleadas, 136; DNT, *Organización sindical*, 9).

†If one eliminates white-collar workers from the calculation—few of whom belonged to the UOEM—the UOEM represented 25 percent of the work force.

THE UF

As a result of the arbitration award by President Justo in October 1934, the UF had had to accept concessions which the rank-and-file greatly disliked. While the railroad companies were determined to maintain the concessions, the UF, under pressure from the rank-and-file, struggled to roll them back. Severely weakened by internal conflict, the union was cautious, unwilling to antagonize the government, afraid that the regime would sever connections and permit layoffs.

The seizure of the CGT sharply divided the UF: while it had been the driving force behind the takeover, those involved were not a large group and the opposition was vociferous. The union was paralyzed. It came very close to being torn in two. Moreover, a four-month judicial intervention of its headquarters—a response to the internal struggle—limited maneuverability. Elected officials handled daily affairs, but they could not plan steps against a presidential arbitration award.

By 1937 the internal conflict had been papered over, and rail traffic had temporarily increased. Many railroads stopped withholding a proportion of wages, and many of those that continued returned the money.[52] The rail unions demanded an end to wage retentions; to back their demands, a five-minute work stoppage was scheduled for 20 August, with hints of stronger action to follow. Two days before the strike the companies expressed a willingness to go back to the 1931 contracts or negotiate new ones. The unions felt this offer was adequate, but the stoppage went on as scheduled. The unions claimed there was not enough time to stop it. Charges were hurled that the strike had been timed to aid the Socialist Party—it was two weeks prior to the presidential election—and that government pressure stopped the movement after the five-minute strike. It is unclear how a strike could have helped the Socialists, nor is it likely that the UF's leadership would have jeopardized the union for any political group, but the charges may account for President Ortiz's hostility to the UF leadership.[53]

The UF conducted an endless series of talks with the companies and the government, but these achieved nothing. At the grass roots feelings ran high, especially on three railroad lines which continued to retain wages; strikes occurred on all three. The union had missed a golden opportunity: the financial position of the other lines worsened in 1938, and these companies once again began to retain wages. Workers responded with local stoppages, but the unions did little beyond appealing to the government and calling for the nationalization of the railroads.[54]

New problems arose in part because of the inability to improve conditions. In mid-1938 the Syndicalists withdrew from the UF and formed a new union, the Federación Obreros y Empleados Ferroviarios (FOEF—discussed in detail in Chapter 7). Ironically a breakdown of discipline, which accompanied any problem within the UF, allowed railroaders to apply pressure on the government because worker unhappiness disrupted much local rail traffic.[55] Yet the government moved slowly, asking the unions for their opinions. All three unions—the UF, FOEF, and La Fraternidad—equivocated, saying they wanted the 1931 contracts and Justo's 1934 arbitration award annulled but also wanted workers to be protected from layoffs and a deterioration of working conditions. The government, obviously stalling, called for studies.

The UF's leaders feared forceful steps which might cause them to lose control of the membership. The union began peaceful agitation. Locals adopted motions and held rallies and meetings against the Justo arbitration award. They even obtained the support of the Chamber of Deputies, which voted to ask the president to nullify the decision. The FOEF failed to supplant the UF, and attention again focused on the arbitration award. In February 1940, when the schism among the railroaders finally ended and the FOEF dissolved, President Ortiz ordered a study of the feasibility of eliminating the arbitration award and the 1931 contracts.[56]

The report came out. The government waited, and so did the unions, while the railroad companies asked to be allowed to cut costs through layoffs. The parties met with the government, but nothing happened. The union leadership remained cautious:

> If the [UF's] Comisión Directiva was certain that paralyzing the railroads for several days would resolve our problem, the *compañeros* could be certain that this measure would already have been adopted, but the truth is that with an attitude of this nature, the lifting of the [wage] retentions would not be obtained and instead it would damage the railroad workers and the country; at the same time it would harm the organization's reputation.[57]

Afraid of failure, the UF did little, and those who favored militant action were fiercely attacked by the leadership.

In 1940 a bitter split developed in the UF between the Communists and other elements. Not surprisingly, the dissenters (i.e., the Communists and their allies) focused much of their attack on the 1934 arbitration award, blaming the leadership that the decision still stood. They managed brief stoppages on some lines, but the dominant faction expelled dissenting members and took over locals to keep the dissidents under control.[58]

La Fraternidad and the UF were able to use a propitious situation to finally make progress. Rail traffic was increasing rapidly. More important, the political situation was unsettled. Castillo was acting president, but the possibility of Ortiz's return still existed. Castillo's hold on power was too shaky, and he could not afford a disruption of the flow of exports. On 26 November 1941 in a meeting with Castillo, the two unions asked formally for an end to the retention of wages. While the leadership conferred with government authorities, the locals, in a carefully orchestrated campaign, stated that they were ready to undertake whatever action the unions might desire. When negotiations appeared to have failed, railroaders stopped work for half an hour on 25 February 1942. It was to be an incremental strike, with the stoppage increasing by fifteen minutes each day. While the unions did not publicize their role, the stoppage was centrally directed and was forceful enough to impress Castillo. That afternoon he met with the unions and promised a favorable response within a week. The unions called off the strike.

Castillo decreed that railroad tariffs would be increased; a portion would be used to pay the workers a full salary, while the remainder would go to the railroad pension fund, to which the companies had consistently paid less than their share. The UF and La Fraternidad were pleased, but the companies were not since they did not theoretically receive the increased revenues for which they had been arguing, though in fact they received some of the money.[59]

The UF and La Fraternidad had demonstrated their power. Castillo's government was cracking down on other unions, but it gave the railroaders what they wanted. The February stoppage had not been a contest between employers and workers to see which would be overcome first by economic distress, but rather a political demonstration during which the unions reminded the government what they could do.

The UF pressed ahead. In 1942 its annual congress set salary demands: a 20 percent raise for salaries up to 160 pesos a month, 15 percent for salaries of 161–250 pesos, and 10 percent for those who earned more. It also called for the return of retained wages. The companies were in no mood to grant wage increases since they were petitioning for higher rates and claiming that the government was mistreating them.[60] On 28 February 1943 the UF planned to begin a series of short incremental stoppages similar to those called the previous year. However, a few days before that date, union leaders met with the minister of public works, who offered the government's good offices in finding a solution. The UF accepted and a mixed commission was formed. No common ground could be found, so the matter was handed back to the government.[61] Only after the rise of Perón did the railroaders receive increases and their retained wages.

Again the UF had proceeded cautiously, but it had good reasons to accept the government's offer to jointly seek a solution. For one thing, the government had been responsive to its desires. For another, the struggle for control of the union had intensified, with an alliance of Radicals, Communists, and some Socialists seriously challenging the leadership. The dissidents rejected the idea of salary increases that depended upon a raise in railroad tariffs, claiming this would be inflationary. For the same reason, the Communists had opposed the scheme for ending wage retentions. Given the stance against inflation, a strike would have been difficult to end in an orderly fashion because any solution would have involved raising shipping charges. Disorder would have invited government repression and the disintegration of the union.[62]

The UF had been active on other fronts as well. In 1938 after a long effort, it signed a contract with the private railroads which covered the lowest paid category—the road and track maintenance workers. These railroaders had finally achieved the same rights as their brethren in the other major job categories.[63] In addition, keenly aware that it was a strong union in a failing industry and that workers in other modes of transportation were poorly paid and unorganized, the UF helped create a national organization intended to represent all transportation workers. It failed. No attempt was made to organize truckers, the chief competitors of the railroads. The major unions that joined the new organization—La Fraternidad and the trolley-car workers' union—already had a close working relationship with the UF. The waterfront union that joined was not the Federación Obrera Marítima, the largest and most prestigious organization, but the Unión Obrera Marítima, which many considered a yellow union.[64]

Stymied in the attempt to change conditions through traditional means, the railroaders turned increasingly to social programs to improve their lives and strengthen the sense of group solidarity that already existed. In 1936 in conjunction with La Fraternidad, the UF began to create a health plan. In mid-1940 the unions purchased a hospital in the capital and in 1942 opened a clinic in Rosario. The facilities were intensively used. By December 1942, 44,677 railroaders were associated with the health plan—a little under a third of the railroad work force. The UF also provided recreational facilities for its members. In 1939 it began to build a vacation resort in the hills of Córdoba which was ready for use by summer 1943. Also in 1939 it acquired property in an outer suburb of Buenos Aires for use as a recreational facility by the many members living in the metropolitan area.[65]

Social programs helped the UF weather an extremely difficult period. The number of monthly dues-payers averaged 67,456 between 1936 and 1942. Only in 1939, a year of intense strife, did the membership dip drastically (see Table 6-4). The UF represented almost 60 percent of eligible workers in 1941.*

The last years of the Neo-Conservative era were extremely difficult for the UF. The union tried to recover lost ground but was not sure how. Its traditional cautious methods, which depended on the government, brought few results. Failures stoked the fires of dissent, which threatened not only to destroy the union, but also made it harder to achieve desired changes.

Table 6-4

Average Number of Monthly Dues-Payers in the UF, 1935-44

Year	Average of Dues-Payers
1935	71,001
1936	70,862
1937	72,490
1938	71,637
1939	57,704
1940	67,980
1941	64,812
1942	66,707
1943	65,688
1944	74,721

Sources: *El Obrero Ferroviario*, 16 May 1939; UF: *Memoria y balance correspondiente al año 1940* (Buenos Aires, 1941), 102; *Memoria y balance correspondiente al año 1942* (Buenos Aires, 1943), 121; "Libro de actas de la Comisión Directiva," 1 (2 Feb. 1945), 18.

*Workers earning over 500 pesos a month are excluded from this estimate, as are those who could be members of La Fraternidad (Caja Nacional de Jubilaciones y Pensiones de Empleados Ferroviarios, *Memoria correspondiente al año 1942* [Buenos Aires, 1943], 172).

THE UOT

Using the tactics first tested in 1935, the UOT expanded its influence. It was hindered, however, by ideological conflict, as well as growing employer and government resistance.

The entrance of the Communists into the UOT combined with the general growth of labor militancy to produce a strike wave in the textile industry in the mid-1930s. In 1936 government authorities counted 26 stoppages in greater Buenos Aires. (Only the construction industry, in the midst of the greatest explosion of union activity of the period, had more.) Several of the strikes were large and violent and marked by failure. According to Luis Sommi, a key leader of the Communist Party, elements in the party were trying—despite the popular front strategy—to make strikes as violent as possible in order to make them revolutionary.[66] The most conspicuous was at the firm Casa Gratry: 621 workers struck for higher wages and the rehiring of recently fired factory leaders. Pitched battles ensued between workers and strikebreakers, and sympathy strikes began in neighborhoods surrounding the plant. The arrest of strike leaders and government determination to protect strikebreakers led to the strike's collapse, as did government pressure on the UOT for its role in this and other strikes. The police shut three union neighborhood centers. Meetings were forbidden outside the UOT's headquarters. Only after the CGT conferred with the authorities did repression ease, allowing the union to open two new locals.[67]

In April 1936 the UOT renewed its push for collective contracts, especially in the wool sector. In November the union presented a list of demands that called for a minimum wage, the right of association, suppression of favoritism, rotation of workers instead of layoffs, rehiring of workers fired for union activity, and the creation of mixed commissions to settle disputes.

In what was to become standard procedure, the UOT requested that both the national department of labor and that of the province of Buenos Aires become involved in union-employer negotiations. Both agencies consented, but the largest employers' organization favored the DNT. The DNT helped establish a mixed commission of employers and union members, but only after the former had refused to allow the union leadership on the commission because they were not woolworkers. Barely able to prevent the rank-and-file from striking, the UOT leadership, advised by the CGT, continued the talks with employers and the DNT. The very ability to negotiate without calling a strike was a major breakthrough. On 2 February 1937 a provisional agreement was reached which established a minimum wage. According to *La Vanguardia*, the DNT had made it clear that it wanted to avoid a serious conflict. The employers' organization lacked the power to enforce the agreement, so the DNT and its provincial equivalent urged companies to cooperate.[68]

A final agreement in the wool sector was reached rapidly because of pressure from the authorities in the province of Buenos Aires. They gave employers and the union eight days to present their positions. On 17 February a contract was signed at the provincial department of labor. The pact set minimum wages, forbad strikes or lockouts without a reasonable period for negotiations, and called for submission of disagreements about the contract to the department of labor. Two days later the same agreement was signed in the capital. Subsequently a permanent mixed commission to interpret the agreements was established for the wool sector.[69] In the province of Buenos Aires, the government of Manuel Fresco wanted a contract and obtained it, pushing the DNT into action. The provincial maneuverings were the beginning of a rivalry between the national and local authorities that greatly aided the UOT.

The stunning victory—establishing an industry-wide contract without a strike—came only partly because of increased government interest and UOT strength. Establishing minimum wages was in the best interest of some firms as well because it lessened price competition created by lowering salaries. In 1941 a textile employers' association requested that congress establish a minimum wage for the industry.[70]

Success brought an increase in the average number of dues-payers, which rose sharply from 1,510 in the first half of 1935 to 2,351 in the first quarter of 1936 and to 4,249 in the next. In the first three months of 1938 the paid membership averaged 5,255.[71] As membership rose and the number of union meetings increased sharply, the frequency of strikes declined, reflecting the UOT's strategy of collective contracts (see Table 6-5).

After its success in the wool sector, the UOT began preparing demands in the dyeing, cotton, silk, and stocking sectors. The focus rapidly became cotton, and in July 1937 the UOT presented a petition to cotton-sector employers. The firms responded by establishing minimum salaries—an acknowledgment of the union's growing power. However, they refused to negotiate with either the UOT or the CGT, calling them professional agitators; they even spurned a DNT offer to mediate. Lacking the strength to shut down the cotton factories, the UOT called an industry-wide twenty-four–hour strike. Despite police efforts to prevent

Table 6-5

Strikes and Union Meetings in the Textile Industry in Buenos Aires, 1935–45

Year	Number of Strikes	Number of Union Meetings
1935	13	460
1936	19	506
1937	12	574
1938	7	539
1939	4	737
1940	10	682
1941	3	448
1942	10	431
1943	12	155
1944	3	119
1945	7	315

Sources: DNT, División de Estadística: *Estadística de las huelgas* (Buenos Aires, 1940), 49; *Estadística de las huelgas 1940* (Buenos Aires, 1941), 9; *Investigaciones sociales 1940*, 45; *Investigaciones sociales 1941* (Buenos Aires, 1942), 88; *Investigaciones sociales 1942* (Buenos Aires, 1943), 88, 95; Dirección de Estadística Social, *Investigaciones sociales, 1943–1945*, 17, 56–59.

the spread of propaganda, the union claimed that the stoppage was a success, but the results were far from optimal. Five hundred workers from the Grafa plant were fired, and the employers abandoned the wool industry's mixed commission.[72] The cotton firms still refused to negotiate, and many even abandoned the minimum wages that had been established.

The collapse of the drive in cotton coincided with the recession of 1937–38. Plant closings and layoffs made organizing difficult. Nonetheless, the UOT's commitment to sector-wide contracts intensified in 1938, when the Communists, with the help of the Partido Socialista Obrero, took over the UOT and assumed complete control in the following year. The Communists strongly believed in moving away from plant-by-plant organization.

When the economy improved, the UOT returned to the offensive. As in 1935 the first attempts at establishing a collective contract were in the knitting sector. In December 1938 workers demanded uniform salaries in order to stop wage cuts. Negotiations proved impossible because the employers' association dissolved rather than accept DNT mediation.

More than one thousand workers in two hundred establishments struck, but production in larger factories could not be halted. After two weeks contracts were signed where possible. The UOT claimed that even in firms that refused to sign workers received a slight increase in salary.[73]

This partial defeat was followed by a series of dramatic victories. Since 1935 conditions in the silk industry had declined continually, despite the UOT's efforts to uphold them. In early 1939 the UOT pressed harder for a contract. The employers refused to negotiate or allow the mediation of the DNT, but they offered a raise. On 2 July 1939 the workers rejected the wage offer and authorized a strike. Threatening a strike and claiming to be ending the chaos in the industry, the union attempted to force negotiations. In the capital it failed, but in the province of Buenos Aires an agreement was signed because of pressure from the Fresco government. However, the contract could go into effect only if it were also adopted in the capital, which it was not.

On 27 July the workers walked out. In the capital, according to the DNT, 2,000 out of 2,500 workers in 90 plants struck.[74] The strike was less effective in Buenos Aires province. The companies refused to capitulate, and the UOT looked consistently to the government for a way out. Pushing for a contract, Fresco got one on 8 September which established a minimum wage and a mixed commission. This spurred on the DNT, and on 20 September an agreement was reached in the capital.[75] According to the CGT, the national government coerced the employers into a settlement:

> In the end the workers' iron discipline, shown in the maintenance of the strike without any sign of weakening, and the determination of the DNT, obliged the industrialists to abandon their intransigence.[76]

The triumph had a domino effect. On 9 November 1939, after a long period of bargaining, a contract establishing minimum wages for cotton-spinning was signed in the province of Buenos Aires. In December the same agreement was approved for the capital. Like the agreements discussed above, these contracts would have been impossible without pressure from government authorities.[77] On 27 March 1940 all 1,500 workers in belts and elastics—the vast majority women and/or minors—struck. After 42 days the minister of interior separately called in both employers and union representatives. Two days later at the DNT a contract was signed which set minimum wages and established equal pay for equal work.[78]

Success brought some of the expected dividends. For example, the number of neighborhood centers increased from 5 in 1939 to 10 in 1940.

GROWTH & FRUSTRATION, 1936-1943   121

However, the UOT did not grow: from April 1939 to March 1940 dues-payers averaged 4,373 a month, and from April 1940 to November 1941, 4,908. (In contrast, there were more than 5,000 dues-payers in early 1938.)* The UOT was plagued by what had become the normal pattern for it: workers joined and then dropped out.[79]

The onset of World War II undermined the UOT's progress. Some branches of the industry faced severe dislocations. Either because of such problems or because of easy and large profits, employers moved against the union, firing officials, including one of the highest, Prospero Malvestitti. More important, the uneasy coexistence between Communists and Socialists shattered after the Hitler-Stalin Pact. Tensions rose in 1939. In 1940 Socialists and Syndicalists pulled out of the organization, and in mid-1941 they established their own union, also called the Unión Obrera Textil. (Henceforth we shall retain the name UOT for the Communist-dominated union and designate the Socialist-dominated union the UOT[SP].)[80]†

After the split the UOT became more pugnacious; it is difficult to urge restraint when another union can issue a call to action. The new Communist strategy—hard-line anti-imperialism—led to frequent strikes against foreign-owned firms. The industry became ensnared in constant turmoil. Long, bitter stoppages distracted the union from efforts to obtain collective contracts and destroyed the image that it had tried to create of a union producing order out of chaos.

The most important of the strikes against foreign-owned companies started on 15 October 1940 at Ducilo, the large rayon producer owned by Dupont and Imperial Chemical, located in an isolated part of Quilmes, Buenos Aires province (a suburb of the capital). The UOT had organized the plant after the signing of the 1939 silk contract, but relations with the company had never been easy; workers had walked out twice prior to the October stoppage.[81] The strike started because of the company's unwillingness to negotiate and because of firings, suspensions, and Ducilo's alleged refusal to establish a six-hour day for workers in unhealthy jobs—as required by law. Ducilo employed strikebreakers, and the UOT tried to stop their use. Violence was an important tactic of both sides. Two workers were killed and as many as 280 were held by the police at one time. The provincial government (without the goals of

---

*Figures calculated from percentage of dues-payers in each category given in *El Obrero Textil*, Dec. 1941.

†The unions were usually identified as UOT Entre Ríos and UOT Independencia respectively.

Fresco, who had been removed from office in March 1940) declared the stoppage illegal and made no serious effort to force negotiations. *El Obrero Ferroviario* described the impact of the stoppage as follows:

> The towns near the factory . . . are practically "seized" by police forces. . . . A worker has been killed by thugs who have been protected by concealed interests. The inviolability of the home has disappeared. Women are insulted and attacked by police. . . . A brief inspection of the surroundings have convinced us of a sad reality . . . we believe we find ourselves before a picture of war. Europe obsesses the mind and creates an illusion of bloody reality, armored cars in the peaceful zone of Quilmes, cavalry with carbines, police with rifles.[82*]

The strikers were making no headway and wanted to demonstrate local support, so a regional grouping of unions in Quilmes called a twenty-four–hour general strike, which (according to *La Nación*) was a success.[83] With the exception of butcher shops and bread stores, which stayed open half a day, all retail establishments shut. Only some public transport operated, and in many factories most employees failed to show up. The general strike forced the provincial government to press for a settlement that allowed the union to save face. On 13 February 1941 the UOT signed an agreement providing for the rehiring of striking workers within ninety days; if they were not taken back, the company was to pay them two and one-half months' salary. An already existing grievance committee was to continue to function.

Anti-Communists claimed that the Communists used the Ducilo strike as a showcase for anti-imperialism. (In the 1970s Jorge Michellón, the UOT's secretary general during the Ducilo strike, made a similar comment.) The Communists' aggressive anti-war stance clashed with pro-Allied sentiments, leading to intensified conflict. The UOT's legal advisor resigned because of anti-war statements. A verbal brawl erupted between the union and the CGT over whether the latter had aided the UOT sufficiently. The confederation had played a vital role in the recent victories, providing advice and lending its prestige, but the war drove a wedge between the two organizations.[84]

The government matched the UOT's aggressive attitude. As mentioned, the DNT refused to deal with the UOT for much of 1941 and 1942, depriving the union of a vital source of leverage. Communists faced increasing harassment from the police; two members of the executive

---

*Two weeks later, *El Obrero Ferroviario* printed an angry denunciation of the Communist Party and its role in the strike.

board were arrested. Employers used this atmosphere to rid their firms of union leaders.[85]

Despite a deterioration in working conditions and a return to single-plant strikes, the UOT continued to be an important force in the industry. It helped organize a campaign for the reform of laws concerning expectant mothers and pushed for the creation of a pension fund.[86] (The former undoubtedly appealed to the large number of women in the industry.) It also fought for paid vacations. Because of the reformed commercial code, industrial workers in the capital had the right to paid vacations, but the courts had not definitively decided the issue in the province of Buenos Aires. In any case, the law was implemented only when unions applied pressure. In 1938 and 1942 (both difficult years for the UOT) the union pressed hard for the law to be implemented and had some success. For example, in 1942 in the municipality of San Martín, the UOT signed an agreement that secured vacations in thirty-four firms and covered three thousand workers.[87]

In response to the war-induced inflation, the UOT launched a drive to increase wages, but employers uniformly refused to negotiate. Yet the union was still feared, and the government, anxious to avoid unrest, had the DNT strenuously lobby employers to grant higher wages. In 1941 wool workers received a 10 percent raise, while cotton spinners in the province of Buenos Aires got 15 percent. Several non-cotton or wool firms also increased wages. In 1942 employer associations gave across-the-board wage increases in wool, silk, and cotton-weaving. In none of these cases was a union directly involved. Only the UOT(SP) won a new collective contract, which covered its stronghold, the stocking industry.[88]

Despite the setbacks, the UOT grew, although the reasons for its increasing membership are unclear. Between December 1941 and May 1943 it averaged 7,672 dues-payers per month. It remained larger than the UOT(SP), which was limited to the Socialists' traditional bastions—the stocking industry and a few large plants. Nonetheless, in 1943 only approximately 8 percent of textile workers belonged to the UOT.[89]

The UOT well represents the dilemma of industrial unions during the Neo-Conservative era. Given good leadership and government cooperation, progress could be made. However, the government did not have a genuine interest in labor, and it was difficult to organize a high percentage of workers. Thus unions remained vulnerable.

Despite the labor movement's tribulations, in 1941 it had a total membership of 441,412—a growth of 19.3 percent since 1936. While the increase was substantial, it just outpaced the growth of the nonrural working population. Only 12 percent of the nonrural economically active belonged to unions. However, the union movement had changed. In 1932 the UF had represented a high percentage of all union members, but by 1941 the construction workers' union claimed 48,680 members, the CGEC 35,000, and the food workers' union 19,513. Only 35.1 percent of those organized worked in transportation, while 32.8 percent were in industry, and the remaining 26.7 percent in services.[90]*

In the massive surge of union activity during the mid-1930s, led by the Communists, unions had established a firm foothold in new areas, especially in manufacturing. Unions moved from plant-oriented to industry-wide mobilization. National organizations became more common. The changes occurred because the urban economy was growing and a popular front spirit pervaded the union movement. The government left unions room to maneuver, while maintaining its lack of interest in the labor movement. However, the propitious conditions ended. The economy weakened and became plagued by inflation. Partly owing to World War II, the labor movement divided into two competing camps. Under Castillo, there was little room for dissenting voices. The Communists suffered from repression, while the Socialists already had been hurt by the changes in the political system after 1935. The labor movement was increasingly dissatisfied with the unions' inability to grow faster, creating tensions. Ironically, dissatisfaction grew as the unions were becoming stronger, winning an increasing percentage of strikes and signing more contracts. To an ever larger number of workers, unions had become legitimate organizations. Nonetheless, the dominant mood in mid-1943 was frustration and a desire for change.

---

*I have used the categories established by Miguel Murmis and Juan Carlos Portantiero, *Estudios sobre los orígenes del peronismo*, I (Buenos Aires, 1971), 128, fn. 15.

Chapter 7

UNION RELATIONS WITH THE GOVERNMENT, 1930–1943

Interaction between a government and a labor movement helps define the nature of unions. Repression, cooperation, or a lack of either—all are important in shaping union tactics and ideology because they help set the limits of the possible. The relationship between government and unions should not be viewed as one-dimensional. It cannot be reduced to obvious forms of intervention in a conflict between capital and labor since the working class is an actor—even if a minor one—in a multidimensional political game.[1]

In the Neo-Conservative era unions in Argentina did not play an important political role, nor were they an accepted part of the political system. The government did not attempt to define the unions' place in the society but continued the Radical tradition of dealing with them in an ad hoc manner. Yet the role of government loomed large. Unions could approach the government in many ways. They could use the various branches of the state to put pressure on decisionmaking bodies. Union allies in congress could pass favorable legislation. Government agencies could be induced to implement laws that had been passed or to put pressure on employers. The executive could act. Provincial governments played a substantial role. Thus it is impossible to understand the unions without an explication of their relationships with the government.

Prior to 1943 the ruling elites did not view the working class as a potentially important actor, although—in comparison to the rest of Latin America—the labor movement had considerable strength and the modern economic sector was substantial. Yet the Argentine elites—unlike their counterparts in Chile or Mexico, for example—did not systematically define the role of unions by labor laws or encourage organized labor to join the political system.[2] Nevertheless, by the 1930s the government's role in the labor movement was extensive and not limited to police powers. As most employers refused to negotiate with unions, the government became the only source of outside leverage, leading to increasing union dependence on it. And as the unions became more powerful, government interest increased.

The phenomenon of government interest growing along with the labor movement is by no means limited to Argentina; in many societies governments define the limits of the struggle between capital and labor. This becomes increasingly necessary in the view of many elites and labor leaders when the number of unskilled urban workers increases and a consciousness of union power spreads. The simple withholding of labor is no longer sufficient to make employers grant concessions. The ability to readily replace strikers leads to violence and the use of the state's repressive apparatus. Then some form of friendly intervention is needed. J. David Greenstone has hypothesized that in the United States it was the need of the less skilled workers of the Congress of Industrial Organizations (CIO) for friendly government intervention that led that confederation to increased political involvement.[3] In Argentina union ideology and the Neo-Conservative political system delayed political mobilization, but almost the entire labor movement constantly sought government intervention, even unions representing the highly skilled.

While governments from Justo through Castillo remained essentially indifferent—when not hostile—to labor, they remembered the lessons the Radicals had learned: cooperation could be easier than repression. As the 1930s progressed and unions became stronger, governments began to favor collective contracts and to intervene more actively in conflicts between labor and capital. Even though their basic attitudes did not alter, they were forced to pay attention, and there were key differences from government to government. The regimes of Justo and Ortiz were less hostile than those of Uriburu and Castillo.

The seeming contradiction between increasing government involvement and indifference is an illusion. Governments remained untouched by a concern for unions, but a perception of the disruptive power of unions began to penetrate. The Neo-Conservative governments were too weak to permit widespread labor unrest; violent repression had high political costs. Moreover, the dominant landed interests had little to lose from minor concessions to urban workers.

The interests of government and labor could be made to converge. The Neo-Conservatives wanted to maintain tranquility and to keep the opposition within the political system, while the unions desired improved working conditions. The rail unions and a few others, because of their strategic position, were able to maintain an ongoing relationship similar to the one achieved under the Radicals. To fuse these desires most unions needed to challenge the government and catch its attention but stop short of inducing repression.

Union challenges could assume two basic forms: strikes and political pressure. The government had three major options in responding to strikes: 1) ignore them and allow the police to hinder demonstrations; 2) suppress them outright; 3) force owners to make concessions. The third option depended not only on the unions attracting government attention, but also on various other factors, including the current political situation, the character of the union involved, the industry involved, the extent of disruption, and the visibility of a particular strike. However, the government never clearly indicated what its criteria were in reaching a particular decision, nor was the average union sufficiently strong to push the government toward a favorable action. Only unions in industries where strikes affected large numbers of people could do so. Moreover, a danger existed in attracting the regime's attention: one time it could bring government aid, and the next time, the police. Political pressure was particularly effective in the period prior to the return of the Radicals to the electoral process because the Socialists had substantial power and their desires had to be considered. The regime granted concessions on what it considered minor matters but which were important to the Socialists.

While the government intervened increasingly in the struggle between capital and labor, it was inconsistent. For example, the DNT was committed to easing tensions, but it lacked support from more powerful sectors of the state apparatus. If employers were unwilling to negotiate, the DNT could do little. Moreover, ministries frequently operated at cross purposes, and rivalries existed between provincial and national agencies. At times legislative bodies placed pressure on the executive branch to side with unions. In the following sections we shall discuss how the unions dealt with changing governments and policies.

THE FOET

The FOET provides the best example of a union challenging the government without stepping over the invisible line that brought repression. The 1932 telephone strike disrupted a vital means of communication through the use of violence, but the government did not repress it, as it did many others. Rather it forced the UT to come to terms.

The FOET's relationship with Yrigoyen helped shape the union's view of the state. As discussed in Chapter 4, its first contract was signed after Yrigoyen's personal intervention. Through Luis Gay, the union's dominant figure, the FOET had other ties to the Radicals. While Gay has said that he was not a Radical during the 1930–43 period, he claims that he always admired Yrigoyen's social philosophy.*

After the 1930 coup, faced with the UT's determination to crush it and unwilling to help the company by striking, the FOET turned frequently to the government. Twice delegations met with Uriburu. The union tried appealing to the government's nationalism; it accused the UT of the following:

> making use for the benefit of its unlimited avarice any situation, even if it is prejudicial to the country, and this despite much flying of flags from the fronts of its buildings by which it wants to demonstrate its patriotism. In reality it imposes hunger, sows injustice, and commits outrages in the same country that it pretends to appreciate so much.[4]

Nationalistic appeals could have an impact. When the UT indefinitely suspended some workers for refusing to work overtime, FOET representatives approached the capital's chief of police, Admiral Ricardo Hermelo. The admiral, who had a reputation of being anti-labor, called them agitators and told them they could be shot if they disturbed the martial law. Assuring him that until recently they had worked for the company, they stressed that a foreign corporation (i.e., ITT, which controlled the UT) should not be allowed to use the coup to injure Argentines. Much to their surprise, Hermelo negotiated a settlement in which the UT agreed to take back the suspended employees. The victory was short-lived since within several months the UT had again laid off many workers.[5]

A long string of failures followed. The DNT was unable to force the UT to discuss layoffs, work rules, or other major problems. The agency's impotence is clear from the following: In January 1931 the FOET presented a proposal to the DNT that addressed some of the government's worries about rising unemployment. The union suggested that the UT rehire all laid-off workers and everyone work one day less a month, thereby taking a pay cut. Still under Maglione's control, the DNT presented these suggestions to the UT with a plea that they be

---

*Gay received his first job—working for the Chamber of Deputies of the province of Buenos Aires—through the influence of his father, who was a Radical. Moreover, he claims he participated in the unsuccessful Radical conspiracy of December 1932, although there is no corroborative evidence of his role (author's interviews with Luis Gay, 17 Oct. 1975 and 31 Mar. 1976). Atilio E. Cattáneo, *Plan 1932* (Buenos Aires, 1959), does not mention Gay. See below.

accepted, but they were not. The company claimed that the lower salary would be nullified by the day off and objected to the restraints on its right to dismiss workers.[6]*

The government remained inaccessible during the rest of 1931, but the FOET greeted the Justo regime with some hope and issued an ultimatum to the UT. As a precautionary move against a walkout, in early May 1932 the company "asked" its staff to remain overnight in the exchanges. While the UT claimed that it had twice the number of "volunteers" it needed, the union charged that the company kept the workers at their posts with threats. Because women could not legally work at night, the FOET went to the DNT for help. Eduardo Bullrich (Justo's choice for president of the DNT), a Socialist deputy, Gay, and some others investigated and found women in the offices, but nothing was done. Similar violations occurred later in the same month.[7]

The DNT's ineffectuality went still further. On the day that the FOET's ultimatum expired, the agency offered mediation. The union accepted, saying it sought a peaceful solution and wanted to stop the rumors that the threatened strike was merely political maneuvering. The UT accepted as well. The DNT held numerous meetings with both sides, but the UT remained unwilling to compromise on the rehiring of laid-off workers. Bullrich, after telling the UT that he hoped it would cooperate in solving the unemployment problem, proposed the company immediately rehire seventy workers, an additional seventy within sixty days, and rehire others according to need. The UT rejected the proposal, and the DNT ended its attempt at mediation.[8]

The strike began without warning on 23 May 1932 at 5:00 p.m. As shifts changed, squads of laid-off workers converged on the offices to spread the news. At some exchanges, bombs and stink bombs were hurled to drive operators out of the buildings. The number of strikers was small. The company claimed that only 1,479 workers out of 9,126 went out, and Gay's estimate of 1,800 is not much larger. Most were skilled workers in repairs and installation. The union's inability to organize women exacted a heavy price. For example, at the foreign and long-distance exchange only about thirty of three hundred female operators struck.[9]

With the operators still working, the FOET depended on sabotage and the hope that the government would intervene. As noted, lines were destroyed, and the destruction continued throughout the strike, severing

---

*The union tried to see the minister of interior but failed (*La Vanguardia*, 28 Feb. 1931; *Federación*, Mar. 1931).

communication between the capital and many of its suburbs. The UT informed the U.S. Embassy that as of 1 June 39,486 telephones had been put out of service and only one third had been repaired. Strikers and their supporters frequently exchanged gunfire with strikebreakers. The FOET accused right-wing nationalist organizations of supplying guns and cars to the strikebreakers.[10]

The government's reaction was measured, except during the first days, when a police picket surrounded the FOET's headquarters and arrested strikers entering and leaving. The first post-strike meeting was banned, but pressure soon eased and the arrest rate declined. Harassment continued but unevenly. The union headquarters was raided twice. The police used violence against strikers but made only 120 arrests, none of which were of key leaders—despite the efforts of the UT, which offered a 500 peso reward for the arrest of anyone damaging its property and tried unsuccessfully to prosecute the union leadership for sabotage.[11]

The UT accused the government of not controlling the strikers. It complained to the U.S. Embassy that it did not receive full protection:

> The company considers that it is receiving very full and effective assistance from the police, but that there is a point beyond which that force cannot go without the backing of the Ministry of Interior, and this support apparently is absent. It is evident that these acts of destruction are not isolated, but obey a central direction, hence the arrest and detention of those caught in flagranti delictu [sic] will not stop the trouble. On the other hand the representatives of the Company consider that if some ten agitators were either put under lock and key, or warned to behave, on the pain of being held personally responsible for subsequent happenings, sabotage would entirely stop. The Government, however, is not so far apparently willing to go to this length.[12]

Major newspapers and other commentators echoed the UT's remarks.[13]

The government tried to settle the strike. On 1 June Bullrich offered mediation through letters which made it clear that the matter had been discussed with Justo; they threatened that if the offer was not accepted, "the government [would] have to apply the dispositions and regulations intended to assure the correct functioning of public services compromised by the present conflict."[14] The UT accepted but claimed that practically no strike existed and that it considered all those who had walked out to have lost their jobs. It rejected the rehiring of those who had been laid off, but it consented to arbitration on the issue of whether it had the right to dismiss its staff. The FOET did want negotiations.

The UT's representatives failed to attend the first meeting on the grounds that some of the FOET delegation had been dismissed by the company for bad conduct and had published defamatory statements about the UT's directors. Moreover, the company questioned whether the FOET represented the workers and whether it would be legally bound by a contract since the union did not have personería jurídica. The union changed its representatives, negotiations started, but soon ground to a halt. The UT refused to meet with the FOET until the sabotage ended. The DNT's urgings were of no avail, and the agency ended its attempt at mediation.[15]

On 18 June Bullrich sent a heated letter to the minister of interior, calling on him to see that all laws and regulations concerning telephone service were carried out and that the 1929 contract be taken into account. "Enforcing the rules" had become a euphemism for ending the strike on terms favorable to the FOET.[16] Furthermore, Bullrich accused the UT of flouting Argentine sovereignty; he felt it imperative that the state have the right to control and inspect a public service, as well as assure that it operated normally.[17]

The minister of interior, who took over the conciliation effort, called for two studies, one on disrupted telephone service and the other on the number of strikers and the working conditions. The UT was hopeful that a verdict would go its way, while the FOET believed that the minister was trying to wear it out. Finally, the minister called on both parties and the DNT to meet with him on 30 June. The UT gave its version of the meeting to the U.S. Embassy:

> The proposition was there made on the part of the Department of Labor that the Company should take back 150 strikers immediately ... and this number should be continually increased; further that those restored should receive pay for the period during which they had been striking. This proposal is of course quite unacceptable.
>
> The inference placed upon this ... is that, whereas the Minister of Interior is considered to be sound at heart in this affair, the Department of Labor has the backing of the President.[18]

No progress was made until the matter was handed back to the DNT. Justo appointed Roberto M. Ortiz as his personal representative, and the UT was told that a solution was desired in forty-eight hours. A contract was signed on 14 July.[19]

The contract was only part of the settlement. A major obstacle had been the disposition of the legal cases against those who had been arrested since the company refused to drop charges. Ortiz promised that within fifteen days of the strike's end all prisoners would be given conditional releases while awaiting trial and that the charges pending against Luis Gay would not be dropped but Gay would be cleared. The pledges were carried out.[20]

The FOET had little choice but to accept government mediation, but why the government behaved favorably toward the union is a more complex question. The key to the agreements was the desire of Bullrich and Ortiz to settle the strike on terms that did not necessitate the FOET's capitulation. They had Justo's support, despite violence and pressure from newspapers and representatives of the foreign community in Argentina for firmer action to protect the U.S.-owned, British-based UT. The North American and the British chambers of commerce had sent a joint protest to the minister of interior. The United States's chargé d'affaires had backed the UT in a meeting with the minister of foreign affairs.[21]

One reason for the regime's behavior was the UT's arrogance. Its lack of respect for the DNT had a significant impact on government sensibilities. When talking with the North American ambassador, the minister of foreign affairs compared the UT's intransigence unfavorably with the attitude of the British-owned Ferrocarril Oeste, where the government had taken firm steps to end a slowdown. Also, the UT was unpopular due to poor (if improving) service. The unpopularity was recognized in the U.S. diplomatic correspondence.[22] In addition, because the UT was North American–owned, local political ramifications were not serious.

Another factor was the political situation. The easing of repression in 1932 led to a strike wave, leaving the government with two major options: continuing the policies of Uriburu—i.e., repression of almost all attempts at sociopolitical expression—or conciliation. The latter meant helping (or at least tolerating) unions whose interests were not anathema to the government. The telephone strike was a good opportunity to try this option. For one thing, it was one of the first major stoppages. For another, the FOET was dominated by Syndicalists and belonged to the CGT and was therefore not as threatening as simultaneous strikes by Anarchist or Communist unions.

A crisis that erupted during the strike, with the right opposing Justo and the left supporting him, further limited the regime's options. A rumor (apparently not totally groundless) spread that the right was going to overthrow the "constitutional regime." The telephone strike contributed to the uneasiness. The right worried about the increase in union activity and sabotage. As the *Review of the River Plate* pointed out,

> The national fuss which is being made over the epidemic of "rumours" is intense. Telephonic isolation of thousands of subscribers at a time when the flu is prevalent and the children's doctors are wanted over the wire which happens to be cut is much worse, and had a psychological effect which may be left to the imagination.[23]

The Socialists responded to the threat of a coup by calling a rally to reaffirm faith in democracy—i.e., the existing system. Joining the Socialists were the Independent Socialists, the Progressive Democrats, the Anti-Personalist Radicals, and the Entre Ríos Radicals. Labor organizations also lent their support—the CGT, UOEM, and UOT among others. The FOET declared that it would physically resist all attempts at governmental change contrary to the country's democratic sentiments or the well-being of the working class. The rumors of a coup ended after a rally of about 100,000 people.[24]

The FOET and its allies had supported the regime. In a debate on the strike in the Chamber of Deputies, Socialists, Independent Socialists, and Progressive Democrats supported the union's position—and they represented 68 of the 158 seats in the lower house. They could not therefore be alienated needlessly, as contemporary observers noted:

> The present tendency in labour disputes is obviously one of relative acquiescence to the viewpoints of the trade unions. That there are political factors in operation is fairly evident, and a quick glance at the political situation ought to be sufficient to prompt the realization that any development likely to antagonize the Socialists is likely, whenever possible, to be religiously avoided.[25]

Toleration did not extend to all labor organizations. After shootings and bombings, a simultaneous strike by an Anarchist bread bakers' union was crushed. The government declared the union an illegal association, raided its headquarters, and arrested over five hundred workers. Eventually only eleven were tried, but the strike was disrupted.[26]

The government's attempt to establish a working relationship with the FOET continued. It even survived the planned participation of key FOET members in a foiled revolt of the Radicals led by Lieutenant Colonel Atilio Cattáneo in December 1932. The FOET's role would have been to take over key exchanges. After the plot was uncovered, Gay fled Buenos Aires. When a FOET delegation visited Ortiz, he expressed the view that the FOET had participated due to inexperience and that Gay could return without charges being pressed.[27]

The government's support of the FOET did not earn it any direct political benefits. Indeed an article in the union's newspaper was entitled "I Whistled at the President at a Soccer Match":

> I whistled [the equivalent of catcalls] at His Excellency the president of the Nation. I whistled because he fooled the people with his campaign promises, with his false protests of constitutional normality and many other "little things" that he did not hesitate in promising when he was only a candidate.[28]

Nonetheless, for the regime the telephone strike was not a complete loss. A pattern of labor relations had been set. Unions knew that the government would not automatically crush a major strike. Organizations not perceived as a threat could obtain favorable intervention. However, from the unions' perspective, a major problem had not been resolved: the line between acceptable and unacceptable behavior was very thin and never defined.

THE FEC

Receiving government support through political pressure is best demonstrated by the FEC. The FEC recognized that it needed basic laws enacted because it was unable to call strikes or to set conditions without undermining the establishments where it had won concessions. Through a series of political campaigns built on but expanded beyond Socialist support, the retail clerks were able to acquire favorable legislation. Once the legislation was enacted, the union worked with the government to ensure enforcement.

Three successful campaigns—for uniform closing laws, the English Saturday, and the reform of the commercial code—in the period prior to the Radicals' return were based on the need to set basic conditions through legislation. The union lacked the strength to help enforce the eight-hour day. Moreover, it had difficulty holding on to gains made in smaller stores in outlying neighborhoods because once improvements had been won, the employees abandoned the union and old conditions returned. As noted, the DNT lacked the resources to help. The FEC needed to make violations obvious. The solution to its inability to help enforce the eight-hour day was ingenious, if not foolproof: legislation requiring the closing of all stores at 8:00 p.m. While not eliminating long days, this would limit them. When the Senate considered exempting stores that did not have employees, the FEC objected strenuously, arguing that those stores would have a competitive advantage and that easy enforcement of the law would be impossible.[29] The union wanted flouters of the law to be so obvious that the government could not ignore them. The FEC desired the legal establishment of the English Saturday because it knew that only legislation could reimpose the custom that had broken down in the wake of the depression. The solution was controlling competitive instincts.[30] On a more elaborate plane, with the reform of the commercial code the FEC saw to it that minimum conditions were imposed on an entire industry—a move inconceivable outside the political arena. It was the FEC's ability to mobilize political strength that permitted these victories.

Aware that laws did not change conditions, the FEC fought for enforcement. It even advocated that the government give the union's executive board the power to investigate infringements and obtain police cooperation.[31] More realistically, the union urged employees to bring it signed denunciations of violations; after investigating their validity, it forwarded the charges to the DNT. Between 1 August 1939 and 31 July 1941 the FEC forwarded 349 such charges. In addition, it made sure that transgressors received unfavorable publicity: friendly publications printed the names of the businesses and their infractions, sometimes describing violations in graphic detail.[32]

The complaints of the FEC to the DNT—unlike those of many unions—had an impact. For example, in April 1933 the FEC informed the DNT that Artela, García y Cía. worked its employees nine to ten hours a day. The agency dispatched an inspector who confirmed this, and for a time the company complied with the law. In July, however, employees had to work nine to ten hours a day plus all day Saturday and some Sundays as well. At the request of the FEC, the DNT sent several inspectors to the company on a Saturday afternoon when they knew that employees would be working:

> When the inspectors appeared to fulfill their mission, the *concierge* made all sorts of objections before permitting their entrance. This was due to an attempt to gain time so that the employees might be hidden in a basement. Therefore, upon entering, the DNT representatives did not find the personnel, who minutes before had been working, but

the presence of several overcoats and hats, plus the fact of finding all the heaters burning, made them certain that the employees had been forced to hide. They attempted to find them [the employees] in the various parts of the establishment, but lack of knowledge of the building prevented locating them.[33]

Despite being caught in open violation of the law, the manager claimed that he knew someone who could fix these matters. The FEC appeared to have no fear of this.

Like other unions, the FEC used the government as a mediator. When M.S. Bagley y Cía. changed the routes of its traveling salesmen, the salesmen felt they would earn less from commissions. Suspecting that the reroutings were illegal under the reformed commercial code, they turned to the FEC for help. The company refused to yield. The union applied pressure by issuing unfavorable publicity and urging its members to write letters threatening a boycott of the company's products. It also went to the minister of interior and the DNT; with the latter's mediation an agreement was finally reached. The company consented to compensate for any decline in the salesmen's income created by the reroutings.[34]

Throughout the Neo-Conservative era the FEC depended on its ability to achieve gains through the political system. To some extent as it grew larger, it could operate without the regime, but on most matters it depended upon a working relationship.

THE UOEM

The UOEM's relationship with the government is in some ways unusual; for one thing, the government was also the employer; for another, an ongoing relationship had been developed as early as the 1920s. In other ways, however, the relationship resembled that between the FEC and the government. Like the FEC the UOEM depended for much that it did on a legislative body—in this case, the city council.

The key activity of the UOEM was the settling of grievances. On many issues the union negotiated directly and often successfully with the municipality. Pérez Leirós claimed that talks with the municipal bureaucracy solved small problems while larger ones were discussed with the city council.[35] Even during the Uriburu dictatorship when there was no city council, the union dealt with the intendente and his subordinates. For example, in November 1930 a delegation discussed a new rule prohibiting workers from staying in the shops during the two-hour midday break. According to the union, this caused great inconvenience because many workers lived far away and had no place to go after eating in the nearby establishments. Furthermore, the lack of a place to rest caused workers to spend their time in establishments where they drank and played cards. The intendente quickly pointed out that the ruling had not been intended to be anti-worker but to prevent fires. He ordered a site prepared where workers could rest during the midday break.[36]

While always received respectfully by the municipal bureaucracy, the UOEM was far from universally successful. For example, it protested that lamplighters had been subject to a speedup; they had been required to light forty or more blocks in fifty minutes instead of the previous sixty-five. The union was informed that the change had been made after a long study and would not be reversed, but that an investigation would be conducted on ways to make the work less strenuous.[37]

When necessary, the UOEM applied pressure through the city council. (As noted, the city council had limited powers but was a vital ally of the UOEM.) On large issues such as pay raises the council had little influence, but on smaller matters, the intendente frequently found it easier to yield. In March 1932 the UOEM asked the municipality to provide waterproof boots to workers who frequently had to stand in water. At the Socialists' prompting, seven months later the council passed a resolution calling on the city to provide the boots. When the municipality failed to do so, a councilor from a minor party introduced a similar request, which also passed. A year after the initial resolution, the council was informed by the intendente that the boots had been acquired and would be distributed as needed.[38]

The UOEM's relationship with the municipal government was solid and deep. The union accepted government participation in many of its activities. City representatives attended important union events. The UOEM felt close enough to one intendente to present him with a photo album of its activities.[39]*

As has been stressed, the UOEM's social programs received government subsidies. Its recreational facility was built on land ceded by the municipality, and in 1930–31 the city granted the union 6,000 pesos for it. The municipality also contributed trees, built a wading pool, and financed the construction of dressing rooms. The union received 25,000

---

*Similar gifts by other unions to Perón created storms of protest. Such gestures to either the government or employers were considered outside union norms.

pesos from the national government and the municipality to help build its vacation resort.⁴⁰ The government had two reasons for contributing to these programs: they helped maintain the employees' health and limited the potential for militancy since clashes with the government could provoke the revocation of rights. It should be emphasized that the relationship enabled the union to achieve many things, but it worked only as long as the government felt it was in its best interest.

THE UF

An unstated mutual understanding existed between the UF and all governments since the mid-1920s—i.e., the flow of exports was vital to the country, and the UF did not propose to deter it. Moreover, the union paid little heed to larger issues and concentrated on its industry. In return for peace on the railroads, the government helped the railroaders achieve relatively good conditions. It was in the interest of both parties that there be a strong union because when discipline weakened, disruption of traffic increased.

The structure of the railroad industry dictated heavy government involvement. Government-established working conditions and regulations were spelled out in such detail that they filled a 220-page book. Changes had to be approved by the General Railroad Board. In January 1939 the board ruled on 763 issues.⁴¹ As discussed, the government was highly involved in all negotiations over wages and layoffs.

While the UF maintained regular contact with the railroad companies, both sides knew that even on minor issues the government could become involved. For example, in 1940 workers in the Ferrocarril Oeste's engine sheds at Haedo protested a failure to follow correct promotion procedures. When the railroad did not heed their complaints, an assembly voted to call an incremental strike, initially fifteen minutes, with fifteen minutes to be added each day. After several days the workers halted the stoppages in the hope that an agreement could be reached. When it was not, they began their protest again. They stopped only after the director of railroads promised to intercede for them with the company.⁴² The railroaders had achieved a favorable intervention, which many unions could not produce at any cost.

The government's policies were partly shaped by the union's attitudes toward politics. While many of the UF's leaders belonged to political parties, a vast majority saw the UF as more important. No ideology ever completely controlled the executive committee. The dominant approach was expressed by Antonio Tramonti, longtime president of the UF: "We are not Socialists, and if some are, we do not take it into account."[43]

The UF's refusal to align with any political party can be best seen in a 1931 controversy surrounding the candidacy of Bernardo Becerra for the Chamber of Deputies on the list of the Conservatives in the province of Buenos Aires. Becerra had helped found the UF and had always held key positions. In 1931 he also was serving on one of the CGT's governing bodies. His decision to run on the Conservative list produced a storm of criticism from UF locals and from other unions, as well as calls for his immediate removal from all his posts. Open support for the Conservatives was seen as a betrayal of the union movement. Not only did support for an elite-dominated party break with union norms, but also the Conservatives were perceived as generally unfriendly to labor. The union's executive board unanimously reaffirmed the UF's noninvolvement in politics and pointed out that it did not support Becerra's candidacy. A UF press release had earlier stated the union's line:

> The position of our organization on political matters is well known and events more far-reaching, varied, and unforeseen have not succeeded in modifying it.
>
> Many of the workers that belong are at the same time militants in political parties, and, who until today, are filling and have filled elective public offices, without this preventing them from taking an active part in the tasks of the organization, together with those who belong to their opposition. . . . This is possible because the UF does not belong to any tendency.[44]

The UF could take no other position if it wanted to remain above politics. In the same election six railroaders won seats in the Chamber of Deputies on Socialist lists. One, Marcelino Ganza, was as prominent as Becerra, but no fuss was raised. Nor was there any controversy over the election on Socialist lists of numerous important members of the UF to municipal posts in the province of Buenos Aires. Despite pressure the UF took no action against Becerra. He took a leave of absence during the campaign, but so did Ganza. Becerra was forced to resign from his CGT post *despite* the UF's actions.[45]*

---

*Not all of the six railroaders who won on the Socialist lists were UF members. At least one, Marcelino Buyán, had been expelled from the UF (FOEF, *Motivos de su creación* [Buenos Aires, 1939], 26).

The UF also held itself at a distance from other unions. The railroaders never struck in solidarity, and their financial contributions to other unions were relatively small. The UF would not endanger its position for any group. The union's position was allegedly epitomized by José Domenech, the leader of the Socialist faction in the UF. At a CGT congress Domenech was approached by the delegate of the *medialuneros* (croissant-makers) with a request to call a general strike. Domenech replied as follows: "Look *compañero*, we are railroad workers, and if we strike we paralyze the country; if there are no croissants, people will eat cake or bread, but with the railroads it's different."[46]

The UF did take stands on some public issues: democracy in Argentina, opposition to fascism, support for the Allies during World War II. However, if anything, it was statist.[47] It cooperated with both Yrigoyen and Uriburu, just as it would with any regime that did not try to destroy it. For governments with no desire to institutionalize the labor movement, the UF was an ideal union.

The relationship between the government and the UF is best shown by Ortiz's attempts to create a rail union closer to him politically. While Ortiz came to the presidency intending to eliminate fraud, he needed to create a base because he had undercut those who had elected him. An obvious potential source of support were the UF's Syndicalist leaders, with whom Ortiz had developed a good relationship when he was Alvear's minister of public works. The Socialist leaders had no personal bonds with Ortiz; the president resented Domenech (who had become the UF's president in 1934) because he refused to rig UF elections as requested. Moreover, the Socialists' political orientation made them appear threatening.[48] The growing power in both the UF and the CGT of men considered Socialists represented the potential threat that their influence would be transferred to the political arena, enabling the Socialists to escape their confinement to the capital.

Ortiz's goals for a railroad union and the labor movement are summed up by Manuel V. Ordóñez, an attorney for the State Railroads who had close ties to the Syndicalists: "My job consisted of creating an independent CGT but one that sympathized with the government or—better said—with the objectives of the government."[49] The lessons that Ortiz had learned as a Radical had not been forgotten. In April 1938 Ortiz appointed Tramonti (a Syndicalist) to the presidency of the railroad pension board, the first labor leader to hold such a post.

In June 1938 at the UF's annual congress, twenty-four of the ninety-seven delegates walked out, claiming that the union had been taken over by the Socialists and that the congress had met just to rubber-stamp the leaders' decisions.[50] Three days later the dissidents held a convention and formed a new union, the FOEF. Its constitution resembled the UF's except that it placed greater emphasis on separation from politics, banning internal groups and forbidding the simultaneous holding of posts in the union and in parties or the state. There were also some differences in the way members were elected to office.[51]

The UF charged that the FOEF had government backing, and it was correct. On 18 August 1938 the government granted the FOEF personería jurídica, just two months after it had been requested. Even the union itself had to acknowledge the rapidity with which the regime had acted. Less than a month later the FOEF received the right to represent its members before any government agency, and a short while later the State Railroads gave it permission to form grievance committees. At the end of November the private railroads granted the FOEF all the rights that the UF possessed.[52] According to the UF, Tramonti used his position as head of the pension board to further the cause of the dissidents by speaking at meetings and allowing his name to appear on propaganda. The UF feared that while he headed the board, no fair elections could be held. Its vigorous protests forced Tramonti to keep a lower profile.[53]

By creating a new union, Ortiz hoped to bolster his political position, but unrest spread along rail lines, driven by competition between the unions and a collapse of the normal firm discipline. The FOEF accused the UF of provoking job actions each time the FOEF's grievance committees met with the companies. Larger conflicts also occurred. On the Central Argentino a change in work regulations for switchmen (to which the UF had agreed) led to unrest when the FOEF refused to accept the new rules. FOEF members worked to regulation in Rosario and surrounding stations to protest the agreement.[54]* Friction between the two unions exacerbated a conflict with the Sud line over car-cleaning by an outside contractor, disrupting service for fifteen days.[55]

To end the unrest the regime decided to force a merger. On 31 March 1939 the minister of public works told representatives of both unions that their rivalry was disruptive and had harmed the general welfare. He gave the two unions ten days to establish a merger agreement which had to include four points: both executive boards would resign; future boards would be elected proportionally according to job type; matters pertaining to a branch of the industry would be decided by that branch;

---

*The UF hid its organizing of the stoppages in order not to provoke the government's wrath.

and the new union would refrain from politics and not join a confederation.[56]

The conditions favored the FOEF. They put the unions on an equal footing despite the UF's being commonly acknowledged as much larger. The resignation of both executive boards would have been a victory for the FOEF, which had complained of the UF leadership's iron control. The restructuring of decision-making and elections also reflected the dissidents' desires. The ban on joining a confederation would have seriously weakened the labor movement by depriving the CGT of its primary source of dues but would not have aided a resurrection of the Syndicalists.[57]

The UF's locals protested, and they were joined by many unions. The Radical Party's organization for railroaders opposed unity on the terms outlined by the government. The Socialists savagely attacked the plan, calling it an attempt to develop a labor movement along Fascist lines, but they carefully directed their remarks at the minister of public works and not at Ortiz. Even the conservative paper *La Prensa* felt that the government had gone too far.[58]

On 10 April a UF delegation met with the minister of public works and expressed a desire for unity but wanted it to be voluntary, stressing that if there had been problems, the government was responsible, for it had encouraged the growth of the FOEF. The UF rejected all the points on which the minister insisted. The next day the CGT hinted at some type of action if the government continued to press its proposals. The FOEF replied favorably to the government's initiative. The government authorities retreated rather than having to face rail stoppages or possibly a general strike. On 15 April a UF delegation visited Ortiz, and he urged that the unions settle their own problems. The UF asked La Fraternidad to mediate, but negotiations failed.[59]

The government continued to favor the FOEF. On 9 May 1939 Ortiz postponed the elections to the railroad pension board that had been scheduled for the following week. He claimed they would aggravate tensions and make unification more difficult, but he in fact wanted to save the FOEF from defeat. The move increased tensions because the UF and La Fraternidad began to agitate for elections.[60]

Union discipline crumbled even further. On 18 July stoppages and work to regulation began on both the Pacífico and the Compañía General—after the railroads announced a return to a 10 percent retention of wages. The protests were not initiated by any of the unions, though the FOEF endorsed them. An agreement was quickly reached with the

Compañía General, but unrest on the Pacífico intensified. On 22 July the government gave the Pacífico railroad twelve hours to return service to normal, allowing it to fire workers who did not cooperate. The FOEF called for a return to normal work procedures; the UF felt it did not have to because it had not backed the stoppages. The participation of UF locals seems to have ended (at least officially), but FOEF members continued to slow train service. The Pacífico fired fifty-eight railroaders. The FOEF retaliated with support of the strikers and even threatened to widen the movement. A fifteen-minute stoppage occurred on the Central Buenos Aires. On 25 July the government threatened to revoke the FOEF's personería jurídica. The next day the FOEF capitulated, and the following day service returned to normal.[61]

The FOEF had made its last stab for power. The government was angry that the union had disturbed the peace. "Respectable" sectors of public opinion began attacking it. For example, an editorial in *La Nación* noted the following:

> The two large and traditional unions in the industry have not participated in this decision [on stoppages] nor consented to the use of means foreign to the tranquil discussion of existing problems. . . . One organization . . . imparted these orders of hostility. . . . In this circumstance the minister of public works . . . [indicated] the need to withdraw its personería jurídica. This resolution was enough for the directing committee . . . to . . . immediately declare an end to the conflict. If the conflict had had real support among the workers and responded to profound and justifiable motives, it would not have been so easy to end.[62]

Agitation for ending wage-retentions and for pension board elections increased. A change in government attitude could first be seen when the executive branch named Domenech as the workers' representative to the Pan American Conference on Labor in late 1939—a sure sign of government favor. Workers had begun to drift back to the UF. With the FOEF an obvious failure, unity talks began in the first months of 1940.[63]

The FOEF could not cut its umbilical cord to the government. When the two unions could not agree on an interim executive committee, the FOEF insisted that the question be submitted to Ortiz. The government pressured the unions to come to an agreement.* On 28 February 1940 an agreement was reached: the FOEF dissolved and had its members enter

---

*Andrés Cabona claims the government forced the unification (author's interview with Cabona, 6 Aug. 1976).

the UF; executive committee posts would be divided according to each organization's size. A secret agreement apparently existed as well: Domenech would not run for reelection to the executive board and therefore would give up the UF presidency; he would remain the secretary general of the CGT.[64] The day after the agreement, Ortiz called pension board elections, modified certain work regulations that had long irritated workers, and initiated a study that could lead to the end of wage retentions.[65]

Despite the UF's statist attitudes and its nonthreatening behavior, Ortiz did not hesitate to move against it when he saw it as an impediment to his political objectives. However, since the costs for a weak government of not maintaining rail service were higher than any long-range benefits, Ortiz abandoned his plans to eliminate the UF and establish a union to his liking. Such a campaign against an established union was not duplicated during the Neo-Conservative era; no other union was important enough to warrant such attention. However, remarkably similar—and more skillful—maneuvers were carried out after 1943 by a much stronger government. The UF had achieved a relationship with the government that no other labor organization had. It became part of the political system, and governments dealt with it on a regular basis. In many ways it was a forerunner of what was to come.

THE UOT

The relationship between the UOT and the government is typical of most union-government ties. Interaction was sporadic and often negative. Prior to the major breakthrough—the 1937 contract in the wool industry—the government paid little attention to the union since textile workers seemed incapable either of causing major disruptions or of being of political value. The industry's growth as well as the union's changed the government's stance. For a time the national government and that of the province of Buenos Aires dealt with the UOT in order to limit disruption, but dealings ended during World War II.

During the first Neo-Conservative years the UOT turned regularly to the government, but the results were frequently disappointing. Even the enforcement of labor laws was not forthcoming. *La Vanguardia* reported that one firm, La Libanesa, almost totally ignored the rules: the plant remained open on Sundays; an apprentice worked four months without pay; not only did the company hire underaged children, but also legal minors worked more than the permissible hours. The paper charged that the owner knew ahead of time when provincial inspectors would visit, enabling him to send illegal workers home.[66] Even when the union received government cooperation, it had little impact. In 1935 the UOT prevailed upon the provincial department of labor to investigate violations in the suburban industrial belt. The department uncovered a long list of infringements. While large fines were levied, they were suspended until the next transgression was discovered.[67]

Whether the government would help settle strikes was crucial because many employers refused to negotiate with the textile unions. A strike in a textile plant essentially affected only those directly involved, and the government had little reason to consider such a strike important. The DNT attempted to settle many conflicts, but (as we have seen) it lacked the power to force solutions. For example, in July 1935 the Casa Gerino lowered salaries by 50 percent; the workers struck and asked the DNT to mediate. The agency accepted, but when the employer refused to negotiate, it withdrew.[68]

When employers permitted the DNT's participation, the union fared better. A good example is a series of conflicts with Muñoz Sauca y Saltzman. On 22 September 1930 the company lowered wages by as much as four pesos a day. More than one thousand workers walked out, 80 percent of whom were women or minors. A delegation immediately explained the strike to the DNT's Maglione, who agreed to intervene. The DNT proposed that a commission mediate; in the meantime conditions would remain as they had been before 22 September. Both the employer and the union accepted, and work resumed on 29 September. However, salaries were lowered, workers laid off, and new ones hired. Despite the DNT's attempts to enforce the status quo arrangement through constant inspections, the company behaved as it wished. On 28 October the workers struck and again immediately informed the DNT. Two days later, through the DNT's efforts, a new proposal was accepted. Nonetheless, the company continued to lower salaries and dismiss workers.[69]

In March 1932 workers in one section of the Muñoz Sauca y Saltzman plant walked out to protest cuts in salary. The employer then locked out the entire work force. Following its now traditional pattern, the union went immediately to the DNT. Once again a mixed commission was proposed, but while the UOT accepted, the company did not. Soon with the DNT's help the parties reached an agreement in which the firm promised to let all workers return at their old salaries and to obey all labor laws.[70]*

The state acted as the necessary intermediary, providing the union with access to owners, as well as pressuring them (at least to a limited extent) to deal reasonably with their workers. Unfortunately the government's most conspicuous function in any strike was the keeping of the peace, and almost inevitably this entailed the use of police against strikers. Most textile workers were unskilled and could easily be replaced by strikebreakers. Therefore, the strikers' presence outside factories became extremely important. They informed the wider public of the stoppage, attempted to block plant entrances, or practiced physical intimidation. Police response was predictable; the union complained regularly of harassment.

In strikes such as the one at Gratry in 1936 (in which the firm attempted to break the strike), violence was the workers' only hope. The only access to the plant was a single road, and after women and children blocked the trucks carrying strikebreakers, the men attacked them. The response was equally blunt. The factory was turned into a fortress; police hounded the strikers and arrested large numbers, including the leaders. Strikers were expelled from company housing. The repression became so bad that it was impossible to continue the strike, and the union called it off.[71] Since textile strikes affected only a small sector of the economy, and the violence was isolated in a single community, significant positive government intervention was unlikely.

The growth of the textile industry and the drive for sector-wide contracts produced a shift in the relationship with the government. The UOT became capable of causing significant disruption, but it tried to create order in a chaotic industry. Sector-wide agreements would lessen the number of conflicts. As long as the UOT acted "responsibly," the government was willing to deal with a union that had come under Communist control.

It is worth reemphasizing the vital role that the departments of labor played in obtaining sector-wide contracts. In Buenos Aires province Governor Fresco wanted to prevent strikes, but when he could not, he wanted them ended first in the province. The officials of the DNT were undoubtedly instructed not to be upstaged. For example, in 1939 Jorge Michellón went to speak to Fresco about the silk strike and conversation turned to the cotton sector. Fresco made it clear that he did not want

---

*The company continued to threaten to lower wages, however (*La Vanguardia*, 20 Dec. 1932; *El Obrero Textil*, Nov. 1933).

another strike and would have the head of the provincial labor department arrange an agreement. With the agency's help and without a stoppage, an accord was reached covering spinning. In the capital the industrialists resisted, but the DNT made a determined effort, calling in each one separately, and they bowed to the pressure. The UOT failed to achieve a contract in cotton-weaving because the sector was concentrated in the capital and it lacked the leverage of a provincial contract.[72]

The charged atmosphere created by World War II again altered the relationship. The Communists' shift in tactics begun in 1939 led to several long and violent strikes, destroying the image of an organization producing order. This coincided with Castillo's assumption of the powers of the presidency; he was much less tolerant of Communists than Justo or Ortiz. Furthermore, the split with the Socialists left the Communists more exposed to government anger. As long as repression did not go beyond certain levels, government measures against Communists were received by their opponents with quiet satisfaction. Unfortunately for the UOT it had become quite dependent on good relations with the government. From April to December 1939 the UOT brought 188 pleas for mediation, requests for inspections, and the like to the DNT, while 143 petitions were presented to the Buenos Aires provincial agency.

The government severed the relationship with the UOT. The exact date is unclear, but in January 1941 *La Hora* advocated removing the president of the DNT.[73] In March in its periodical the UOT charged that

> the launching of splinter groups and employer [controlled] organizations . . . has become frequent. The increasing intensity of police and governmental persecution takes as a pretext these employers' provocations and is thus creating a climate of opinion to accuse the union's directors of being "professional agitators" and "Communists." . . . By a suspicious coincidence the authorities of the DNT, in almost all conflicts, try to exclude the UOT from negotiations for a settlement, but they blame us for the strikes.[74]

On the same page an article called for Ortiz's return to the presidency.

At some point during 1941 the DNT refused to receive the UOT and the construction workers' union, which was also Communist-controlled. When the CGT tried to negotiate an end to this policy, the DNT replied that both unions were led by legally recognized Communists who were manipulating the union movement not for the benefit of the working class but to further their political ideology. The DNT did not deny the validity of workers' demands for improvements, but it considered that such demands should be prepared and presented by acceptable organizations with whom employers and the DNT would be willing to negotiate.[75] By April 1942 the DNT had eased its stand somewhat and dealt on a limited basis with the UOT, although it did not return to the more cooperative earlier interaction.* Police harassment had increased and the state of siege hindered union activities.[76]

The impact of the government's unwillingness to mediate is evident in a conflict between the UOT and the Manufactura Algodonera Argentina in 1941. Problems started when the management fired 17 workers, including the grievance committee and UOT factory leadership. A delegation went to the DNT seeking a solution but was received hostilely. The agency's president (now Emilio Pellet Lastra) blamed the union for the problems and called the delegation agitators and Communists. When a worker protested that they had not come to discuss politics, he was expelled from the meeting and later fired by the company. Not surprisingly, a violent strike broke out, with as many as 1,900 out of 2,000 workers participating. At least 119 workers were arrested. After three months of stalemate, an offer was made which would have allowed all workers to return except those originally fired, who would be compensated. The union rejected the offer.[77]†

The UOT called on the government for aid, including Castillo and the president of the Chamber of Deputies, but to no avail. The Socialists tried to help; one of their deputies requested an interpellation of the minister of interior on the strike. Political pressure had no impact; the minister's reply was a clear statement of the government's unwillingness to aid the UOT and an excellent example of the Castillo regime's view of unions. It clearly divided organizations into two categories, acceptable and unacceptable:

> The executive power shows consideration to and helps workers' associations that exhibit a clear line of conduct in such a respect [maintaining relations with employers and benefiting the workers], and favors the signing, between them and their employers, of collective contracts which contribute to the easing of working relations and to lessening the number of conflicts.

*The government's more tolerant attitude roughly coincides with the forging of alliances between the Communists and segments of the Socialists and Radicals.

†According to *La Vanguardia* (16 and 18 Mar. 1941) and *El Obrero Textil* (Apr. 1941), the offer was tailored by the minister of interior. CGT, *Memoria 1939–1942*, 48–49, claims it was the company's and was passed on by the DNT.

UNION RELATIONS WITH THE GOVERNMENT   149

But there now are workers' associations, whether by preconceived plan of social and political agitation, or because of the effects of relaxed internal discipline, in which are not found the spirit which makes possible their useful function in the working world.

An example of this latter class of association is the one which has sponsored and directed the strike that preoccupies Your Worthiness.[78]

The strike continued for another three weeks. After 120 days, the minister of interior mediated a solution. Two hundred of the 2,000 workers were to return immediately, while the others were to be taken back in 15 days or paid an indemnity.[79] The workers' willingness to make tremendous sacrifices enabled the union to avoid complete capitulation; however, faced with a determined employer and an unfriendly government, it could achieve little. The UOT had to struggle with government and employer hostility throughout the period 1941–43.

The UOT's relations with the government demonstrate the limits of the political system's interest in unions. When the organization did not have to be taken seriously, it was neglected. After the union and the industry had grown and the UOT began to reduce chaos in the industry, the regime supported these attempts. When the government perceived the UOT as a threat to stability, it withdrew its cooperation.

Past examinations of the Neo-Conservative governments have seen them as blindly anti-labor or (as in the works of Gaudio and Pilone) developing a consistent policy regarding labor. From our analysis of individual unions, it is clear that Neo-Conservative policies were inconsistent and developed on an ad hoc basis. While largely uninterested in unions, the government could not afford to ignore them.

Only the UF and to a lesser extent the UOEM were large enough to be integrated—and then only partly—into the political system. For the unions it was a frustrating system because the ground rules were unclear. Unions had to demand attention, whether through strikes or political agitation. The government intervened favorably in strikes only when it found the unions unthreatening, but the stoppages exacted a political cost, and the line between acceptable and unacceptable union behavior was narrow. The Socialist Party alone lacked the strength to push through labor legislation, and few unions possessed the skill or the middle-class respectability that the FEC had to rally wider support. However, as the unions became stronger, an evolution took place. Mediation became more important. Unions became more heavily dependent upon the state. The government took tentative steps toward molding the labor movement by backing the FOEF and refusing to deal with Communist unions. The government never fully carried through on these union-related objectives. Government aid in achieving contracts was diluted by a failure to enforce them. New labor laws had an impact only where strong unions helped enforce them. Efforts to change union orientation were too politically costly.

The unions' hopes for government aid remained largely an unfulfilled dream. With hindsight one can only be struck by the limited realization by all classes of the workers' potential power. Only when Perón recognized it were government labor policies applied consistently. But the very recognition of labor's potential marked a major shift in the relationship between the government and the unions.

Chapter 8

DECISION-MAKING AND INTERNAL POLITICS, 1930–1943

In part the constant turmoil that wracked the union movement reflected frustration with an inability to grow as quickly as might be expected. The Syndicalists became vulnerable to attack in the Neo-Conservative era because their continued use of tactics developed during the Radical years no longer produced results. After the Radicals' return to political participation, Socialist progress slowed. The shifts in Communist tactics in response to World War II undermined the successful unionizing drives.

Many works on Argentine unions—even recent ones—have accepted the ideological rhetoric used to justify intra-union quarrels that had other origins.[1] While ideology played a major role, an examination of individual unions makes clear that causes for turmoil were much more complex. Added to the frustration with the lack of progress and with the political system were personal rivalries, but the unions' systems of governance did not permit a peaceful transfer of power. These clashes provide the key to comprehending union functioning. In addition, they show not only the frustration with traditional union practices and the political system, but also how union leaders were capable of delivering support to Perón.

The decision-making process affected many facets of union existence. On paper all unions had open democratic structures, but there were no guarantees since the state had no legislation controlling the internal workings of unions. The few organizations that possessed personería jurídica had in theory to conform to certain norms, but the government usually had no interest in enforcing adherence.

While union constitutions called for democratic decision-making, reality did not conform to the rules. Bodies that were supposed to decide issues frequently did not. Dissent was stifled or at least the leadership attempted to stifle it. Power was concentrated. While there tended to be rapid turnover on executive boards, many board members—usually the key decision-makers—held office for extended periods. It is important to note that similar office-holding patterns existed in the United States and elsewhere.[2] In Argentina leaders might have to consult with others, but they frequently had their own way until they lost control of the union. One man frequently came to personify the union.*

Powerful leaders do not preclude effective, open decision-making, but dissent was not tolerated. Union statutes provided mechanisms for the suppression of opposition. Slander of the union or its leaders was grounds for expulsion. In the UF the central authorities could intervene in disobedient locals. Interventions were often blatantly political. The members' basic source of information, the union newspaper, was frequently used by the dominant group to attack challengers.

The motivation for suppressing opposition was not a lack of belief in democracy; almost all union leaders cherished it. Nor can the differences between theory and practice be blamed on an inadequate understanding in Argentina of the democratic process; union intolerance of dissent and leaders' ability to retain power have been noticed in many parts of the globe. Beyond a natural desire for power lies a fear of what would happen to a union if it were not unified.

Argentine unions existed in a hostile atmosphere, and they believed that employers and the government would prop up challengers to weaken or destroy them. The FOET charged that dissident groups were financed by the UT, and the UF claimed that the government was behind the formation of the FOEF.[3] The leadership felt that discipline was essential if unions were to survive. One of the few things that a union could offer employers and the government was freedom from labor unrest if certain concession were granted. Similar fears exist in societies that are more open politically than was Argentina in the 1930s. William M. Leiserson used analogous terms to explain the lack of democracy in unions in the United States:

> Anyone who follows the speeches and public statements of union leaders must be impressed by their emphasis on threats to the security of the organizations. While leaders may stimulate such fears for their own advantage, the fact is that membership by and large shares in this feeling of apprehension for the safety of their organization. . . . It is in this feeling of insecurity that the explanation of undemocratic trends in union government must be sought.[4]

---

*While dominant, a leader obviously depended on a coterie of allies, and his exact power was difficult to gauge.

Another factor operating against democracy in Argentine unions was the increasing bureaucratization. Despite a lingering mistrust of paid leadership, unions had grown too large to be run after work and on Sundays. Of the unions in our study only the UF could afford a complete bureaucracy, but paid officials became common. They could devote all their time to the organization, giving them a decided advantage in any power struggle. The principle that Robert Michels has called "the iron law of oligarchy" came into effect: "At the outset, leaders arise *spontaneously*; their functions are *accessory* and *gratuitous*. Soon, however, they become *professional* leaders, and in the second stage of development they are *stable* and *irremovable*."[5] In other words, those at the center of the organization became difficult to dislodge.*

Despite these impediments to democratic decision-making, counterbalancing factors existed. Union membership was totally voluntary. Unions had to depend on workers handing over their dues every month since no automatic (checkoff) system of collection existed. No legislation made anyone belong to a union, and the union shop was almost nonexistent.† Joining a labor organization was an active, conscious decision, and members could withdraw easily. V. L. Allen argued as follows in a discussion of checks on the authority of union leaders:

> So long as trade-union members have the right to "contract out" of membership if they are dissatisfied with the union they belong to, then a continuous impulse will operate to impel trade-union leaders to retain them. Obviously in a free organization of this nature workers would retain their membership only if they were satisfied with the work the organization was doing. Dissatisfaction would be reflected in a declining membership and in the interests of self-preservation union leadership would be compelled to stem the tide.[6]

Bureaucratization enhanced this form of control over the leaders since they could be paid only if revenues from dues remained high.

In industries in which unions were not well established, joining often meant making sacrifices. Employers frequently harassed union members. A member unhappy with a union might even be rewarded by the employer for leaving the organization. With some exceptions—such

---

*It does need to be emphasized that compared to the Perón era, the union bureaucracies were quite small.

†Construction workers did have something resembling a union shop; see Celia Durruty, *Clase obrera y peronismo* (Córdoba, 1969).

as the UOEM and the UF, which had extensive social programs—membership offered few immediate tangible benefits. Contracts would benefit all workers, members or not, and while unions handled grievances, their success rate varied greatly.

In many industries workers had a choice of unions. Both the UOEM and the UOT faced the threat of competitors throughout or during much of the 1930-43 period. Most other unions were challenged—if weakly—by Anarchist, Catholic, or splinter groups that did not normally present a danger to the dominant organization, but could. Even the UF and the FEC struggled against parallel unions. The existence of such unions meant that the leadership could not allow the rank-and-file to become too dissatisfied, for they might join the competitor organization.[7] Union leaders also had to confront resistance from opposition groups. Communists, Socialists, and Syndicalists—all to some extent played this role. Normally this type of dissent had little chance of success unless the rank-and-file could be mobilized around issues. The easiest way to block the opposition was to eliminate the reasons for which it had gained support.[8] Clearly little held workers to their unions and their leaders except commitment.

Still the unwillingness to allow challenges to the leadership was a serious problem. The society was being transformed; unions were becoming larger and their systems of governance more complex; there were shifts in ideological tendencies; there was chronic frustration with the lack of progress. Yet only rancorous struggles could alter leadership that would not or could not adjust to different times.

While ideology was undoubtedly an important factor, it did not mobilize the rank-and-file, who was more attached to its leaders than to any political group. Socialist and Communist union leaders did not convert their followers. For example, Socialist Party affiliates always held a significant percentage of key offices in the UF, but everyone agreed that the vast majority of railroaders were not Socialists.[9] The Socialists were supported because of union activities and not ideology. The average worker seems to have had little interest in ideological quarrels, becoming involved only when dissidents hit upon a key issue that had not been addressed adequately. Indeed while such issues might not have been of primary concern to militants, they motivated a sizable portion of the membership.[10]

Ideology has been used to explain strife because (among other reasons) it provided an acceptable justification for conflict in a movement in which solidarity was the stated norm. In addition, ideology could be used as a weapon. Political parties provided meeting rooms, publicity, and volunteers. The success of the party-based ideologies—Socialism and especially Communism—was partially due to such participation.[11] Below we shall take a closer look at the inner workings of unions.*

THE UF

Internal strife convulsed the UF during almost the entire Neo-Conservative era. The chief cause was the economic crisis of the railroads, but the union's position within the labor movement also contributed because any group wanting to dominate the labor movement needed to control the UF. In addition, as noted, the government took an active interest in the UF.

The centralization of union power exacerbated conflicts. The UF was national in scope, but power rested in the headquarters in Buenos Aires. The locals—of which there were at least 220—had little authority. A handbook carefully defined their duties. Even locals in the same community were not supposed to communicate with each other, except with special permission. When locals broke the rules, the union's national leadership could intervene (take over a local)—a procedure usually accompanied by wholesale expulsions and suspensions.[12] Dues went directly to Buenos Aires. Money had to be requested from headquarters for everything, including changing locks and paying increased lighting costs. In 1930 the central authorities turned down a request for a telephone from the giant Rosario local of the Central Argentino because if it had one, other locals would also want one.[13]

The responsibility for daily affairs lay with the executive board (Comisión Directiva—CD).† The CD's decisions could be reviewed only by annual congresses, which were supposed to pass judgment on the

---

*In this and the following chapter we depart from the order of discussion used in preceding chapters. We begin with the UF bcause it is pivotal to this analysis. The group who controlled the UF became the dominant force in the union movement, so that decisions made in the UF affected many other unions.

†The CD had seventeen members who served two-year terms, with half elected each year. Elections went by company, according to the number of union members, with the smaller lines grouped together. In 1940 a new system was established: on lines with more than one board member, representation was divided among the occupational categories (UF, *Memoria 1940*, 2–35; *El Obrero Ferroviario*, 16 Jan./1 Feb.1941).

actions of the past year and to set policy. However, real power lay with the CD. As discussed in Chapter 5, the CD disregarded even the extraordinary congress of 1932. In 1934, when the congress tried to investigate electoral fraud, the CD denied it the necessary information, claiming that the congress lacked the power for such an investigation.[14]

The UF was actually run by the Mesa Directiva, members of the CD elected to specific offices by the full board. As the CD averaged only eighteen meetings a year, the Mesa decided what issues should be presented to it. Moreover, the Mesa normally took a stand on an issue prior to presenting it, thereby influencing the outcome. Important decisions were often made and presented to the CD as *faits accomplis*. For example, in 1935 a CD member was accused of using undue influence to obtain a pension for a relative, and this became a central issue in the conflict between Syndicalists and Socialists. The Mesa first took a public position and then submitted it to the CD for approval.[15]

One reason for the Mesa's power was that its members were full-time employees of the UF, on leave from the railroads. However, this cannot fully explain the Mesa's power because as many as five other CD members worked full-time for the union in the early 1930s.[16] Another reason is that the Mesa was in a good position to take advantage of the UF's large staff. As early as 1928 the UF had forty-eight employees at its headquarters and nineteen more in the locals, though some of the latter worked only part-time. In 1945 eighty-seven employees worked in the headquarters. The bureaucracy played a key role in decision-making—especially Rafael Kogan, who was in charge of the staff and often presented issues to the CD. Kogan had held the same position in one of the UF's predecessors, and he remained on the job through the rise of Perón.[17]

As we have indicated, the top leaders accumulated power and were reluctant to surrender it. Tramonti, the UF president from 1922 to 1934, openly stated his belief that the leadership of the union ought to be for life and in well-known hands. Moreover, as the leadership gained power, it freely used suspensions, expulsions, and interventions. More pernicious was electoral fraud. The best known case was committed in 1930 by Luis Cerutti, a railroader who faked the vote of the COA in favor of labor unity. As Cerutti said, "The unity of the working class was made by me."[18]

Because losers in union elections often claimed fraud, the frequency with which it determined outcomes is unclear. It was an important issue in 1933 during a struggle between Socialists and Syndicalists over three seats on the CD. In one contest on the Oeste line Luis M. Rodríguez, a Radical and key Syndicalist on the CD, defeated a Socialist by 93 votes. Rodríguez carried his home local 1,474 to 95—which was more ballots than there were members. In the second, on the Pacífico line, Ceferino López, an incumbent and staunch Socialist, won because of fraud in his home local. The third involved a contest between two nonincumbents. The CD allowed the reelections of Rodríguez and López to stand, but in the third contest, it disqualified the highest vote-getter because of disorder and corruption in his local.[19]

In 1934 the secret ballot was introduced, and further reforms were enacted in 1940. Nonetheless, frequent charges of fraud continued. In 1943 in some locals the number of annulled ballots was greater than the total for any candidate.[20] Electoral fraud was pandemic in Argentina, and the UF could not escape it.

The structure of the political process helped the top leadership. An examination of longevity on the CD from the first board in 1923 until 1943 reveals a twofold pattern: over half of the members served just one term, while 11 percent served eight or more years. The latter were the most important leaders.[21] This pattern contributed greatly to union unrest: revolts against the dominance of a few men played a vital role in two major conflicts—one between Socialists and Syndicalists and the other over Socialist domination.

The struggle between Socialists and Syndicalists rent the UF between 1933 and 1940 and was only peripherally connected with ideas. Indeed there were scarcely any differences in beliefs on major issues. Both factions cooperated with the authorities and neither was willing to sacrifice the union to politics. According to a judicial official who investigated the UF in 1936, there were no political differences between the two factions. In 1933 the CD was split eight to eight (it was missing one member). The Syndicalist faction had two Radicals, four Socialists, and two with no affiliation. The Socialist group included six who belonged to no party and two Socialist Party members. The leaders of the Socialist faction, José Domenech and Luis González, had no party affiliation at this time.[22]*

If ideology was not the source, what caused the conflict? There was a great deal of personal antipathy, but it is unclear whether it helped generate the problem or resulted from it. A major factor was a generational division—not of age, but of time in power. Tramonti and his

---

*Domenech joined the Socialist Party in 1942 (José Domenech, IDTOHP, 72–73).

Syndicalist allies had controlled the UF since its founding, and the outs wanted in. In addition, rivalry between the Central Argentino and the Sud lines played a part. The two railroads had approximately the same number of workers and were the largest private companies. Domenech and González represented the former and Tramonti the latter. Those from the Central Argentino felt they had been excluded from a fair share of power since no one from this line had worked at headquarters until 1930.[23]*

The Syndicalist and Socialist factions depended on support from other lines, especially the two next most important, the Oeste and the Pacífico, where politics was unstable (as illustrated by the 1933 fraud). In contrast to the Central Argentino and the Sud, where locals at Rosario and Remedios de Escalada, which contained the shops, controlled politics, no dominant local existed on these lines. On the Pacífico the locals at Alianza and Junín struggled for supremacy, while on the Oeste the large Buenos Aires local was challenged by those at Liniers and Haedo.[24]

Tensions between the Syndicalists and Socialists had appeared as early as 1928 but came fully into the open only in 1933, prodded by the disagreements over contracts with the companies. On economic issues the factions had been in basic agreement until the 1932 extraordinary congress rejected a proposed contract with the Sud railroad due to grass-roots discontent. The Syndicalists decided to ignore the congress and accept the Sud contract, while the Socialists tried unsuccessfully to uphold the congress's decision.[25]† The Socialists fanned the railroaders' anger over their economic situation. The discontent, while not always coordinated, was evident not only when locals rejected the CD's positions, but also in more militant protests, such as antistatutory regional congresses and partial stoppages. Despite expulsions and interventions in locals, the authority of the dominant faction was undermined. Personal tensions on the CD rose.[26]

The Syndicalists, who had always opposed the intervention of political parties in union affairs, charged in the early 1930s that the Socialist Party was attempting to take over the UF. According to a November 1934 circular of the coordinating committee of Socialists active

---

*Domenech denied that the rivalry between the two railroads was a cause of friction, but the lineup of Tramonti and Antonio Melani (a key leader of the Syndicalist faction) versus Domenech and González is too obvious to ignore (José Domenech, IDTOHP, 104–6). When Tramonti lost control of the Sud, the political situation in the UF became more complex as no group was able to control it.

†The contract is discussed in detail in Chapter 5 above.

in the labor movement, party members had established caucuses, and the new CD had emerged from these organizations. The party even expelled two CD members who backed the Syndicalist faction.[27] To what extent the gains of the Domenech faction can be ascribed to such efforts is impossible to say, but they increased the hostilities.

In this atmosphere the UF's strict discipline fed the fire instead of dampening it. For example, a team investigating problems created by election irregularities on the Oeste line uncovered statements protesting the fraud by three men from the Liniers local in the minutes of the Villa Luro local. The comments were not particularly inflammatory and were largely—if not totally—accurate. The investigating committee recommended that the three men be expelled. The Socialists admitted that the men had broken the rules by addressing another local but claimed that they were good union members; two had helped found the Liniers local. Moreover, they pointed out that the shops at Villa Luro and Liniers were separated essentially by a sheet of metal and that members tended to go to either local since they in fact worked together. However, politics, not justice, was the prime consideration. The accused had supported the Socialist position, and the Syndicalists expelled them.[28]

In the 1934 elections the Socialists did well. This plus the retirement of Tramonti tipped the balance to the Domenech group. Tramonti was a popular and powerful figure whom no one had openly challenged for the leadership, and his departure left a vacuum. Presidents were elected by a majority vote of the CD, and candidates did not vote for themselves. That year balloting for president deadlocked for twenty-five rounds with Domenech receiving eight votes, Luis Rodríguez seven, and the candidates voting for two others. Finally a compromise was reached: Domenech became president, Rodríguez first vice president, and the Socialist faction took four of six seats on the Mesa.[29] The Socialists moved quickly to consolidate their power, installing a new committee (which they controlled) to oversee the union publication. The number of CD members employed full-time by the union was reduced to the Mesa and a representative of the State Railroads, giving the Socialists an added advantage. At the same time, the Socialists attempted to ease the increasing ill feelings. Domenech did not challenge an incumbent belonging to the Syndicalist group in the internal election for candidates for pension board elections, and meetings were held between leaders of the factions.[30]

The 1935 elections placed the Socialists in firmer control, and they showed no mercy. A Syndicalist CD member, Angel Basteri, had helped obtain a pension for an aunt by marriage because she was blind and unable to work. However, the aunt had worked as a concierge in a whorehouse and was therefore ineligible. Basteri claimed ignorance of her past, but the Socialists, wanting him off the CD, took an extremely moralistic stance against prostitution. The discussion turned ugly. Despite a committee of inquiry report that found Basteri essentially innocent of wrongdoing, the Socialists were determined to oust him. The Syndicalists then left a CD meeting and failed to attend the next session as well. A quorum could be obtained only after Basteri resigned—at the suggestion of his allies. The ploy failed because the key Syndicalist, Rodríguez, refused to serve as first vice president, Basteri charged Domenech with wrongdoing in 1930, and some members of the board sought (unsuccessfully) to expel Basteri from the union. The Socialists then moved against Basteri's home local, Alianza, the Syndicalist stronghold on the Pacífico line. On the grounds that procedures to elect the local's executive board had been wrong—though no charges of fraud had been made—the CD called for new elections. When the local refused, the Mesa intervened in the local without informing the Syndicalist CD member who represented the Pacífico.[31] There was no going back, and the split became definitive. What had inflamed the struggle was not ideology but the majority's vindictiveness, no matter which group controlled the union.

The UF's internal struggle spilled over into the CGT. When the CGT was created, the UF's representatives had voted as a bloc, believing that they should control the confederation. The practice broke down with the increasing friction. The CGT's governing board, the Comité Confederal, was composed of representatives of the COA and the USA, with additional delegates representing independent unions. The Syndicalist railroaders allied with the USA representatives to control the confederation.

The Syndicalists' decline had no impact on the CGT.* Several Syndicalist delegates to the Comité Confederal had ceased to represent the unions that had appointed them. Two had been selected by organizations that no longer existed and had subsequently acquired jobs with the government and become self-appointed representatives of the state employees' union. Another had switched unions. At the same time, the Comité Confederal refused to allow the UF to replace its own delegates. (Only those who resigned could be replaced.) The replacement issue first arose in 1933 but became more important in 1935 after the Domenech faction had secured a clear majority on the CD and was not permitted

*Due to a failure to hold a convention and adopt statutes, no mechanisms for replacing board members existed.

to replace delegates who were no longer members of the CD.[32] Wanting the new Socialist majority to be reflected in its delegation, the UF retaliated by withholding its dues—a serious step since it was by far the CGT's largest source of funds. The UF's reprisal might have stopped there because a constituent congress was scheduled for March 1936 which would have permitted the selection of new delegates. However, the Socialists seized the CGT first. The Syndicalists charged that the Socialists had done so because the congress would have enacted statutes (which the Socialists opposed) barring elected officials from the confederation's councils and political interference in the labor movement. The statutes were likely to have passed, but they do not appear to have been the reason for the seizure. The proverbial straw that broke the camel's back was a CGT plan to send delegates into the provinces; while never openly stated, their purpose was to campaign for Syndicalist candidates for positions in the UF. The Socialist majority in the UF was shaky, and elections were scheduled for the constituent congress as well as other posts. This unprecedented interference in the UF's internal affairs sparked action. Without informing its Syndicalist members, the Mesa met and invited representatives of sympathetic unions to help seize control of the CGT on 12 December 1935. A majority of the CD approved the action ex post facto.[33]

The seizure divided the UF, as discussed in Chapter 6. Tramonti became secretary general of the CGT of the Calle Catamarca, and many important Syndicalists in the UF joined him. Numerous locals rejected the takeover, but the exact number is impossible to determine because both sides issued wildly different claims. Delegations toured the interior to shore up support for both sides. The CD expelled rebellious members and intervened in some locals.[34] Attempting a countercoup, dissidents assaulted the UF's headquarters on 5 February 1936. A large crowd broke down the doors but was repelled by gunfire and water from fire hoses. The government appears to have countenanced the attack: according to the UF, despite repeated requests, the police did not protect the headquarters but threatened instead to arrest the defenders.[35]

Both sides took the unprecedented step of involving the judiciary. While the leadership used the courts against some of its members, the dissidents requested that the judiciary intervene in the UF on the grounds that an accidental majority had no right to expel CD members. The investigating authorities held that while on the whole the UF was run according to its statutes, the CD had overstepped its prerogatives in expelling board members and candidates for office; such decisions had to be left to congresses. The government intervened in the union and returned the expelled members to the CD but let the CD run the UF.³⁶

The extraordinary congress, which met in May 1936 to deal with the crisis produced by the seizure of the CGT, reveals how evenly the union remained divided. The CD ruled that two opposition-dominated locals which previously had had two representatives would have only one because five larger locals also had only one. The government overseer ruled in favor of the old system, but by two votes the congress accepted the CD's position. The overseer declared that the congress lacked legal standing; the congress, over the objections of the Syndicalists, voted to adjourn—again by a margin of two votes—to await an appeal of the ruling. Just when the split seemed definitive, a compromise was reached. The Syndicalists dropped their court case, and the UF paid all legal expenses. The congress reconvened and agreed with little rancor to accept the CGT's seizure, while condemning the methods used. A general amnesty was issued, but all members did not return.³⁷

The compromise just hid the antagonisms, and in 1938, as discussed in Chapter 7, the Syndicalists created the FOEF. They again hoped to use the issue of wage reductions, as they had when they had been challengers for power in the UF. However, the FOEF needed results, and the Syndicalists could not produce any. The compromise which led to the dissolution of the FOEF and the reentry of most of its members into the UF did not heal the wounds. While the UF's CD was supposed to be divided between the adherents of the two unions, the FOEF's supporters did not take their seats. The Syndicalists were finished as serious contenders for power, though they made a final effort after the 1943 coup.³⁸

The essential problems of the UF remained: wage retentions and the domination of the union by a small clique around the leader—currently Domenech. Even in a union with a tradition of centralized power, Domenech loomed large. A man without subtlety, he did not tolerate opposition and gathered power. Spanish-born, he began work in the railroad shops in Rosario at a young age. There he was a leader during the 1917–19 strike wave. He was first elected to the CD in 1926. He became more powerful than Tramonti had been as president of the UF since for a time he combined his union post with that of secretary general of the CGT. He also served for two periods as worker representative to the pension board. Even Luis González's assumption of the presidency— part of the arrangement that ended the schism between the UF and FOEF—did not diminish Domenech's influence greatly. González was tightly allied to Domenech, and the latter continued to control the CGT.

The Syndicalists had complained about the tight control by the UF leadership; later some of Domenech's allies admitted that the concentration of personal power had been a mistake.[39]

The second major conflict in the UF concerned a challenge from the Communists. Like previous power contenders, they used rank-and-file discontent with wage reductions. Member frustration with the dominant faction was also important. The Communists had been allied with the dominant group since 1935. However, in the wake of the Hitler-Stalin Pact, tensions rose. In October 1940, when the Central Argentino increased the percentage of salaries being retained, a few locals initiated a thirty-minute strike; they did so against the wishes of the CD but with the Communists' blessing. The Communists supported a growing discontent that resulted in several other stoppages. The CD accused the dissidents of practicing revolutionary gymnastics, which was in a sense true because the Communists were using the railroaders' unhappiness to gain support. The CD moved to restore discipline in the usual fashion—i.e., expelling dissidents and intervening in important locals such as Alianza, Liniers, and Mar del Plata. Nonetheless, even in the home local of González and Domenech the Communists created problems.[40]

Despite the hostility a major break had not yet occurred; the dissidents supported the official UF candidate in the 1941 pension board elections. By early 1942 the split had become much deeper. The Communists attacked the CD for accepting Castillo's method of ending wage retentions because railroad tariffs would increase, thereby intensifying inflationary pressures. During the internal elections slightly later in 1942, vitriol reached new heights, with the Communists accusing the dominant group of fraud.[41]

The bitterness reflected the stakes. By themselves the Communists could not have taken over the union. They had elected only two men to the CD, and the government would not have allowed the Communists to control the board. After the invasion of the Soviet Union, the Communists sought allies, and they allied with the Radicals. The majority of railroaders supported the Radical Party in the political arena, but only in the late 1930s did the party begin to organize effectively within the industry. The Radicals provided respectability and votes, while the Communists contributed experience and a dedicated corps of workers.

By late 1942 the Communists were supporting the head of the Radical railroad organization, Julio Duró Ameghino, against Domenech in the internal election to choose the UF's candidate for the pension board.[42] Duró Ameghino did not have an outstanding union record. According to the UF, he had joined in 1926 but was dropped from the rolls in 1927 for not paying his dues. He reentered in 1934 and a year later was again expelled for nonpayment. He rejoined in 1937.[43] However, he was backed for the pension board because of his political activities. Domenech won the internal election by 1,595 votes, but only because he carried the Central Argentino by a wide margin. Immediate charges of fraud arose.[44]

The struggle within the UF then merged with a revolt against the domination of the CGT by Domenech and the UF. Those opposing the CGT leadership also worked to loosen its grip on the UF. Communist-controlled unions in the CGT composed the heart of the opposition to Domenech, but they received support from the more politically inclined Socialists, such as the leadership of the FEC and the UOEM. These Socialists felt that the almost Syndicalist norms calling for the separation of unions from politics, which were supported by Domenech and his allies, were obsolete. They felt that the unions needed to strongly oppose the government and become more tightly tied to political parties. The alliance among Radicals, Communists, and some Socialists was part of a larger movement to form a united front.[45] Moreover, the unions headed by the more political Socialists had grown tired of the UF's insistence on having its own way and its failure to recognize that it was no longer the only large union. For example, according to Borlenghi, Domenech told a meeting of commercial employees that they ought to use the tactics of the UF:

> [Domenech claimed] that ... we ought to have followed the directives of the Unión Ferroviaria, that we should have been guided by the same tactics that the Unión Ferroviaria had followed, and in a few words that we should subordinate ourselves to the Unión Ferroviaria. We answered that we did not have disagreements with the Unión Ferroviaria, but neither did we think that we ought to be subject to it, ... that there was no reason why we should follow anyone.[46]

The personal ambitions of Pérez Leirós and Borlenghi cannot be ignored either because both wanted a share of power. General dislike of the concentration of power in Domenech's hands was also important.[47]

By the end of 1942 the entire labor movement was clearly divided into two camps, although the formal division did not take place until 1943. On one side stood the Radicals, the Communists, and the more politically active Socialists; on the other were those who supported

Domenech. Each side was intent on destroying the other, and the UF was the prime battleground since if Domenech lost his base in the railroad union, he was finished. Against all union norms, the UOEM provided space in its headquarters to the dissident railroaders.[48] The UF's leadership fought back. The CD intervened in locals and expelled members. The opposition increased its charges of fraud (probably with good reason). The CD purged the CGT's central committee of UF representatives who did not promise to vote correctly, thereby setting the stage for the formal division of the confederation.[49]

The creation of two separate CGTs removed any remaining restraints on behavior since both sides now had little to lose. The dissidents within the UF threatened its lifeblood by paying dues to a separate committee. The UF leadership moved beyond its normal iron-fisted tactics by supporting parallel unions that challenged established Communist organizations. It helped create a non-Communist metallurgical union, the Unión Obrera Metalúrgica, and backed the UOT(SP).[50]

The struggle also raged in the most open forum available—the elections for the pension board. Duró Ameghino and José Pipino, an incumbent member of the board, challenged the nominees of the two railroad unions.* The voting took place during the change in government in 1943. Despite a vigorous effort by the UF, the dissidents received 21,903 votes to the leadership's 20,698.[51] It appeared that a new day was dawning for the UF.

Dissidents had continued to mobilize unhappiness with the UF leadership's inability to improve conditions. The centralized structure of the union hindered their seizure of power, but it also made their challenges more serious by preventing peaceful transfers of power. Only a tradition of unity kept the UF in one piece. It should be clear that while ideology was important, it was not the cause of the conflicts.

THE FEC

Governance in the other unions in our study was very different from that in the UF. Smaller unions did not need a sophisticated system of locals and annual congresses, nor were they the center of interest of the government or political parties. In the FEC the basic unit of government was the general assembly, a meeting of all members. This was

*Pipino had represented La Fraternidad but had been denied renomination.

impractical for an organization as large as the FEC became, but it functioned because no quorum was needed and turnouts were extremely low. In November 1937 only 1,049 members voted, and the union had claimed a membership of over 18,000 in 1936.[52] As a result of low turnouts, general assemblies were relatively easy to control by groups that could assure the attendance of supporters and could supply speakers who followed a strategy. Meetings tended to be one-sided.

The CD of the FEC was the center of power. It was the only body that existed apart from the general assemblies, for which it controlled the agendas. General assemblies met infrequently—twice a year until 1935, once a year until 1939, and after that every two years. While extraordinary assemblies could be called, the long intervals between meetings left tremendous power with the CD. It maintained a firm grasp on all aspects of union life. Union delegates in individual firms only collected dues and passed along information. They were not allowed to deal with employers; that had to be done by the CD.[53]

The core of leaders remained stable. An examination of the elected officers—members of the CD, alternates, and auditors of accounts—shows that while numerous men held office for brief periods, others held the same post for many years or shifted among the different positions. The most important change came in 1931, when secretary general Miguel Navas was deposed, permitting Borlenghi to come to power. Borlenghi became the dominant figure around which everything revolved. He was aided by the FEC's success in improving the conditions of the retail clerks. There was so little dissent that in 1933 a list of candidates for the CD was elected unanimously. Socialists became so deeply entrenched that it seemed almost inconceivable to challenge their predominance.[54]*
The Socialists took no chances. They had a caucus that met prior to general assemblies. Its purpose was to avoid "the little pleasing spectacle of seeing Socialists in an assembly of the union sustaining opposite points of view."[55] Key leaders played a role in the caucus, as well as in the party's union organization, the Comisión Socialista de Información Gremial.[56]

Despite the FEC's relatively close identification with the Socialist Party, the party's problems were not reflected in the union; the schism that produced the Partido Socialista Obrero created little more than a ripple. Ludovico Fazio signed a manifesto attacking conditions inside the Socialist Party and identified himself as a member of the FEC's CD. He was suspended from the CD for tying his position to the FEC. If he

---

*In the early 1930s the Socialists did face some challenges.

had not been attacking the Socialist Party, it is unlikely that such a fate would have befallen him. In the next executive board election the established leadership swept to victory with only minimal opposition.[57]

Problems nonetheless existed between the Socialist Party and the FEC. As mentioned in Chapter 5, the party was suspicious of Borlenghi and never used his considerable political talents. Conflicting testimony exists on how much power Borlenghi allowed the party once he had consolidated his position. It is clear that he loosened ties to the Socialists. One source claims that he never attended caucus meetings and drew up his own lists of candidates.[58] Another claims that Borlenghi followed party directives.[59] In any case, he certainly had the power to do things his way. Tensions were usually carefully hidden, but in February 1943 Borlenghi's relations with a portion of the Socialist leadership were clearly strained. *La Vanguardia* carried a long letter from Borlenghi attacking it for printing an article on the bad conditions in the industry that his union served, while ignoring a recent CGEC congress.[60]

Problems between the union and the party were exacerbated by the union's cooperation with the Communists and its position on the CGT. The FEC's motives for allying with the Communists in 1942 and 1943 resembled those of other unions, but another reason may have existed. According to Ernesto Janín, a long-time labor leader active in the CGEC, a strong dissident alliance existed in the FEC composed of left-wing Socialists and Communists who had organized small stores in neighborhoods such as Once, Canning, and La Boca, which had been neglected by the leadership. The alliance planned to present a slate of candidates in the election for representatives to the convention of the CGEC. If it won, with the support of the interior it could control the confederation. Just prior to the election the Communists made a deal with Borlenghi and withdrew their support from the slate.[61]

The FEC had created the CGEC to bolster its agitation for labor law reform, and it continued to dominate the confederation. In 1939 five of the seven members of the CGEC's executive board belonged to the FEC. The FEC maintained control due in part to the prestige it had earned in its campaigns for labor law reform and in part to its size. The unions that composed the CGEC retained considerable autonomy. National negotiations were impractical because almost all employers were limited to one locality. Common interest lay in agitating for legislation. The CGEC wanted new member organizations; it did not want to repel them with stiff regulations. The CGEC's statutes gave it little power over its affiliates. No provisions existed for interventions, and while unions could be expelled, this was not very threatening. The CGEC provided little beyond coordination, speakers, and occasional subventions. The loose structure helped prevent the tensions that rent the UF.[62]

Success helped limit strife among the retail clerks. There was little against which to rally the rank-and-file. The small store employees had been neglected, but to have a significant impact they would have had to be organized in large numbers. Despite the FEC's successes, an unhappiness with the role of unions in the society existed, and the leaders were attempting to take the union in new directions.

THE UOEM

While the UOEM was organized in a manner similar to the FEC, the union lacked the FEC's triumphs to insulate it from internal problems. Tensions also arose because more than any other union, the UOEM was dominated by one person—the secretary general, Francisco Pérez Leirós.

The executive power resided in the Comisión Administrativa (CA), composed of the secretary general and fourteen others. The secretary general had unusual power because only he was elected by the entire union. The others were elected by the smaller units into which the union divided the municipal work force. These units also elected delegates to act as links between the rank-and-file and the CA. Unlike delegates in the FEC, UOEM delegates handled grievances; only if they failed did the CA intervene.[63]

According to UOEM member Pedro Otero, a person could dominate or be powerful in a union if he could bring 500 people (members or not) to meetings.[64] Otero's assessment was particularly true in the UOEM. The general assembly, which met frequently and was the ultimate authority, was often sparsely attended. Vote totals were as low as 149 in a union that averaged five or six thousand members. At times no one challenged Pérez Leirós in the elections for secretary general.[65]

Because of parallel unions and the UOEM's unwillingness to seek unity, non-Socialists had alternatives. Such alternatives, a politicized work force, the spoils system, and the union's dependence on the city council produced extremely close ties to the Socialist Party. The link was informal, but Pérez Leirós was probably the most important trade unionist within the party apparatus, and another member, José Marotta, was twice elected to the city council by the Socialists. Other members also had good party connections.⁶⁶ The close identification with the Socialist Party and the availability of parallel unions fostered unity within the UOEM.

There was little continuity on the CA, however. Only Pérez Leirós and Pedro Pérez Villar served continuously between 1931 and 1943; with several exceptions, the turnover was rapid. Key members—Juan Brennan, Juan B. Ugazio, and Domingo Mastrolorenzo—did not sit on the CA or sat for only brief periods and instead served the union elsewhere. The pattern of office-holding suggests that power lay not inside the CA but with Pérez Leirós.

Pérez Leirós brooked no challenges. He was the only official responsible to the entire union. Moreover, he had an extremely strong personality; he seemed to hold the union in his hand. Not only did he serve as secretary general from 1919 to 1944, but he was also elected to congress four times on Socialist slates. When he was not serving as a deputy, Pérez Leirós was a full-time employee of the union; none of the four other union employees was on the CA.⁶⁷ Indeed Pérez Leirós was the only union leader employed by the UOEM; this gave him an advantage, as did his party ties.

Pérez Leirós confronted two serious threats to his authority—one from Concentración Obrera and the other from among the Socialists themselves. In the early 1930s Concentración Obrera challenged the dominant Socialists. While it was an extremely small party, it had significant support within the union: at least two members had been elected to the CA. In 1932 one of them, Beniamino Semiza, secured a spot on the UOEM slate for the pension board election and was subsequently elected. In October 1934 the two parties openly battled to place their candidates on the UOEM slate for the pension board election. The Socialists won by 135 of the 1,777 votes cast.⁶⁸ Concentración Obrera supported the UOEM's candidates in the election, but a split developed nonetheless. In the general assembly of 16 February 1935 a motion was made that the vote for secretary general be secret (contrary to normal procedures), but this was turned down 408 to 260. Then Pérez Leirós almost unanimously defeated Semiza for the position. At the next meeting of the CA the two members of Concentración Obrera moved that future meetings not be held at the Socialist Party's Casa del Pueblo because individuals who did not belong to the union but to the party had participated in the general assembly. The motion was defeated, with only the sponsors voting in favor. In subsequent meetings the CA resolved to tighten control of assemblies, but Semiza resigned from the board.⁶⁹ The way was paved for the formation of the FOEM. Concentración Obrera's strength in the internal elections in 1932 and 1934 seems out of line with the extent of the party's popularity, but the voting undoubtedly reflected unhappiness with Pérez Leirós and his allies.

The challenge within the Socialist camp was still inchoate in 1943. Criticism had surfaced about several major issues. A few long-time militants expressed unhappiness with the UOEM's lack of success, particularly in not attempting to unify the unions representing municipal workers. Others were unhappy with the UOEM's role in challenging the Domenech faction within the CGT and then causing a split in the confederation. The CA reprimanded one of the union's representatives to the CGT's central committee—Ugazio—for his actions on it. Ugazio continued to criticize the union's position on the confederation. In the May 1943 general assembly he held that the UOEM should be neutral in the quarrel over the CGT. The members voted 139 to 24 with 3 abstentions to back the CA's position. Meanwhile, Otero led a personal crusade against Pérez Leirós, arguing that he was unfit to hold union office because he dealt in real estate. The accusation was not new and it was now undoubtedly aimed at getting rid of the leader.

The CA responded to these challenges with disciplinary proceedings against the dissidents.⁷⁰ When the 1943 coup occurred, the outcome of the challenges was still uncertain. While it is unlikely that the dissidents could have unseated Pérez Leirós, they provided crucial support for Perón's intervention of the union in 1944.

Why had the dissatisfaction with Pérez Leirós surfaced? He was undoubtedly authoritarian. According to two sources, he always fought the Comisión Socialista de Información Gremial and did what he wanted.⁷¹ In an interview in the early 1970s, Otero charged that Pérez Leirós often lost votes in the Socialist caucus, yet it felt compelled to defend him against other forces in the Neo-Conservative era. He also claimed that the secretary general foisted incompetents on the union and did not work to win a retirement board election when a personal opponent was nominated. The latter charge had already been made in 1943.⁷² Pérez Leirós believed his problems started during the Spanish Civil War, when Communist organs began to praise him constantly. Envy and fear that he would go over to the Communists arose.⁷³ In all probability the causes lay deeper. Pérez Leirós's tight control did not leave room for the personal ambitions or the visions of others. Even service on the CA did not mean a share of power. This intertwined with the union's lack of success and unwillingness to seek unity to produce a current of unhappiness.

THE UOT

Decision-making in the UOT differed from that in the FEC and UOEM. No political faction continuously controlled the UOT, nor was it dominated by a single figure. Control was harder to maintain than in the other unions in our study. While membership grew substantially, it was not attracted by stunning success. The new members came from different sectors of a diverse industry. Finally, unlike in the other unions, the major upheavals in the UOT had a direct connection to ideology, stemming from clashes between two distinct political traditions—Communist and Socialist.

Prior to 1935 the UOT was governed by the typical structure of a general assembly and a CD. This was found to be inadequate, and the union experimented with new forms in order to secure a voice for those who worked in the suburbs and in the various branches of the industry. The union set up locals which were subordinate to the CD but had their own councils. By 1942 there were twelve locals. In each plant members elected a committee that handled grievances, collected dues, and acted as a link between the central authorities and the membership. In addition, the union formed advisory boards for each branch of the industry.

The general assembly lost importance as the union grew. Voting for the CD moved from the assembly to a general vote of the membership. The UOT tried to eliminate general membership meetings and rely on annual congresses, but only one was held (in 1940) due to problems stemming from the intra-union clashes in the wake of the Hitler-Stalin Pact. However, meetings of delegates from factory committees were held periodically, as were sector assemblies; general assemblies still met as well.[74]

The CD remained the controlling body. Prior to 1938 CD membership changed constantly, but no evidence exists of internal conflict. The Socialist leaders appear to have rotated posts among themselves. Since union work was done exclusively on the leaders' own time, there was a desire to share an unenviable burden. Paid leadership was viewed suspiciously and in any case could not have been afforded. The first union employee was hired in late 1934 but earned only 60 pesos a month. The union's growth permitted an expansion of paid staff. By 1937 the secretary general received a salary, and the following year two CD members were on the payroll. A paid leadership brought some stability to the CD since the employees could devote all their energies to the union. The money spent on employees increased significantly; from April 1940 through March 1941 it was between 859 and 1,111 pesos each month. Despite the shift to paid leadership (which occurred almost simultaneously with Communist control) there was constant turnover on the CD, except for the top leaders.[75]

As discussed, the union split along party lines in 1929, with both Communist and Socialist segments creating distinct bases. The popular front era had allowed the Communists to join the UOT. However, a struggle for control was inevitable since the Communists wanted at least a share of the power. Conditions made the Communist push relatively easy. The Communists did not have to convince members that they could provide a better future for the organization, but only to attract new members from an expanding pool of workers. The Socialists did not receive help from their party; in any case they were suspicious of party aid and depended on their base in the stocking industry. The Communists relied on an effective outside network. The party placed reliable men in the industry and propelled them quickly to the top union posts—including such leaders as Michellón and Malvestitti. (Michellón was what the party needed in an industry in which many Communists were foreigners. Tall and dark, he not only was native-born, but he also looked like a creole—an Argentine whose family had been in the country for several generations. In addition, he was a good orator.) Party strategy called for members to organize the largest factory in a neighborhood—frequently a textile plant.[76] It also made the Communists more aware of women's role in the industry. They pushed harder for equal pay for equal work, supported changes in the law governing pregnant workers, and helped elect women to union office.

In 1937 the Communists elected only one person to the CD, and he received almost five hundred votes less than the front runner. However, he became pro-secretary. The next year, in alliance with the Partido Socialista Obrero, the Communists gained control of the eleven-member board. The five Communists elected included Michellón, Malvestitti, and Ida Pechini, the first woman to serve on the CD. The secretary general, Juan Armendares, was a member of the Partido Socialista Obrero, and, unlike the Communists, had a long history of service to the UOT. To quiet the Socialists' fears, a Socialist was made treasurer. The situation was more favorable to the Communists than it appears because Armendares preferred not to give up his well-paying job to become a union employee, while Michellón and another Communist worked full-time for the organization.⁷⁷* Armendares soon realized he had been outmaneuvered, and he resigned his post prior to the next election. Some of the Socialists stopped participating in union affairs. The next election placed the Communists solidly in control. The Socialists continued to control only the position of treasurer and some of the auditors of accounts.⁷⁸

Tensions grew, and events in Europe made the situation worse. By November 1939 the Socialists were openly attacking the union, and Armendares publicly complained of the methods used to elect representatives to the CGT.⁷⁹ The Communist and Socialist factions moved inexorably toward a schism. The Socialists protested what they claimed was Communist manipulation of the UOT's first and only congress and did not participate. (Ironically *La Vanguardia* praised the congress.) Two auditors of accounts—Basilio Dimópulos, a Socialist leader, and Armendares—refused to sign over the union's bank accounts to their successors, which led to their expulsion. In one of the largest plants, Piccaluga (Suárez), a movement began to stop paying dues. Both the Communists and Socialists appealed to the CGT to mediate, but it could not intervene effectively. Its leaders were anti-Communist, but its charter forced the recognition of elected officials and gave the confederation no power over members' internal affairs.⁸⁰

Any hope of a compromise ended when the UOT claimed that the CGT had not done enough to help the Ducilo strike, while the confederation charged that the union used the stoppage for political purposes. Shortly after the strike ended, the CGT terminated all relations with Michellón and for a short time with the UOT because of what it considered slanderous remarks. Despite frantic efforts by UOT leaders, on 24 May 1941 the dissidents founded a new union (the UOT[SP]).⁸¹ Each side retained the loyalty of those it had organized, leaving the Communist union much the larger.†

World War II played a major role in the schism. At first the UOT actively backed neutrality, heaping scorn on both sides. While its stance changed quickly after the invasion of the Soviet Union in June 1941, when it pledged solidarity with the Soviet people, the Socialists, who were strongly pro-Allied, felt that the Communists had betrayed antifascism. Moreover, the Socialists claimed they had been driven from power by unfair tactics. They believed that a political party had injected

*Party identifications were made by Michellón.
†Details are in Chapter 6.

itself into the union's internal affairs. One Socialist leader even denounced the union for hanging a poster in its headquarters announcing the forthcoming publication of *La Hora*. The Socialists had an almost Syndicalist belief in the need for an independent labor movement.[82]

The German invasion of the Soviet Union eliminated one cause of friction. Soon afterward the UOT called for unity to help defeat the Nazi-Fascists, but only in mid-1942, under pressure from the rank-and-file, was a serious effort made to heal the split. It was too late for reconciliation since the UOT and UOT(SP) lacked a way to divide power and the atmosphere had been further fouled by competition for members. Furthermore, the tradition of unity was weak, and the Socialists had reason to fear a similar competition for power if reconciliation was achieved. The conflict raging in the labor movement as a whole made unity even more difficult. The division of the CGT allowed the UOT(SP) to achieve more legitimacy when it joined the CGT I.[83]

Unity in the textile industry was artificial. Both factions had bases of support and could not completely dominate the other, nor were they capable of sharing power. No figure emerged to unify the workers and overcome the divergent traditions. Discipline could not be maintained because expulsion was not a threat. The leaders had their own bases, which the central authorities could not take away. As long as organizing continued and both groups retained legitimacy, the contest for control remained.

THE FOET

The FOET's Syndicalist leanings did not have a major impact on its structure or problems. Its constitution resembled that of the other small unions, and power did not follow statutory lines because strong personalities played a key role.

The FOET had a three-tiered government: a CA, a council of delegates and subdelegates, and a general assembly. In a union the size of the FOET, the general assembly remained a manageable component, and at times over half the membership attended. Theoretically basic decisions were made in the general assembly. As in other unions, they were usually made elsewhere and then presented to the assembly—sometimes too late for the assembly to stop a proposed action.[84]

The council of delegates and subdelegates comprised the elected representatives from the branches of the industry. This body had more control over the CA than the general assembly. While the council's principal duties were to meet once a month and act as a conduit between the CA and the membership, it chose the members of the CA. It nominated eight members to be reelected and seven new members each year. Its nominations were submitted to the general assembly, but there never seems to have been a problem in getting the recommendations ratified.[85]

The CA was the locus of power, but a group of men who were always on the council—except when political infighting pushed them off—had tremendous influence. Luis Gay, thin, bespectacled, and a self-taught intellectual with a charismatic air, was the FOET's dominant figure. Gay, unlike his counterparts in other unions, did not always hold the top post. He shared the secretary generalship with his close ally Modesto Orozco, and José Cabrera held it twice. Still Gay was almost always the FOET's spokesman. He represented the union in the CGT and the USA and was for a time secretary general of the latter. When Gay left the secretary generalship of the FOET in 1933, one publication proclaimed that "Gay was the soul of the Federation."[86] The sharing of leadership makes it difficult to fully assess Gay's influence, but it was very large.

Many of the men who sat on the CA served only one or two terms, while others served for long periods despite the internal upheavals and the manner of selection. Those in power had a decided advantage: they could use the union's machinery to protect their position. Discipline was extremely tight. Any cooperation with the UT—e.g., an appearance at a company dinner or membership in its mutual aid society—was sufficient for expulsion. Political opposition produced similar results.[87] However, UT pressure on the membership sharply circumscribed the leaders' ability to do as they wished. It was all too easy to leave the union and be rewarded by the company.

The FOET's political problems can be divided into two categories—ideological conflicts and the more serious struggles within the Syndicalist group. The FOET had a nucleus of Communists, and friction developed between them and the leadership just prior to the strike called in May 1932. When a shortage was discovered in the treasury in December 1931, the Communists attempted to exploit the issue, but the leadership did not permit it. The treasurers were not allowed to resign; when the investigating committee became embroiled in a controversy with the CA, the CA stripped the committee of its powers with the aid of the delegates and subdelegates. Those who protested too vigorously were denied the right to hold union posts. Nevertheless, immediately prior to and during the strike the Communists criticized the FOET's tactics.

The settlement of the 1932 strike gave the Communists an issue around which to rally support. The future of those who had been arrested had been left undecided, and the UT had no intention of rehiring them. The Communists charged that not enough was being done to help these men. The leadership accused the Communists of interjecting politics into the union by forming a caucus. In September 1932 the union ended the agitation by expelling seven Communist leaders. While the loss of the Communists had little impact, as late as 1934 they still maintained a separate union.[88]

A group that called itself the "opposition" proposed candidates for the CA to the general assembly in January 1933. The opposition had ties to the Socialist Party; the FOET's leadership accused the party of trying to take over the union, but the party denied it. The opposition's bid to be elected to the CA failed, and a short time later its members were expelled. The CA had used all its powers to block the opposition—including the union paper, which took a stridently antidissident stance. The opposition continued to exist after its expulsion, and the FOET charged that it received funds from the UT.[89]

The dissidents had not found issues that could lead the rank-and-file away from leaders who had just conducted a reasonably successful strike. Later conflicts were more serious because they split the core leadership. In some ways they resemble those that beset the UF between 1932 and 1940 but without the overlay of ideology.

A major conflict erupted in 1937 and 1938. On one side were members of the CA who had been fired after the 1930 coup, had not been rehired by the UT, and were employed by the FOET—Gay, Orozco, Adolfo Varela, and Florencio Farré. On the other were CA members who still worked for the UT. A suspicion of paid leaders lingered, and the leaders employed by the UT charged that the paid union officials abused their positions by, for example, making meetings last so long that those who had to get up the next morning had to leave before the sessions were over.

With the exception of a short period in 1933, when José Cabrera was secretary general, those who had been fired held that position. In 1937 the most important of the UT-employed leaders—Cabrera, Rafael Fabiano, and Raúl Barros—were not reelected to the CA, but the four union employees were. The following year Varela and Farré lost their seats; the UT-employed leaders returned to the board and occupied all the top positions. The balance had completely changed. In 1938 Gay was in Santa Fe when the delegates and subdelegates drew up recommendations for the CA.[90]

The election for the CA took place in January 1938, and in April the first signs of trouble surfaced. An assembly was informed that problems existed but they would not be discussed because the CA had unanimously decided to postpone presenting them until a solution had been reached. The next hint of trouble was in July, when *Federación* railed against a proposed contract with the UT which would permit a particular contractor to perform certain tasks and would reclassify some workers. The agreement, backed by the CA, had been rejected by the delegates and subdelegates. At the end of September a general assembly met to elect a new CA because many members of the old board had resigned. While the assembly was not informed why an election was necessary, it accepted the list drawn up by the delegates and subdelegates. Those who had not been rehired by the UT recaptured power. Only after the election did the membership learn the basis of the quarrel.

The *casus belli* was the contract signed with the UT. The use of contractors had long bedeviled the FOET because workers not directly employed by the UT received none of the benefits the union had gained. The group around Gay (the minority on the CA in early 1938) felt not only that the agreement was a sellout, but also that the UT-employed union leaders had betrayed the organizing effort in Santa Fe. The latter claimed that the contract settled a specific problem and felt that the Gay faction was being obstructionist in order to regain power. The union employees had retained control of *Federación* and thus had a forum in which to argue against the contract.

In April 1938, meetings were held by the delegates and subdelegates, as well as by a special body of active members which included delegates, former CA members, representatives from the interior, and other militants. The Gay faction won in both bodies, but the UT-employed leaders refused to concede the active members authority. The union practically ceased to function. Instead of its constitutionally required weekly meetings the CA met three times in May and once in each of the next four months.

The opportunity to elect a new CA came because of a tactical error: the resignation of the majority (the UT-employed leaders) faction. The minority then became the majority. A series of general assemblies and meetings of delegates and subdelegates followed in which the Gay faction won easily, and a significant group of militants—some of whom had been important since the union's founding—were expelled.[91] Thus while the issue in dispute was important, underlying it was a nonideological struggle between two factions for control.

The FOET's politics did not remain tranquil. In late 1940 and early 1941 the union was again torn by feuding. Charges of misuse of funds were leveled against the top leadership by less important leaders. Investigations by both the union and the USA found the accused innocent, but the accusers refused to accept the verdict, insisting, among other things, that a general assembly had been packed and they had not been allowed to speak. Again, one of the root causes was a desire to share power: the dissidents resented the control of Gay and Orozco. After being expelled, the dissidents created a parallel union with the help of the Socialist Party and a considerable portion of the FOET's treasury. They were joined by some who had been expelled earlier. The new union remained small, but it received the support of the La Plata union. As late as 1946, the new union was still trying to break the hold of the FOET on the loyalty of the telephone workers.[92]

Challenges by political factions did not gain rank-and-file support in the FOET because the leadership developed a reputation for the aggressive defense of workers' rights with the 1932 strike. Challenges from within the Syndicalist group presented a more serious problem because the dissidents held positions within the union, and shared credit for what the organization had done in the past. Moreover, the leadership was vulnerable because of its inability to make major gains. Lying behind the divisions were frustrations over a lack of progress and the unwillingness of leaders to share power. Both challenges were withstood because of the leadership's prestige and its skillful use of the union's powers.

As unions grew, the rank-and-file had less to say about daily affairs. Decision-making largely lay with a few leaders on the executive boards. While the phenomenon of decreasing democracy in expanding unions is international, it became a problem in Argentina because of rapid changes in the society to which unions had to adapt. Members demanded change, but dissent was not tolerated; attempts to replace leaders through constitutional means frequently met with heated opposition. The nature of unrest varied, although the concentration of power was remarkably similar. In three of the five unions studied, the power concentration was a principal cause of conflict. However, control from above did not automatically lead to internal struggle. Ideology, personalities, relations among the leaders, and the union's overall success—all played a role.

The constant upheavals were a sign of frustration. Many in the rank-and-file and in the leadership had begun to search for new ways to increase union influence. There was a growing dissatisfaction with the Socialist Party's policies, as can be seen in Borlenghi's attitude in 1943. The Domenech group was unhappy with the support that the staunchly Socialist UOEM gave to the dissidents in the UF. Even the Socialists within the UOEM were divided. The Communist Party had alienated many union leaders, making it difficult for it to widen its base. At the same time, those who supported the CGT II and Duró Ameghino in the UF attempted to align unions with political parties, moving them away from Syndicalist-like norms that had been dominant since early in the century. The Socialist militant Jacinto Oddone perceived a move to establish the CGT as an independent political power.[93] Change seemed inevitable, but in 1943 it was unclear where it would lead. It is quite possible that if there had not been a military coup in 1943, the politicization of the labor movement would have occurred under very different auspices.

We have shown that some of the apparently ideological quarrels were partly masks to hide other types of conflicts. We have also seen that power frequently failed to follow constitutional lines, that individual leaders were crucial to the decision-making process, and that many of the leaders were searching for new approaches for the union movement by 1943. It was some of these men who provided critical initial support for Perón.

Chapter 9

PERON'S IMPACT ON THE UNIONS, 1943–1945

The period between June 1943 and the workers' demonstration of 17 October 1945 was the most decisive in the history of Argentine labor. Unions began a new trajectory. They did not suddenly abandon ideals or goals, but the realm of the possible altered drastically. Juan Perón increased government involvement with unions. The dream of recreating the relationship with the government that had existed under the Radicals was fulfilled and surpassed. The state shifted the balance between labor and capital in favor of the former. Perón tapped a long-standing union desire for better relations with the government and a growing dissatisfaction with old norms and existing political parties.

Suddenly unions became important political actors. They changed: they had funds; their leaders became national figures; they received the constant (if not always benevolent) attention of the government. Yet it is important to note that both unions and the government built on established traditions. On the one hand, the changes in 1943–45 masked the continuities that existed between the Neo-Conservative and the Perón eras. On the other hand, they should not be underestimated.

Union reaction to the changing circumstances varied from a tight embrace of Perón to watchful waiting to revulsion. Underlying the reaction was a union's ideology, internal problems, personalities, pressure from the government, and experiences during the 1930s. It is difficult to hypothesize in the abstract about which unions would support or oppose Perón; too much depended on the decisions of a few individuals. Moreover, the response was not constant and varied over time. Nonetheless, by September 1945 Perón had forged a working alliance with the majority of established unions.* Without the legitimacy and organizational support they provided, Perón would have been consigned

---

*With one or two exceptions, new unions had a major impact only after 1945 (Louise M. Doyon, "Organized Labour and Perón [1943–1955]"; Ph.D. dissertation, University of Toronto, 1978, 254–56).

to oblivion in October 1945 and would not have been elected president the following year. Unorganized workers had less importance than has frequently been thought; it was the established unions which provided critical support.

In June 1943, when the military overthrew President Castillo, unions, like other sectors, were neither surprised nor saddened. While new measures such as rent reductions were well received, all union factions reacted hesitantly—but in accordance with the tradition of dealing with any government.[1] Both CGTs sent delegations to the new authorities. A CGT II delegation informed the minister of interior that "The working class has felt a true relief at the fall of the deposed rulers, and it will aid the present government's plans to comply with the National Constitution, to clean up the public administration and the judiciary."[2] The confederation also supported measures to control the cost of living and asked only that unions be permitted to carry out their normal functions. According to later accounts, the CGT II promised to organize a rally for the government if the regime permitted unions to operate freely, released political prisoners, and broke relations with the Axis. The CGT I frequently cooperated with the government. It proposed a representative to sit on the rent control board of Buenos Aires province, did not oppose a new law that imposed tight restrictions on unions, and supported the regime's drive against inflation. [3]

Initially the military's union policies did not seem much different from Castillo's. The jailing of Communist labor leaders and the harassment of their unions increased, seemingly just an intensification of past persecutions. Large meetings could not be held, but this was not unexpected in a coup's wake.

The atmosphere changed radically in mid-July 1943. The government dissolved the CGT II. (The CGT I once again became the CGT.) The restrictive new union law (among other measures) forbad participation in politics and mandated that union officials work in their industry. Labor organizations were required to register with the DNT. Repression and arrests increased. When President Ramírez went to Rosario, sixteen unions were raided and shut down. Union activity became more difficult.[4] These moves could be seen as anti-Communist, but it quickly became apparent that the military had a wider vision of its mission. On 23 August the DNT warned that strikes should be avoided and problems with employers settled at the agency. The same day the government placed the UF and La Fraternidad under state control, limiting the possibility of worker defiance. Moreover, it forced the UF to withdraw from the CGT, and thus the confederation lost its strongest member and its primary source of funds. The CGT debated whether it should continue. It did, and it moved from the UF's headquarters to that of the trolley-car workers' union.

The regime intervened in or shut down other unions, including those of the retail clerks of Rosario and the meatpackers. Persecution of militants intensified. While far from the only target, Communists remained the primary one, and their unions were forced underground. The labor movement's most dynamic sector had been shattered. The CGT stiffened its opposition, denouncing the new labor law and the limitations on free union activity, as well as calling for changes in foreign policy, but it was powerless.[5]

The situation again altered because the military was not united. A group of young army officers, of whom Perón was the most important, had been meeting secretly with union leaders, including Communists, in a quest to find out what the unions wanted. The officers' motivation seems to have been a fear of communism and social conflict and an awareness of many workers' poor living conditions, learned from contacts with conscripts who were drawn from all walks of life. The desire for contact was a two-way street. For example, a UF leader, Luis Monzalvo, attempting to help his union, met with the head of the police's special section (which was in charge of dealings with groups seen as a threat to society); Monzalvo knew the special section head from obtaining permission for rallies. The policeman introduced him to the chief of police and the latter to Perón.[6] From these early meetings Perón built his initial union connections.

In early October 1943 Perón helped settle a strike in the meat-packing industry. More important, on 23 October Perón had his friend and close collaborator, Colonel Domingo A. Mercante, appointed as the UF's new interventor. Mercante soon assumed control of La Fraternidad as well.[7] The first indications of a changed labor policy came from these unions.

On 27 October Perón had himself appointed president of the DNT. Given the agency's limited powers and labor's peripheral role, it appeared an odd choice for a man with towering ambitions, but it legitimized contacts with labor leaders and gave him a staff with an unsurpassed knowledge of union and working-class conditions. The key staffer was José Figuerola, a Spaniard who had worked on labor questions in his native country during the dictatorship of Miguel Primo de Rivera (1923–30). Primo de Rivera's labor policies bear a superficial resemblance to Perón's. According to Raymond Carr, Primo de Rivera's reputation "was based on the liquidation of the red spectre combined with sympathy for virtuous labor."[8] This similarity did not escape Argentine contemporaries. In November 1944 the CGT compared its support for Perón to that of Francisco Largo Caballero, the longtime leader of Spain's Socialist labor confederation and the Second Republic's wartime prime minister, for Primo de Rivera.[9]

In November 1943 the DNT was superseded by the Secretaría de Trabajo y Previsión. Unlike its predecessor, the Secretaría was national in scope; the provincial departments of labor became regional branches. In addition, the Secretaría controlled social welfare agencies and oversaw labor relations in the ports and on the railroads, where the DNT had had no say. The greatly expanded powers of the new agency made it a more fitting base from which to build labor support. However, Perón did not immediately begin a headlong pursuit. He was not yet totally committed to unions. He first tried to build a coalition that included employers. The restrictive law controlling unions was abrogated, much to the unions' delight. Mercante began to improve conditions for railroaders. Nevertheless, measures favoring labor came slowly; between 27 November 1943 and 30 June 1944 only twenty-seven labor contracts were signed in the capital.[10]

Despite the slow progress, the groundwork for the future was being laid. As they had during the Neo-Conservative era, most unions turned frequently to the government. In contrast to the earlier period, the Secretaría had more power and was more sympathetic than had been the DNT. The principal holdouts to working relations with the government resisted for ideological reasons—the Communists and a handful of others, including the UOEM. Unions that later opposed Perón, such as the UOT(SP) and La Fraternidad, developed good relations with the Secretaría.

Unions played a dual game, going to the Secretaría and opposing some government policies at the same time. The CGT called vigorously for union independence and an immediate end to government control of the rail unions. A number of leaders who met with Perón relayed his thinking back to the labor movement. The unions were willing to throw down the gauntlet. Unions that had belonged to the CGT II and still operated openly—e.g., the FEC, the UOEM, and the printers' union—suggested a march and rally for May Day 1944 in protest against the regime's domestic and foreign policies. The CGT and USA agreed to participate in what would have been a unique moment of unity, but the regime did not permit it.[11]

According to Luis Gay, the banned May Day demonstration marked a turning point. The government reacted to labor's almost unanimous repudiation by making a determined effort to attract labor leaders and by helping unions achieve long-sought goals.[12] Circumstantial evidence supports Gay's assertion. Pérez Leirós in 1946 claimed that Gay and Borlenghi desisted from active opposition in June or July 1944.[13] Union militants began to be placed on government commissions. A special committee composed of Gay, Borlenghi, and Alcides Montiel of the beer workers' union was created to help draw up legislation. During the third quarter of 1944, contracts signed in the capital increased dramatically to ninety-seven, while union meetings and attendance also went up.[14] Perón intensified his attempt to convince unions and workers of his sincerity, using his charismatic charm to good effect.

A rapid shift in union behavior occurred which was not entirely due to increased support for Perón. The CGT participated in Independence Day celebrations, issued a statement, and held a rally supporting the government's foreign policy. Numerous independent unions and the USA supported the rally after drawing up a slightly weaker statement. Why did the unions back a foreign policy of which they disapproved? Their disapproval was clear from other statements both before and after the rally. Using pressure, the government posed support for its foreign policy as an issue of patriotism; in addition, it threatened to take over the trolley-car workers' union, which had become the CGT's bulwark. A number of resignations from the CGT followed, including the secretary general. In the UF and some other unions a few Socialists began to move into open opposition. The support for the regime marked a sharp break with union norms and can only be compared to support for Justo in 1932 and Ortiz in 1940.[15]

Perón's use of the proverbial carrot and stick helped hold the opposition in check. Unions that cooperated did well. Elected union authorities again ran the two railroad unions. The number of contracts expanded rapidly. In the last three months of 1944, 131 were signed in the capital—a total of 255 since the formation of the Secretaría. In the interior 279 pacts were signed in 1944. In 1945 there were 184 agreements in Buenos Aires and 121 in the interior. Many only raised wages by a set percentage or called for the enforcement of labor laws and did not change basic relations between workers and employers. However, others fundamentally altered relations between workers and management by giving workers some control over conditions. Some established elaborate pay scales and defined jobs, while others required such alterations as the building of separate locker rooms for male and female employees or the provision of notebooks for those doing piecework so that workers could keep track of their production. As important, the Secretaría assumed the responsibility of enforcement; for the first time, not only unions defended contracts. Conditions were further revolutionized by the Secretaría's enforcement of labor laws. As Maglione realized in 1930, the codes could have a significant impact. (Perón claimed that the enforcement of the labor codes was his most important reform.) The Secretaría also helped key unions achieve long-sought goals. The railroaders received pay raises and the telephone workers the escalafón. By making it clear that it preferred to deal with unions and not unorganized workers, the Secretaría encouraged unionization.[16] Perón's tactics were only partly successful. While some unions became strong supporters, others attempted to stake out a middle ground, but increasing contact with the government made them more dependent. Moreover, they realized that joining the opposition would entail large costs.

Harsh repression was the regime's stick. In contrast to 1943, the repression became more selective, allowing cooperating organizations some latitude. They were permitted to organize. Pressure on the Communists did not ease, and their unions remained underground until mid-1945. Opponents of the government, no matter what their ideology, faced arrest and persecution. For example, the police raided the printers' union and arrested 150 members in an attempt to block the reelection of René Stordeur (a Communist) to the union's executive board. (Stordeur won, but shortly thereafter he left or was expelled from the Communist Party for dealing with the Secretaría on economic matters.) The regime also took over the UOEM in order to weaken the government's most vigorous Socialist opponent, Pérez Leirós.[17] No union could fully carry out normal activities, and any increase in police attention could prevent operations.

As part of its pressure on established unions, the Secretaría supported parallel unions but prior to 1945 did not create new ones. It helped existing unions such as the Unión Obrera Metalúrgica, founded in early 1943 by Socialists dissatisfied with a Communist-controlled union. With government aid, it grew to be the largest union in Argentina. The UOT(SP) cooperated with the Secretaría and with its help expanded rapidly. The threat of government-supported parallel unions was clear.[18]

In mid-1944 the Socialist Party ordered its members to take the course of maximum resistance to the regime's policies, but the call had little immediate impact. Until 1945 the chief opposition within the unions came from the Communists, who saw Argentina as part of the Axis-Allied struggle in Europe, with themselves as the resistance. They organized covert union groups and called general strikes. A stoppage scheduled for 31 October 1944 was intended to be revolutionary but was barely noticeable. They even rejected any improvements in workers' conditions that had been made with government help. Among other things, the Communists hinted at assassination:

> In these months the Argentine working class has been able to unmask various Judases, whose names they have sought to hand over to their respective unions and they should not be forgotten. . . . To aid this memory, we publish a list of names that is still not complete . . . [14 names]. REMEMBER THEM and . . . imitate the French Maquis and select yours, in order to dedicate to him a "special" remembrance when the time comes.[19]

This type of belligerence made wavering from support for Perón difficult. Nonetheless, a reluctance to go too far in endorsing the government lingered. When the CGT sponsored a rally on the first anniversary of the Secretaría's establishment, attendance was not massive, despite a major effort by the agency to attract workers. Doubt remains about how hard the CGT labored to bring them out. A short time later the CGEC attracted a tremendous crowd to salute a new pension fund for commercial employees. However, this occasion was different, a celebration of a hard-won victory. It did not differ markedly from the organization's traditional demonstrations. Perón addressed the crowd, but politicians had frequently spoken at CGEC rallies, including President Justo. Moreover, Perón had helped achieve a long-sought goal.[20]

The ability to use the Secretaría but not fully support the regime ended in mid-1945. With the lifting of many restrictions and the Allied victory in Europe, the opposition gathered strength and seemed determined to undo everything that had happened since 1943. Labor leaders returned from exile and jail. Communist-dominated unions reemerged and competed with organizations that had attempted to replace them. Anti-Peronist factions within loyal unions began to form in a way that flouted tradition because openly organized dissent had always been frowned upon.[21]

One of Perón's greatest advantages lay in who his enemies were. On 16 June 1945, 319 industrial and commercial organizations—the so-called *fuerzas vivas*, productive forces, which represented most businesses in the country—issued a manifesto which they had sent to President Farrell. It denounced vigorously the economic policies of the government, claiming that they had severely hurt business by restricting commercial liberties; it also accused the government of stirring up social tensions that had lain dormant since the Tragic Week of January 1919. Supporting advertisements by rural interests (among others) soon followed. The attack aimed at the heart of what had changed since 1943: the government had favored the unions over capital. Employer groups, cheered on by the opposition, wanted to return to the status quo of 1943. The unions saw the manifesto for what it was and replied with a barrage of statements and newspaper advertisements. Except for the Communist unions, which saw the regime as an embodiment of fascism which had to be defeated at all costs, the recoil from the manifesto was universal. Even the UOT(SP) and the DUSA—which would soon join the opposition—attacked it, and the former even defended the Secretaría.

On 12 July the unions organized a mass rally to defend the gains that had been made with the Secretaría's help. The speakers failed to mention the head of the agency, while defending it, but the crowd, not governed by old union norms, called for Perón to be president. Even if the speakers did not mention Perón, a political agenda existed. For example, the FOET adopted the slogan "For the active and direct participation of the workers in the solution of the country's social, economic, and political problems."

The supporters of the Secretaría had taken to the streets but then abandoned them to the students and the middle class until October. Why? In part it was a new game, and the unions were not sure how to play. Elections were scheduled, but no established party supported the workers' gains, and the unions were not yet ready to create their own. The tide had apparently turned against Perón, and many leaders wanted to be on the winning side. Furthermore, many agreed with some criticisms of the regime and began calling for the release of political prisoners and the full restoration of civil liberties.[22]

In early September four organizations with close ties to the Socialists—the UOT(SP), the CGEC, La Fraternidad, and the shoemakers' union—responded to the party's call for breaking relations with any group affiliated with Perón and withdrew from the CGT—a dramatic blow. All four had cooperated on some levels with the Secretaría and had held almost 30 percent of the seats on the CGT's central committee. The decision had been difficult since they had benefited from cooperation with the Secretaría. Despite important gains, the CGEC's provincial affiliates had revolted against Borlenghi's support for Perón, and withdrawal from the CGT was an attempt to restore unity. In the other three, overall tensions forced a resolution of conflicts between political convictions and the use of the Secretaría. For example, the shoemakers' union had protested the CGT's cooperation with the government. In late 1944 its two representatives resigned from the administrative commission in protest. Nonetheless, the shoemakers' union continued to meet with officials of the Secretaría and in 1945 signed a major contract with employers at the agency, though it later claimed that the signing was despite the indifference of the government. Success almost doubled the number of dues-payers between August 1944 and September 1945.[23] However, by the latter month, unions could no longer half-heartedly oppose the government; they had to define their positions.

Perón's support seemed to be crumbling, and he moved to shore it up. On 2 October 1945, after extensive consultation between Perón and the leadership, a comprehensive law governing unions was decreed. It included a number of features that the organizations wanted, such as the establishment of a system in which union dues were automatically deducted from wages and limitations on the existence of parallel unions. At the same time, it gave the government more control over unions. The state could dictate the form unions had to take, and only organizations recognized by the state would have the right to represent workers vis-à-vis employers or the state.[24]

Perón's sacking by military rivals on 9 October 1945 mobilized large segments of the labor movement and the working class. The response grew out of the sharply defined lines etched into the society in the previous months. The middle and upper classes considered Perón's changes threatening to their way of life and were determined to set the clock back to 1943. They set the tone for much of 1945, practicing politics in the streets. The workers sat by quietly until Perón's fall from power. Then they captured the streets and for the first time determined the country's future. Their response culminated in the giant workers' demonstration of 17 October. Since the events surrounding that uprising will always partially be concealed by myths and contradictory evidence, they will be presented here only in a schematic fashion.[25]

Perón's removal from his posts created a vacuum, but workers and unions rapidly saw what their fate would be. At the plant level gains were quickly reversed, and employers immediately began erasing recent improvements in conditions—for example, they refused to acknowledge the new Columbus Day holiday. The Secretaría's new head made it clear that the agency would no longer function as it had.[26] The civilian opposition demanded that power be given to the supreme court, but the unions saw that as giving power to the most reactionary forces.

Union leaders moved in two directions. Delegations spoke with government officials (and received assurances that social gains would be protected). Meanwhile, groups of leaders met secretly to plan resistance, gathering—for example—at night in the recreational facility of the beer workers' union in Quilmes. As early as 15 October rumors of a general strike appeared in the press. That same day worker demonstrations began in the southern industrial suburbs and the following day reached the capital. The CGT's administrative commission voted to call a general strike upon the approval of the central committee. On 16 October the central committee voted 16 to 11 to strike on 18 October. The main opposition to the strike came from the UF, which maintained its cautious, statist attitudes. Despite the crisis, the leaders clung to union norms and failed to mention Perón in the strike proclamation; rather they expressed opposition to giving power to the supreme court, supported the recent gains, and called for raises, minimum wages, profit-sharing, and the distribution of land to those who worked it.[27]

On the hot spring morning of 17 October tens of thousands of workers poured into Buenos Aires, especially from the industrial suburbs to the south. The crowd was in a determined but good mood. They seized streetcars to take them to the downtown area. They came any way they could to pack the plaza in front of the presidential palace and call for Perón's return. As can be seen from photographs, despite myths to the contrary, the crowd was exceedingly well dressed, the men wearing ties and jackets despite the heat. A few took off their jackets and some even their shirts; some waded in the fountain. Yet only in a city as proper as Buenos Aires could the upper and middle classes have expressed shock—which they did—at the workers' dress. For the first time the city seemed to belong to the workers, and *that* was what the upper and middle classes found upsetting.

As night fell, makeshift torches lit the sky. Heated negotiations went on between union and military leaders. Faced with the prospect of massive violence, the military relented and freed Perón.* The way was clear for Perón to be elected president.

Why after being quiet for so long did the workers take to the streets? Why on 17 October and not the next day, when the CGT strike

---

*While in the city the demonstration was remarkably peaceful, in the southern industrial suburbs there was considerable violence.

was planned? Popular mythology—adopted as well by some scholars—has long held that Evita, Eva Duarte (Perón's friend and future wife), played a major role by rallying the workers to Perón's defense. Marysa Navarro has shown that this is not true.[28] A spontaneous combustion of the masses can also be ruled out because similar demonstrations took place in widely different parts of the country. The call for the CGT general strike came too late to directly affect the demonstration on 17 October. While the decision to strike gave the protest legitimacy, elements both in and out of the CGT had been working to mount a strike and demonstration for a number of days. In any case, several key unions, especially that of the meatpackers, were not affiliated with the CGT. Over the past fifteen years unions had built a legacy of legitimacy, and their networks reached everywhere that workers lived. They had in the past organized large demonstrations, and this time effervescence flowed through working-class neighborhoods. The workers did not need much encouragement.[29]

With a successful strike on 18 October, the labor movement capped a triumph that surpassed its wildest dreams. It had escaped marginality and emerged victorious over the traditional political elites. Perón owed it his chance at the presidency. Within days, with a tremendous surge in self-confidence, union leaders founded the Partido Laborista. Talk of such a party had circulated before, but only now was anything done.[30]

The model for the Partido Laborista was the British Labour Party because it espoused social-democratic ideals and was controlled by unions. The Argentine unions had greeted the Labour Party's electoral triumph in July 1945 almost as if it were their own. The relationship of the British party to local experience is summarized in a CGT declaration:

> The [CGT] has evolved and will continue evolving in the most absolute independence from political organizations and governments, but it demands the right of participation in the political, economic, and social solutions of the country, of which is a living example the clamorous triumph of the British Labour Party.[31]

A fascination even existed with Labour Party theorists. During a presidential campaign trip, Montiel, not only a leader of the beer workers' union, but also a former secretary general of the CGT and a prime mover of the October 1945 mobilization, read Harold Laski.[32]

The Partido Laborista not only took its name from its British counterpart, but its creators also made unions an integral part of the party structure. They tried to create an independent organization, not just one dependent on Perón. While the party made a vital contribution to Perón's victory and did well in the congressional elections, those who wanted to create an independent force were no match for Perón. Directly after Perón became president, he decided that an independent party threatened his power, and he easily overcame any resistance to its dissolution.[33] Too many leaders had wanted to be close to power for too long and went along with Perón. Moreover, he had the working class with him. Perón needed unions to build a connection with the workers, but once president and with relations established, labor leaders became much less important. Below we shall analyze the specific ways in which Perón affected the unions between 1943 and 1945.

THE UF

The UF's strategic importance did not alter, and it remained a focus of government attention. However, the military regime used the state's powers more fully and was able to successfully alter the UF's course.

After the 1943 coup the UF tried working with the regime, as it had with all previous ones. It welcomed Ramírez's attacks on speculation. Delegations met several times with high government officials. The UF accepted the new restrictive union law and requested registration.[34]

Despite the UF's compliance, on 23 August 1943 the government intervened in the UF. The official justification was that the union's leadership lacked legitimacy and that because of internal problems stoppages had occurred and these were unacceptable. While the regime's thinking remains obscure, it is fairly evident that it did not care about the UF's legitimacy but undoubtedly found the unrest worrisome. In addition, the government may have feared that a strike in meatpacking would spread to other sectors; with the railroad unions under its control, this would have been difficult if not impossible. Moreover, the government intended to weaken the labor movement by dividing the UF into four craft-specific unions and at the same time hamstring the CGT by removing its strongest affiliate. Certainly the UF's internal problems played an important role. The faction led by Luis González and Domenech was losing control. According to its own analysis, it had lost the last pension board election because of apathy. Evidence exists that the dissidents urged the government to take action and greeted the intervention warmly.[35]

The interventor, Captain Raúl J. Puyol, steered the union in a surprising direction. While calling for unity and urging all railroaders to rejoin the union, Puyol fired key employees, including Rafael Kogan and Juan Bramuglia, the UF's long-time Socialist lawyer and Perón's future foreign minister. Puyol attempted to revive the Syndicalist faction, appointing Syndicalists such as Domingo Santiago Diz and Bernardo Zugasti (who had supported the FOEF and had not rejoined the UF after the merger) to union posts. Puyol intervened in all large locals and reconstituted the grievance committees with substantial participation from the Syndicalists. If the intervention had been intended to attracted worker support, as attempts to settle minor problems indicate, these actions and the plan to divide the union were a serious blunder.[36]

The UF's executive committee (CD) members returned to jobs on the railroads, but key railroaders met clandestinely to discuss the situation. Contacts were made with elements in the military. The initial probes were made by those who had to work closely with the state, leaders from the State Railroads, and the port of Buenos Aires. According to an account in *El Obrero Ferroviario*, the crucial contact was made by Plácido Polo, a Socialist Party member who had represented the State Railroads on the CD. Through a friend who was a major in the army, Polo was introduced to a Major Eracilo Ferrazzaro; with the latter's help he began making repeated visits to the seat of government. He was accompanied by three leaders of the local of the port of Buenos Aires—Juan N. Olivera, Juan A. Carugo, and Florencio Soto. On 18 October 1943 they met with Perón, Mercante, and other officers in what Polo claimed was a decisive meeting. On 20 October the former CD met with President Ramírez and presented a long reply to the charges against the UF. Less than a week later, Puyol was replaced by Mercante, who was in a sense a railroader. His father had been a member of La Fraternidad, and a cousin was a member of the UF and had played a major role in establishing contacts with the military.[37]

Mercante immediately accepted the resignations of Puyol's appointees and reinstated those who had previously held the positions. He also restored locals and grievance committees to their elected officials, though locals still could not hold meetings of their members. He appointed as advisors Polo, Soto, and Carugo, who had engineered the change in direction. They were later joined by Monzalvo, who had also been active in establishing contacts, was a Socialist, and had represented the UF in the CGT.[38] Mercante wanted the prestige and experience of those in power at the time of the 1943 coup. He had little real choice.

An alliance with the Syndicalists had stirred discontent, and one with the Communists was impossible.

Mercante created support by returning the union to its leaders and by solving long-term problems. Relatively quickly he convoked elections for the locals' executive committees. After some delay he called elections for the UF's CD. The voting appears to have been without major incident, but the candidates were vetted. All those who had fallen behind in their dues—a serious matter because the dissidents prior to the coup had withheld their dues—as well as those who were having problems with the police were stricken from the lists. Forty-eight nominated candidates were vetoed, including three former CD members and the most important Communists. The group that had just won the pension board election could not present its strongest candidates, but the Communists and their allies continued to campaign, claiming that they could win. When the CD regained power in September 1944, twelve of seventeen members of the previous CD had been reelected and three had not run. However, Polo, the only advisor to Mercante to seek reelection, finished a distant second in the first round of voting and obtained the necessary majority in the second only after favorable publicity in *El Obrero Ferroviario*.[39]

Almost immediately Mercante satisfied some of the union's oldest desires: The government recognized the UF's right to represent white-collar workers. Annual leaves were regularized and applied equally to all specialties. On 10 January 1944 Perón announced a plan to build a large hospital for railroaders in Buenos Aires. The hospital and the railroad unions' health-care service would be financed by a large contribution from the government and obligatory payments by workers and the companies. By the end of 1946 the hospital was under construction and clinics existed in ten cities. In return for financial support, the unions surrendered control of the health-care system to a government agency.[40]

The regime also moved to make improvements by intervening in the State Railroads and the General Railroad Board, which had been viewed as anti-worker. Numerous favorable adjustments were made in working conditions and salaries. Eduardo Rumbo, the General Railroad Board's interventor, so won the confidence of the UF's leadership that in mid-1945 it publicly lamented his removal from the post. (In 1946 he was elected to congress on the list of the Partido Laborista.) In March 1944 President Farrell had been presented with a sixteen-point petition, and during the next two years all the demands were at least partially fulfilled.[41]

Not surprisingly, under Mercante the UF closely followed the government's line. While he permitted the UF to rejoin the CGT, he forced it to withdraw for a time when the confederation manifested some independence. Not only were union representatives present when Perón was sworn in as vice president, but also the UF called a half-hour work stoppage while the ceremony took place. A homage was organized for Perón. *El Obrero Ferroviario* became sycophantic; its front page was dominated by the national colors, azure and white. Perón's picture frequently adorned its pages.[42] Such behavior broke traditional norms, but only Domenech of the precoup leaders never cooperated with the intervention; however, in December 1943 he called Perón "the first Argentine worker."[43] Some leaders—such as Camilo Almarza and Roberto Testa—broke away and joined the opposition because of what they considered unacceptable union behavior and their growing opposition to Perón. Both Almarza and Testa had represented the intervention in the CGT and were Socialists. However, neither had served on the CD. Almarza had been Domenech's protégé in the CGT, while Testa had been one of the most active Socialists among the leading railroaders and had held positions in the CGT.

There is no way to judge the popularity of the Mercante-led UF, but the huge crowd that presented the sixteen-point petition—claimed to be 30,000—was unprecedented.[44] More telling is the 1944 reelection of the majority of the 1943 CD. Despite the restrictions on candidates, the results were in effect an endorsement of the intervention since Mercante clearly backed those in power prior to the coup.

When the new CD took power in mid-September 1944, it had to decide about its relations with the government. No sharp course correction occurred, but the UF began to behave more traditionally. *El Obrero Ferroviario* lost its patriotic colors. The CD urged that railroaders held for political reasons be freed and that locals be permitted to hold meetings. At the same time, it called Mercante's intervention "a stage of clarification and of constructive work whose results it would be childish to deny."[45] The leadership accepted Mercante's suggestion to appoint two delegates to the Secretaría who would handle the union's affairs and whose expenses would be paid by the agency.[46] Accepting this suggestion might be ascribed to the traditional willingness to cooperate with any government, but the CD's decision in September 1944 to make Farrell, Perón, and Mercante honorary UF members clearly broke tradition. Even within the CD this stirred strong opposition because it breached the barrier between the government and the union. Opposition to the gesture did not necessarily mean disapproval of Perón. A key critic of the idea later won election to congress on a Partido Laborista slate. Perón's enemies also disliked the gesture; in a clandestine Communist paper a headline to a story about the honorary membership read, "The railroaders will place the traitors against the firing squad wall."[47]

The regime's wooing of the union did not end when the UF was returned to its officials. Shortly thereafter the government decreed that up to one thousand pesos per worker of retained wages (part of the 1934 Justo arbitration award) were to be returned by the end of 1944. Moreover, it granted wage increases that went beyond what the UF had demanded in 1942. It established a minimum wage of 140 pesos a month and mandated raises of up to 20 percent, with the lower paid receiving the higher increases. The opposition, especially the Communists, attacked the increases, claiming they were inflationary because the companies were permitted to raise tariffs.[48] The rejection of the idea of wage increases was a difficult position to defend, especially at a time of inflation. As important, it limited the leaders' ability to move away from Perón. Without Perón's support they would need allies, and no common ground existed between the leadership and the opposition.

The UF continued to win small victories, but the big ones became more difficult. The union pressed for major changes in the work rules, a complete revision of all agreements, and a contract for white-collar employees. The last was the immediate objective, but the companies were adamantly opposed, putting pressure on employees to resign from the UF and negotiating with another organization. Despite a half-hour stoppage on 7 June 1945, union agitation had no impact. In its usual fashion, the UF did not want to upset the government and feared that a protest once started could not be controlled. Only in mid-1946 did the UF achieve these major goals. Nonetheless, the mood of many labor leaders was summed up by Luis González at the end of 1944: "In the time span of approximately 15 months, including the period of the intervention, we can say that the organization has done ... what it could not do in 20 years."[49]

In 1944 visible opposition to Perón and the union leadership was limited to the Communists and their allies, who formed special cells and supported various strikes. During 1945 opposition became more vocal and widened to include elements from the Socialist and Radical parties. Almost all who were active primarily in the union continued to support Perón. The extent of opposition is unclear, but in September *La Vanguardia* claimed that one hundred locals had attacked the CD.[50] The CD's response was low key, frequently just verbal. The restraint seemed motivated by fears of splitting the union and a desire not to create new problems. However, the CD prolonged its term by postponing elections until 1946 and then having the entire board up for reelection. In addition, no union congress was held in 1945. The leadership's rationale was that the CD's term would have been truncated and that the congress could deal only with the short period between September and December 1944. While technically accurate, the true motivation was fear of electoral agitation and of the verdicts.[51]

Problems did exist within the CD because of the Mesa's failure to consult members of the larger board. The failure provoked deep anger; in early March 1945 Luis González resigned the presidency, but the gesture was rejected. Later that month the CD nominated González for a position in a new government institute controlling pensions, despite comments that no one should hold two important posts and that when it had happened in the past—a reference to Domenech—there had been trouble. González again submitted his resignation, and it was accepted 7 to 4, with several board members leaving just prior to the vote. Telmo Luna, the first vice president, assumed the higher office. Luna had been a union activist prior to the UF's formation and had served on the CD since 1935. Like his two predecessors, he came from Rosario, but he represented the State Railroads. Support for Perón was not an issue, but style was. Some CD members had felt that González had not consulted them, and after Luna's ascension, advocacy for Perón seemed more subtle.[52]

Under Luna the UF's behavior became even more traditional. The UF effusively praised U.S. President Roosevelt and warmly greeted the end of the war in Europe. Moreover, it attacked the "so-called 'nationalists'"—who were allied with Perón—for being the servants of those whom the Allies had just defeated in Europe and defended the vociferously anti-Peronist de facto opposition leader, U.S. Ambassador Spruille Braden. It also waged an active campaign to free political prisoners and lift the state of siege. Despite these positions, the union continued to favor the regime. *El Obrero Ferroviario* reprinted the CGT's call for calm when Berlin fell because the government feared that a demonstration would be used to launch an attack on it. The UF participated in the movement against the fuerzas vivas. At the end of August 1945 it held a homage for Perón, Mercante, and Farrell, as well as other authorities. A special album with thousands of railroaders' signatures was presented to Perón.[53]

The UF's dual approach appears to have been dictated by a desire to distance itself from a regime with which it differed on such issues as political prisoners and limitations on the press and which seemed about to fall, but which had aided it greatly. The CD was torn as well between a desire to support Perón and traditional union norms. This is clearly demonstrated when the CGT debated whether to call a general strike in October 1945. All the UF delegates voted against the strike—the unanimity a requisite of UF rules—arguing that while they supported Perón, a strike should not be undertaken, especially because the new government had promised to retain previous gains.[54] This stand combined the UF's view of the proper role for unions in politics with its statist beliefs. (The UF did join the 18 October strike.)

Even after the unions' victory in October 1945 the UF attempted to behave traditionally. Unlike much of the labor press, *El Obrero Ferroviario* strictly limited its electoral coverage, but at the same time the UF leadership helped establish the Partido Laborista. On the founding board, three of the fifteen members belonged to the UF, as did thirteen of the thirty-four labor leaders the party elected to the Chamber of Deputies. The rail unions played a vital role in setting up the party because they were national unions and railroaders could travel throughout the country.[55]

As it had in the Neo-Conservative era, the UF helped set the tone; its early support for Perón was key in bestowing legitimacy on him. It made going to the Secretaría respectable. Given the statist norms of the UF and the gains achieved for its membership, support for Perón should not be surprising. However, because it retained some of the old values—unlike many of the unions—the UF refrained from tightly embracing Perón in late 1945.

THE FEC

During the Neo-Conservative era the retail clerks had depended heavily upon the goodwill of the government. At the same time, the FEC—despite distancing itself somewhat from the Socialist Party—had maintained a reasonably good relationship with it. In the period after 1943 it became impossible to maintain good relations with both the regime and the Socialist Party, and the CGEC came close to being destroyed.

After the June 1943 coup the CGEC continued—within the limitations imposed by the government—its campaign for a pension plan. Delegations met with high officials, including President Ramírez and Perón soon after he took over the DNT. The union did not hide its disagreements with the regime. For example, at the meeting with Ramírez, Borlenghi stressed that the government was backed by the working class, but that the workers "fervently desire the greatest cordiality and collaboration with all the American countries."[56] In other words, the union wanted a change in foreign policy.

The FEC was moved by the logic that had propelled it during the 1930s. It lacked control over conditions in most stores and depended on the state for legislation and enforcement. Hostility to the government would end any hope for gains and might jeopardize past achievements. Even the loss of the expectation of new victories weakened the union, as is evident in the following comment from a retail clerks' periodical from Bahía Blanca:

> The suppression of the legislature, as a consequence of the revolutionary movement of 4 June, has spread a feeling of uncertainty and dismay among the rank-and-file of our union; closing the congress, it is said, virtually ended the possibility of obtaining new rights by the legislative route. And not a few members, hasty or lacking in consciousness, hurried their resignations because they could not see the prospect of obtaining legal benefits through our organization.[57]

The union was not confined to formal meetings with the government. According to Alfredo López, Perón established his first contact with Borlenghi through a series of personal connections. When speaking with a retired first lieutenant, Perón discovered that the lieutenant had gone to secondary school with a leader of the traveling salesmen's union, an organization belonging to the CGEC. A message was then passed that Perón wanted to speak to the leader on a matter of importance. The meeting took place, and the leader convinced Borlenghi that he ought to see Perón.[58]

Borlenghi began meeting regularly with Perón toward the end of 1943. Mercante claimed that Borlenghi's first contacts with the Secretaría were reserved; according to Pérez Leirós, Borlenghi played a dual game, acting as a conduit for information to other unionists.[59] The CGEC continued to stress its differences with the regime's union policies. However, Rodolfo Puiggrós, who in 1944 was one of the leaders of the Communist Party, has written that Borlenghi laid out his position in a meeting with Communist leaders in February 1944. The Communists argued for unity against the dictatorship—which meant giving up the quest for immediate gains because it distracted from the formation of a united front and the overthrow of the government. Borlenghi replied, "With this or any other government, I am not disposed to abandon the fight for immediate gains."[60] After May 1944 Borlenghi began to consult regularly with Perón on key legislation, although his complete support came much later. In December 1944 the Communist Party described Borlenghi as trying to stay neutral.[61]

The FEC's contacts with the Secretaría did not bring spectacular results, but a threat to the reformed commercial code was turned back. On 27 January 1944 five thousand retail clerks petitioned Perón for a minimum wage, raises, and a pension plan. Perón replied that while he favored a minimum wage, raises should be set by contracts signed with the aid of a union. He called for a commission to study the feasibility of a pension plan. Chances of success seemed very high because the CGEC was represented on the commission and Bramuglia, an expert on pensions, was co-chair. However, the commission did not meet until June; moreover, a Catholic employee's union was also represented, much to the CGEC's distress.[62]

The change in government powers and attitudes had a tremendous impact in the interior. For example, at the urging of the local retail clerks' union, the government of Mendoza had set a high minimum wage for the industry. When employer opposition prevented full implementation, a delegation came to the capital. With Borlenghi's help, they saw a functionary of the Secretaría and the original decree was restored. In the capital the FEC continued to push for better conditions in the stores, but it seemed to do so without significant intervention by the Secretaría.[63]

The CGEC's major goal remained the pension plan, and it continued to campaign. On 22 November 1944 a decree established such a plan. It is significant that despite earlier promises, enactment came after May 1944, when a more serious attempt to attract labor support began. To commemorate the establishment of the plan, on 4 December the CGEC held a rally in downtown Buenos Aires that was broadcast over state radio to three hundred celebrations around the nation. The crowd in the capital was estimated at 200,000. The union had every reason to be satisfied since it had attracted probably the largest crowd that Perón had yet seen. When Perón addressed it, he spoke well of the next target—minimum wages. Almost immediately the CGEC began to campaign for minimum wages, raises, profit-sharing, and equal pay for equal work.[64]

According to several sources, the establishment of the pension plan placed Borlenghi firmly in Perón's camp. At the victory rally Borlenghi gave the Secretaría a ringing endorsement. He was pushed in this direction by his critics, who not only attacked him for going over to the enemy (an accusation to be expected), but attacked the pension plan as well. Critics proclaimed that nothing should be accepted from the regime as well as that raises should have been obtained.[65] Among other reasons for Borlenghi's support of Perón was that he was getting from Perón the personal recognition that he had never received from the Socialists.

The achievement of a long-sought goal did not prevent internal unrest. In mid-1945 the easing repression allowed objections to be voiced. Given the middle-class aspirations of many CGEC members and the union's relations with a Socialist Party that was hardening its stance against Perón, discontent is not surprising. For those retail clerks who viewed with suspicion Borlenghi's ever closer relationship with Perón, the breaking point came when the CGEC openly backed Perón after he was attacked by the fuerzas vivas. Union norms had been breached. Starting in July, criticisms of the leadership began to appear regularly in *La Vanguardia*. Groups of retail clerks denounced Borlenghi in both the provinces and the capital. They were seconded by some of the CGEC's affiliated unions, including those in Rosario and Mendoza. In the capital in August a committee of "free" employees was formed; similar organizations already existed elsewhere. In September the committee became the Unión de Empleados de Comercio, headquartered in the Casa del Pueblo of the Socialist Party. José Arriba Hojas, who had been active in the FEC since at least 1929, resigned from the CD.[66]

In the interior dislike of the identification of Borlenghi and the CGEC with Perón was intense, as was the feeling that Borlenghi ignored constitutional procedures and ran the union as a dictatorship. During the CGEC convention in late August and early September, the vast majority of affiliated unions voted to reject the executive committee's report on the preceding period. The ruling officials were saved from a serious loss of face by a statutory provision that permitted each union to have as many votes as members. The FEC weighed in with 27,000—an inflated figure—enough to sway the outcome. Borlenghi won several other key votes in the same fashion. It appeared that the organization might divide. However, a compromise was reached and three important decisions were made by acclamation: recently renewed relations with the CGT would be suspended; participation in electoral politics would be forbidden unless a special congress approved it; and the CGEC would continue to approach the government for legislation. No one seemed to want to split the union. Moreover, the opposition won much of what it wanted. For example, prior to the congress the Bahía Blanca affiliate had opposed political participation, a return to the CGT, and the procedures of the CGEC's executive committee, but it had endorsed campaigns for improvements.[67]

Sketchy but convincing evidence exists that Borlenghi, seeing which way the wind was blowing, tried to trim his sails and advocated turning over power to the supreme court during the crisis of October 1945. On 15 October the CGEC stated that the country should return as quickly as possible to constitutional rule but that labor's gains should be respected. The FEC supported the 18 October general strike. Once the October crisis ended, Borlenghi and his allies backed Perón's candidacy; unlike others in the labor movement, they seemed interested only in victory and not in establishing an independent party. Borlenghi was proposed for the presidency of the Partido Laborista but was perceived as Perón's candidate and received little support.[68]

Despite the convention's vote against political participation, the CGEC's leadership openly backed Perón's presidential candidacy. In late November delegates from twenty-five member unions gathered in Rosario to protest. The opposition was strong enough to win elections in the interior. Borlenghi rode out the storm partially by disregarding the restrictions placed on him. Moreover, on 20 December 1945 the government issued a decree (33.302) which established for all workers many of the benefits that the CGEC had been fighting for, such as immediate raises and minimum wages. Fierce opposition by employers—including a refusal to acknowledge the decree and lockouts—not only helped Perón's presidential campaign by showing what would happen if he lost, but also allowed Borlenghi to hold his organization together. In early January 1946 the CGEC held a special congress to defend decree 33.302. Borlenghi's positions won easily. By acclamation the congress voted that decree 33.302 should be defended and that it was not demagogic. In addition, it supported the retail clerks who tried to get the decree enforced by taking over work places. The argument of the most vociferous dissidents that the decree should be repudiated and gains made through negotiations with employers did not get much support.[69]

The problems that shook the CGEC had a major impact on it. According to government statistics, the number of organized workers in commerce, offices, banking, and insurance declined drastically from July

1941 to December 1945—from 60,841 to 29,849.[70] Yet many dissident leaders returned to the fold after Perón's election. Of the four who presided over the dissident congress in Rosario in November 1945, two served on the CGEC's executive board between 1951 and 1953. *Ritmo*, the paper of the Bahía Blanca union, edited by one of the returnees, David Diskin, hinted that a desire for unity and better conditions overcame other objections. In 1946 Perón appointed Borlenghi minister of the interior; in consequence the CGEC acquired prestige, and Borlenghi used his power to help the union. With time and state aid, loyalists took over affiliates that continued their opposition.[71]

The retail clerks' unions depended upon the government, and Borlenghi and those around him were not willing to give up this relationship. Moreover, they had somewhat distanced themselves from the Socialist Party, and Perón offered much more. Borlenghi's personal ambitions also may have played a role: during the 1930s he never received political recognition, but this changed with Perón's rise. Other activists—especially in the interior, where they had had less contact with the national government—remained loyal to union norms and the Socialist Party. They were no match for Borlenghi and Perón.

THE UOEM

The UOEM had behaved similarly to the FEC throughout the Neo-Conservative era (though with considerably less success), but during the military dictatorship their paths diverged. Ascribing this divergence totally to the differing reactions of Pérez Leirós and Borlenghi to Perón would be an oversimplification. While both unions remained connected to the political process, the FEC had moved away from total identification with the Socialist Party. On the other hand, Pérez Leirós remained closely tied to the party and his personal decision largely determined the UOEM's reaction to Perón. He broke with the norm of dealing with any government and refused to talk with the Secretaría. His attitude stands in sharp contrast to most Socialist leaders and is parallel only to the Communists'. Pérez Leirós's decision placed the union in an awkward position: not only would the government do nothing for a hostile union, but also it was the employer.

After Castillo's overthrow, the UOEM took a wait-and-see attitude and tried to proceed normally. It participated in the CGT II delegations that visited regime officials. The dissolution of its confederation did not lead to strong public opposition—impossible in any case for a union that wanted to continue to function. The executive board (CA) voted to comply with the restrictive new union law, while the union paper reprinted an attack on it from *La Vanguardia*.[72] The UOEM continued to make appeals for such necessities as straw hats and winter uniforms. The city's response did not differ greatly from the period after the closing of the city council, and it finally granted sanitation workers the right to a vacation.[73] Larger questions still posed a problem. Despite a surplus in the municipal treasury, the campaign for 10 percent raises went nowhere. The goals laid out by the UOEM at the end of 1943 had a familiar ring since they were unchanged from past years.[74]

Not only had the UOEM not achieved its earlier goals, but it also failed to prevent a deterioration of conditions. The city altered annual vacations from 20 days for everyone to 10–30 days based on seniority, thus reducing vacations for many. The municipal retirement fund restricted its loans to housing. For the first time, hospital workers had to buy their uniforms. Workers did receive an increase in the amount paid for each child under 15, but the UOEM stated bluntly that it preferred a raise. The city planned medical facilities, a vacation resort, and a library for its workers and their families. The UOEM was unhappy because all workers had to participate in these programs and the fees were deducted directly from salaries, placing a burden on those earning the minimum wage.[75] Moreover, the city was encroaching on the programs that the UOEM used to retain members. Attempting to divert attention from its weakness, the UOEM advocated a series of grandiose projects. It proposed building facilities for ailing children and for retired municipal workers on its property in Córdoba. It planned a ten-story headquarters that would include a library, a meeting hall, legal and medical offices, and inexpensive apartments for members.[76] However, it lacked the money to carry out such schemes.

The UOEM's problems lay in Pérez Leirós's stance: he supported the Socialist Party's opposition to Perón and refused to negotiate with him. The regime responded first by not cooperating and then with intervention on 15 June 1944. For several reasons the government did not support one of the parallel unions. For one thing, the UOEM was by far the largest and had legitimacy. For another, in 1944 the regime had not taken such a step except where Communists controlled a union. Moreover, to shift union loyalties the government would have had to make a larger expenditure than it seemed willing to do. The intervention of the UF and La Fraternidad had worked so well that the government had every reason to try again. Most important, the intervention occurred soon after the attempted May Day rally and sent a clear message by punishing the most visible opposition union leader. Pérez Leirós is undoubtedly correct when he claims that he could have prevented the intervention, even the night before, by going to the Secretaría.[77]

The official reasons for the intervention can be summarized as follows: the union was controlled by a political party "whose doctrine unpiously attacks the underpinnings of citizenship"; the UOEM was run like a dictatorship; the municipal workers' lack of unity prevented the bettering of their condition; and Pérez Leirós had business ventures that were incompatible with his union post. Through the intervention the government pledged to achieve unity among the workers, go over the books, improve conditions, and revise the union constitution.[78]

For the intervention to have the aura of legitimacy, it needed support from established leaders. As discussed in Chapter 8, Pérez Leirós was facing a revolt when the June 1943 coup occurred. In the uneasy period after the coup the dominant group, afraid of splitting the organization, had suspended disciplinary actions against the dissidents, who were not appeased. Otero made his first contact with Perón toward the end of 1943. This was followed by a public appeal by dissidents for intervention.[79] The interventor appointed the leaders of the movement against Pérez Leirós as advisors. Almost all had held positions in the union. The most important were Ugazio and Otero.* Ugazio had joined the union between 1917 and 1919, represented it on the retirement board and the CGT, and served on the CA. Otero had been a delegate and represented the union at a CGT congress.[80] They were men with experience and could provide legitimacy to the intervention. All the dissidents had been Socialists. Their motivation for supporting Perón seems to a large extent to have been determined by their desire to rid the union of Pérez Leirós.

The intervention began ineptly. Its initial issue of *El Obrero Municipal* had a photograph of the first Argentine-built tank with an accompanying article extolling it. The paper improved, although it gave increased coverage to sports and social events. Since the government both controlled the union and was the employer, union propaganda was at times little more than announcements for the city.[81]

While making slow progress in some areas—e.g., a few minor alterations in work rules—the intervention made major strides in others.

*Advisors changed repeatedly, but Ugazio and Otero remained.

On 16 August 1944 the union opened a five-room clinic in its headquarters; workers could now receive medical attention at reduced prices. (The clinic was partially underwritten by 25,000 pesos the interventor had raised from the elite Jockey Club of Buenos Aires province.) When the clinic opened, Perón addressed the crowd, stressing the benefits of unity.[82]

Shortly after Perón's speech, it was announced that at the interventor's initiative unity among the four municipal unions had been achieved within the UOEM. From this point on only the UOEM was recognized by the municipality. The immediate impact is unclear. In the first half of 1943 the average number of dues-payers had stood at 6,009, declined in the six months after the coup to 4,869, and climbed to 5,291 in the first half of 1944. After unification there was an increase, but it had begun earlier; in the last half of 1944 the union averaged 6,708 monthly dues-payers. A special category of income from the FOEM is listed in *El Obrero Municipal*; for one month it approximately equaled the income that the FOEM had received before tailing off. No evidence could be located to indicate that the top Concentración Obrera leadership of the FOEM joined the UOEM, nor that the principal leaders of the Asociación Trabajadores de la Comuna switched allegiance.[83]*

The government also responded to other long-standing union desires. As of 1 January 1945 it raised the monthly minimum wage for blue-collar workers to 180 pesos and to 200 for white-collar employees; in addition, it eliminated certain pay categories, thereby pushing workers into higher levels. Salaries below 500 pesos were adjusted and promotion procedures altered. Municipal slaughterhouse workers joined the pension system and began to have vacations. Hospital maids were permitted to take the tests to become nurses, and in some cases substitutes were incorporated into the regular work force.[84]

In January 1945 the intervention established a system in which the municipality collected the union dues so that the UOEM had a more reliable flow of funds (though there remained large month-to-month variations). During the first four months of 1945 membership averaged 9,424 and climbed to 10,628 for the next four months before it dropped slightly in September through November. The growth cannot be totally ascribed to support for the intervention. When receipts plunged in

---

*Concentración Obrera opposed Perón. The two former FOEM members who became advisors to the intervention appear not to have belonged to Concentración Obrera.

August 1945, the Socialist Party urged its members to stay in the union, and the numbers went back up.[85]

The national confederation of municipal workers' unions had lain dormant since the coup and had never been a vibrant organization. In mid-1945 it was revived. Connections to the government intensified the impact of touring delegations and radio propaganda. A speaker could tell the founding meeting of a local union in Buenos Aires province that the interventor of their province, Juan Bramuglia, had once drafted a national pension plan for municipal workers—a major goal of the confederation. At the request of a recently formed union of municipal workers in Chaco, the UOEM dispatched two delegates to assist the new organization. Once there, the delegates arranged meetings with the appropriate local authorities, who essentially capitulated to the union demands, including one for rehiring fired workers. Such endeavors frequently met with success.[86]

The government's growing interest in the UOEM was a two-edged sword because while the regime brought about improvements, its control also increased. For example, the UOEM ceded its new medical service to the municipality, which funded it and provided service only to union members. The authorities helped improve the recreational facility (e.g., installing a swimming pool), but they barred use by other unions because of potential damage.[87] (Offering access to other unions had been a common gesture of solidarity.)

Opposition to the intervention existed, but its depth is impossible to estimate. The charged mood after June 1945 made those who supported Perón nervous. On 15 October *La Prensa* learned that the new head of the Secretaría was going to relieve the interventor; he did so the following day. When the CGT's central committee met on 16 October to debate a general strike, the four UOEM representatives failed to attend. The only reasonable explanation is that they did not want to take a stand given the unsettled situation in their union. Only a week later did the old interventor regain his post, and Ugazio still had to deny a rumor that the union was to be handed back to the old leadership.[88]

The strength of the opposition could to some extent be measured when the intervention tried to amend the UOEM's statutes to require secret general elections for CA members and the secretary general in order to make control by a small group more difficult. The intervention planned to have a general assembly adopt the new rules and then call an election. The opposition mobilized with the aid of *La Vanguardia*. When the general assembly was held on 19 December 1945, between

1,049 and 2,000 members attended. Both sides put up respected champions to preside over the assembly. Peréz Leirós's faction proposed Juan Brennan, who had joined the union in 1916, been elected to the CA several times, and had represented the UOEM on the retirement board as well as in all the confederations to which the union had belonged. He had retired and had not been visibly active in the years just prior to 1943. Perón's supporters put forward José Marotta, an advisor to the intervention who had been active in the labor movement since 1902, was a founding member of the UOEM, had represented Argentina in the International Labor Organization, and twice had been elected to the city council on the Socialist slate. Brennan won and the intervention's proposal was overwhelmingly defeated.[89]

The group that had dominated the union from its beginning could still control it, and a strong core could still be mobilized by the Socialist Party's opposition to Perón. The dilemma of being controlled by the government and representing government workers contributed to the strength of the opposition. In addition, Pérez Leirós continued to out-organize his opponents; his group brought the majority of the relatively small number of attendees to the general assembly.

Because of his commitment to the Socialist Party and his own perception of Perón, Pérez Leirós abandoned the UOEM's practice of dealing with any government. This permitted his opponents to use the Secretaría to depose the longtime leader. The forces that struggled for control of the UOEM in 1945 were as much divided by their views of Pérez Leirós as they were of Perón.

THE TEXTILE UNIONS

The survival of the textile workers' unions depended on a willingness to cooperate with the government. While the UOT confronted massive repression, the UOT(SP) at first benefited from government attention; then, because of its refusal to support Perón, it suffered a fate not much different from its rival's.

The Ramírez regime's anticommunism had an immediate impact on the UOT. The government arrested and jailed numerous important militants. Others—including the secretary general and the treasurer—went into hiding. Traditional activities became difficult, though the UOT continued to press for improvements in existing contracts. Employers used the repression to fire activists, but the organization resisted with some success.[90]

The UOT established contacts within the military. Two delegates accompanied a large group of union leaders to a meeting with Perón and Mercante at the Ministry of War. More important, soon after the coup an envoy approached the union. After clearing it with the Communist Party, Michellón and CD member Clemente Traverso went to the Ministry of War and met with Mercante and some associates. Six or seven meetings were held, with the union leaders trying to explain what the Communists wanted, as well as reporting back to the party. The party broke off the meetings, not giving credence to Michellón's belief that more could be gained from cooperating with the regime than from opposing it. Michellón was subsequently suspended from the party's central committee. While he retained his union post, the UOT seems to have fallen from the party's grace and never again received sizeable publicity in party organs.

The UOT declined. On 29 September 1943 the Communists called a general strike to support a stoppage in meatpacking and to protest the general repression. The central committee's clandestine periodical lists textile plants that participated, but the number is much smaller than during a similar strike in March, and—unlike on the previous occasion—no numbers of participants are given.[91] The union ceased publishing its paper after the October/November 1943 issue; except for two numbers in September 1944, publication began again only in September 1945. The UOT had gone underground.

The UOT showed few signs of life during 1944. In June it petitioned manufacturers for raises of 10–15 percent and requested discussions of existing contracts. It blamed the poor response—only a few establishments responded favorably—on pressure from the Secretaría. It claimed that the agency not only had refused to meet with the union, but also discouraged companies from doing so. A meeting scheduled for September in Luna Park (the Madison Square Garden of Buenos Aires) had to be cancelled because the union could not obtain permission. The union called for preparation for a general strike in the industry.[92] In essence it was preparing for the revolutionary general strike of 31 October 1944 which failed miserably.

The UOT(SP) faced vastly different problems. As a relatively small Socialist union, it had little to fear from the regime. Soon after the June 1943 coup, three top leaders—Candido Gregorio, Juan Pardo, and Lucio Bonilla—accompanied by Camilo Almarza of the CGT I met with the minister of interior to request that the government prevent the importation of foreigners to work in the stocking industry. This was followed by a visit to the DNT to request enforcement of the 1942 stockings contract. Informal contacts with the regime also began early.⁹³

The UOT(SP)'s relations with the DNT under the military regime did not differ from what they had been. For example, in September 1943 the union went to the DNT to obtain the enforcement of the stocking contract and the segment of the reformed commercial code covering paid vacations for workers in the firm of Julián Zacarias. Before the DNT's president, the company agreed to meet the union's demands, but then refused to comply. The union replied with partial strikes and another appeal to the DNT. The company retaliated by firing two workers and suspending three. The DNT summoned the firm, upon which the owner said he would do everything except hire back the two who had been fired. On 27 October the workers struck, and two days later, at the urging of the DNT's new president (Perón), the owner conceded all points. Perón—like DNT presidents before he took over—was not always so efficient.⁹⁴

The early efforts of the UOT(SP) were largely confined to the stocking industry, but after the creation of the Secretaría the union's scope became broader and it was spectacularly successful. One year after the Secretaría took over, textile workers had benefited from 34 contracts, arbitrations, and conciliations covering 39,193 workers—more than any other industry. Most were plant-level contracts—one covered only 17 workers—but in many ways these were revolutionary. Not only did they deal with raises and enforcement of labor laws, but some also addressed minor daily issues—for example, the recognition of seniority when ownership was transferred and when work places should be cleaned.⁹⁵ It was more difficult to say no to a union when it had the support of the Secretaría.

Industry-wide agreements were also signed. On 21 August 1944 the UOT(SP) presented a petition to the Secretaría calling for improvements in existing collective contracts. On 19 September, with the help of a Secretaría employee, Luis Cerutti (a former secretary general of the CGT), an agreement was reached updating the 1937 wool contracts with a 10 percent raise. Contracts in stockings and belts and elastics quickly followed and again were based on previous agreements. One striking sentence appeared in the belts and elastics pact: it stated that both parties agreed with the regime's social policies.⁹⁶

Major breakthroughs came with sector-wide contracts in industrial dyeing in January 1945 and knitting in September. After eight months of fruitless negotiations with cotton manufacturers, the union called its only massive strike of the period on 2 July 1945. The police estimated that on the first day 30 percent of the plants had to close because they lacked workers. After fifteen days the union sent the workers back to the factories pending final negotiations. The contracts were signed at the end of the month, setting wages and establishing mixed commissions.[97]

The strike came at the height of the crisis over the fuerzas vivas. The UOT(SP) had published a ringing endorsement of the Secretaría; however, according to later accounts, its refusal to take part in the 12 July demonstration led the government to close the union headquarters the next day. It was reopened after the union threatened an industry-wide twenty-four–hour strike. The UOT(SP) had rejected political support for the regime previously as well. Its two delegates had resigned from the CGT after the confederation decided to take part in the government-sponsored celebration of independence day. It had participated in the discussions on the Secretaría's first anniversary celebration, made no objections, but then did not endorse the festivities.[98]

The UOT(SP) had been walking a tightrope, attempting to maintain the traditional distance between politics and unions while benefiting from close contact with the regime. It signed a large number of contracts with government help. Candido Gregorio, its secretary general—who acquired a reputation for intransigence—met with government officials and even served on a state commission. Despite holding itself to some extent aloof from the government, its Communist rival charged that the UOT(SP) was an officialist union—a charge with some validity since the UOT(SP) had benefited from government help.[99]

As tensions rose, ambiguity became impossible. In September 1945 the UOT(SP) withdrew from the CGT, primarily on the pretext that unions had lost their independence. The union's leadership had retained its loyalty to the Socialist Party and responded to its increasing pressure to break relations.[100] The long ideological struggles had confirmed the leadership in its political beliefs. They retained them despite the union's sudden expansion. The UOT(SP) had grown from a small organization to one—according to several sources—with 25,000 members by the beginning of 1945. These estimates vastly overstate its size, but growth had come rapidly because of government aid and the repression of the UOT, its main rival. As Lucio Bonilla recognized, the growth was so quick that the members did not develop loyalty to the UOT(SP).[101]

In the second half of 1945 the UOT(SP) once again had to face rivals. As the repression receded, the UOT resurfaced. The Communists criticized the handling of the cotton strike, but after 17 October they both called for unity and pressed ahead on a wide range of issues. The UOT claimed credit for two new contracts in November in wool and silk. The wool agreement mentions no union, and the silk employers' association requested that its members raise wages. It is unlikely that the UOT had retained the power to force employers to make concessions. The UOT is rarely listed among participants at Communist functions; when listed, it is not given the publicity that strong unions received.[102] In part this may have reflected a desire not to anger the Socialists and a distrust of Michellón, but it also indicated the union's decline.

Newer unions and government wrath posed a greater challenge to the UOT(SP). As early as mid-1944 textile workers began forming new unions, but only after the UOT(SP) joined the opposition did the threat become serious. In late June 1945 its most important rival was founded, the Asociación Obrera Textil. It did not take its definitive form until October; however, the founders had been meeting with the Secretaría for some time.* The Asociación's strength lay in cotton spinning. It had an opportunity to grow when the UOT(SP) did not take part in the strike of 18 October. The Secretaría then refused to receive its delegations, and the UOT(SP) ceased to function effectively. Only in its stronghold in stockings did the UOT(SP) maintain its base. Despite government disfavor, it signed two major stocking contracts in December 1945. The Asociación did not expand quickly, but it soon joined the CGT and won recognition from the government.

Deprived of government support, the UOT(SP) quickly fell apart. At the end of December 1945 according to a government census, there were 8 textile unions with only 2,613 members. Even if the survey understates the strength of the unions, the decline came extremely rapidly.[103] The disintegration is not surprising. The UOT(SP) had grown rapidly because it had been successful, but outside of its core support, little loyalty had developed. The workers had joined because the union brought change, and it could only do so with government support.

In textiles no one union had created a dominant tradition and the government's role was crucial. The UOT had grown faster than its rival because it was more effective. When it was repressed, the UOT(SP) could attract support because it obtained better conditions. However, the

*The founders of the Asociación were young and had not held important positions in other unions—an exception to the general rule.

Socialist union's successes came during a brief period, before loyalty could be created. When the government removed its support, the UOT(SP) crumbled. While union ideals had penetrated the work force, no union developed mass loyalty. The government, with intelligent use of its powers, could shift support among the organizations.

THE FOET

The FOET's relationship with the military regime is archetypical of many unions. While dealing with the government—as it had before—it kept at a distance from the Secretaría until mid-1944. Then it moved to support Perón and achieved long-sought goals.

The FOET responded cautiously to the change in government. It had not applied for personería jurídica in 1942 on the grounds that the government ought to have no say in the internal workings of a union; under the terms of personería jurídica—which were rarely enforced—unions had to conform to certain standards. However, the FOET petitioned for recognition under the new decree regulating union activity, even though it had objections to the law. The FOET first needed to reform its statutes. Prevented by government restrictions on meetings from holding the general assembly required by its constitution to change its rules, the CA altered them without one. The FOET later greeted the repeal of the new law with joy.[104]

On 21 October 1943 an FOET delegation joined leaders of other USA unions in an interview with President Ramírez. Shortly afterwards Gay and Orozco met with the DNT's new president (Perón) and requested help in achieving an escalafón, as well as in the rehiring of the fired workers. Perón promised to help, and the organization was enthusiastic. It welcomed the creation of the Secretaría, but the relationship did not get off to a good start. One of the agency's first moves was to suggest that companies provide their lower-paid workers with traditional foods for the year-end holiday season—sparkling cider, fruitcake, and marzipan. The union—which considered the handouts demeaning—complained that the UT had bought low quality goods but suggested that the workers accept anyway. More important, the Secretaría did not take action on the FOET's petitions, and when the union requested an interview with Perón, it could speak only to Mercante.[105]

The relationship improved after the foiled May Day rally in 1944. Gay claims that he moved into permanent contact with Perón, consulting about union matters of all types.[106] Improvements in conditions seem to have been slow but important. In the interior the union began an organizing drive. The chance for success had altered drastically with the creation of the Secretaría's regional branches: no longer did union organizers have to face hostile local authorities. Unions were founded in provinces such as Córdoba, Tucumán, Mendoza, and Entre Ríos. The government helped. In Córdoba the UT, attempting to set up a yellow organization, held a meeting which had not received the necessary authorization. The participants were arrested and held overnight. Moreover, the Secretaría's regional branch recognized the organization affiliated with the FOET.

In late July 1944, in order to build national support for an escalafón (among other things), the FOET helped found a confederation, the Federación Obrera de Telecomunicaciones de la República Argentina. It was modeled on the CGEC, but its task was easier because the UT controlled so much of the telephone network. In August, when the FOET met with Mercante, it brought along confederation representatives from the interior.[107] The FOET could now claim to represent workers nationally.

On 3 October 1944 negotiations began with the UT under the Secretaría's supervision. Just three days later, Perón addressed a union meeting, expressing happiness that the telephone workers were united and stating that he considered Gay and Orozco true union representatives, although they no longer worked for the company. He added that the workers' desires would be considered first, then the state's, and last of all the company's. A contract was not agreed upon quickly. One reason may have been the FOET's reluctance to totally abandon its traditional view of union-state relations. It had endorsed only the weaker manifesto supporting the government's foreign policy in mid-1944 and played an inconspicuous role in the celebration of the Secretaría's first anniversary. As late as December 1944 the Communist Party noted Gay's attempts to stay neutral.[108]

It would have been difficult for the FOET to stray from its support for Perón for two major reasons: it faced a challenge from former dissidents for the loyalty of the telephone workers, and it recognized that it needed government help with the UT. The dissidents, who had been expelled from the FOET in the last years of the Neo-Conservative period, reactivated their parallel union during the military regime. They printed a newspaper, attempted to bargain with the UT, and tried to see Perón. They failed to see him, but they met with Mercante and requested that the government intervene in the FOET. The UT's traditional reluctance to make concessions meant that a contract could come only with government aid. However, unlike in earlier periods, the government was now much more likely to act in the workers' favor, as the union well knew.[109]

Several factors impelled the regime to help the FOET. Gay and Orozco had a great deal of prestige, as had the FOET itself; it was the USA union closest to the Secretaría.* In addition, telephone service was strategic and vital. Amidst the crisis created by the fuerzas vivas (in which the FOET abandoned any pretense of neutrality), a contract was signed on 7 and 8 July 1945. The pact established an escalafón, grounds for disciplinary actions, and salaries for the entire UT system. It also instituted a national grievance committee. These concessions could have been wrested from the UT only with government help. Moreover, the Secretaría made the FOET the sole representative of telephone workers to state agencies.

The FOET grew slowly, reaching an average of 2,314 members per month between March and August 1945—the highest since 1935. It claimed that large numbers of women and administrative personnel were joining.[110] Expansion in the interior was more vigorous. In Rosario a union affiliated with the FOET had collapsed in 1932 and could not be revived because of management opposition. The switch in government policy changed what was possible. In 1945 the union was reactivated; its first meeting was held in the Secretaría's regional headquarters and was addressed by Demetrio Figueiras, an employee of the Secretaría and longtime president of the UF's Rosario local on the Central Argentino. (He was elected senator in 1946.) By September 1945 the FOET had links with seventeen unions in the interior and three organizations representing other telephone-related companies in the capital.[111]

During the October 1945 crisis the FOET leadership strongly supported Perón. Gay participated in the secret union meetings called to plan a response to Perón's downfall. Support for Perón continued. Gay became president of the Partido Laborista, while Orozco was elected to the Chamber of Deputies on the party's list.

Support for Perón seems driven by three factors. First, the parallel union, which was willing to play either side, posed a major threat. It attacked the FOET for collaborating with the government and even

---

*The prestige of Gay and Orozco is evident in their positions with the Partido Laborista (see below).

rejected the 1945 contract, but it did so only after it had failed in its own attempt to cooperate with the regime.[112] In addition, it appeared that Perón was going to help create a society in which the workers would play a large role. Finally, the FOET had made major strides toward achieving long-sought goals. During the Neo-Conservative era it had been stymied by a combative employer and difficulties in striking a means of communication. It had looked to the government for help but had received little. Perón's shifting of the balance between capital and labor enabled the FOET to win an escalafón and organize the interior.

The environment changed when the government became interested in unions. However, Perón committed himself to the labor movement gradually, as his options became more limited, rather than all at once. Most unions did not make major gains until the second half of 1944. Of the unions in our study, only the UF had made substantial progress before May 1944. After mid-1944 changes came swiftly. Wages and working conditions improved significantly. As important as concrete measures, a change was evident in the workers' position in the society. The government obviously considered them significant. Perón used his charisma to convince them that they were important. Workers were appointed to positions within the Secretaría, and (as noted) Bramuglia even became interventor of the province of Buenos Aires. While intangible, these changes were vital.

Outside of the almost instantaneous rejection of Perón by the Communists and Pérez Leirós, union reactions were complex. Almost all labor leaders cooperated to some extent with the Secretaría—some wholeheartedly, others with reservations. Ideology and the leaders' relations with political parties and past governments heavily influenced their views of Perón, but except for Communist unions, there was no clearcut determining factor. The FEC and the UOEM behaved similarly during the Neo-Conservative era but responded differently to Perón. The reactions of individual union leaders were very important. Moreover, union relations with Perón varied over time. At two key periods—mid-1944 and June–October 1945—unions had to define their positions. In the first period, after May 1944 the government increased its attention to the labor movement, both demanding and giving more, but some unions managed to retain a traditional relationship with government. In the political caldron of the second period unions had to define which side they were on. Most sided with Perón, and the union movement began a rapid trajectory away from where it had been in 1943.

CONCLUSIONS

An examination of individual unions lays bare the diversity of responses to the Neo-Conservative era and the rise of Perón. Cooperation and struggle marked the path of unions as they groped to find ways of bettering the lives of their members.

During the Neo-Conservative era the unions had grown and become more powerful. Employers frequently had to negotiate with unions rather than deal directly with employees (bypassing unions) or simply ignore workers' demands. Unions gained considerable legitimacy among workers—a fact not always reflected in quantifiable indices such as the paying of dues. In industries where wages were so meager that workers had trouble feeding their children, dues, however low, represented a burden that many could not shoulder. Moreover, union membership could bring the unwanted attention of employers or the police. Nonetheless, workers increasingly knew about unions, turning to them when faced with problems.

The labor movement had changed by 1943. Anarchism and Syndicalism had declined dramatically. The crafts and archaic industries, the strongholds of Anarchist and Syndicalist unions, had declined. As important, connections to the political system and to nonunion organizations became vital. Socialist-dominated unions were strong in the services and transportation because of their ability to deal with the government and long-standing traditions. The Communists were most successful in low-paying industries due to their daring tactics and the party's willingness to provide organization.

Despite some gains, however, both the union rank-and-file and the leaders were frustrated with what unions could achieve under the Neo-Conservatives. The state's semi-authoritarian structure and its ad hoc relationship with unions provided few opportunities for steady growth. Many union leaders felt a growing unhappiness with their exclusion from "acceptable" society and the political system. By 1943 some leaders were preparing to politicize the unions by creating a union-led political movement. Many others proposed breaking norms by rejecting the Syndicalist-like stance of keeping unions out of open politics and aligning them more tightly to the political parties on the left. To engage in some counterfactual history, it is possible that if those committed to tying the unions more closely to political parties had in 1944 taken over the UF and the Communists had not been repressed, worker mobilization would have taken place under the influence of the Socialist and Communist parties. Worker integration into the political system would have been under the auspices of the left, much as it had been in Europe. Argentina would have avoided the populist model but would have faced a different set of problems after the coming of the cold war.

Union leaders had seen that the government played a crucial role in the labor movement's development. Lacking leverage over employers and usually not strong enough to use strikes to bring companies to their knees—especially because of police intervention on behalf of employers—unions turned regularly to the government for assistance. The response was inconsistent, and unions could not fully comprehend the rationale. Decisions were based primarily on the regime's analysis of its political situation. That the Neo-Conservatives should at times favor unions, despite their lack of interest in labor, should not be surprising. The presence of Anti-Personalist Radicals in the regimes meant that the lessons learned during the 1920s were not forgotten. It was frequently far simpler and less politically damaging to force employers to make concessions than to face violent strikes. Because many employers, such as the UT or the railroad companies, were foreign corporations and highly unpopular, they carried less weight than they might have in domestic politics. Moreover, the government was dominated by rural elites, whose direct economic interests were not damaged by concessions to urban workers.

The Neo-Conservative governments are far from the only semi-authoritarian regimes which, while unwilling to deal with unions in a consistent fashion, have dealt with them so that some could survive in a manner which seems to contradict the restrictive nature of the society. As in Argentina, favorable gestures toward labor seem motivated by practical political considerations. Such governments have realized that it would be difficult to eliminate unions and easier to make concessions to nonhostile factions within the labor movement than always to use repression. This perfectly sensible tactic frequently has been hidden by conspicuous repression and by commentators' identification with the repressed unions. To make my point it will be sufficient to give two brief examples, one from Europe and another from Latin America.

In Admiral Miklós Horthy's semi-authoritarian interwar Hungary during the ten-year prime ministership of Count István Bethlen, a three-part strategy toward labor was adopted: right-wing unions were seen as useful because they served as a constructive and loyal opposition; other unions were dealt with by the police; and certain key industries, such as the railroads, were considered off limits to unions. The government at times interceded in conflicts between capital and labor, much as the Neo-Conservatives did in Argentina. In 1930 it intervened in a major strike in the metallurgical industry and helped arrange a settlement. Under Bethlen's successor, who was much more antilabor, the political importance of unions was recognized in an unusual way. Unemployed union members did not have to go to the municipal soup kitchens created to cope with the depression, but received cash equivalents. The measure created such a stir among the right that it was ultimately withdrawn. While the government was capable of brutal force, it remained willing to coexist with and even aid unions when it was in its interest to do so.[1]

In Venezuela in the years after the death of long-time dictator Juan Vicente Gómez in 1935, the political system began to open up but remained semi-authoritarian. Like other sectors, the working class took the opportunity to organize. (Previously union organizing had been impossible.) Under the presidencies of Eleazar López Contreras and Isaías Medina Angarita certain types of unions were recognized by the government; there were 111 such unions by 1941. However, the government refused to tolerate unions perceived as threatening, including any connected to a political party and therefore possibly having an agenda that might undermine the regime. The government did not hesitate to use force when it felt it should, as during a major petroleum strike in 1936. Yet the government's performance during the strike had an Argentine air to it, as different government branches worked at cross purposes. According to Julio Godio, despite the president's attempting conciliation, the military used force. While never laying out a clear union strategy or attempting to encourage unionization, the immediate post-Gómez governments established their behavior toward unions on the basis of immediate political gain.[2]

In Argentina the style of the semi-authoritarian Neo-Conservative regimes set the stage for Perón. Government inconsistency was a major irritant. For example, the Neo-Conservatives offered increasing aid in establishing contracts, as Gaudio and Pilone have pointed out.[3] However, not only were the contracts less important than Gaudio and Pilone have argued, but also the government failed to see that they were enforced, thus frequently reducing such pacts to exercises in futility. Dissatisfaction with the government combined with frustration at slow union growth and with existing political parties led many union leaders to accept help from a man—i.e., Perón—with whom they disagreed on key issues, such as the war or free speech. As indicated, Borlenghi stated quite bluntly that he would not give up the hope of immediate gain for any reason.[4]

The rise of Perón is surprising *not* because he recognized the political potential of the working class and saw the unions as an excellent mechanism for organizing support, but because others had *failed* to do so. No political party had given a major role to workers. The Socialists refused to run a popular union leader like Borlenghi for office and in general did not use their excellent contacts with labor in the political arena. The Conservatives abandoned attempts at attracting worker support after the 1931 elections, when they ran two UF leaders for congress. The Radicals seemed content to be the majority party and paid little attention to organized labor. The Communists lost their one serious opportunity to join the political system and emerge from illegality when they passed up a chance to merge with the Partido Socialista Obrero.[5] In ignoring the workers and their unions, the parties failed to escape the morass of the Neo-Conservative era and build wider support. In part this blindness may have been due to deformities in the political system created by fraud. More likely it was because the parties did not recognize the value of the growing pool of eligible voters who were workers. These were not just migrants; immigration had practically ceased in 1930, so that any new male worker was likely to be a voter.

From the time he emerged as a public figure, Perón seems to have wanted to reach the presidency by election. While workers always loomed large in his calculations, he planned originally to build a broad coalition. When he failed to do so, he began to depend more heavily on the working class than he had intended. He used the unions as the vehicle to appeal to the workers. Workers were mobilized not only through improvements in wages and working conditions, but also because they now received a type of respect and consideration that they had never had before. They were being integrated into the larger society. However, with the exception of the Communist unions, few organizations responded immediately and consistently to Perón's efforts. They continued to seek aid from the government without offering support for the regime. The planned anti-government rally of May Day 1944 is ample proof. The subsequent intensification of government aid and pressure swung union support to the regime. Moreover, the heated political atmosphere in mid-1945 forced unions to take sides. Had unions not provided crucial support in October

1945 and during the subsequent elections, Perón would have been relegated to a minor place in Argentine history.

Perón's method of attracting working-class support is part of a Latin American tradition that has been labeled populist. He mobilized popular support, but at the same time worked to control the organizations that made mobilization possible. He won support by integrating workers into the larger society, giving them pride in themselves, and improving their living conditions, but he made no attempt to fundamentally alter the basis of the society. It was perhaps a more just society, but not one with a new economic basis.

The early period of Peronism differs from other political movements usually labeled populist in two ways. First, while there is little agreement on the attributes of populist movements, most commentators have called them multi-class coalitions. Peronism in urban areas in 1945 lacked wide support; the bourgeoisie and the true middle class rejected Perón in 1945. As a result of the lack of multi-class backing, unions were in a critical position: they were the only means of mobilizing popular support.[6] Second, the fact that Perón did not create the unions but won over a movement of considerable power meant that they played a much more crucial role than did their counterparts in such populist experiments as that of (say) Lázaro Cárdenas in Mexico. Cárdenas could balance union power with that of the peasants, but in Argentina unions remained the keystone of the Peronist movement even after Perón became president and demonstrated an ability to manipulate the union leadership. While he could weaken union power, he could only go so far without destroying his own regime.

THE UNION MOVEMENT AFTER 1944

A new union movement did not emerge in 1944 and 1945; labor retained many of its old leaders and values. However, unions were greatly transformed, in part because they ceased being invisible to the society and vaulted onto the center of the political stage; this altered the way they operated and began to change their nature as well. Change intensified as Perón consolidated his hold on the unions and stripped them of much of their independence.

There are thus substantial grounds for arguing that the period 1943–45 is a turning point in the history of organized labor in Argentina.

Unions at specific points take on certain characteristics that may be retained for long periods of time.[7] The initial investigators of Peronism—for example, Alexander and Germani—considered that the rise of Perón created a sharp disjuncture in the labor movement, in large part because the old union establishment had been overwhelmed by migrants from the interior.[8] A subsequent critique of this migration theory focused on whether there was a discernible difference in behavior between migrants and other workers, but it did not analyze change within the unions.[9] An alternative theory of union behavior, presented in the pioneering work of Murmis and Portantiero, was based on the now undeniable premise that it was the old unions that provided key support for Perón. The Murmis and Portantiero argument was fleshed out by such recent analysts as del Campo, Matsushita, and Tamarin. Gaudio and Pilone made an important contribution by pointing out an increasing level of government involvement in the conflicts between capital and labor in the pre-Perón period.[10]

As I have argued elsewhere, there was continuity between the Neo-Conservative period and the initial stages of Peronism.[11] As we have mentioned above, the same leaders controlled the unions, and they retained a desire to cooperate with the government. This should not be surprising: history rarely leads to complete breaks with the past; tradition and people linger. However, after more intensive study of the period 1943–46 it has become clear that I and others who argued for continuity overstated its extent. The loss of independence, the breaching of established norms, and the changed union role in society meant that the unions did after all become different.

There was continuity because much of the leadership during the early Peronist years had been active prior to 1943. Almost all of the Partido Laborista's first leaders had been union activists for years. Workers with some leadership experience ran even the parallel organizations since some standing was needed to achieve legitimacy. (The Asociación Obrera Textil was an important exception.)[12]

While the older textile unions ceased to be important organizations, the other unions in our study retained an important core of leaders. Of the seventeen members of the UF's CD elected for the 1946/47 term, eight had been serving on the board when the government intervened in the union in 1943, while at least four others had been active at other levels prior to 1943. Two additional members of the 1943 CD had been reelected in 1944 but resigned in early 1946 prior to the elections—Angel Ponce to run for congress on a Partido Laborista slate and Plácido Polo to accept a government job. In 1946/47 the Mesa was, with one exception, composed of CD veterans; the exception, Francisco Verde, had represented his local at the annual congress in 1941. As important, Rafael Kogan still served as the top employee.[13]

The situation in the FOET was similar. Eight of the fifteen members of the CA elected in April 1946 had served on the board just prior to the coup, while a ninth had sat on an earlier board. Veterans were predominant despite the inclusion of representatives of other telephone companies for the first time. Continuity in the CGEC was even greater: in late 1946 at least six of its eight representatives to the CGT had been active in the CGEC prior to 1943, and a seventh was Angel Borlenghi's brother. Due to a lack of elections, the UOEM's situation is not strictly analogous, but when the national confederation of municipal workers was reconstituted in 1946, the three titular officers had been active prior to 1943. The advisors that assisted the interventor had almost all served in union posts in the Neo-Conservative era.[14]

Given this continuity, a sharp ideological break did not occur. Modifications were made, but many ideas that have been considered Peronist go back to the Neo-Conservative era. Two have been discussed in some detail above: unions eliciting government support and creating social programs for the working class. During the 1930s and even before, unions had turned to the government for help. What changed the most after 1943 was the *government's* attitude, not that of the unions. In a startling shift the regime began to take the unions seriously and to carry out their agenda. The social programs—clinics, vacation resorts, and the like—had long been a cherished goal, and a handful of unions had begun to implement it in the Neo-Conservative era. After the military took over, unions could carry out their plans more quickly because they now had the funds.[15]

Yet the events of 1943–46 also altered the labor movement. One major change was the greater visibility of unions. Prior to 1943 unions were very independent, partly because the government, the political parties, and the media had ignored them much of the time. Government interest was sporadic, frequently unfriendly, and unpredictable, and the parties did not try to integrate them into the political system. As Perón rose to power, the government's attention became constant. Its dual policy of repression and attraction is best symbolized by the unions' integration into the legal system in early October 1945 with the enactment of the law governing unions. At last unions had a special status, but at the same time the government defined which organizations could represent workers and it delineated their scope. Only one union could exist in each industry and a system of dues checkoffs was established. The government was interjected into the life of unions, and many restraints on the leaders disappeared. No longer could unhappy members join parallel unions, and the flow of funds became more constant. With greater government interest came control of social programs, such as the railroaders' health-care system. In addition, workers lost their complete freedom to choose their leaders.

The labor movement became politicized. During the Neo-Conservative period the accepted norms had limited overt political participation. Unions demonstrated for Justo in 1932 and Ortiz in 1940, but participation in politics remained of minor importance—although the conflicts in 1942 and 1943 sprang partly from differing views on political involvement. With Perón's labor policies and the society's reactions to the military regime, the unions had to choose sides. This resulted in the demonstration of 17 October 1945, the general strike of the following day, and the formation of the Partido Laborista. Unions had become integrated into the political system and were to remain so.

Prior to 1943 the unions' style had been simple and puritanical, in part because funds did not exist for large staffs or fancy offices, though ideology also played a role. All the major ideological tendencies advocated self-help, education, and high moral standards. There was a lingering mistrust of union employees and of anything not austere. As mentioned, Borlenghi, though representing many workers who considered themselves middle class, was attacked for being well dressed and having a rug on his office floor.

Increased income from dues checkoffs and new members altered the realm of the possible. Between May 1943 and November 1945 the UOEM's income increased by 57 percent, while between June 1943 and May 1946 the FOET's revenues from dues went up 240 percent.* As union income soared over the next few years, the organizations' style began to reflect the relative affluence. In the short run increased income permitted the fulfillment of plans that had been held in abeyance by insufficient funds. Gradually attitudes began to change as well. For example, previously leaders had attempted to be as like their members as possible, but this norm began to be broken. In November 1944 the CD of the UF—a union that still had financial problems—established a special dining room for itself and other UF leaders—an action unthinkable just one year before.[16] Increased income and its predictability plus

*A portion of the FOET's rise in income came from an increase in dues.

gradually changing norms of behavior created a widening gap between officeholders and the rank-and-file. No longer did leaders have to worry that mildly alienated members would cease paying dues. The bureaucracy could increase and further tighten the leaders' hold.

During the 1930s the union movement had been strongest in greater Buenos Aires with only isolated pockets of activity elsewhere, but in 1944 and 1945 it became truly national. With government help, organizations such as the FOET and UOEM established branches throughout the interior. Strong unions were created in Mendoza, and the sugar workers in Tucumán established a formidable organization. An indication of the interior's new importance can be seen in the celebration of the Secretaría's first anniversary: two of the six speakers came from outside Buenos Aires.[17] Government support permitted the fulfillment of yet another union dream: the unionization of the entire nation. An inevitable consequence was the rise of leaders with little experience.

As indicated above, the key factor in continuity was the leadership. New leaders, however, had not been steeped in the old norms. Therefore, they were less likely to value independence from the government. Even if they did, they were less likely to be able to withstand government pressure since their ties to the workers were recent.*

The assumption of political posts by experienced union leaders and their frequent appointment to government jobs undermined continuity in two ways. In some cases these leaders left their union posts, depriving the organization of skilled, experienced people with close ties to the members. In others, they retained their positions in the union, but problems arose when the interests of the workers and the government did not coincide. In the UF simultaneously holding a leadership position in the union and an outside political or government post became an issue of contention. As already discussed, the appointment of Luis González to a state pension organization helped lead to his resignation as president of the union, though he remained on the CD. In June 1945 Pablo López asked permission to serve simultaneously on the CD and as interventor of Gobernador Gálvez, a town in Santa Fe province. The Mesa saw no problem as long as he returned to work on the railroad and was no longer a union employee. However, a majority of the CD felt that this would compromise the union's neutrality. Ponce pointed out that members who now saw no incompatibility between the holding of the two

---

*The rise of new leaders whose position was weaker vis-à-vis the government was encouraged by the regime.

positions had severely criticized Pérez Leirós for being both a national deputy and the UOEM's secretary general. Despite clear orders from the union to give up one position, López continued to hold both posts. In the ensuing controversy it came out that a number of railroaders held posts in the locals or the grievance committees as well as government jobs. With the exception of positions to which members were nominated by the union, the CD pressed railroaders to make a choice. As mentioned, Ponce and Polo resigned from the CD in 1946, and a third member resigned in 1947—all because of the greater opportunities that existed elsewhere. At the lower levels the turnover was also high.[18] Even a union with a large corps of leaders found its stock quickly depleted, especially given the struggles that had pushed aside so many.

Other unions faced similar problems. The FOET's leaders became totally involved in politics. Gay had become president of the Partido Laborista, while Orozco and Ernesto Cleve of La Plata won seats in congress on that party's slates; Gay and Orozco continued to serve the union as well. As a result (among other things), *Federación*, the union newspaper which had appeared regularly since 1929, ceased to appear between December 1945 and June 1946. The leaders lacked the time to put out a paper. After the government nationalized the UT in 1946, two union members sat on the governing board; in addition, Gay represented the state and was vice president of the company. Gay also served as president of the postal savings bank. While these men continued their union activities, they obviously not only had less time to spend on them, but also their loyalties became somewhat divided. This is not to say that they were coopted. In 1947, when Perón had Gay unceremoniously deposed as secretary general of the CGT because of his independent stance, the government felt it necessary to have the CGT intervene in the FOET, and Orozco and Cleve strenuously defended Gay.[19]

Other unions maintained less independence than the FOET. The CGEC leaders remained close to the government, with Borlenghi both secretary general of the union and the regime's minister of interior, while José Argaña served the union and was a national deputy. Roberto Marrone accused the government of gaining the support of two leaders of Rosario's retail clerks by giving them jobs with the pension organization.[20]

In late 1946 the government began appointing labor attachés to serve in Argentine embassies abroad. These were largely drawn from the second echelon of labor leaders. The large number—fifty-two by 1947—strained the ranks of experienced leaders, and the appointments were undoubtedly used to remove independent leaders from where they might cause problems.[21] As should already be clear, union leaders were also appointed to the new institutions created to control the pension systems. While their roles did not differ markedly from that of workers on elected boards prior to 1943, the government made the appointments at the suggestion of the unions, which implies a very different relationship.[22] The new opportunities not only stretched the relatively small group of experienced leaders, but also in some cases compromised their independence.

All these factors initiated within the labor movement a new trajectory away from the paths that it had taken earlier. While a product of its past, the Peronist labor movement was something very different.

LOSS OF INDEPENDENCE

In the 1930s the unions had been an independent force. The two government attempts to change the direction of the labor movement by persuasion—i.e., the shoring up of the Syndicalists by giving Syndicalist leaders jobs and the establishment of the FOEF—had failed. The Argentine labor movement had been the most powerful in Latin America even prior to 1943 and had played a crucial role in the events of 1945 and 1946. Yet Perón's ability to manipulate the unions was evident. Because Perón willed it, the Partido Laborista—the answer to a dream of many labor leaders for an independent labor party—was superseded by a party more directly controlled by Perón, with little controversy. Why was he able to impose his will on the unions?

The explanation lies to a large extent in the charisma of Juan Perón and the position he held. Once he had the reins of power firmly in his hands, he could fully use the state's organizing power, which was far greater than the unions'. Moreover, the devotion and loyalty that workers had come to feel for him bypassed the unions: they knew from where their gains really came. In his long political career Perón attempted to destroy anyone who might challenge his leadership, and old-line union leaders had their own bases, potentially threatening his hegemonic control over the workers. Therefore, Perón displaced union leaders who attempted to remain independent. While the unions stood at the front of the political stage and remained important symbols, power lay with Perón. Unions were still capable of independent actions, but these had high costs.²³ The fate of the unions that are the focus of this book is a good indication. Only the FEC retained its old leaders.

As mentioned, the government had the FOET intervened in 1947. In March of the same year the advisory council of the UOEM resigned, frustrated by the government's unwillingness to end the intervention in that union and the continued postponement of wage negotiations. A wildcat strike followed. Also in 1947, after a wildcat strike in cotton, the Asociación Obrera Textil suffered an intervention.²⁴* In 1948 Pablo López became secretary general of the UF. According to Samuel Baily, López was a favorite of Evita Perón and the election was of dubious honesty. In 1950–51 unhappiness with the union's inability to achieve wage increases led to wildcat strikes, arrests, intervention, and marginalization of those in power.²⁵ The most conspicuous demonstration of Perón's power was the deposing of Gay as secretary general of the CGT. The labor confederation removed a popular and legitimate leader because Perón wanted it to do so. This is a far cry from the 1930s, when Ortiz failed to change the political orientation of the UF; while Domenech was forced out of the presidency of the union, he still controlled the CGT.

Not all unions suffered massive government interference. Unions that went along with the government managed to retain their leaders. The CGEC was stable. During 1951–53 at least eight of the eleven-member executive board had been active prior to the 1943 coup, and Borlenghi remained minister of interior.²⁶ Despite the continued importance of the unions, they had lost considerable control of their destiny.

During the 1930s unions had to adjust to an intensification of industrialization that rapidly enlarged potential membership and to a semi-authoritarian government with little sustained interest in workers. Some adjusted by becoming national in scope, uniting various crafts, or using strikes as organizing tools. Others used the political system to overcome obstacles. Many others were stymied. Despite an overall growth of the labor movement, a sense of malaise had set in by 1943; progress was slower than expected. Workers remained outsiders, both politically and in the society. The government, which had become a focus of union attention, continued an ad hoc relationship with the labor movement. It also became more unfriendly under Castillo. In the labor movement the search for a coherent response had led away from the

---

*The new unions in construction, shoemaking, and tobacco suffered a fate similar to that of the textile union (*CGT*, 1 Dec. 1947).

Syndicalists and toward the Socialists and Communists. Even the traditional relationship with the Socialist Party began to appear less satisfactory. By 1943 it appeared that strong support existed both for tying unions tightly to the Socialist and Communist parties and for establishing the unions as an independent force.

This was not to be. Through a combination of repression and reward, Perón reshaped the labor movement. Unions that resisted felt the full wrath of the state. Many were willing to cooperate. For years they had looked to the government and received very little. Now the regime offered a way of solving long-standing problems and permitted an escape from political and social marginalization. In many cases cooperation did not at first mean overwhelming support; this developed gradually, as Perón wooed them more intensely and they had to choose sides. By mid-1945 most unions strongly backed Perón, but resistance increased as well. Yet it was workers, partially mobilized by their unions, who turned the tide in October 1945 and then played a key role in electing Perón president in 1946.

Without the changes in the society and in the unions produced by the great depression, Peronism would have been impossible—at least in the form it took. The increased strength and legitimacy of unions made them a useful mechanism to rally popular support. They provided the essential link between Perón and the workers. Union leaders' attitudes gave Perón his opportunity; they too were searching for allies, and what Perón offered went beyond their wildest dreams. The relationship was not static but changed over time. Not all leaders liked what they saw; these believed that Perón was trying to control the unions, and they rejected cooperation with the regime. During the Neo-Conservative era the unions had simultaneously cooperated with and struggled against the government. Under the military, because of Perón's increased interest in labor, union leaders had to cooperate *or* resist. Most unions cooperated, and they and Perón have been intertwined ever since.

NOTES

Introduction

1. James R. Scobie, *Buenos Aires: Plaza to Suburb* (New York, 1974), 220. The social exclusion of the working class cannot be addressed fully here.

2. Gino Germani, *Política y sociedad en una época de transición*, 5th ed. (Buenos Aires, 1974).

3. Robert J. Alexander, *The Perón Era* (New York, 1951); George I. Blanksten, *Perón's Argentina* (Chicago, 1953).

4. See Manuel Mora y Araujo and Ignacio Llorente, eds., *El voto peronista* (Buenos Aires, 1980), 13–364, which includes articles by Germani, Smith, and Kenworthy; Walter Little, "Popular Origins of Peronism," in *Argentina in the Twentieth Century*, ed. David Rock (London, 1975), 162–78. See also José Enrique Miguens, "The Presidential Elections of 1973 and the End of an Ideology," in *Juan Perón and the Reshaping of Argentina*, ed. Frederick C. Turner and J. E. Miguens (Pittsburgh, 1983), 150–59. Torcuato S. Di Tella is practically the only major scholar who continues to support the migrant theory, and he does it with great skill in "Working-Class Organizations and Politics in Argentina," *Latin American Research Review* 16, 2 (1981), 47–51.

5. Miguel Murmis and Juan Carlos Portantiero, *Estudios sobre los orígenes del peronismo*, I (Buenos Aires, 1971); Ricardo Gaudio and Jorge Pilone: "El desarrollo de la negociación colectiva durante la etapa de modernización industrial en la Argentina, 1935–1943," *Desarrollo Económico*, no. 90 (July/Sept. 1983), 255–86, and "Estado y relaciones laborales en el período previo al surgimiento del peronismo, 1935–1943," *Desarrollo Económico*, no. 94 (July/Sept. 1984), 235–73; Hiroschi Matsushita, *Movimiento obrero argentino 1930/1945* (Buenos Aires, 1983). See also Hugo del Campo, *Sindicalismo y peronismo* (Buenos Aires, 1983), and David Tamarin, *The Argentine Labor Movement, 1930–1945* (Albuquerque, N.M., 1985).

6. Calculated from Departamento Nacional del Trabajo (DNT), *Boletín informativo*, Sept./Oct. 1936, 4728–54.

7. Charles Bergquist, *Labor in Latin America* (Stanford, 1986); Peter Winn, *Weavers of Revolution* (New York, 1986).

8. See Matsushita, esp. 185–209.

9. Tamarin, esp. 86–88.

10. Gaudio and Pilone; Matsushita; del Campo; Tamarin.

11. Joel Horowitz, "The Impact of pre-1943 Labor Union Traditions on Peronism," *Journal of Latin American Studies* 15, 1 (May 1983), 101–16.

12. Alexander; Alberto Belloni, *Del anarquismo al peronismo* (Buenos Aires, 1960); Samuel L. Baily, *Labor, Nationalism and Politics in Argentina* (New Brunswick, N.J., 1967).

13. For differing opinions, see S. L. Baily, 76; Tamarin, 180–81; Matsushita, 277–79.

Chapter 1: Argentine Politics, 1930–1945

1. Kenneth Paul Erickson, *The Brazilian Corporative State and Working class Politics* (Berkeley, 1977), 34–35.
2. Ezequiel Gallo and Roberto Cortés Conde, *Argentina: La república conservadora*, 81–89, 187–211; vol. 5 of *Colección historia argentina*, ed. Tulio Halperín Donghi (Buenos Aires, 1972); Natalio R. Botana, *El orden conservador* (Buenos Aires, 1977); José Luis Romero, *A History of Argentine Political Thought*, trans. Thomas F. McGann (Stanford, 1963), 188–213.
3. Gallo and Cortés Conde, 212–23; David Rock, *Politics in Argentina 1890–1930* (London, 1975), 41–55; Peter G. Snow, *Radicalismo argentino*, trans. Ana Noboa de Dufaux (Buenos Aires, 1972), 29–41; Ezequiel Gallo and Silvia Sigal, "La formación de los partidos políticos contemporáneos," in *Argentina, sociedad de masas*, ed. Torcuato Di Tella et al. (Buenos Aires, 1965), 124–76.
4. Felipe Cárdenas(h), "Ese enigmativo conductor," in *Los radicales*, ed. Félix Luna (Buenos Aires, 1976), 87–99; Ysabel F. Rennie, *The Argentine Republic* (New York, 1945), 188–219.
5. Romero, 217–18; Snow, 37–38; Alberto Ciria, *Parties and Power in Modern Argentina (1930–1946)*, trans. Carlos A. Astiz (Albany, 1974), 133.
6. Richard J. Walter, *The Socialist Party of Argentina, 1890–1930* (Austin, 1977); Jacinto Oddone, *Historia del socialismo argentino*, 2 vols. (Buenos Aires, 1934); Alfredo Galletti, *La realidad argentina en el siglo XX* (Buenos Aires, 1961), 51–75; Horacio Sanguinetti, *Los socialistas independientes* (Buenos Aires, 1981), 19–135.
7. Rock, 35–40; Gallo and Cortés Conde, 194–223; Botana, 217–345.
8. The best account of the Radical period is Rock, 95–217. See also Darío Cantón, José Luis Moreno, and Alberto Ciria, *Argentina: La democracia constitucional y su crisis*, 1–100, vol. 6 of Halperín Donghi, ed.; Anne L. Potter, "Political Institutions, Political Decay and the Argentine Crisis of 1930" (Ph.D. dissertation, Stanford University, 1978), 181–270; Ana María Mustapic, "Conflictos institucionales durante el primer gobierno radical," *Desarrollo Económico*, no. 93 (Apr./June 1984), 85–108.
9. Félix Luna, *Alvear* (Buenos Aires, 1958), 56–73; Rock, 218–40; Beatriz Alonso, *La presidencia de Alvear* (Buenos Aires, 1983); Snow, 65–72; Cantón, Moreno, and Ciria, 100–105; Potter, "Political Institutions," 271–338.
10. Darío Cantón, *Elecciones y partidos políticos en la Argentina* (Buenos Aires, 1973), 269; Rennie, 221–22; Robert A. Potash, *The Army and Politics, 1928–1945* (Stanford, 1969), 29–30; Roberto Etchepareborda, "Aspectos políticos de la crisis de 1930," *Revista de Historia*, no. 3 (Buenos Aires, 1958), 29–30.
11. Tulio Halperín Donghi, *Argentina en el callejón* (Montevideo, 1964), 17; Rock, 235–44, 247–50.

12. Etchepareborda, 28–29; Anne L. Potter, "The Failure of Democracy in Argentina, 1916–1930," *Journal of Latin American Studies* 13, 1 (May 1981), 83–109; Carl E. Solberg, *Oil and Nationalism in Argentina* (Stanford, 1979), 113–55, esp. 153–55.

13. Etchepareborda, 1–15; Horacio Sanguinetti, *La democracia ficta, 1930–1938* (Buenos Aires, 1975), 14–15; Federico Pinedo, *En tiempos de la república* (Buenos Aires, 1946), I, 69–70. For the Independent Socialists, see Sanguinetti, *Los socialistas independientes*, and Walter, *The Socialist Party*, 193–226.

14. Rock, 252–64.

15. Cantón, Moreno, and Ciria, 106–12, 159–62; Walter, *The Socialist Party*, 214–27; Etchepareborda, 31–37; Ciria, 4–7; Nidia Areces, "La revolución de 1930," in *La década infame*, ed. Alberto Ciria (Buenos Aires, 1974), 11–18.

16. *La Vanguardia*, 7–8 Sept. 1930; *La Nación*, 7–8 Sept. 1930; *La Prensa*, 7–8 Sept. 1930; Dardo Cúneo, *El desencuentro argentino, 1930–1955* (Buenos Aires, 1965), 174–78.

17. In this section, in addition to the works cited, I have relied considerably on Potash's analysis of the military. See in particular his pp. 42–98 (for an overview of the Uriburu and Justo presidencies), pp. 104–83 and 193–209 (for the presidencies of Ortiz and Castillo, plus the coup of 1943), and pp. 224–55 and 269–82 (for the 1943 military regime). See also Marysa Navarro Gerassi, *Los nacionalistas* (Buenos Aires, 1968), 59–68; Cúneo, 179–82; Alain Rouquié, *Poder militar y sociedad política en la Argentina*, trans. Arturo Iglesias Echegaray (Buenos Aires, 1983), I, 229–51.

18. See *La Vanguardia*, 1 and 10 Feb. 1932; *La Prensa*, 10 Feb. 1932.

19. See *La Vanguardia*, Sept. 1930–Feb. 1932, esp. Sept. 1930–Jan. 1931 and July 1931. See also José Peter, *Crónicas proletarias* (Buenos Aires, 1968), 140–42; Pascual Vuotto, *Vida de un proletario (El proceso de Bragado)* (Buenos Aires, 1975), 40–50; Roberto Marrone, *Apuntes para la historia de un gremio (Empleados de Comercio de Rosario)* (Rosario, 1974), 126–27; Diego Abad de Santillán, "El movimiento obrero argentino ante el golpe de estado del 6 de septiembre de 1930," *Revista de Historia*, no. 3 (Buenos Aires, 1958), 131–32; Sanguinetti, *La democracia ficta*, 52–54; Tulio Halperín Donghi, "Crónica del período," in *Argentina 1930–1960*, ed. Jorge A. Paita (Buenos Aires, 1961), 32–33; *Review of the River Plate*, 12 June 1931, 5; Fernando Quesada, *El primer anarquista fusilado en la Argentina* (Buenos Aires, 1974), 82; Sanguinetti, *Los socialistas independientes*, 187–96.

20. U.S. Embassy, Buenos Aires, Robert Woods Bliss to Secretary of State, 30 Oct. 1930, National Archives Record Group 59, File No. 835.00B/34, p. 4. See also *La Vanguardia*, 11, 19 Sept. and 14 Dec. 1930; Sebastián Marotta, *El movimiento sindical argentino* (Buenos Aires, 1970), III, 308–10; Andrés Cabona, Instituto Di Tella Oral History Program (IDTOHP), 60–67.

21. Halperín Donghi, "Crónica del período," 30–32; Luna, *Alvear*, 79–82; Nicolás Repetto, *Mi paso por la política: De Uriburu a Perón* (Buenos Aires, 1957), 15–17; María Dolores Béjar, *Uriburu y Justo* (Buenos Aires, 1983), 33–36.

22. Ciria, 14; Snow, 79–81; Sanguinetti, *La democracia ficta*, 54–55.

23. Galletti, 101–11; Carlos R. Melo, *Los partidos políticos argentinos*, 4th ed. (Córdoba, 1970), 58–60; Ciria, 118–23.

24. Galletti, 96–101; Melo, 59–60; Rennie, 226–28; Ciria, 12–13, 133–35; Sanguinetti, *La democracia ficta*, 57–59.

25. *La Vanguardia*, 9–15 Nov. 1931; Cantón, 270.

26. For details, see Chapter 7 below.

27. Rouquié, I, pp. 263–74.

28. Potash, 96.

29. For details, see Chapter 7 below. For the military threat, see Potash, 95–98.

30. Peter H. Smith, *Argentina and the Failure of Democracy* (Madison, 1974), 80–83. Also see Béjar.

31. The passage of such laws is discussed in Chapters 5 and 7 below. Also see Joaquín Coca, *El contubernio* (Buenos Aires, n.d.).

32. See *Review of the River Plate*, 26 Feb. 1932, 5–9.

33. José Luis Imaz, *Los que mandan*, trans. Carlos A. Astiz (Albany, 1970), 13–16; Daniel Drosdoff, *El gobierno de las vacas (1933–1956)* (Buenos Aires, 1972). As Peter H. Smith has pointed out, the government favored one portion of the cattle industry over another (*Politics and Beef in Argentina* [New York, 1969], 142–227).

34. Luna, *Alvear*, 140–41; Halperín Donghi, "Crónica del período," 37.

35. Cámara de Diputados, División Archivo, Publicación y Museo, *Composición de la Cámara de Diputados de la Nación* (Buenos Aires, 1956), 34–40; Rennie, 262; Ciria, 112–18; Mario Justo López, "Poder legislativo," in Paita, ed., 108–12.

36. *Review of the River Plate*, 3 Jan. 1936, 3 and 3 Dec. 1937, 24–25; Félix Luna, *Ortiz* (Buenos Aires, 1978).

37. Pinedo, as quoted in Ciria, 47.

38. Roberto A. Ferrero, *El fraude a la soberanía popular, 1938–1946* (Buenos Aires, 1976), 13–19; Rouquié, I, 288–92; Rennie, 285–87.

39. Manuel A. Fresco, *Cómo encaré la política obrera durante mi gobierno* (La Plata, 1940); Ronald Howard Dolkart, *Manuel A. Fresco, Governor of the Province of Buenos Aires, 1936–1940* (Ph.D. dissertation, University of California, Los Angeles, 1969).

40. Ferrero, 109–11; Luna, *Ortiz*, 192–94.

41. Miguel Angel Scenna, "CHADE: El escándalo del siglo," in *Los grandes negociados*, ed. Félix Luna (Buenos Aires, 1976), 11–60; Luna, *Alvear*, 196–221, 233–71; Ferrero, 42–48.

42. Rodolfo Puiggrós, *Historia crítica de los partidos políticos argentinos* (Buenos Aires, 1956), 416–29; Enrique Dickmann, *Recuerdos de un militante socialista* (Buenos Aires, 1949), 235–41; Jorge Abelardo Ramos, *Historia del stalinismo en la Argentina* (Buenos Aires, 1974), 114–15; Partido Comunista de la Argentina, *Ezbozo de historia del Partido Comunista de la Argentina* (Buenos Aires, 1947), 84.

43. For recent discussions of the war's impact, see Mario Rapoport, *Gran Bretaña, Estados Unidos y las clases dirigentes argentinas, 1940–1945* (Buenos Aires 1980); Carlos Escudé, *Gran Bretaña, Estados Unidos y la declinación argentina* (Buenos Aires, 1983); C. A. MacDonald, "The Politics of Intervention: The United States and Argentina, 1941–1946," *Journal of Latin American Studies* 12, 2 (Nov. 1980), 365–96; R. A. Humphreys, *Latin America and the Second World War* (London, 1982), II, 129–202.

44. Luna, *Ortiz*, 194–209; Osvaldo Bayer, "Palomar: El episodio que conmovió a un régimen," in Luna, ed., *Los grandes negociados*, 67–120; *El Obrero Ferroviario*, 1 Sept. 1940.

45. Ferrero, 109–30.

46. Cámara de Diputados, *Composición de la Cámara de Diputados*, 38–39; Ferrero, 128–57; Juan J. Llach, "El Plan Pinedo de 1940, su significado histórico y los orígenes de la economía política del peronismo," *Desarrollo Económico*, no. 92 (Jan./Mar. 1984), 528–31.

47. For repression, see Cámara de Diputados, *Diario de sesiones*, IV, 17 Sept. 1941, 539–68. For the text of the closure of the city council, Comisión Interventora de Vecinos del Concejo Deliberante de la Ciudad de Buenos Aires, *Actas*, III, 17 Oct. 1941, 1869.

48. Ferrero, 159–62; Rouquié, I, 302–30.

49. Marvin Goldwert, *Democracy, Militarism and Nationalism in Argentina, 1930–1966* (Austin, 1972), 58–65; Rennie, 289–307; Ferrero, 184–91, 233–38.

50. Luna, *Alvear*, 292–332; MacDonald, 273–74.

51. Mario Rapoport, "Patrón Costas y la revolución del 43," *Todo es Historia*, Nov. 1979, 8–21; Rennie, 344; Juan Antonio Solari, *Parias argentinos* (Buenos Aires, 1940); Pinedo, *En tiempos de la república*, I, 182–83; Ferrero, 247–50.

52. Ferrero, 251–63; *Unidad Nacional*, 12 and 24 June 1943. Rouquié, II, 15–46, has a strong discussion of the beginnings of the military regime.

53. *Unidad Nacional* is an excellent source because it was the clandestine publication of the Communist Party's central committee; see July 1943–Jan. 1944. See also Ray Josephs, *The Argentine Diary* (New York, 1944), 185–354, for an interesting if strange account; Tulio Halperín Donghi, *Historia de la Universidad de Buenos Aires* (Buenos Aires, 1962), 165–72; *La Vanguardia*, 7 Jan. and 7, 8 Apr. 1944; Chapter 9 below.

54. Robert A. Potash, ed., *Perón y el GOU* (Buenos Aires, 1984).

55. The best study of Perón is Joseph Page, *Perón: A Biography* (New York, 1983). For an excellent discussion tying Perón's actions to political circumstances, see Juan Carlos Torre, "El rol del sindicalismo en los orígenes del peronismo" (Spanish version, doctoral dissertation, Ecole Pratique des Hautes Etudes, 1983).

56. See Chapter 9 below; Potash, 224.

57. Rapoport, *Gran Bretaña*, 183–87; Ferrero, 280–89.

58. Page, 60–62.

59. Joel Horowitz, "Latin American Populism Reconsidered: Peronism as a Test Case"; paper delivered to the New England Council of Latin American Studies, 1987.

60. Repetto, 274–305; "Reportaje a Jorge Michellón," *Controversia*, Suplement 1, Dec. 1979, ix–x; *Unidad Nacional*, 1943–45, esp. second week Mar. 1945. For Paris, see any Buenos Aires paper, 25–27 Aug. 1944.

61. Halperín Donghi, *Historia de la Universidad*, 172–78; Félix Luna, *El 45* (Buenos Aires, 1969), 85–175. *La Vanguardia* reappeared on 10 Apr. 1945.

62. Luna, *El 45*, 176–273; Chapter 9 below.

63. Rouquié, II, 63–72; Luna, *El 45*, 273–428. For the workers' side, see Chapter 9 below.

Chapter 2: The Economy and Society

1. Federico Pinedo, *Siglo y medio de economía argentina* (Mexico, 1961), 107–8; Carlos F. Díaz Alejandro, *Essays on the Economic History of the Argentine Republic* (New Haven, 1970), 94.

2. For the founding of Argentine industry, see Adolfo Dorfman, *Historia de la industria argentina* (Buenos Aires, 1970); Ricardo M. Ortiz, *Historia económica de la Argentina*, 4th ed. (Buenos Aires, 1974), 547–82; Javier Villanueva, "El origen de la industrialización argentina," *Desarrollo Económico*, no. 47 (Oct./Dec. 1972), 451–76.

3. Adolfo Dorfman, *Cincuenta años de industrialización en la Argentina, 1930–1980* (Buenos Aires, 1983), 148; Díaz Alejandro, *Essays*, 422.

4. Gino Germani, *Estructura social de la Argentina* (Buenos Aires, 1955), 139–225, esp. 219.

5. Díaz Alejandro, *Essays*, 62; H. S. Ferns, *The Argentine Republic, 1516–1971* (New York, 1973), 89; Alejandro E. Bunge, *Una nueva Argentina* (Buenos Aires, 1940), 126. Robert E. Shipley, "On the Outside Looking In" (Ph.D. dissertation, Rutgers University, 1977), has a harsher view of working-class conditions in the 1920s, but this does not invalidate the concept of relative well-being.

6. For an excellent discussion of the worldwide impact of the depression, see Charles P. Kindleberger, *The World in Depression, 1929–1939* (Berkeley, 1973).

7. Javier Villanueva, "Economic Development," in *Prologue to Perón*, ed. Mark Falcoff and Ronald Dolkart (Berkeley, 1975), 60–61; Arturo O'Connell, "La Argentina en la depresión," *Desarrollo Económico*, no. 92 (Jan./Mar. 1984), 487–90; Guido Di Tella and Manuel Zymelman, *Las etapas del desarrollo económico argentino* (Buenos Aires, 1967), 380–412; Díaz Alejandro, *Essays*, 479.

8. DNT, División de Estadística, *Investigaciones sociales 1939* (Buenos Aires, 1940), 38 (hereafter DNT, *Investigaciones sociales year*); DNT, *Investigaciones sociales 1940*, 35; DNT, *La desocupación en la Argentina 1932* (Buenos Aires, 1933), 20. The percentages are calculated from population figures in Díaz Alejandro, *Essays*,

428; Bunge, 141; and from the average of economically active in 1914 and 1947 in Germani, *Estructura*, 120.

9. U.S. Embassy Buenos Aires, 29 Dec. 1933, National Archives Record Group 59, File No. 835.504/90; Enrique Siewars, "Unemployment in Argentina," *International Labor Review* 31, 6 (June 1935), 798–99; Angel Perelman, *Cómo hicimos el 17 de octubre* (Buenos Aires, 1961), 30; Juan José Real, *30 años de historia argentina* (Buenos Aires, 1962), 35; *La Vanguardia*, 5 Feb. 1931.

10. David Rock, *Politics in Argentina 1890–1930* (London, 1975), 253–58; Ferns, 116–19, 123; G. Di Tella and Zymelman, 380–84; Villanueva, "Economic Development," 62–63.

11. Pinedo, *Siglo y medio*, 112–13; *La Vanguardia*, 24 Jan. and 20 Feb. 1931.

12. Díaz Alejandro, *Essays*, 57–58, 101; Villanueva, "El origen de la industrialización argentina."

13. Javier Villanueva, "Aspectos de la estrategia de industrialización argentina," in *Los fragmentos del poder*, ed. Torcuato S. Di Tella and Tulio Halperín Donghi (Buenos Aires, 1969), 339–40; Carlos F. Díaz Alejandro, "The Argentine State and Economic Growth," in *Government and Economic Development*, ed. Gustav Ranis (New Haven, 1971), 226–27; Miguel Murmis and Juan Carlos Portantiero, *Estudios sobre los orígenes del peronismo*, I (Buenos Aires, 1971), 3–55.

14. Murmis and Portantiero, 20–23; Pinedo, *Siglo y medio*, 113–18; Ferns, 125–31; G. Di Tella and Zymelman, 421–52.

15. Díaz Alejandro, *Essays*, 94–102, 420; Dorfman, *Historia de la industria argentina*, 365–86.

16. Dirección Nacional de Estadística y Censos, *Cuarto censo general de la Nación* (Buenos Aires, 1949), III, 26–27.

17. Murmis and Portantiero, 33–34; Díaz Alejandro, *Essays*, 406; *Revista de Economía Argentina*, March 1944, 88; DNT, División de Estadística: *Ocupación y desocupación* (Buenos Aires, 1943), 18, and *Investigaciones sociales 1940*, 36.

18. G. Di Tella and Zymelman, 459–91; Villanueva, "Economic Development," 76–79.

19. G. Di Tella and Zymelman, 488; Díaz Alejandro, *Essays*, 478–79; DNT, División de Estadística: *La desocupación en la Argentina 1940* (Buenos Aires, 1940), 11–16, 20, 40; *Adaptación de los salarios a las fluctuaciones del costo de la vida* (Buenos Aires, 1943), 42; and *Ocupación y desocupación*, 18–19.

20. DNT, *Ocupación y desocupación*, 7–8, 17; Ferns, 143; Cornelio Oswald, Instituto Di Tella Oral History Program (IDTOHP), 8; Thomas C. Cochran and Rubén E. Reina, *Capitalism in Argentine Culture* (Philadelphia, 1962), 176–94.

21. Dirección de Estadística Social: *El índice del costo de la vida* (Buenos Aires, 1945), appendix 1, and *Investigaciones sociales 1943–1945* (Buenos Aires, 1946), 35.

22. Germani, *Estructura*, 75.

23. See below and Torcuato S. Di Tella, *El sistema político argentino y la clase obrera* (Buenos Aires, 1964), 21.

24. I am not implying that a labor aristocracy existed. For a discussion of this term, see Joel Horowitz, "Occupational Community and the Creation of a Self-Styled Elite," *The Americas* 42, 1 (July 1985), 58–59.

25. DNT, División de Estadística, *Condiciones de vida de la familia obrera* (Buenos Aires, 1937), 14; unless otherwise indicated, translations are mine. The DNT's surveys are probably not statistically accurate but convey a good impression of conditions.

26. DNT, *Condiciones de vida*, 25.

27. Instituto de Estudios Económicos del Transporte, *Salarios ferroviarios y costo de la vida* (Buenos Aires, 1943), 25; DNT, *Investigaciones sociales 1938*, 19.

28. DNT, *Condiciones de vida*, 28; Ministerio de Hacienda, Dirección General de Estadística y Censos de la Nación, *Estadística industrial de 1941* (Buenos Aires, 1943), 46.

29. Torcuato Di Tella, "¿Cómo vive el obrero de la industria argentina?," *Revista de Economía Argentina*, Jan. 1941, 25–26.

30. Armour Research Foundation, *Technological and Economic Survey of Argentine Industries with Industrial Research Recommendations* (Ann Arbor, 1943), 65–76.

31. Carl C. Taylor, *Rural Life in Argentina* (Baton Rouge, 1948), 294–97; DNT, División de Estadística: *Costo de la vida* (Buenos Aires, 1935), and *Condiciones de vida*; Manuel A. Fresco, *Cómo encaré la política obrera durante mi gobierno* (La Plata, 1940), I, 226–27; Provincia de Buenos Aires, Departamento del Trabajo, *Condiciones de vida de la familia obrera* (La Plata, 1943), 36–44.

32. T. Di Tella, "¿Cómo vive el obrero?, 25–26. For dress, see pictures of strikes and union meetings appearing in the press, especially of the demonstration of 17 October 1945.

33. Alcides Greca, "El problema de la vivienda económica en la República Argentina," *La Habitación Popular*, July/Sept. 1938, 265; Emilio Lenhardtson, "El problema financiero de la vivienda, para la población de medianos recursos," *La Ingenería* 48, 9 (Sept. 1943), 643–44; DNT, *Condiciones de vida*, 28, 56–58. The number living in one room was an improvement over 1913; see Bunge, 351–52.

34. Ysabel F. Rennie, *The Argentine Republic* (New York, 1945), 233–34; T. Di Tella, "¿Cómo vive el obrero?," 26; Fresco, I, 253–67.

35. DNT, *Condiciones de vida*, 28.

36. For a relatively complete listing of labor laws, see Luis Ramicone, *Apuntes para la historia: La organización gremial obrera en la actualidad* (Buenos Aires, 1963), 66–67. Some of the laws applied only to the capital and the national territories.

Chapter 3: Conditions in Five Industries

1. For the early history of telephones in Argentina, see Ricardo T. Mulleady, *Breve historia de la telefonía argentina (1886–1956)* (Buenos Aires, 1956); Cía. Unión

Telefónica del Río de la Plata, *Cincuenta años de vida, 1887–1937* (Buenos Aires, 1937); Enrique Wolfenson, *El problema de los teléfonos* (Buenos Aires, 1956).

2. Mulleady, 27–28, 43–45; Universidad de Buenos Aires, Instituto de Economía de los Transportes, *Los servicios públicos de teléfonos de la Argentina*, publication no. 8 (Buenos Aires, 1942), 145, 152–54; *Review of the River Plate*, 5 May 1939, 5; Cámara de Diputados, Comisión Especial de Estudio del Régimen Legal de Telecomunicaciones, *Publicación de antecedentes* (Buenos Aires, 1936), 13, 49, 163–65 (hereafter *Antecedentes*). For friction with the union, see *Federación*, esp. Nov. 1934.

3. *Federación*, esp. May 1936; Cámara de Diputados, *Antecedentes*; Cía. Unión Telefónica, 40; Universidad de Buenos Aires, 142–51.

4. Cámara de Diputados, *Antecedentes*, 13; *La Vanguardia*, 17 June 1932; Dirección General de Correos y Telégrafos, *Estadística telefónica año 1939* (Buenos Aires, 1940), 105; Caja Nacional de Jubilaciones y Pensiones de Empleados y Obreros de Empresas Particulares de Servicios Públicos, *Publicación informativa* (Buenos Aires, 1943), cuadro 20.

5. Universidad de Buenos Aires, 282–310, esp. 300; Dirección General de Correos y Telégrafos, *Antecedentes de la situación económica, financiera, industrial, etc. de la Compañía Unión Telefónica* (Buenos Aires, 1937), 131–33, 170.

6. Cámara de Diputados, *Antecedentes*, 178, 263, 272–76; Cía. Unión Telefónica, 44; Luis Gay, "Historia de la FOET," 36 (unpublished manuscript; title and pagination mine). See also *Federación*, esp. July 1931 and *Revista Telefónica Argentina*.

7. Dirección General de Correos y Telégrafos, *Estadística telefónica*, 104–5.

8. *Anales de legislación argentina* (Buenos Aires, 1953), III, 59–65 and IV, 263; Juan Antonio Solari, *Previsión social argentina* (Buenos Aires, 1941), 50.

9. FOET, *Luchas y conquistas* (Buenos Aires, 1944), 206–19.

10. Gay, "Historia de la FOET," 57.

11. Cámara de Diputados, *Antecedentes*, 266.

12. Dirección Nacional de Estadística y Censos, *Cuarto censo general de la Nación* (Buenos Aires, 1949), III, 254–64.

13. Roger Gravil, "British Retail Trade in Argentina 1900–1940," *Inter-American Economic Affairs* 24 (Autumn 1970), 26.

14. See *La Vanguardia*, 1930–33, esp. 31 Jan., 2–10 Apr., 21 July, and 7, 29 Sept. 1932 and 29 Sept. 1933; DNT, *La desocupación en la Argentina 1932* (Buenos Aires, 1933), 96–103.

15. *CGT*, 9 Sept. 1938 and 17 Feb. 1939; FEC, *Informe del Concejo Administrativo. Asamblea general ordinaria, 1º de agosto de 1938 al 31 de julio de 1939* (Buenos Aires, 1939; hereafter FEC, *Informe year*); Gravil, 26; *La Vanguardia*, 1937–38; DNT, *La desocupación en la Argentina 1940*, 15.

16. Dirección Nacional de Estadística y Censos, *Cuarto censo*, III, 260; DNT, División de Estadística, *Investigaciones sociales 1941* (Buenos Aires, 1942), 55, 115.

The study of the ages of women commercial workers was not confined to retail establishments.

17. DNT, *Investigaciones sociales 1941*, 52, 112–15.

18. FEC, *Informe 1930*, 20; DNT, *Crónica mensual*, Jan. 1930, 3076.

19. *La Vanguardia*, 15 Oct. 1935; FEC, *Informe 1935/1936*, 23–31; *Ritmo*, Sept. 1944.

20. Camilo Almarza, Instituto Di Tella Oral History Program, 1–2 (hereafter IDTOHP); FEC, *Informe 1930*, 30–31; *La Vanguardia*, 26 July 1932, 23 Mar. and 1 Apr. 1933; Angel Borlenghi, *La ley más beneficiosa para los empleados de comercio* (Buenos Aires, 1935), 13–17.

21. Gravil, 11; *La Vanguardia*, 15 Oct. 1935.

22. For numbers of employees, see Municipalidad de la Ciudad de Buenos Aires, *Presupuesto general de gastos y cálculo de recursos* (hereafter Buenos Aires, *Presupuesto year*). For diversity, see Municipalidad de la Ciudad de Buenos Aires, *Memoria del Departamento Ejecutivo 1933 y 1934* (Buenos Aires, 1935), 180–83, 578–82 (hereafter Buenos Aires, *Memoria del D.E. year*).

23. Buenos Aires, *Memoria del D.E. 1933 y 1934*, 115, 129; *La Prensa*, 1, 24, and 28–30 Jan. 1931; Buenos Aires, *Presupuesto, 1930* and *1931*, esp. pp. 4–6 for pay cuts. For late payments, *La Vanguardia*, 31 Dec. 1930, 15 Oct. 1931, and 4 June 1932.

24. Concejo Deliberante de la Ciudad de Buenos Aires, *Actas del H. Concejo Deliberante*, IV, 22 Dec. 1933, 4100–22 (hereafter Concejo Deliberante, *Actas*); Buenos Aires: *Presupuesto 1932*, 3, and *1933–35*; *Memoria del D.E. 1933 y 1934*, 113, 142, and *1935*, 33, 102–4; *La Vanguardia*, 13 Feb. 1942.

25. Francisco Pérez Leirós, *Situación del personal de la comuna* (Buenos Aires, 1941), 22–23; Buenos Aires: *Memoria del D.E. 1933 y 1934*, 180–83, and *1936*, 320–21; *Presupuesto 1937*, 49–51.

26. Municipalidad de la Ciudad de Buenos Aires, Caja Municipal de Previsión Social, *Ordenanzas y reglamentos en vigor*, 3d ed. (Buenos Aires, 1940); Pérez Leirós, *Situación*, 20; Buenos Aires, *Memoria del D.E. 1936*, I, 508–14, and *1933 y 1934*, 189–200.

27. Francisco Pérez Leirós, IDTOHP, 29–30.

28. Concejo Deliberante, *Actas*, IV, 22 Dec. 1933, 4115–16.

29. For UOEM leaders, *La Vanguardia*, 7 July 1939; *El Obrero Municipal*, Nov. 1942; for hiring of Radicals, Félix Luna, *Alvear* (Buenos Aires, 1958), 236. See also Buenos Aires, *Memoria del D.E. 1933 y 1934*, graph following 182; Gino Germani, *Política y sociedad en una época de transición*, 5th ed. (Buenos Aires, 1974), 281.

30. For firings and escalafón, see note 24. For harassment, see *La Vanguardia*, Apr.–June 1931. For complaints about the new system, Concejo Deliberante, *Actas*, I: 18 May 1934, 164–68; 24 June 1938, 966–74; 14 June 1940, 253–55.

31. For example, Concejo Deliberante, *Actas*, IV, 21 Nov. 1933, 3476, and 19 Dec. 1933, 4028; III, 29 Nov. 1938, 3637.

32. Concejo Deliberante, *Actas*, IV: 22 Nov. 1932, 4223–26; 23 Dec. 1932, 4879–80; 28 Dec. 1933, 4694–95.

33. Concejo Deliberante, *Actas*: III, 11 Oct. 1932, 5376–77; IV, 4 Nov. 1932, 3825–27.

34. *CGT*, 16 Dec. 1938 and 6 Jan. 1939; *La Vanguardia*, 14 May 1931 and 13 Apr. 1939; Pérez Leirós, *Situación*, 26; Concejo Deliberante, *Actas*: IV, 24 Nov. 1933, 2530–31; I, 26 May 1936, 206–10; III, 29 Nov. 1938, 3580–81; IV, 23 Dec. 1938, 4153; II, 20 Oct. 1939, 2203–4.

35. Pedro Otero, IDTOHP, 25; author's interview with Dora Genkin de Michellón and Jorge Michellón, 24 June 1976; *La Vanguardia*, 20–21 Aug. 1932 and 6 Sept. 1939; *CGT*, 1 Mar. 1940; Concejo Deliberante, *Actas*: IV, 28 Dec. 1933, 4694–95; I, 16 June 1939, 563–64.

36. Emilio Llorens and Rafael García-Mata, *Argentina económica 1939* (Buenos Aires, 1939), 137. For the early history of Argentine railroads, Raúl Scalabrini Ortiz, *Historia de los ferrocarriles argentinos*, 7th ed. (Buenos Aires, 1975); William Rögind, *Historia del Ferrocarril Sud* (Buenos Aires, 1937); Colin Lewis, *British Railways in Argentina* (London, 1983).

37. Paul Goodwin, *Los ferrocarriles británicos y la UCR* (Buenos Aires, 1974); Winthrop R. Wright, *British-Owned Railways in Argentina* (Austin, 1974), 70–157; Julian S. Duncan, "British Railways in Argentina," *Political Science Quarterly* 52, 4 (Dec. 1937), 574.

38. For the board, see Goodwin, 16–17, and *Boletín de la Dirección General de Ferrocarriles*, Apr. 1939, 275–98. The board dictated 763 resolutions in January 1939 (*Boletín de la Dirección General de Ferrocarriles*, Feb. 1939, 139). For the government's ability to defy the companies, see Raúl García Heras, "Hostage Private Companies under Restraint," *Journal of Latin American Studies* 19, 1 (May 1987), 41–67.

39. *El Obrero Ferroviario*, 1 Mar. 1943; *Review of the River Plate*: 29 Sept. 1939, 9–15; 24 Oct. 1941, 5; 5 Feb. 1943, 11; 20 Dec. 1944, 14–15; 23 Nov. 1945, 19; José Beltramé, *La crisis de los ferrocarriles argentinos de propiedad privada* (Buenos Aires, 1946), 61–64.

40. Duncan, 574; Pedro Skuptch, "El deterio y fin de la hegemonía británica sobre la economía argentina," in *Estudios sobre los orígenes del peronismo*, II, ed. Miguel Murmis and Juan Carlos Portantiero (Buenos Aires, 1973), esp. 19, 35, 73; Daniel Drosdoff, *El gobierno de las vacas (1933–1956)* (Buenos Aires, 1972), 23–25.

41. Cámara de Diputados, *Diario de sesiones*, II, 8 Aug. 1941, 951.

42. García Heras; Wright, 172–96; *Review of the River Plate*, 29 Dec. 1944, 14–15, and 20 July 1945, 17–19.

43. Scalabrini Ortiz, 266–78; Wright, 197–214.

44. See Joel Horowitz, "Occupational Community and the Creation of a Self-Styled Elite," *The Americas* 42, 1 (July 1985), 58–61.

45. Juan Manuel Santa Cruz, *Ferrocarriles argentinos* (Santa Fe, 1966), 33; *CGT*, 30 May 1941.

46. Caja Nacional de Jubilaciones y Pensiones de Empleados Ferroviarios, *Memoria correspondiente al año 1941* (Buenos Aires, 1942), 65–66, 157–75.

47. *El Obrero Ferroviario*, 1 and 15 Oct. 1942.

48. For the problems that occurred because of one appointment, see Ferrocarril Oeste de Buenos Aires, *El "trabajo a reglamento" ante el poder ejecutivo, la justicia federal y la opinión pública* (Buenos Aires, 1932). For government regulations, see *Ley y reglamento general de los ferrocarriles nacionales, Publicación oficial* (Buenos Aires, 1936).

49. See any contract and *El Obrero Ferroviario*, 1 May 1931.

50. *El Obrero Ferroviario*, 16 Oct. 1937; Juan Rodríguez, IDTOHP, 24–25; Horowitz, "Occupational Community," 67–69.

51. *El Obrero Ferroviario*, 1 Mar. 1940; for complaints about conditions, see 1/16 June 1939, 1/16 June 1942, and 1 May 1943; *La Vanguardia*, 7 Feb. and 19 Mar. 1940.

52. *El Obrero Ferroviario*, 16 Apr. 1938 and 16 Mar. 1942; Antonio di Santo, IDTOHP, 3; Comisión Especial de Representantes de Empresas y Obreros Ferroviarios, *Revisión de escalafones, convenios y reglamentos* (Buenos Aires, 1930), 239–40.

53. Adolfo Dorfman: *Evolución industrial argentina* (Buenos Aires, 1942), 83, and *Historia de la industria argentina* (Buenos Aires, 1940), 340–42.

54. Guido Di Tella and Manuel Zymelman, *Las etapas del desarrollo económico argentino* (Buenos Aires, 1967), 359; Great Britain, Department of Overseas Trade, *Economic Conditions in the Argentine Republic 1930* (London, 1931), 44–45; *La Vanguardia*, 1930–33.

55. Enrique Siewars, "Unemployment in Argentina," *International Labor Review* 31, 6 (June 1935), 789; *Review of the River Plate*, 22 June 1934, 5. Employers were adding shifts rather than buying machinery. Great Britain, Department of Overseas Trade, *Economic Conditions in the Argentine Republic 1935* (London, 1936), 67.

56. Dorfman, *Historia de la industria argentina*, 373; Cámara de Diputados, *Diario de sesiones*, VI, 30 Sept. 1938, 192; Junta Nacional del Algodón, *Memoria anual 1943* (Buenos Aires, 1943), 40.

57. Cámara de Diputados, *Diario de sesiones*, II, 4 Sept. 1941, 948; CGT, 1 May 1942; *El Obrero Textil*, July 1942; Adolfo Dorfman, *Evolución de la economía argentina* (Buenos Aires, 1939), 231.

58. Cámara de Diputados, *Diario de sesiones*, III, 27 July 1938, 165; DNT, División de Estadística, *Industria textil: Capacidad normal de trabajo de los obreros* (Buenos Aires, 1939), 55–56; author's interviews with Jorge Michellón, 8 Jan. and 24 June 1976; *El Obrero Textil*, July 1939.

59. Carlos F. Díaz Alejandro, *Essays on the Economic History of the Argentine Republic* (New Haven, 1970), 446; Ministerio de Hacienda, Comisión Nacional del Censo Nacional, *Censo industrial de 1935* (Buenos Aires, 1938), 447–56; Dirección Nacional de Estadística y Censos, *Cuarto censo*, III, 66–67.

60. DNT, *Industria textil*, 37–64; CGT, *Acta del primer congreso ordinario* (Buenos Aires, 1940), 71–74.

61. Cámara de Diputados, *Diario de sesiones*: III, 27 July 1938, 162–86, 189–91, esp. 168–69, and 28 July 1938, 215–20; VI, 30 Sept. 1938, 191–204.

62. See *El Obrero Textil*, 1939–43, esp. second fortnight May 1941, Dec. 1941, and Apr. 1943; *Review of the River Plate*: 10 Nov. 1944, 5–6; 23 Mar. 1945, 9; 20 July 1945, 14–16; Dirección de Algodón, *Boletín mensual*, Mar./Apr. 1946, 82; *La Prensa*, 26 June 1945.

63. DNT, *Industria textil*, 20–21, 24–25, 87; CGT, *Acta del primer congreso ordinario*, 73; Lucio Bonilla, IDTOHP, 3–4; author's interview with Jorge Michellón, 8 Jan. 1976; Dirección Nacional de Estadística y Censos, *Cuarto censo*, III, 44–45.

64. See Table 2-3; DNT, *Industria textil*, 8; CGT, *Acta del primer congreso ordinario*, 71, 73.

65. Chapter 6 below; DNT, *Industria textil*, 85; Mariano Tedesco, IDTOHP, 4–8; *La Vanguardia*, 15 and 22 Aug. 1935.

Chapter 4: The Labor Movement Prior to 1930

1. For the early years of the labor movement, see Ricardo Falcón, *Los orígenes del movimiento obrero (1857–1899)* (Buenos Aires, 1984); Iaacov Oved, *El anarquismo y el movimiento obrero en la Argentina* (Mexico, 1978); Jacinto Oddone, *Gremialismo proletario argentino*, 2d ed. (Buenos Aires, 1975), 30–368; Sebastían Marotta, *El movimiento sindical argentino*, I, II, III (Buenos Aires, 1960, 1961, 1970); Diego Abad de Santillán, *La FORA*, 2d ed. (Buenos Aires, 1971), 7–239.

2. Samuel L. Baily, *Labor, Nationalism and Politics in Argentina* (New Brunswick, N.J., 1967), 26; David Rock, *Politics in Argentina 1890–1930* (London, 1975), 86–87.

3. This analysis is primarily based on the pathbreaking work of Rock. Also see Joel Horowitz, "Ideologías sindicales y políticas estatales en la Argentina, 1930–1943," *Desarrollo Económico*, no. 94 (July/Sept. 1984), 275–96.

4. Robert E. Shipley, "On the Outside Looking In" (Ph.D. dissertation, Rutgers University, 1977), 282–87; Rock, 89–91, 129–31; Marotta, II, 202–6.

5. Heidi Goldberg, "Railroad Unionization in Argentina, 1912–1929" (Ph.D. dissertation, Yale University, 1979), 158–71; Rock, 138–43; Alfredo Fernández, *El movimiento obrero en la Argentina* (Buenos Aires, 1936–37), I, nos. 4–5, 217–28; Paul Goodwin, *Los ferrocarriles británicos y la UCR* (Buenos Aires, 1974), 74–86.

6. Rock, 152–53, 288–98; Peter H. Smith, *Politics and Beef in Argentina* (New York, 1969), 71–73.

7. Marotta, II, 207–87; Rock, 125–79.

8. Edgardo J. Bilsky, *La Semana Trágica* (Buenos Aires, 1984); Oddone, *Gremialismo*, 403–14; Abad de Santillán, *La FORA*, 243–54.

9. FOET, *Luchas y conquistas* (Buenos Aires, 1944), 8–18.

10. Rock, 180–217; Shipley, 292–312; Marotta, III, 38–49; Osvaldo Bayer, *Los vengadores de la Patagonia trágica*, 3 vols. (Buenos Aires, 1972–74).

11. Rock, 216–17, 245–46.

12. See Antonio Tramonti's comments in UF, "Libros de actas de la Comisión Directiva," 22 (20 Dec. 1933), 44, 53–55, and below; also UF, *Memoria y balance de la Comisión Directiva, 1922/23* (Buenos Aires, 1924), 35 (hereafter UF, *Memoria year*); UF, *Memoria 1930*, 18.

13. Partido Socialista, *Anuario socialista 1930* (Buenos Aires, 1929), 149–51; Unión Tranviarios, *Reseña de la labor sindical (1919–1933)* (Buenos Aires, 1933), 11; and below.

14. Richard J. Walter, *The Socialist Party of Argentina, 1890–1930* (Austin, 1977), 202; Marotta, III, esp. 206, 250.

15. Goldberg, 315–20; Walter, *The Socialist Party*, 203–4, 225; Marotta, III, 125–27, 176–78, 191–203.

16. Alfredo López, *¿Qué pasa en la Confederación General del Trabajo?* (Buenos Aires, 1943), 6–9; Partido Socialista, *Anuario socialista 1930*, 53–54; Val Lorwin, *The French Labor Movement* (Cambridge, 1966), 35.

17. Rubens Iscaro, *Historia del movimiento sindical* (Buenos Aires, 1973), II, 200–206; U.S. Embassy, Buenos Aires, 8 Sept. 1930; National Archives Record Group 59, File no. 835.00B/30 (hereafter U.S. Embassy, Buenos Aires, date, file no.); Confederación Sindical Latino-Americana, *Bajo la bandera de la CSLA* (Montevideo, 1929), 7, 299.

18. *El Trabajador Latino Americano*, Aug./Sept. 1930, supplement, 10–11; Confederación Sindical Latino-Americana, 256–57; Carlos M. Silveyra, *El comunismo en la Argentina* (Buenos Aires, 1936), 140–48.

19. Alfredo López, *Historia del movimiento social y la clase obrera argentina* (Buenos Aires, 1971), 275; Lewis Lorwin, *Labor and Internationalism* (New York, 1929), 408–9; Alberto Belloni, *Del anarquismo al peronismo* (Buenos Aires, 1960), 39.

20. *La Vanguardia*, 1 May 1930; Rock, 220; A. López, *Historia del movimiento social*, 275; Partido Socialista, *Anuario socialista 1930*, 140; Moises Poblete Troncoso, *El movimiento obrero latinoamericano* (Mexico, 1946); Diego Abad de Santillán, "El movimiento obrero argentino ante el golpe de estado del 6 de septiembre de 1930," *Revista de Historia* 3 (Buenos Aires, 1958), 130.

21. Rubén Rotandaro, *Realidad y cambio en el sindicalismo* (Buenos Aires, 1971), 96; Partido Socialista, *Anuario socialista 1930*, 162–65, 241; Abad de Santillán, *La FORA*, 276–77; Rock, 71–91, 210–16; Marotta, II, 217–18, 280; Martín Casaretto, *Historia del movimiento obrero argentino* (Buenos Aires, 1946), I, 123.

22. Marotta, III, 287–99; Oddone, *Gremialismo*, 450–55; Andrés Cabona, Instituto Di Tella Oral History Program, 37 (hereafter IDTOHP); CGT, *Acta del congreso general constituyente* (Buenos Aires, 1936), 41–47.

23. FOET, 22–33; Luis Gay, IDTOHP, 1–8; author's interview with Luis Gay, 11 Nov. 1975; Marotta, III, 265–66.

24. Author's interview with Luis Gay, 17 Oct. 1975; Gay, IDTOHP, 2–5; FOET, 34–37, 206–19; Cámara de Diputados, Comisión Especial de Estudio del Régimen

Legal de Telecomunicaciones, *Publicación de antecedentes* (Buenos Aires, 1936), 67; U.S. Embassy, Buenos Aires, 25 Sept. 1930, 835.504/67.

25. FOET, 40–50; Marotta, III, 267–69; *La Vanguardia*, 9 May 1930.

26. *Review of the River Plate*: 3 Jan. 1930, 25; 31 Jan. 1930, 9; 14 Mar. 1930, 4, 7; U.S. Consulate, Rosario, 6 Feb. 1930, 835.504/54, 3–4; U.S. Embassy, Buenos Aires, 2 Apr. 1930, 835.504/56, and 25 Sept. 1930, 835.504/67.

27. *Federación*, Aug.–Nov./Dec. 1930; FOET, 63–71.

28. *Federación*, Mar.–Aug. 1930; FOET, 53–61.

29. *CGT*, 11 Dec. 1936; Marotta, II, 253–55; Rotandaro, 83.

30. Ernesto Janín, IDTOHP, 14–16; Partido Socialista, *Anuario socialista 1928*, 164–66, and *Anuario socialista 1930*, 139; FEC, *Informe del Concejo administrativo. Asamblea general ordinaria, 26 de agosto de 1930* (Buenos Aires, 1930), 20–31; FOEF, *Motivos de su creación* (Buenos Aires, 1939), 20.

31. Casaretto, I, 179–81; Francisco Pérez Leirós, IDTOHP, 13; Rock, 132–34; Partido Socialista, *Anuario socialista 1930*, 209–11; Dario Cantón, José Luis Moreno, and Alberto Ciria, *Argentina: La democracia constitucional y su crisis*, 87; vol. 6 of *Colección historia argentina*, ed. Tulio Halperín Donghi (Buenos Aires, 1972).

32. Richard J. Walter, "Municipal Politics and Government in Buenos Aires, 1918–1930," *Journal of Interamerican Studies and World Affairs* 16 (May 1974), 176; Casaretto, I, 181.

33. Partido Socialista, *Anuario socialista 1930*, 211–12; Concejo Deliberante de la Ciudad de Buenos Aires, *Actas del H. Concejo Deliberante*, II, 28 June 1932, 2277; Municipalidad de la Ciudad de Buenos Aires, *Presupuesto general de gastos y cálculo de recursos 1930* (Buenos Aires, 1929), 173; *La Vanguardia*, 26 Oct. 1930.

34. Pedro Otero, IDTOHP, 25; *La Vanguardia*, 20 Nov. 1932; Liga Patriótica Argentina, "Sindicatos obreros de la Capital Federal," enclosure in U.S. Embassy, Buenos Aires, 3 Oct. 1932, 835.00B/69.

35. Marcelino Buyán, *Una avanzada obrera* (Buenos Aires, 1933), 9–10, 28–29; Juan B. Chiti and Francisco Agnelli, *Cincuentenario de "La Fraternidad"* (Buenos Aires, 1937), 22–25, 457; Goldberg, 10, 41–52; Ruth Thompson, "The Engine Drivers' and Firemen's Strike of 1912" (unpublished); A. Fernández, *El movimiento obrero*, I, nos. 4–5, 184–87; William Rögind, *Historia del Ferrocarril Sud* (Buenos Aires, 1937), 481–83.

36. Goldberg, 53–193; A. Fernández, *El movimiento obrero*, I, nos. 4–5, 217–45; II, 251–53; Goodwin, 69–148; Rock, 138–52; Chiti and Agnelli, 319–28, 383–404; Ruth Thompson, "The Making of the Confraternidad Ferroviaria" (unpublished); Manuel F. Fernández, *La Unión Ferroviaria a través del tiempo* (Buenos Aires, 1948), 83–101, 117–26; Rögind, 563–65.

37. Chiti and Agnelli, 404–6; Goldberg, 194–257; M. Fernández, 125–48.

38. UF, *Memoria 1922/1923*, 4–6; Goldberg, 257–72.

39. Goodwin, 194–95; M. Fernández, 132–33.

40. *Review of the River Plate*, 21 Mar. 1930, 23; Partido Socialista, *Anuario socialista 1931*, 134–35; Camilo Almarza, IDTOHP, 65–67; José Domenech, IDTOHP, 28–29, 97; M. Fernández, 281–82.

41. Goodwin, 219–59; Goldberg, 278–83; Félix Luna, *Ortiz* (Buenos Aires, 1978), 41–42, 96; *El Obrero Ferroviario*, 16 Oct. 1942.

42. *El Obrero Ferroviario*, 16 Mar.–1 Apr. 1930; *Review of the River Plate*, 14 Mar. 1930, 11, and 21 Mar. 1930, 5, 7; M. Fernández, 236–37; Comisión Especial de Representantes de Empresas y Obreros Ferroviarios, *Revisión de escalafones, convenios y reglamentos* (Buenos Aires, 1930); Rögind, 663–65; Goodwin, 276–83.

43. Chiti and Agnelli, 408–14; Goldberg, 324–34.

44. Fábrica Argentina de Alpargatas, "Libro de Actas," 1, 12 Aug. 1901, 235 (kindly provided by Donna Guy); A. Fernández, *El movimiento obrero*, I, no. 1, xxxix; *El Obrero Textil*, Nov. 1933; Adolfo Dorfman, *Historia de la industria argentina* (Buenos Aires, 1970), 266; Iscaro, II, 209; author's interview with Jorge Michellón, 24 June 1976; Edgardo Bilsky, "Etnicidad y clase obrera: La presencia judía en el movimiento obrero argentino," paper presented to the Latin American Labor Conference, 1988.

Chapter 5: The Difficult Years, 1930–1935

1. Diego Abad de Santillán, "El movimiento obrero argentino ante el golpe de estado del 6 de septiembre de 1930," *Revista de Historia*, no. 3 (Buenos Aires, 1958), 127–30; David Rock, *Politics in Argentina 1890–1930* (London, 1975), 261.

2. *La Vanguardia*, 8, 9, and 11 Sept. 1930; *Federación*, Sept. 1930.

3. *La Vanguardia*, 28 Jan. 1931; U.S. Embassy, Buenos Aires, 7 Oct. 1930, National Archives Record Group 59, File No. 835.00B/31 (hereafter U.S. Embassy, Buenos Aires, date, file no.); José Peter, *Crónicas proletarias* (Buenos Aires, 1968), 140–42. See also Pascual Vuotto, *Vida de un proletario (El proceso de Bragado)* (Buenos Aires, 1975), 153–55, Roberto Marrone, *Apuntes para la historia de un gremio (Empleados de Comercio de Rosario)* (Rosario, 1974), 126–27; Chapter 1 above.

4. U.S. Embassy, Buenos Aires: 7 Oct. 1930, 835.5045/226; 9 Oct. 1930, 835.5045/227; and 30 Oct. 1930, 835.00B/34; *La Vanguardia*, Oct. 1930; *Review of the River Plate*, 10 Oct. 1930, 13.

5. Author's interview with Jorge Michellón, 29 Mar. 1976; Rufino Gómez, *La gran huelga petrolera de Comodoro Rivadavia (1931–1932)* (Buenos Aires, 1973), 20–28. For the advantages of unions with party backing, see Joel Horowitz, "Ideologías sindicales y políticas estatales en la Argentina, 1930–1943," *Desarrollo Económico*, no. 94 (July/Sept. 1984).

6. *Federación*, Sept. and Oct. 1930; FOET, *Luchas y conquistas* (Buenos Aires, 1944), 64–66; René Stordeur, Instituto Di Tella Oral History Program, 55–56 (hereafter IDTOHP); Luis Ramicone, IDTOHP, 8–9; *La Vanguardia*, esp. 15 Sept. and 24 Dec. 1930 and 13 June 1931; *El Obrero Ferroviario*, 1 Oct. 1930.

7. See, for example, David Tamarin, *The Argentine Labor Movement, 1930–1945* (Albuquerque, N.M., 1985), 85–88.

8. DNT, *Crónica mensual*, Sept. 1930, 3310–11.

9. *La Vanguardia*, 2 Oct. 1930.

10. Eduardo F. Maglione, "Mi experiencia en el Departamento Nacional del Trabajo," *Revista de Derecho Social*, July 1931, 143–52; *La Vanguardia*, esp. 6 Dec. 1930 and 20 Jan., 24 May, and 29 July–2 Aug. 1931; Chapter 7 below.

11. *El Obrero Ferroviario*, 1 Nov. 1930.

12. *La Vanguardia*, 20 Jan. 1931.

13. FOET, 80–81; author's interview with Luis Gay, 28 July 1976.

14. *La Prensa*, 22 Aug. 1931; DNT, *Boletín informativo*, Apr. 1934, 3918–19.

15. For union strength in 1932, Liga Patriótica Argentina, "Sindicatos obreros de la Capital Federal," enclosure in U.S. Embassy, Buenos Aires, 3 Oct. 1932, 835.00B/69.

16. *Review of the River Plate*, 26 Feb. 1932, 5–9; Sebastián Marotta, *El movimiento sindical argentino* (Buenos Aires, 1970), III, 323–26; Gómez; Peter, 141–73.

17. See Celia Durruty, *Clase obrera y peronismo* (Córdoba, 1969); *El Trabajador Latino Americano*, Oct./Nov. 1935; *El Obrero Ferroviario*, 16 Aug. 1935; Partido Comunista de la Argentina, *Ezbozo de historia del Partido Comunista de la Argentina* (Buenos Aires, 1947), 82–83.

18. *La Vanguardia*: 14 Dec. 1930; 1 Jan., 1 June, and 3 Nov. 1931; 16–20 Jan. 1932; *La Nación*, 10 Dec. 1930; Andrés Cabona, IDTOHP, 60–67; Marotta, III, 309–10.

19. Liga Patriótica Argentina; *El Obrero Ferroviario*, 16 Apr. 1933.

20. *La Vanguardia*, 9 Nov. 1933.

21. *El Obrero Ferroviario*, 16 Mar.–16 May 1934; Marotta, III, 376–84; *La Vanguardia*, Nov.–Dec. 1933.

22. Horowitz, "Ideologías sindicales"; *El Obrero Ferroviario*, 20 Dec. 1935 and 1 Mar. 1936; *La Vanguardia*, 13 Dec. 1935; Andrés Cabona: IDTOHP, 93, and "Un homenaje y una reivindicación," in *Vida, obra y trascendencia de Sebastián Marotta*—collected work of various authors (Buenos Aires, 1971), 144.

23. See *La Vanguardia*, 13–24 Dec. 1935; *Federación*, Dec. 1935; Chapter 8 below.

24. *Federación*, Sept.–Nov./Dec. 1930; FOET, 63–77; author's interview with Luis Gay, 1 Nov. 1975; *Revista Telefónica Argentina*, Sept. 1930; Cámara de Diputados, Comisión Especial de Estudio del Régimen Legal de Telecomunicaciones, *Publicación de antecedentes* (Buenos Aires, 1936), 13 (hereafter *Antecedentes*); *La Vanguardia*, 17 June 1932.

25. For contrasting views, see *Federación*, esp. Nov. 1933, and *Revista Telefónica Argentina*. See also Cía. Unión Telefónica del Río de la Plata, *Cincuenta años de vida, 1887–1937* (Buenos Aires, 1937), 47.

26. Luis Gay, IDTOHP, 25–26; author's interviews with Luis Gay, 10 Dec. 1975 and 17 Feb. 1976; *La Vanguardia*, 26 Aug. and 25 Sept.–1 Oct. 1931.

27. Dues calculated from *Federación*, 1930–32.

28. *La Vanguardia*, esp. 5 Nov. and 16 Dec. 1930, Oct.–Nov. 1931; *Federación*, esp. Nov./Dec. 1930 and Nov. 1931; FOET, 91–95; Rodolfo Araoz Alfaro, *El recuerdo y las cárceles (memorias amables)* (Buenos Aires, 1967), 53.

29. *Federación*, 4 Dec. 1931, Feb. and Mar. (special issue) 1932; *La Vanguardia*, 10 Dec. 1931.

30. Author's interviews with Luis Gay, 11 Nov. and 10 Dec. 1975; Luis Gay, IDTOHP, 17; *La Nación*, 24 May 1932; *La Vanguardia*, 25 and 26 May 1932; U.S. Embassy, Buenos Aires, 3 June 1932, 835.5045/235; FOET, 162. For a day-to-day account of the violence, see *La Nación*.

31. Amancio Spagnuolo, "Lo que piensa la gente de la huelga telefónica," *Atlántida*, 30 June 1932, 53 (scrapbook Gay). See also Ricardo T. Mulleady, *Breve historia de la telefonía argentina (1886–1956)* (Buenos Aires, 1956), 27; Dirección General de Correos y Telégrafos, *Antecedentes de la situación económica, financiera, industrial, etc. de la Compañia Unión Telefónica* (Buenos Aires, 1937), 167.

32. *Federación*, Aug. 1932; *La Nación*, 15 July 1932; *La Vanguardia*, 16 July 1932; FOET, 225–26; Chapter 7 below.

33. Gay, "Historia de la FOET," 5 (unpublished manuscript; title and pagination mine); *Federación*, esp. Oct. 1932, Feb.–Mar. 1933, Aug. and Oct. 1934, and Sept.–Nov. 1935; FOET, 165–69; Cámara de Diputados, *Antecedentes*, 67.

34. Dues-payers calculated from *Federación*, 1932–36; see also *El Obrero Ferroviario*, 1 May 1933; Gay, "Historia de la FOET," 31–32; *Federación*, Oct. 1935.

35. *Federación*, Nov. 1934–Sept. 1935; FOET 227–33.

36. *La Vanguardia*: 29 Sept., 19 Nov., and 24 Dec. 1930; 8 Jan. and 7 Feb. 1931; *La Prensa*, 28 Jan. 1931; *Review of the River Plate*, 30 Jan. 1931, 11.

37. Ernesto Janín, IDTOHP, 16–17; René Stordeur, IDTOHP, 462–64; *La Vanguardia*: 11–15 Mar.; 2–6, 11, 19 Apr.; and 23 Sept. 1931.

38. Personal communication from Michael F. Mullaney; *La Vanguardia*, 5 Jan. 1932; Juan Rodríguez, IDTOHP, 34–35; Camilo Almarza, IDTOHP, 41–42; Pedro Otero, IDTOHP, 55–57; Francisco Pérez Leirós, IDTOHP, 129–30.

39. *La Vanguardia*, 21 May 1935.

40. For example, *La Prensa*, 1, 3 Sept. 1932, and 4, 9 Sept. 1934; *La Nación*, 27 Dec. 1935.

41. *La Vanguardia*, 28 Jan.–30 Sept. 1932; Cámara de Diputados, *Diario de sesiones*, VI, 27–28 Sept. 1932, 834; *Anales de legislación argentina* (Buenos Aires, 1953), III, 270.

42. Cámara de Diputados, *Diario de sesiones*, III: 24 June 1932, 421–31; 6 July 1932, 615–45; 11 July 1932, 681–703; *Anales de legislación argentina*, III, 516–17. For detailed information on the campaign, see *La Vanguardia*.

43. *Anales de legislación argentina*, III, 477–83; Angel G. Borlenghi, *Beneficios del nuevo artículo 157 del código de comercio* (Buenos Aires, 1934), 9–13.

44. *La Vanguardia*: 29 Jan.; 3, 9 Feb.; and 10, 16 Mar. 1932.

45. *La Vanguardia*, 24 June and 17, 20 July 1932; Borlenghi, *Beneficios del nuevo artículo 157*, 14.

46. See *La Vanguardia*; esp. Feb.–July 1932 and 28 Sept. 1933.

47. *La Vanguardia*: 4, 20, 26 June; 7, 8 July; and 7 Aug.–11 Sept. 1932.

48. Marrone, 133; *La Vanguardia*, 13, 15 Sept. and 18 Nov. 1932.

49. *La Vanguardia*, 5–12 Oct. 1932 and Apr.–Sept. 1933.

50. Cámara de Diputados, *Diario de sesiones*: I, 7 May 1934, 179–80, and III, 18 July 1934, 411–34; Cámara de Senadores, *Diario de sesiones*, II, 18 Sept. 1934, 329–44; *La Vanguardia*, Oct. 1933 and Feb.–Sept. 1934; Borlenghi, *Beneficios del nuevo artículo 157*, 13.

51. See *La Vanguardia*, 8 Jan., 18 June, and 25 July 1933; DNT, *Boletín informativo*, Sept./Oct. 1936, 4736; Liga Patriótica Argentina.

52. FEC, *Memoria de la Comisión Directiva, febrero de 1935–octubre de 1936* (Buenos Aires, 1936), 25–34; *La Vanguardia*, 17 June, 15 Oct., and 3 Dec. 1935.

53. Concejo Deliberante de la Ciudad de Buenos Aires, *Actas del H. Concejo Deliberante*: I, 4 Mar. 1932, 58–66; II, 28 June 1932, 2213–32; III, 27 Sept. 1932, 3065–80, esp. 3066 (hereafter Concejo Deliberante, *Actas*); *La Vanguardia*: esp. 5, 23 Feb.; 20 May; 24, 25 June; and 14–18 Nov., 1931.

54. *La Vanguardia*, 19 Dec. 1930 and 20 Nov. 1932.

55. See Chapter 7 below; *La Vanguardia*, 11, 20 Sept., 26 Oct., and 7 Nov. 1930; 19 Jan., 31 Oct. 1931; 2 Feb. 1932.

56. Concejo Deliberante, *Actas*, I: 19 Feb. 1932, 1–3, and 1 May 1934, 1–3. For the UOEM's political ties, see Chapters 3 above and 8 below.

57. Concejo Deliberante, *Actas*: I, 26 Apr. 1932, 796–97; III, 11 Oct. 1932, 3376–77; IV, 4 Nov. 1932, 3825–27; *La Vanguardia*, 28 Apr. 1932.

58. *La Vanguardia*, 23 Dec. 1933; Concejo Deliberante, *Actas*, IV, 22 Dec. 1933, 4100–22; *Boletín municipal*, 30 Dec. 1933, 2620–21.

59. Concejo Deliberante, *Actas*, IV: 2 Dec. 1932, 4404, and 20 Dec. 1932, 4773.

60. Joel Horowitz, "The Impact of Pre-1943 Labor Union Traditions on Peronism," *Journal of Latin American Studies* 15, 1 (May 1983), 110–15. For examples of social activities, *La Vanguardia*, 5, 15 Feb., 27 May 1932, and 8 Sept. 1935; also Unión Obreros Municipales, *Dignificado en vacaciones* (Buenos Aires, 1940); *El Obrero Ferroviario*, 16 Feb. 1935.

61. *La Vanguardia*, 11 Dec. 1932; *El Obrero Municipal*, 16 Dec. 1934.

62. Membership figures for 1932 from *La Vanguardia* and for 1933–35 from *El Obrero Municipal*.

63. *La Nación*, 11–13 Sept. 1930; *Review of the River Plate*, 12 Sept. 1930, 28; *La Vanguardia*, 9 and 13 Sept. 1930; *El Obrero Ferroviario*, 16 Sept. 1930.

64. Juan Manuel Santa Cruz, *Ferrocarriles argentinos* (Santa Fe, 1966), 33; Dirección General de Ferrocarriles, *Estadística de los ferrocarriles en explotación, 1934*, 43 (Buenos Aires, 1936), 315.

65. *La Vanguardia*, esp. 28 Nov. and 3 Dec. 1930; *El Obrero Ferroviario*, esp. 16 Dec. 1930 and 1 Aug. 1931.

66. *La Prensa*, esp. 15 Aug. and 20 Nov. 1931; *La Vanguardia*, esp. 9, 10 Sept. and 3 Oct. 1931; *El Obrero Ferroviario*, 1 Sept.–16 Oct. 1931; UF, "Libros de actas de La Comisión Directiva," 13 (20 Aug. 1930), 4–8, and 18 (21 Oct. 1931), 4–13 (hereafter UF, "Actas").

67. *El Obrero Ferroviario*, 16 Oct. 1931–1 Mar. 1932; UF, "Actas," 18–21 (21 Oct.–9 Dec. 1931); *La Vanguardia*, esp. 3 Oct. and 20 Nov. 1931; *La Prensa*, 18–20 Nov. 1931; Chapter 8 below.

68. For dissent, see *El Obrero Ferroviario*, 1 Feb. and 1/20 June 1932; for the seniority dispute, Ferrocarril Oeste de Buenos Aires, *El "trabajo a reglamento" ante el poder ejecutivo, la justicia federal y la opinión pública* (Buenos Aires, 1932); *La Nación*, 18 May–12 June 1932; *La Vanguardia*, 18 May–12 June 1932; Cámara de Diputados, *Diario de sesiones*: II, 1 June 1932, 673–79, and 8 June 1932, 870–75, 981–87; III, 13 June 1932, 122–33.

69. *El Obrero Ferroviario*, 16 May 1932–1 Feb. 1933, esp. 16 Jan.; also 1/16 June 1933; *La Vanguardia*, 14 May 1932–1 Feb. 1933, esp. 30 Dec. 1932; UF, "Actas": 1 (3 Jan. 1933), 1–25; 3 (26 Jan. 1933), 2–9; Robert Potash, *The Army and Politics, 1928–1945* (Stanford, 1969), 82; Félix Luna, *Ortiz* (Buenos Aires, 1978), 157.

70. *El Obrero Ferroviario*, 1/16 July 1934.

71. *La Prensa*, 8 Aug.–26 Sept. 1934; *La Vanguardia*, 8 Aug.–26 Sept. 1934; *El Obrero Ferroviario*, 1 Sept.–1 Oct. 1934.

72. *El Obrero Ferroviario*, 1/16 June 1935; UF, "Actas," 14 (24 Sept. 1934), 6–19.

73. Manuel F. Fernández, *La Unión Ferroviaria a través del tiempo* (Buenos Aires, 1948), 190–96.

74. Instituto de Estudios Económicos del Transporte, *Salarios ferroviarios y costo de la vida* (Buenos Aires, 1943), 20; *El Obrero Ferroviario*, 1 Jan.–1 Aug. 1935.

75. UF, *Memoria y balance de la Comisión Directiva, 1930* (Buenos Aires, 1931), 18; *El Obrero Ferroviario*, 16 May 1939.

76. *La Vanguardia*, esp. 23–27 Sept. 1930; DNT, *Crónica mensual*, Oct./Dec. 1930, 3338–45; Lucio Bonilla, IDTOHP, 22–23, 54–55; Mariano Tedesco, IDTOHP, 12–13; interview with Jorge Michellón conducted by Juan Carlos Torre; author's interview with Jorge Michellón, 29 Mar. 1976.

77. *La Vanguardia*: 12 Mar., 7 Aug., and 6 Oct., 1931; 29 Feb.–15 Mar. 1932.

78. *La Vanguardia*: 24 Dec. 1930; 24 Feb., 1 May–5 July, and 14 Aug. 1931.

79. *El Obrero Textil*, June 1938; DNT, *Boletín informativo*: Apr. 1934, 3913, 3919.

80. *La Vanguardia*, 14 and 16 Apr. 1932; *El Obrero Textil*, Nov. 1933 and Aug. 1934.

81. *La Vanguardia*, 23 Feb.–6 Apr. 1933; *El Obrero Textil*, Apr. 1933 and 1 May 1934; *Federación*, Apr. 1933; *El Obrero Ferroviario*, 16 Apr. 1933.

82. DNT, *Boletín informativo*: July/Sept. 1935, 4353, 4359; Apr./June 1936, 4596; Liga Patriótica Argentina; *El Obrero Textil*, 1 May and Aug. 1934, July 1935, and Dec. 1941; Camilo Almarza, IDTOHP, 96.

83. The first post-suppression reference to the FOIT (except for its presence at conferences) appears in *La Vanguardia*, 1 Mar. 1933. See also *El Trabajador Latino Americano*, Nov./Dec. 1931 and Nov. 1932. For friction between the two unions, see *El Obrero Textil*, Aug. 1934.

84. *La Vanguardia*: 21, 23 June; 17, 27 July; and 6, 12 Aug. 1935; 6 Jan. 1936; author's interview with Jorge Michellón, 24 June 1976.

85. *El Obrero Textil*, July 1935; *La Vanguardia*, 15 June and 12 July 1935.

86. *El Obrero Textil*, Mar. 1935, May 1936, and May–June 1937; *La Vanguardia*, Feb.–Sept. 1935, esp. 13 June; author's interview with Jorge Michellón, 8 Jan. 1976.

87. *El Obrero Textil*, Mar. 1935; author's interview with Jorge Michellón, 29 Mar. 1976; interview with Jorge Michellón conducted by Juan Carlos Torre.

Chapter 6: Growth and Frustration, 1936–1943

1. DNT, *Boletín informativo*, Sept./Oct. 1936, 4728–54; Carlos F. Díaz Alejandro, *Essays on the Economic History of the Argentine Republic* (New Haven, 1970), 428; Arthur M. Ross and Paul T. Hartman, *Changing Patterns of Industrial Conflict* (New York, 1960), 17; Miguel de Andrea, *El catolicismo en la acción gremial* (Buenos Aires, 1945), 181–312; Federación de Asociaciones Católicas de Empleadas, *Reseña de su obra social* (Buenos Aires, 1944).

2. For the Communists, see *La Vanguardia*, Jan.–Mar. 1936.

3. *La Vanguardia*, 1 and 14 Jan. 1936; Andrés Cabona, Instituto Di Tella Oral History Program, 91, 109–10 (hereafter IDTOHP); *Federación*, Aug. 1936; Chapter 7 below; for the political history of the unions, see Chapter 8 below.

4. *CGT*, 12 June 1936, 9 July 1937, 25 Mar. 1938, 14 July 1939, and 11 July 1941; Celia Durruty, *Clase obrera y peronismo* (Córdoba, 1969), 59; José Peter, *Crónicas proletarias* (Buenos Aires, 1968), 182–83.

5. See Tables 5-1 and 5-2 above. Statistics limited to the capital were less valid as the decade progressed. Unfortunately, a complete set of statistics for the province of Buenos Aires could not be located.

6. *La Vanguardia*, 1 and 2/3 May 1936; Marilú Bou, "1936: El fraude, el frente, el fascismo," *Todo es Historia*, Feb. 1987, 8–25; Enrique Pereira, "La guerra civil española en la Argentina," *Todo es Historia*, July 1976, 6–32; *Federación*, Dec. 1936, special issue; see also any union paper from 1936 to 1939.

7. See below; also see *La Hora* and *La Vanguardia*, May–June 1940; CGT, *Actas de las reuniones del Comité Central Confederal: Efectuadas en mayo de 1940 y en octubre de 1942* (Buenos Aires, 1942).

8. Victorio Codovilla, *Nuestro camino desemboca en la victoria* (Buenos Aires, 1954), 414–28; Partido Comunista de la Argentina, *Ezbozo de historia del Partido*

Comunista de la Argentina (Buenos Aires, 1947), 100–101; DNT, División de Estadística, *Investigaciones sociales 1942* (Buenos Aires, 1943), 90–105.

9. Mario Rapoport, *Gran Bretaña, Estados Unidos y las clases dirigentes argentinas, 1940–1945* (Buenos Aires, 1980), 203, n. 254. See also author's interviews with Luis V. Sommi, 24 Aug. 1976, and Jorge Michellón, 8 Jan. 1976; Angel Perelman, *Cómo hicimos el 17 de octubre* (Buenos Aires, 1961), 29–33.

10. *La Vanguardia*, 14 June 1943; *El Obrero Textil*, Apr. 1943, special issue; *Crítica*, 30 Oct.–1 Nov. 1942.

11. Juan Raúl Pichetto, "The Present State of Social Legislation in the Argentine Republic," *International Labor Review* 46 (Oct. 1942), 416; CGT, *Memoria y balance, período 1939–1942* (Buenos Aires, 1942), 32 (hereafter CGT, *Memoria 1939–1942*); Provincia de Buenos Aires, Departamento del Trabajo, *Condiciones de vida de la familia obrera* (La Plata, 1943),103–12; Manuel A. Fresco, *Cómo encaré la política obrera durante mi gobierno* (La Plata, 1940).

12. Ricardo Gaudio and Jorge Pilone: "El desarrollo de la negociación colectiva durante la etapa de modernización industrial en la Argentina, 1935–1943," *Desarrollo Económico*, no. 90 (July/Sept. 1983), 255–86, and "Estado y relaciones laborales en el período previo al surgimiento del peronismo, 1935–1943," *Desarrollo Económico*, no. 94 (July/Sept. 1984), 235–73.

13. Gaudio and Pilone, "Estado y relaciones laborales," provide information on types of negotiations but cover only 1941 and 1942. Information for 1937–40 is available in DNT, División de Estadística: *Estadística de las huelgas* (Buenos Aires, 1940), 13, 67–69, and *Estadística de las huelgas 1940* (Buenos Aires, 1941), 14.

14. Gaudio and Pilone, "El desarrollo de la negociación colectiva," 277. There are numerous examples throughout this volume of flouted contracts.

15. *El Obrero Ferroviario*, 16 Aug. 1936; *Federación*, Apr.–June 1937; DNT, *Boletín informativo*, Sept./Oct. 1936, 4733–54.

16. *Federación*, May 1937, 17 Feb. 1941, 27 May 1942, and 30 Apr. 1943; Jacinto Oddone, *Gremialismo proletario argentino*, 2d ed. (Buenos Aires, 1978), 494–502; Luis Gay, "Historia de la FOET," 56 (unpublished manuscript; title and paginación mine); René Stordeur, IDTOHP, 445–46; Andrés Cabona, IDTOHP, 114–15; author's interviews with Luis Gay, 28 June and 8 July 1976; *CGT*, 11 Oct. 1940.

17. *Federación*, esp. Apr. 1936, Aug. 1939, and 31 Aug. 1942.

18. Camilo Almarza, IDTOHP, 154–55.

19. *Review of the River Plate*, 19 Nov. 1937, 5; see also CGT, *Memoria y balance a considerar por el primer congreso ordinario* (Buenos Aires, 1939), 15; *CGT*, 28 Mar. 1941.

20. For example, *CGT*, 28 Mar. 1941 and 12 June 1942; CGT: *Acta del segundo congreso ordinario* (Buenos Aires, 1943), 127, and *Memoria 1939–1942*, 27, 49–53; *El Obrero Ferroviario*, 16 Mar. and 1 Apr. 1941; *La Hora*, 26–28 Jan. 1941.

21. UF, "Libros de actas de la Comisión Directiva," 3 (16/17 Mar. 1943), 15–16 (hereafter UF, "Actas"); *El Obrero Ferroviario*, 16 Mar. and 1, 16 May 1943; *La Hora*, 4, 5 Feb. and 10 Mar. 1943; *La Vanguardia*, 11–22 Mar. 1943; interview with

Hilario Fernando Salvo conducted by Robert J. Alexander, 7 Nov. 1946; Perelman, 42.

22. *Federación*, Mar. 1936–May 1937; FOET, *Luchas y conquistas* (Buenos Aires, 1944), 234–38.

23. *Federación*, Apr.–Oct. 1936 and Jan. 1937; Gay, "Historia de la FOET," 31–33.

24. *Federación*, esp. Aug.–Sept. 1935, Feb.–Mar. 1936, Mar.–July, Sept. 1937, and Feb./Mar. 1938; Gay, "Historia de la FOET," 20–24, 38–40.

25. *Federación*, Aug./Sept. 1938; see also Provincia de Santa Fe, Departamento del Trabajo, *Boletín mensual*, Aug. 1938, 1132–34, and Sept. 1938, 1152.

26. *Federación*: May–June 1939; June–Nov./Dec. 1940; 17 Feb. and Oct./Nov. 1941.

27. *Federación*, esp. Feb., July, and Aug. 1939; Gay, "Historia de la FOET," 57.

28. *Federación*, Mar.–July 1940.

29. *Federación*, 30 Apr. 1942–30 June 1943. For the text of the proposed escalafón, see 30 Nov. 1942.

30. CGEC, *Memoria del Concejo Administrativo, julio de 1936–mayo de 1939* (Buenos Aires, 1939), 49–110, esp. 66; *La Vanguardia*, esp. 23–25 Dec. 1935 and 18–26 Jan. 1936.

31. *Review of the River Plate*, 22 July 1938, 7, and 29 Oct. 1938, 9; CGT, *Memoria por el primer congreso*, 11–12; CGEC, *Memoria 1936/1939*, 99–100; *La Nación*, 28 and 29 Sept. 1938.

32. FEC: *Memoria de la Comisión Directiva del 1º de agosto de 1938 al 31 de julio de 1939* (Buenos Aires, 1939), 10–11 (hereafter FEC, *Memoria year*); *Memoria 1939/1941*, 9–12; Cámara de Diputados, *Diario de sesiones*, 1940–1941; Cámara de Diputados, División Archivo, Publicación y Museo, *Composición de la Cámara de Diputados de la Nación* (Buenos Aires, 1956), 36–39; Chapter 1 above.

33. DNT: *Boletín informativo*, Sept./Oct. 1936, 4736, and División de Estadística, *Organización sindical* (Buenos Aires, 1941), 6; CGEC, *Memoria 1936/1939*, 181; *La Vanguardia*, 24 Mar. 1942; Pan American Union, Division of Labor and Social Information, *Labor Trends and Social Welfare in Latin America 1941–42* (Washington, D.C., 1943), 3.

34. *La Vanguardia*: 4 Dec. 1932; 16 Jan. and 2 Mar. 1933; 20 Sept. 1935; *CGT*, 15 May 1942; *La Hora*, 9 Mar. 1943; Provincia de Santa Fe, Departamento del Trabajo, *Boletín mensual*, July 1938, 13.

35. *La Vanguardia*, 9 July 1935. See also Fresco, I, 173–97; CGEC, *Memoria 1936/1939*, 17–32.

36. DNT, *Boletín informativo*, Sept./Oct. 1936, 4736; FEC: *Memoria 1935/1936*, 6, and *Memoria 1936/1937*, 51–66, 82–83; *CGT*, 11–25 Dec. 1936; José Domenech, IDTOHP, 121; interview with Morris A. Schefer conducted by Robert J. Alexander, 10 July 1956.

37. FEC, *Memoria 1939/1941*, 25. See also *CGT*, 24 Dec. 1937; *La Hora*, 7 Feb. 1943; FEC, *Memoria 1938/1939*, 43–47.

38. FEC, *Memoria 1939/1941*, 23; see also 24–30.

39. For strikes see *CGT*: 20 Aug. 1937; 9 Sept. 1938–10 Mar. 1939; and 17, 24 Dec. 1940; FEC, *Memoria 1938/1939*, 50–59.

40. *CGT*, 24 Apr. 1942; DNT, *Adaptación de los salarios a las fluctuaciones del costo de la vida* (Buenos Aires, 1943), 43, 45.

41. Pan American Union, 3; Dirección Nacional de Estadística y Censos, *Cuarto censo general de la Nación* (Buenos Aires, 1949), III, 254–57.

42. *La Vanguardia*, 12 Mar. 1936; *La Prensa*, 12 Apr. 1938 and 16 Apr. 1940; Miguel Angel Scenna, "CHADE: El escándalo del siglo," in *Los grandes negociados*, ed. Félix Luna (Buenos Aires, 1976), 11–60.

43. *El Obrero Municipal*, 16 Feb. and 1 Apr. 1936; *La Vanguardia*, 29 and 31 Mar. 1936.

44. For an example of a campaign, see *La Vanguardia*, Oct. 1939–Jan. 1940; Francisco Pérez Leirós, *Situación del personal de la comuna* (Buenos Aires, 1941), 41–45. See also *CGT*, 6 Aug. 1937 and 1 Nov. 1940; Concejo Deliberante de la Ciudad de Buenos Aires, *Actas del H. Concejo Deliberante*: II, 10 Aug. 1937, 1249–1305, and 13 Aug. 1937, 1344–46; III, 30 Sept. 1937, 2123–28 (hereafter Concejo Deliberante, *Actas*).

45. Pedro Otero, IDTOHP, 32; Concejo Deliberante, *Actas*: I, 27 Apr. 1937, 712–13; II, 13 Aug. 1937, 1325; DNT: *Boletín informativo*, Sept./Oct. 1936, 4754, and *Organización sindical*, 6; *La Vanguardia*, 9 Dec. 1934; *El Municipal*, Feb. 1939; *El Obrero Municipal*, 1 Oct. 1944.

46. Pedro Otero, IDTOHP, 25; DNT, *Organización sindical*, 10; *Quién es quién, 1941* (Buenos Aires: Guillermo Kraft, 1940), 204–5.

47. *El Municipal*, esp. 15 Mar. 1937 and Mar. 1938. For pension board elections, see *La Nación*, 7 Dec. 1936 and 5 Dec. 1938; *El Obrero Municipal*, 16 Dec. 1940 and 1/16 Jan. 1943.

48. *La Hora*, 6 Dec. 1940. See estimates of membership and dues collected by the FOEM in *El Municipal*, Nov. 1937, Feb. 1939, Oct. 1940, and May 1941.

49. *El Obrero Municipal*, 15 Sept. 1941; *El Obrero Textil*, second fortnight Aug. 1941; *La Vanguardia*, 17 Aug. 1941; *CGT*, 26 Sept. 1941.

50. See Chapter 1 above; *El Obrero Municipal*, 1 Apr. 1942–16 May 1943; *La Vanguardia*, 2 June 1943; Comisión Interventora de Vecinos del Concejo Deliberante de la Ciudad de Buenos Aires, *Actas*, I, 2 June 1942, 151–52.

51. Municipalidad de la Ciudad de Buenos Aires, *Revista de Estadística*, Jan./June 1942, 111.

52. *El Obrero Ferroviario*, 16 July–16 Nov. 1936 and 1 Mar. 1937; Instituto de Estudios Económicos del Transporte, *Salarios ferroviarios y costo de la vida* (Buenos Aires, 1943), 20.

53. *El Obrero Ferroviario*, 1 July, 16 Aug., and 1 Sept. 1937; *CGT*, 13–20 Aug. 1937; *La Prensa*, 19–21 Aug. 1937; FOEF, *Motivos de su creación* (Buenos Aires, 1939), 47; U.S. Embassy, Buenos Aires, 26 Aug. 1937, National Archives Record Group 59, File No. 835.77/302.

54. *La Prensa*, 19 Aug. 1937; *El Obrero Ferroviario*: 1 Oct. and 16 Nov. 1937; 1 Apr.–1 Sept. 1938; *Review of the River Plate*: 12 Nov. 1937, 5; 19 Nov. 1937, 5, 11; 6 May 1938, 7.

55. *El Obrero Ferroviario*, 1 May–1 Aug. 1939; *La Vanguardia*, 8–21 July 1939.

56. *La Nación*, 25 July 1939–1 Mar. 1940; *La Vanguardia*, esp. 1–2 Aug., 6 Sept., and 17 Oct. 1939 and 3 Jan. 1940; *El Obrero Ferroviario*, 16 Aug. 1939–16 Mar. 1940; Cámara de Diputados, *Diario de sesiones*: III, 18 Aug. 1939, 143–84; 23 Aug. 1939, 254–87; 24 Aug. 1939, 320–24; II, 8 Aug. 1941, 923–30; *Review of the River Plate*, 23 Feb. 1940, 11–12.

57. UF, *Acta oficial de la XVIII asamblea general de delegados* (Buenos Aires, 1941), 37. See also Cámara de Diputados, *Diario de sesiones*, II, 8 Aug. 1941, 930–98; *El Obrero Ferroviario*, 16 Nov. 1940, 16 Apr., 16 June/1 July, and 16 July 1941; *La Nación*, 28 June 1941; *Review of the River Plate*, 15 Aug. 1941, 3–5.

58. *El Obrero Ferroviario*, 1 Nov. 1940–16 Apr. 1941; UF, *Acta de la XVIII asamblea*, 110–17; *La Hora*, 3–5 Jan. 1941 and 1 Nov. 1941–11 Feb. 1942; *La Vanguardia*: 5 Jan.; 2, 19, 27 Feb.; and 12 Mar. 1941.

59. *El Obrero Ferroviario*, 16 Dec. 1941–16 Apr. 1942; *La Vanguardia*, Feb. 1942; *La Hora*, 24–28 Feb. 1942; *La Prensa*, 24–28 Feb. 1942; *CGT*, 27 Feb.–27 Mar. 1942; *Review of the River Plate*, 27 Feb.–3 Apr. 1942; Caja Nacional de Jubilaciones y Pensiones de Empleados Ferroviarios, *Memoria correspondiente al año 1942* (Buenos Aires, 1943), 100.

60. *El Obrero Ferroviario*: 1 May–16 Oct. and 1 Dec. 1942; 1 Jan. 1943; UF: *Acta oficial de la XIX asamblea general ordinaria de delegados* (Buenos Aires, 1942), 159–60, and *Memoria y balance de La Comisión Directiva, 1942* (Buenos Aires, 1943), 14–18 (hereafter UF, *Memoria year*); *Review of the River Plate*, 4 Dec. 1942–5 Feb. 1943.

61. *El Obrero Ferroviario*, 1 Jan.–1/16 June 1943; *La Vanguardia*, Feb. and 4, 6 Mar. 1943; *La Nación*, Feb. and 4 Mar. 1943; *Review of the River Plate*: 26 Feb. 1943, 9; 28 May 1943, 7; UF, *Memoria 1942*, 18–21.

62. *La Hora*: 6–9 Mar. 1942; Nov. 1942–June 1943, esp. Feb. 1943; *El Obrero Ferroviario*, Nov. 1942–June 1943.

63. Ferrocarril Buenos Aires al Pacífico, *Reglamento escalafón para el personal de peones de caudrilla de vía* (Buenos Aires, 1938); *El Obrero Ferroviario*, 16 Mar. and 1 Apr. 1938.

64. *El Obrero Ferroviario*, 1 July, 1 Aug., and 1 Oct. 1939; *Federación*, 27 May 1942; UF, *Acta de la XVIII asamblea*, 26–27; DNT, *Organización sindical*, 6, 10; interview with Manuel Pardo conducted by Robert J. Alexander, 6 Nov. 1946; interview with Antonio Campos conducted by Robert J. Alexander, 6 Oct. 1946.

65. Joel Horowitz, "Occupational Community and the Creation of a Self-Styled Elite," *The Americas* 42, 1 (July 1985), 77–79; UF, *Memoria 1942*, 41.

66. Nora Gatica Krug, "Entrevista a Luis V. Sommi," *Boletín de Investigación del Movimiento Obrero* (Universidad Autonoma de Puebla) V, 8 (Mar. 1985), 159.

67. DNT: *Estadística de las huelgas*, 49, and *Boletín informativo*, Mar./Apr. 1937, 4927–47; Cámara de Diputados, *Diario de sesiones*, I, 9 June 1937, 570–73; *El Obrero*

Textil, 1 May, Oct., and Nov. 1936; Comité de Huelga de la Casa Gratry, *Informe y balance* (Buenos Aires, 1936).

68. *El Obrero Textil*, 1 May 1936–Feb. 1937; *CGT*, 18 Sept. 1936–5 Feb. 1937; DNT, *Boletín informativo*, Jan./Feb. 1937, 4848–54; *La Vanguardia*, 12 Jan.–4 Feb. 1937, esp. 20 Jan.

69. *La Vanguardia*, 8 and 21 Feb. 1937; *CGT*, 19 Feb.–1 Mar. 1937; *El Obrero Textil*, Mar. 1937; DNT, *Boletín informativo*, Jan./Feb. 1937, 4854–57; *La Voz Textil (Organo de los obreros textiles de V. Alsina)*, Aug. 1937.

70. Cámara de Diputados, *Diario de sesiones*, IV, 17 Sept. 1941, 568.

71. *El Obrero Textil*, July 1935, 1 May and Oct. 1936, June 1937, May 1938.

72. CGT, *Memoria por el primer congreso*, 15; *El Obrero Textil*, June–Sept. 1937 and June 1938; UOT, *Memoria y balance correspondiente al año 1939* (Buenos Aires, 1940), 14; *CGT*, 24 Sept.–15 Oct. 1937; *La Vanguardia*, 2–9 Oct. 1937.

73. *El Obrero Textil*, Dec. 1938 and Apr. 1939; *CGT*, 27 Jan.–10 Feb. 1939.

74. DNT, *Estadística de las huelgas*, 17.

75. UOT, 10–14, 46–50; *El Obrero Textil*, May–Aug. 1937, Dec. 1938, and June–Oct. 1939; *La Vanguardia*, 1 July–9 Sept. 1939; interview with Jorge Michellón conducted by Juan Carlos Torre.

76. CGT, *Memoria 1939–1942*, 47.

77. UOT, 14–17, 55–59; *El Obrero Textil*, Nov. 1939 and Jan. 1940; *La Vanguardia*, 14 Oct. –23 Dec. 1939; *CGT*, 17 Nov. 1939; Chapter 7 below.

78. UOT, 18–19; DNT, *Estadística de las huelgas*, 16; *El Obrero Textil*, May and June 1940; *La Vanguardia*, 9 Dec. 1939–11 May 1940; CGT, *Memoria 1939–1942*, 48; Unión Industrial Argentina, Confederación Argentina de Industrias Textiles, *Salarios mínimos en la industria textil* (Buenos Aires, 1946), 53–55.

79. UOT, 24; *El Obrero Textil*, Apr., Aug. 1939, Mar., June 1940, and Jan., May 1941.

80. *El Obrero Textil*: Jan. and July–Oct. 1940; second fortnight May 1 and first fortnight June 1941; Dec. 1942; *La Vanguardia*, esp. 4–20 Jan., 30 Mar., and 17–19 Apr. 1940; *CGT*, 5 Feb. 1941; *La Hora*, 20 May and 30 July 1940; interview with Jorge Michellón conducted by Juan Carlos Torre.

81. *CGT*, 5 Jan. 1940 and 7 Mar. 1941; DNT, *Estadística de las huelgas 1940*, 9; *La Vanguardia*, 7 Nov., 13 Dec. 1939 and 6 Apr. 1940; *El Obrero Textil*, Nov. 1939 and Jan. 1940.

82. *El Obrero Ferroviario*, 16 Jan./1 Feb. 1941.

83. *La Nación*, 29 Jan. 1941.

84. *La Vanguardia*, 16 Oct. 1940–24 Feb. 1941; *El Obrero Textil*, Oct. 1940–Mar. 1941; *CGT*, 25 Oct. 1940–21 Feb. 1941; CGT: *Actas del Comité Central Confederal*, 116–19, and *Memoria 1939–1942*, 49–53; interview with Jorge Michellón conducted by Juan Carlos Torre; author's interview with Jorge Michellón, 29 Mar. 1976; *El Obrero Ferroviario*, 16 Feb. 1941 and 16 July/1 Aug. 1943.

85. For example, *El Obrero Textil*, Nov. and Dec. 1942, Apr. 1943; *Crítica*, 1 Nov. 1942.

86. *El Obrero Textil*, Sept. 1941–Oct. 1942.

87. *El Obrero Textil*, Feb.–Dec. 1938, June 1940, and Jan./Feb. 1942; *CGT*, 30 Jan.–6 Mar. and 5 June 1942; UOT, 23; CGT, *Memoria 1939–1942*, 64; Juan Atilio Bramuglia, *Jubilaciones ferroviarias* (Buenos Aires, 1941), 25.

88. *El Obrero Textil*, Mar. 1941–Dec. 1942; *CGT*: 15 Aug. and 4 Sept. 1941; May, June, and July 1942; DNT, *Boletín informativo*: July/Sept. 1942, 197–205; Oct./Dec. 1942, 329–31; Provincia de Buenos Aires, Departamento del Trabajo, *Condiciones de vida*, 138–40; *La Vanguardia*, 7 May 1942 and 7 Jan. 1943.

89. For dues-payers see *El Obrero Textil*, 1942 and 1943; Dirección Nacional de Estadística y Censos, *Cuarto censo*, III, 26; DNT, *Organización sindical*, 10; Serafino Romualdi, "Notes on the Labor Movement of Argentina and Uruguay," 1 Sept. 1943 (collection of Robert J. Alexander).

90. DNT, *Organización sindical*, 27; Díaz Alejandro, *Essays*, 428.

Chapter 7: Union Relations with the Government, 1930–1943

1. For a discussion of politics as a game, see F. G. Baily, *Stratagems and Spoils* (New York, 1969).

2. See Ruth Berins Collier and David Collier, "Inducements vs. Constraints: Disaggregating Corporatism," *American Political Science Review* 73 (December 1979), 967–86.

3. J. David Greenstone, *Labor in American Politics* (New York, 1969), esp. 47, 67, 72–74; Collier and Collier; Juan Carlos Torre, "El rol del sindicalismo en los orígenes del peronismo" (Spanish version, doctoral dissertation, Ecole Pratique des Hautes Etudes, 1983), ch. 6, p. 15.

4. *Federación*, Sept. 1930.

5. *Federación*, Jan. 1931; FOET, *Luchas y conquistas* (Buenos Aires, 1944), 78–80; *La Vanguardia*, 14 Sept. 1930; Sebastián Marotta, *El movimiento sindical argentino* (Buenos Aires, 1970), III, 306–7; author's interview with Andrés Cabona, 5 Aug. 1976.

6. *La Vanguardia*: 8, 15, 23 Oct. and 5 Nov. 1930; 10 Feb. 1931; *Federación*, Oct. 1930 and Feb. 1931; FOET, 86–87.

7. *Federación*, 4 Dec. 1931, 11 May 1932 and May 1932, special issue; G-2 report from U.S. military attaché Argentina, report no. 4571, 16 May 1932, U.S. Embassy, Buenos Aires, National Archives Record Group 59, File No. 835.5045/240 (hereafter U.S. Embassy, Buenos Aires, date, file no.); *La Vanguardia*, 2/3, 4, and 24 May 1932.

8. *La Vanguardia*, 11 May 1932; *La Nación*, 11 May 1932; FOET, 114–16.

9. Author's interviews with Luis Gay, 10 Dec. 1975 and 17 Feb. 1976; *La Nación*, 24 May 1932; U.S. Embassy, Buenos Aires, 10 June 1932, 835.504/78, 9.

10. U.S. Embassy, Buenos Aires, 2 June 1932, 835.5045/234, 1–2. Daily articles on the strike in *La Nación*, 24 May–14 July 1932, give damage estimates. *Review of the River Plate* gives a more general picture. See *Review of the River Plate*, 3 June 1932, 7, and 8 July 1932, 8; *La Nación*, 17 June 1932; *La Vanguardia*, 7 and 8 July 1932; Luis Gay, Instituto Di Tella Oral History Program, 17 (hereafter IDTOHP).

11. *La Vanguardia*, esp. 24 and 27 May 1932; FOET, 129–31, 165; U.S. Embassy, Buenos Aires, 17 June 1932, 835.75/11, 3; Cámara de Diputados, *Diario de sesiones*, II, 3 June 1932, 824.

12. U.S. Embassy, Buenos Aires, 2 June 1932, 835.5045/234, 2–3.

13. *La Prensa*, 29 May 1932; *La Nación*, 3 and 17 June 1932; *Review of the River Plate*, 10 June 1932, 9.

14. *La Nación*, 2 June 1932.

15. *La Nación*, 3–16 June 1932; *La Vanguardia*, 3–15 June 1932; FOET, 148.

16. See Cámara de Diputados, *Diario de sesiones*, II, 3 June 1932, 821–40.

17. *La Vanguardia*, 19 June 1932. See also *La Nación*, 24 June 1932.

18. U.S. Embassy, Buenos Aires, 1 July 1932, 835.75/13, 1–2; see also 30 June 1932, 835.75/12, 1–2; *La Nación*, 28 June and 1 July 1932; FOET, 161–63; *La Vanguardia*, 1 July 1932.

19. *La Vanguardia*, 9 and 12–14 July 1932; *La Nación*, 10–14 July 1932; U.S. Embassy, Buenos Aires, 15 July 1932, 835.75/15, 1–4; *La República*, 12 July 1932 (scrapbook Gay).

20. FOET, 163–64; *La Vanguardia*, 30 July 1932; *La Prensa*, 20 Aug. 1932; author's interview with Luis Gay, 31 Mar. 1976.

21. U.S. Embassy, Buenos Aires, 2 June 1932, 835.5045/234, 3–4; Luis Gay, IDTOHP, 23–27; author's interviews with Luis Gay, 11 Nov. 1975, 31 Mar. and 5 May 1976; *La Prensa*, 29 May 1932; *Buenos Aires Herald*, 31 May and 2 June 1932 (enclosed in U.S. Embassy, Buenos Aires, 2 June 1932, 835.5045/234).

22. U.S. Embassy, Buenos Aires, 1 July 1932, 835.75/13, 2–3; *Review of the River Plate*, 20 Feb. 1931, 12.

23. *Review of the River Plate*, 17 June 1932, 28.

24. *Review of the River Plate*, 24 June 1932, 7; *La Vanguardia*, 12–21 June 1932, esp. 15 June; *La Nación*, 12–21 June 1932; Nicolas Repetto, *Mi paso por la política: De Uriburu a Perón* (Buenos Aires, 1957), 37–38; Robert A. Potash, *The Army and Politics, 1928–1945* (Stanford, 1969), 95.

25. *Review of the River Plate*, 22 July 1932, 9. See also Cámara de Diputados, *Diario de sesiones*, II, 3 June 1932, 820–40; Table 1-1 above.

26. Comité Pro Presos y Deportados de la FORA, *La FORA ante los tribunales* (Buenos Aires, 1934); *La Prensa*, 1–7 July 1932; *La Nación*, 1–7 July 1932.

27. Author's interviews with Luis Gay, 31 Mar. and 7 Apr. 1976.

28. *Federación*, Dec. 1932.

29. FEC: *Informe del Concejo Administrativo: Asamblea general ordinaria, 26 de agosto de 1930* (Buenos Aires, 1930), 15 (hereafter FEC, *Informe year*), and *Memoria de la Comisión Directiva del 1° de agosto de 1938 al 31 de julio de 1939* (Buenos Aires, 1939), 66 (hereafter FEC, *Memoria year*); *La Vanguardia*: 6 Aug. and 21 Sept. 1932; 24 July 1933.

30. See *Review of the River Plate*, 30 Sept. 1932, 11; *La Vanguardia*, esp. 2, 10, 13 Feb. and 23 Aug. 1932.

31. FEC, *Informe 1930*, 14–15; *La Vanguardia*, 9 Mar. 1933.

32. FEC, *Memoria 1939/1941*, 31–36. For examples, *La Vanguardia*, 5, 14 Nov. 1932 and 15 Apr. 1933; *CGT*, 10 June 1938.

33. *La Vanguardia*, 1 Aug. 1933; see also 15 Apr. 1933.

34. FEC, *Memoria 1936/1937*, 11–18; DNT, *Boletín informativo*, Mar./Apr. 1937, 4912–14. Also see FEC, *Memoria 1938/1939*, 43–47, 50–59.

35. Francisco Pérez Leirós, IDTOHP, 32–33.

36. *La Vanguardia*, 7 Nov. 1930.

37. *La Vanguardia*, 12 Mar. 1931. For other examples of unsuccessful protests, see *CGT*, 16 Dec. 1938; *El Obrero Municipal*, 16 Sept. 1939, Jan. 1940, and 16 Sept. 1942.

38. *La Vanguardia*, 22 Mar. 1932; Concejo Deliberante de la Ciudad de Buenos Aires, *Actas del H. Concejo Deliberante*: III, 23 Sept. 1932, 2994–95; I, 5 May 1933, 516; II, 1 Sept. 1933, 1669 (hereafter Concejo Deliberante, *Actas*).

39. *El Obrero Ferroviario*, 1 Mar. 1937; *CGT*, 22 Oct. 1938; *La Vanguardia*, 18 July 1931.

40. Concejo Deliberante, *Actas*: II, 28 June 1932, 2277; IV, 28 Dec. 1933, 4578; II, 15 Sept. 1937, 1624–25, and 3 Nov. 1939, 2468; Municipalidad de la Ciudad de Buenos Aires, *Presupuesto general de gastos y cálculo de recursos 1930*, 173, and *1931*, 163; *La Vanguardia*, 8 July 1932; *El Obrero Ferroviario*, 16 Feb. 1935.

41. *Ley y reglamento general de los ferrocarriles nacionales. Publicación oficial* (Buenos Aires, 1936); *Boletín de la Dirección General de Ferrocarriles*, Feb. 1939, 139.

42. *La Vanguardia*, 26 Mar.–11 Apr. 1940.

43. Comisión Especial de Representantes de Empresas y Obreros Ferroviarios, *Revisión de escalafones, convenios y reglamentos* (Buenos Aires, 1930), 159.

44. *La Vanguardia*, 14 Oct. 1931. See also *El Obrero Ferroviario*, 16 May 1932; *La Vanguardia*, 10 Oct.–28 Nov. 1931; UF, "Libros de actas de la Comisión Directiva," 18 (21 Oct. 1931), 1–3 (hereafter UF, "Actas").

45. Repetto, 138. For results of municipal elections, see *La Vanguardia*, 25 Jan. 1932. See also UF, "Actas", 18 (21 Oct. 1931), 16–17; Andrés Cabona, IDTOHP, 58–59; *El Obrero Ferroviario*, 1 Dec. 1931.

46. As related by Pedro Otero, IDTOHP, 47. See also Joel Horowitz, "Occupational Community and the Creation of a Self-Styled Elite," *The Americas* 42, 1 (July 1985), 58–61.

47. For examples of the UF's political stands, see José Domenech, "Prologue," in Juan Atilio Bramuglia, *Jubilaciones ferroviarias* (Buenos Aires, 1941), 10; *El Obrero Ferroviario*, 1/16 Aug. 1941. For the UF as statist, see Francisco Pérez Leirós, IDTOHP, 37; Luis Gay, IDTOHP, 49; interview with Jesús Fernández conducted by Robert J. Alexander, 8 Nov. 1946.

48. Félix Luna, *Ortiz* (Buenos Aires, 1978), 41–42, 95–97, 156–74; Camilo Almarza, IDTOHP, 28–30; Francisco Pérez Leirós, IDTOHP, 57–58, 63–64, 75; FOEF, *Motivos de su creación* (Buenos Aires, 1939), 6; Paul Goodwin, *Los ferrocarriles británicos y la UCR* (Buenos Aires, 1974), 238–70; CGT, *Acta del segundo congreso ordinario* (Buenos Aires, 1943), 75.

49. Quoted in Luna, *Ortiz*, 158.

50. *El Obrero Ferroviario*, 16 Apr. and 1/16 June 1938; *La Vanguardia*, 11 June 1938; *CGT*, 17 June 1938; *Federación*, July 1938; FOEF, *Memoria y balance correspondiente al año 1938* (Buenos Aires, 1939), 7–9; UF, *Memoria y balance de la Comisión Directiva, 1938* (Buenos Aires, 1939), 29–31.

51. FOEF: *Estatutos* (Buenos Aires, 1938); *Memoria*, 9, 12–14; UF, *Estatutos* (Buenos Aires, 1934); *La Nación*, 16 June 1938.

52. *El Obrero Ferroviario*, 16 Apr. 1939; FOEF, *Memoria*, 17–20.

53. *El Obrero Ferroviario*, 16 Nov. 1938–16 Jan./1 Feb. 1939.

54. FOEF, *Memoria*, 15, 27–29; *El Obrero Ferroviario*, 16 Mar. 1939.

55. *Boletín de la Dirección General de Ferrocarriles*, Jan. 1939, 40–46; Manuel F. Fernández, *La Unión Ferroviaria a través del tiempo* (Buenos Aires, 1948), 243–44; *Federación*, Nov./Dec. 1938; *Review of the River Plate*: 18 Nov. 1938, 9; 25 Nov. 1938, 5; FOEF, *Memoria*, 25–27.

56. *Boletín de la Dirección General de Ferrocarriles*, Apr. 1939, 299; *La Nación*, 31 Mar. and 1 Apr. 1939; *La Vanguardia*, 2 Apr. 1939; *El Obrero Ferroviario*, 16 Apr. 1939; FOEF, *Motivos de su creación*, 63–64.

57. *La Nación*, 28 July 1939; FOEF: *Motivos de su creación*, 51–57; *Memoria*, 7–8, 11–12; *Estatutos*; Luis M. Rodríguez, IDTOHP, 14.

58. *La Vanguardia*, 1–17 Apr. 1939; *La Prensa*, 2 Apr. 1939. *La Nación*, 1–17 Apr. 1939, indicates that the FOEF locals favored the government's action.

59. *La Vanguardia*, 12, 16 Apr.–3 May 1939; FOEF, *Motivos de su creación*, 63–76; *El Obrero Ferroviario*, 16 Apr. 1939.

60. *El Obrero Ferroviario*, 16 May 1939; *La Vanguardia*, 22 Sept. 1939–3 Jan. 1940.

61. *La Vanguardia*, 18–27 July 1939; *La Nación*, 18–27 July 1939; *Boletín de la Dirección General de Ferrocarriles*, Aug. 1939, 103–10; *El Obrero Ferroviario*, 1 and 16 Aug. 1939; *Review of the River Plate*, 4 Aug. 1939, 3.

62. *La Nación*, 28 July 1939. See also *Review of the River Plate*, 4 Aug. 1939, 3.

63. *La Vanguardia*, 1 Aug. 1939–28 Feb. 1940; *El Obrero Ferroviario*, 16 Nov. and 16 Dec. 1939.

64. *La Vanguardia,* 26 and 28 Feb. 1940; *El Obrero Ferroviario,* 1 Mar. 1940; José Domenech, IDTOHP, 160–61.

65. *La Vanguardia,* 2, 10, and 21 Mar. 1940.

66. *La Vanguardia,* 16 and 22 Aug. 1932; see also 24 Feb. and 14 Aug. 1931, 10 Aug. 1932, and 22 Aug. 1935; CGT, *Acta del primer congreso ordinario* (Buenos Aires, 1940), 71–72.

67. *El Obrero Textil,* July 1935; *La Vanguardia,* 27 June 1935.

68. *La Vanguardia,* July–Sept. 1935, esp. 25 July and 6 Aug.; *Federación,* Aug. and Sept. 1935; *El Obrero Textil,* 1 May 1936.

69. *La Vanguardia*: 23 Sept.–31 Oct. 1930; 12 Mar., 7 Aug., and 6 Oct. 1931; DNT, *Crónica mensual,* Oct./Dec. 1930, 3338–45.

70. *La Vanguardia,* 29 Feb.–15 Mar. 1932.

71. Comité de Huelga de la Casa Gratry, *Informe y balance* (Buenos Aires, 1936); *El Obrero Textil,* Oct. 1936; author's interview with Jorge Michellón, 6 May 1976.

72. Interview with Jorge Michellón conducted by Juan Carlos Torre; *El Obrero Textil,* July 1939 and Jan. 1940; *La Vanguardia,* 14 Oct.–12 Dec. 1939; CGT, 17 Nov. 1939; UOT, *Memoria y balance correspondiente al año 1939* (Buenos Aires, 1940), 14–17.

73. *La Hora,* 4 Jan. 1941; *El Obrero Textil,* Jan. 1940.

74. *El Obrero Textil,* Mar. 1941.

75. CGT, *Memoria y balance período 1939–1942* (Buenos Aires, 1942), as cited in Celia Durruty, *Clase obrera y peronismo* (Córdoba, 1969), 97. See also *El Obrero Textil,* second fortnight July and Dec. 1941; Cámara de Diputados, *Diario de sesiones,* III, 4 Sept. 1941, 890.

76. *El Obrero Textil,* June and Nov. 1942, Apr. 1943, and Apr. 1943, special issue.

77. *La Hora,* 3 and 4 Jan. 1941; DNT, División de Estadística, *Investigaciones sociales 1941* (Buenos Aires, 1942), 85; Cámara de Diputados, *Diario de sesiones,* VI (1940), 18 Apr. 1941, 927. For the strike, see *La Hora,* 7 Jan.–7 May 1941; *La Vanguardia,* 7 Jan.–7 May 1941.

78. Cámara de Diputados, *Diario de sesiones,* VI (1940), 18 Apr. 1941, 928.

79. For the full debate on the strike in the Chamber of Deputies, see Cámara de Diputados, *Diario de sesiones,* VI (1940), 3 Apr. 1941, 853–58; 16 Apr. 1941, 875; and 18 Apr. 1941, 926–33. See also *CGT,* 28 Mar. and 16 May 1941; *El Obrero Textil,* May 1941; CGT, *Memoria 1939–1942,* 48–49.

Chapter 8: Decision-Making and Internal Politics, 1930–1943

1. See, for example, David Tamarin, *The Argentine Labor Movement, 1930–1945* (Albuquerque, N.M., 1985), and Hiroschi Matsushita, *Movimiento obrero argentino 1930/1945* (Buenos Aires, 1983).

2. Eli Ginzburg, *The Labor Leaders* (New York, 1948), 62–66; V. L. Allen, *Power in Trade Unions* (London, 1954), 159; Walter Galenson, *Trade Union Democracy in Western Europe* (Berkeley, 1962), 74.

3. See Chapter 7 above. For other countries, see Galenson; Clark Kerr, "Unions and Union Leaders of Their Own Choosing," in *Labor Management in Industrial Society*, ed. Clark Kerr (Garden City, N.Y., 1964), 21–42; J. David Edelstein and Malcolm Warner, "Research Areas in National Union Democracy," *Industrial Relations* 16 (May 1977), 186–98; Seymour Martin Lipset, Martin A. Trow, and James S. Coleman, *Union Democracy* (Glencoe, Ill., 1956), 3–16.

4. William M. Leiserson, *American Trade Union Democracy* (New York, 1959), 69–70, as cited in Galenson, 88.

5. Robert Michels, *Political Parties*, trans. Eden Paul and Cedar Paul (Glencoe, Ill., 1949), 400–401. For paid leadership, see Lucio Bonilla, Instituto Di Tella Oral History Program, 52 (hereafter IDTOHP); *La Vanguardia*, 19–23 Dec. 1931; *Federación*, Aug. 1931.

6. Allen, 28.

7. *El Obrero Ferroviario*, 16 Dec. 1941 and 16 Feb. 1942; *La Vanguardia*, 27 Dec. 1930, 5 Jan. 1931, and 11 May 1932.

8. See Kerr, 32–34, for a discussion of restraints on union leaders.

9. Camilo Almarza, IDTOHP, 11–12; Juan Rodríguez, IDTOHP, 6–7; José Domenech, IDTOHP, 108.

10. For a similar comment about the French rank-and-file, see Edward Shorter and Charles Tilly, *Strikes in France, 1830–1968* (London, 1974), 172. Militants had a variety of motives; ideology was very important, but it was not the only issue.

11. Joel Horowitz, "Ideologías sindicales y políticas estatales en la Argentina, 1930–1943," *Desarrollo Económico*, no. 94 (July/Sept. 1984), 275–96.

12. UF, *Memoria y balance de la Comisión Directiva*, 1930 through 1942 (Buenos Aires, 1931–43; hereafter UF, *Memoria year*). All information on the UF's constitutional structure is from UF, *Estatutos* (Buenos Aires, 1934). Also see José Domenech, IDTOHP, 94; *El Obrero Ferroviario*, 16 Sept. 1935 and 1 Mar. 1942. Similar centralized relations existed on the French railroads between locals and the national organization (Larry S. Ceplair, "Education of a Revolutionary Labor Union Minority"; Ph.D. dissertation, University of Wisconsin, 1973).

13. UF, "Libros de actas de la Comisión Directiva," 18 (6 Nov. 1930), 18–19; 20 (20 Nov. 1930), 12 (hereafter UF, "Actas").

14. *El Obrero Ferroviario*, 1 Apr. 1936.

15. See UF, "Actas," esp. 18 (28 Oct. 1935), 29–32; 2 (7/8 Mar. 1945), 1–3. The number of CD meetings is listed in the annual *Memoria*.

16. UF, "Actas": 17 (25 Aug. 1933), 5–17; 15 (31 Oct./1 Nov. 1934), 13–28; 20 (18 Nov. 1935), 7.

17. UF: *Memoria 1928*, 45–48; "Actas," 10 (25/26 Oct. 1945), 32; Manuel F. Fernández, *La Unión Ferroviaria a través del tiempo* (Buenos Aires, 1948), 362–65.

18. CGT, *Acta del congreso general constituyente* (Buenos Aires, 1936), 41. See also UF, "Actas," 3 (4/5 Apr. 1934), 34; *El Obrero Ferrroviario*, 1/20 June 1932.

19. UF, "Actas":12 (23 June 1933), 3–6; 14 (31 July/1 Aug. 1933), 1–33; 18 (20 Sept. 1933), 30–34; *El Obrero Ferroviario*, 1/16 July 1934 and 1 Apr. 1936; *La Vanguardia*, 16 Sept. 1933.

20. UF: "Actas"—23 (27 Dec. 1933), 12–14; 10 (28 July 1943), 9–22; *Memoria 1940*, 22–24; *El Obrero Ferroviario*, 1 Feb. 1934.

21. M. Fernández, 149–55.

22. *El Obrero Ferroviario*, 1 Apr. 1936. For different and recent interpretations of the Syndicalist-Socialist conflict, see Matsushita, 131–37, and Tamarin, 108–12.

23. UF, "Actas": 4 (4/5 Apr. 1934), 2–35; 15 (31 Oct./1 Nov. 1934), 27.

24. See election results in UF, "Actas," esp. 14 (31 July/1 Aug. 1933), 1–33.

25. UF, "Actas": 1 (3 Jan. 1933), 1–25; 7 (24 Mar. 1935), 21; *El Obrero Ferroviario*, 16 Apr. 1936.

26. Luis M. Rodríguez, IDTOHP, 3–4; Juan Rodríguez, IDTOHP, 14–15; FOEF, *Motivos de su creación* (Buenos Aires, 1939), 27–28. An examination of *La Vanguardia* and *El Obrero Ferroviario* reveals numerous examples of unrest.

27. FOEF, *Motivos de su creación*, esp. 16–20; *El Obrero Ferroviario*, 16 Mar.–16 May 1934.

28. UF, "Actas": 4 (4/5 Apr. 1934), 2–35; 12 (31 Aug./ 1/3 Sept. 1934), 1–5.

29. UF, "Actas," 9–12 (17 July–31 Aug./ 1/3 Sept.). 1934.

30. UF, "Actas": 13 (6 Sept. 1934), 8; 15 (31 Oct./1 Nov. 1934), 13–28; 17 (5 Dec. 1934), 14–15; 1 (6 Feb. 1935), 7–8; 15 (11 Sept. 1935), 8–9.

31. UF, "Actas," 9–22, 25 June–10/11 Dec. 1935; *El Obrero Ferroviario*, 16 Apr. 1936.

32. Joel Horowitz, "Occupational Community and the Creation of a Self-Styled Elite," *The Americas* 42, 1 (July 1985), 58–61; UF, "Actas": 20–22 (31 Oct.–20 Dec. 1933); 3 (21 Mar. 1934), 33; 6 (17 May 1935), 22–33; 22 (10–11 Dec. 1935), 30–82; Andrés Cabona, IDTOHP, 57, 97.

33. UF, "Actas": 7 (22 May 1935), 44; 16 (18 Oct. 1935), 38–46; 23, 17 Dec. 1935, 1–25; *El Obrero Ferroviario*, 1 Mar. 1936; *Federación*, Dec. 1935; Francisco Pérez Leirós, IDTOHP, 48; FOEF, *Motivos de su creación*, 35–41; CGT, *Anteproyecto de estatutos de la Confederación General del Trabajo* (Buenos Aires, 1934); Sebastián Marotta, *El movimiento sindical argentino* (Buenos Aires, 1970), III, 419–24.

34. *Federación*, Jan.–Feb. 1936; *El Obrero Ferroviario*, 1 Jan.–16 May 1936; CGT (Calle Catamarca), *Informe de la Junta Ejecutiva al Comité Confederal con motivo de la reunión ordinaria del 20 de mayo de 1936* (Buenos Aires, 1936), 2–8; Antonio Tramonti, *Un examen de conciencia* (Buenos Aires, 1936), 8, 22.

35. José Domenech, IDTOHP, 64, 110–12, and interview conducted by Robert J. Alexander, 11 Nov. 1946; *La Vanguardia*, 6 Feb. 1936; *El Obrero Ferroviario*, 16 Feb. 1936.

36. *El Obrero Ferroviario*, 16 Feb.–16 Apr. 1936; Tramonti, 5–17.

37. *La Prensa*, 21–24 May and 2–6 Aug. 1936; *Federación*, May and June 1936; *El Obrero Ferroviario*: esp. 1 June, 1/16 Aug., and 16 Oct. 1936; 1 Oct. 1937; *CGT*: 24 and 31 July 1936; 8 Jan. 1937; Luis M. Rodríguez, IDTOHP, 13.

38. *El Obrero Ferroviario*, 1 May 1940; UF, *Acta oficial de la XVIII asamblea general de delegados* (Buenos Aires, 1941), 63.

39. Domenech, IDTOHP; *El Obrero Ferroviario*, 16 Apr. 1939; UF, "Actas": 4 (28 Mar. 1945), 5–7; 8 (23–24 Aug. 1945), 6–19.

40. *La Hora*, Oct. 1940–Aug. 1941; *El Obrero Ferroviario*, 1 Oct. 1940–16 Aug. 1941; *La Vanguardia*, Jan.–Feb. and 12 Mar. 1941; UF, *Acta Oficial de la XIX asamblea general ordinaria de delegados* (Buenos Aires, 1942), 141.

41. *La Hora*: 29 Mar. and 24 May 1941; 6–9 Mar., 5–31 Aug. and 1, 4, 20 Sept. 1942; *El Obrero Ferroviario*, 1 and 16 Sept. 1942.

42. FOEF, *Motivos de su creación*, 32; UF, "Actas," 3 (16–17 Mar. 1943), 17–28; interview with Julio Duró Ameghino conducted by Robert J. Alexander, 30 Oct. 1946; *La Hora*: 13 June 1940; 16 Jan., 27 May, 1 Aug., and 29 Dec. 1941; 16 and 28 Oct., 3 Dec. 1942; *El Obrero Textil*, Nov. 1942.

43. *El Obrero Ferroviario*, 1 May 1943.

44. *El Obrero Ferroviario*, 1 Jan. and 16 Mar. 1943; UF, "Actas," 1 (3 Feb. 1943), 20–21; *La Hora*, 3–14 Dec. 1942.

45. *La Hora*, Mar.–May 1943, esp. 10 Mar.; *Review of the River Plate*, 18 Dec. 1942–June 1943; *El Obrero Textil*, Apr. 1943, special issue; Francisco Pérez Leirós, IDTOHP, 98–99, and interview conducted by Robert J. Alexander, 30 Oct. 1946.

46. Angel G. Borlenghi, *La verdad sobre lo sucedido en la CGT* (Buenos Aires, 1943), no pagination. See also Francisco Pérez Leirós, IDTOHP, 93; interview with José M. Argaña conducted by Robert J. Alexander, 30 Oct. 1946; CGT, *Actas de las reuniones del Comité Central Confederal: Efectuadas en mayo de 1940 y en octubre de 1942* (Buenos Aires, 1942), 35–105.

47. José Domenech, IDTOHP, 167; Pedro Pistarini, IDTOHP, 31, 37; Luis Ramicone, IDTOHP, 39; author's interview with Andrés Cabona, 5 Aug. 1976; UF, "Actas," 8 (23–24 Aug. 1945), 16–19.

48. *La Vanguardia*, Dec. 1942–Feb. 1943; *CGT*, 16 Oct. 1943; Camilo Almarza, IDTOHP, 156; Francisco Pérez Leirós, IDTOHP, 65–66.

49. UF, "Actas": 1 (3 Feb. 1943), 34–40; 3 (16/17 Mar. 1943), 15–16; *El Obrero Ferroviario*: 16 Sept. and 16 Nov. 1942; 16 Mar. 1943; *La Hora*, 3–9 Dec. 1942.

50. *La Hora*, Mar.–June 1943; *La Vanguardia*, Mar.–June 1943; *El Obrero Ferroviario*, 1 Apr. 16 July/1 Aug. 1943; *CGT*, Apr.–May 1943.

51. Julio Duró Ameghino and José Pipino, *Los directores obreros de la Caja Ferroviaria al gremio ferroviario* (1943); UF, "Actas," 8 (2 July 1943), 15–19.

52. *CGT*, 12 Nov. 1937; DNT, *Boletín informativo*, Sept./Oct. 1936, 4736. Statutes are in FEC, *Informe del Concejo Administrativo: Asamblea general ordinaria, 26 de agosto de 1930* (Buenos Aires, 1930), 39–43.

53. FEC: *Memoria de la Comisión Directiva, febrero de 1935–octubre de 1936* (Buenos Aires), 11–12 (hereafter FEC, *Memoria year*); *Memoria 1938/1939*, 95; *Memoria 1939/1941*, 4–5; interview with José M. Argaña conducted by Robert J. Alexander, 30 Oct. 1946.

54. For office-holding, see *La Vanguardia*; see also *La Vanguardia*, 20 Mar. 1933. The deposing of Navas is discussed in Chapter 5 above.

55. *La Vanguardia*, 24 Oct. 1933. See also *La Vanguardia*, 2–8 Mar. and 9, 14, 16 Aug. 1933; FOEF, *Motivos de su creación*, 19–20.

56. For example, see Partido Socialista, *Anuario socialista 1942* (Buenos Aires, 1941), ii; *La Vanguardia*: 9 Mar., 28 Apr., and 21 Aug. 1933; 10 Apr. 1942.

57. FEC, *Memoria 1936/1937*, 82–83; *CGT*, 12 Nov. 1937.

58. Interview with Pedro Bonatti conducted by Robert J. Alexander, 29 Oct. 1946.

59. Ernesto Janín, IDTOHP, 17.

60. *La Vanguardia*, 24 Feb. 1943.

61. Ernesto Janín, IDTOHP, 19–20, 44–45.

62. CGEC: *Estatuto* (Buenos Aires, n.d.); *Memoria del Concejo Administrativo, julio de 1936–mayo de 1939* (Buenos Aires, 1939), 160–75; *La Vanguardia*: 15 May 1939.

63. UOEM, *Estatutos* (Buenos Aires, 1930); *CGT*, 3 Feb. 1939; *La Vanguardia*: 29 Feb. 1932; 2 and 23 Feb. 1940; 21 Feb. 1943; interview with Francisco Pérez Leirós conducted by Robert J. Alexander, 23 May 1956.

64. Pedro Otero, IDTOHP, 9.

65. *El Obrero Municipal*, 1 Apr. 1935; *El Municipal*, May 1943; *La Vanguardia*: 26 Sept. and 29 Nov. 1932; 12 Feb. 1933; *CGT*, 3 Feb. 1939.

66. *El Obrero Municipal*: 15 May 1937; 16 June–16 Nov. 1940; 1 Feb. 1943; *El Municipal*, 6 Dec. 1938–Jan. 1939; *La Vanguardia*: 22 Jan. and 2 Feb. 1932; 22 Mar. 1934; *CGT*, 1 Oct. 1943.

67. Lists of office-holders can be found in *El Obrero Municipal*. For Pérez Leirós, *El Obrero Municipal*, 1 Oct. 1933 and 14 Sept. 1937; José Luis Imaz, *Los que mandan*, trans. Carlos A. Astiz (Albany, 1970), 239.

68. *La Vanguardia*: 14 Nov. 1932; 13 Jan. and 25 Nov. 1933; 27 and 29 Oct. 1934; *El Obrero Municipal*: 1 June, 1 Aug., 1 Nov., and 1 Dec. 1934; 1 Feb. 1935. The two sources give different vote totals.

69. *El Obrero Municipal*, 16 Mar.–16 May 1935.

70. *El Obrero Municipal*: 1 Nov. and 16 Dec. 1942; 1 Feb., 1 May–16 June, 16 Sept., and 1 Oct. 1943; *El Municipal*, Dec. 1940; *Camarada: En estas páginas hallará sintetizada la nueva orientación y moral sindical que practica la CGT* (Buenos Aires, 1937), 15.

71. Lucio Bonilla, IDTOHP, 7; René Stordeur, IDTOHP, 458–59.

72. Pedro Otero, IDTOHP, 22–27; see also *El Obrero Municipal*, 1 June 1943.

73. Francisco Pérez Leirós, IDTOHP, 40.

74. For the UOT's constitution and its reform, see *El Obrero Textil*, Aug. 1932, Nov. 1933, Aug. 1937, June and Dec. 1938, and July 1942; *La Vanguardia*, 3 Mar. 1932. See also *El Obrero Textil*, Jan. and May 1940, Dec. 1941, and Apr. 1943; Lucio Bonilla, IDTOHP, 50–53; *La Vanguardia*, 2–20 May 1940.

75. Lists of office-holders can be found in *El Obrero Textil*. See also Lucio Bonilla, IDTOHP, 52–53; *El Obrero Textil*, 1 May 1934, Mar. and July 1935, first fortnight July 1941; author's interview with Jorge Michellón, 24 June 1976.

76. Lucio Bonilla, IDTOHP, esp. 11, 16; Mariano Tedesco, IDTOHP, 11, 13; author's interviews with Jorge Michellón, 8 Jan., 29 Mar., and 24 June 1976; interview with Jorge Michellón conducted by Juan Carlos Torre; Joel Horowitz, "Ideologías sindicales"; *El Obrero Textil*, Oct. 1940.

77. *La Voz Textil (Organo de los obreros textiles de V. Alsina)*, Aug. 1937; *El Obrero Ferroviario*, 1 Sept. 1937; interview with Jorge Michellón conducted by Juan Carlos Torre; *El Obrero Textil*, May 1938.

78. *El Obrero Textil*, Apr. 1939 and Sept. 1940; author's interview with Jorge Michellón, 24 June 1976.

79. *El Obrero Textil*, Nov. 1939; *La Vanguardia*, 4, 9 Sept.; 2, 8 Oct.; and 11 Nov. 1939; *CGT*, 3 Nov. 1939.

80. *La Vanguardia*, 12 Mar.–15 May 1940; *La Hora*, 30 July 1940; *El Obrero Textil*: Sept. and Oct. 1940; Apr. and second fortnight May 1941; *CGT*, 27 Sept. and 4 Oct. 1940; CGT, *Memoria y balance período 1939–1942* (Buenos Aires, 1942); 65.

81. *El Obrero Textil*, Dec. 1940 and first fortnight June 1941; *La Hora*, 18 Jan. and 22–25 May 1941; *CGT*, 28 Mar. 1941; *El Obrero Ferroviario*, 16 Mar. and 1 Apr. 1941; CGT, *Memoria 1939–1942*, 27.

82. *El Obrero Textil*: June and Sept. 1940; first fortnight July and second fortnight Nov. 1941; *La Hora*, 1 and 20 May 1940; CGT, *Actas del Comité Central Confederal*, 119; *La Vanguardia*, esp. Sept. 1940 and 9 Feb. 1941.

83. *El Obrero Textil*, Nov. 1941, Apr.–June 1942, and Apr. 1943; *El Obrero Ferroviario*, 16 Apr. 1943.

84. *Federación*, July 1933, Jan. 1934, and Nov. 1937; *La Vanguardia*, 18 Jan. 1932. For the FOET's structure, see FOET, *Luchas y conquistas* (Buenos Aires, 1944), 183–89.

85. *Federación*, Jan., Feb. Dec. 1933 and May 1937.

86. *La República*, 24 Jan. 1933 (scrapbook Gay). See also *Federación*, Oct. 1931 and 17 Feb. 1941.

87. *Federación*, Dec. 1929, Jan. 1931, Feb. 1935, Dec. 1937/Jan. 1938, and Jan./Feb. 1942. Lists of CA members can be found in *Federación*.

88. FOET, 99–103; *Federación*, Jan., Feb., Sept., and Oct. 1932; *La Vanguardia*, 5 and 20 Sept. 1932; *Noticias Gráficas*, 4 Sept. 1932; *La República*, 5 Sept. 1932 (last two items, scrapbook Gay).

89. *Federación*: Jan., Feb., and Nov. 1933; Mar. 1935; *La Vanguardia*, 20 Sept. 1933; *La República*, 16 Jan. 1933 (scrapbook Gay); FOET, 173–76; *El Obrero Ferroviario*, 1 and 16 Mar. 1934; author's interview with Luis Gay, 5 May 1976.

90. *Federación*: May 1937; Jan./Feb. and Apr. 1938; Luis Gay, "Historia de la FOET," 38 (unpublished manuscript; title and pagination mine). Union employees are listed on the balance sheets in *Federación*. Also see Andrés Cabona, IDTOHP, 75-76; author's interview with Andrés Cabona, 5 Aug. 1976.

91. *Federación*, May 1938-May 1939; Luis Gay: IDTOHP, 31-33; "Historia de la FOET," 15-16, 41-50; author's interviews with Gay, 11 Feb., 31 Mar., 8 and 28 July 1976; José M. Cabrera et al., *A los asociados de la Federación Obreros y Empleados Telefónicos* (Buenos Aires, 1938).

92. *Federación*, Nov./Dec. 1940-31 Oct. 1941; *La Vanguardia*, 15, 19 Mar., and 5 Apr. 1941; *Depuración*, 2 Aug. 1943-30 Jan. 1946, esp. 26 Feb. 1944.

93. Jacinto Oddone, *Gremialismo proletario argentino*, 2d ed. (Buenos Aires, 1975), 517.

Chapter 9: Perón's Impact on the Unions 1943-1945

1. *El Obrero Municipal*, 16 June 1943; *CGT*, 11 June and 9 July 1943; *El Obrero Ferroviario*, 1 July 1943; *La Vanguardia*, 20 June 1943; *Unidad Nacional*, 12 and 24 June 1943.

2. *El Obrero Municipal*, 6 July 1943.

3. Francisco Pérez Leirós, Instituto di Tella Oral History Program (IDTOHP), 104-6, 122 (hereafter IDTOHP); Pedro Otero, IDTOHP, 83; *CGT*, 25 June-6 Aug. 1943 and 1 Mar. 1946.

4. Roberto Marrone, *Apuntes para la historia de un gremio (Empleados de Comercio de Rosario)* (Rosario, 1974), 152; *Unidad Nacional*, 29 July-9 Sept. 1943; *El Obrero Ferroviario*, 1/16 June 1943; *Federación*, 31 Aug. 1943; José Peter, *Crónicas proletarias* (Buenos Aires, 1968), 199-200; *Anales de legislación argentina* (Buenos Aires, 1944), V, 227-30; Hiroschi Matsushita, *Movimiento obrero argentino 1930/1945* (Buenos Aires, 1983), 258-59, 299, n. 7.

5. *La Prensa*, 24 Aug. 1943; *Revista de Trabajo y Previsión*, Jan./Mar. 1944, 124-26; *CGT*, 27 Aug. and 16 Sept.-31 Dec. 1943; Matsushita, 260-61; Marrone, 152; Peter, 209; *La Vanguardia*, 8, 9, 15, and 20 Oct. 1943; *Unidad Nacional*, 30 Sept.-18 Nov. 1943 and fourth week Jan. 1944.

6. Robert A. Potash, *The Army and Politics, 1928-1945* (Stanford, 1969), 227-28; Luis Monzalvo, *Testigo de la primera hora del peronismo* (Buenos Aires, 1974), 64-65.

7. Peter, 201-14; Robert J. Alexander, *The Perón Era* (New York, 1951), 26-27; *El Obrero Ferroviario*, 1 Nov. 1943; *CGT*, 1 Dec. 1943.

8. Raymond Carr, *Spain, 1808-1975*, 2d ed. (London, 1982), 570; see also 571-73; *CGT*, 1 Nov. 1943; "Historia del peronismo," VII, *Primera Plana*, 27 July 1965, 53, and VIII, *ibid.*, 3 Aug. 1965, 42, 44; Carlos Fayt, ed., *La naturaleza del peronismo* (Buenos Aires, 1967), 95-97, 104-6.

9. Juan Carlos Torre, "Antes del peronismo: Los sindicatos en los años treinta" (unpublished paper, n.d.), 1.

10. *Leyes obreras de la revolución* (Buenos Aires: Editorial Primicias, 1947), 5–6; *Revista de Trabajo y Previsión*, Jan./Mar. 1944, 127, and Apr./June 1944, 641–71; *Federación*, 31 Dec. 1943; *Crónica mensual de la Secretaría de Trabajo y Previsión*, Nov. 1944, 6–12.

11. *CGT*, 1 Mar. and 16 Apr. 1944; Matsushita, 270; Francisco Pérez Leirós, IDTOHP, 127; "Reportaje a Jorge Michellón," *Controversia*, Supplement 1, Dec. 1979, ix; *El Obrero Municipal*, 16 Apr. 1944; *La Vanguardia*, 16, 19, and 22 Apr. 1944; *Federación*, 30 Apr. 1944.

12. Author's interview with Luis Gay, 29 June 1984; Luis Gay: "El Partido Laborista" (unpublished manuscript), 25–26; IDTOHP, 53–56.

13. Interview with Francisco Pérez Leirós conducted by Robert J. Alexander, 30 Oct. 1946.

14. *CGT*, 1 July 1944; author's interview with Luis Gay, 29 June 1984; *Revista de Trabajo y Previsión*, July/Sept. 1944, 1016–67; Dirección de Estadística Social, *Investigaciones sociales 1943–1945* (Buenos Aires, 1946), 17–18.

15. *Unidad Nacional*, 14 July 1944; *CGT*, 1 Aug. 1944; *El Obrero Ferroviario*, Aug. 1944; *La Prensa*, 29 and 30 July 1944; Lucio Bonilla, IDTOHP, 83–88; Matsushita, 269–73; Jacinto Oddone, *Gremialismo proletario argentino*, 2d ed. (Buenos Aires, 1975), 563–66.

16. *Revista de Trabajo y Previsión*, Oct./Dec. 1944, 1546–660; Dirección de Estadística Social, *Investigaciones sociales 1943–1945*, 32–33; George I. Blanksten, *Perón's Argentina* (Chicago, 1953), 261–62. See Perón's speech to metal workers in Juan Perón, *El pueblo quiere saber de qué se trata* (Buenos Aires, 1944), 173–74.

17. *Unidad Nacional*, first week Apr., fourth week Aug., and fourth week Nov. 1944; *Noticiario Obrero Norteamericano*, 15 Mar. 1947; Rodolfo Puiggrós, *El peronismo* (Buenos Aires, 1969), 127.

18. Angel Perelman, *Cómo hicimos el 17 de octubre* (Buenos Aires, 1961), 43–45; Hugo del Campo, *Sindicalismo y peronismo* (Buenos Aires, 1983), 182–85; Louise M. Doyon, "Organized Labour and Perón (1943–1955)" (Ph.D. dissertation, University of Toronto, 1978), 255–58.

19. *Unidad Nacional*, second week Mar. 1945. See also Roberto A. Ferrero, *El frande a la soberanía popular, 1938–1946* (Buenos Aires, 1976), 276; *Unidad Nacional*, last week Oct.–fourth week Nov. 1944; *La Prensa*, 1 Nov. 1944; Puiggrós, *El peronismo*, 129–30.

20. *CGT*, 1 Dec. 1944; *La Prensa*, 25–26 Nov. 1944; Félix Luna, *El 45* (Buenos Aires, 1969), 54; Rubén Rotandaro, *Realidad y cambio en el sindicalismo* (Buenos Aires, 1971), 194–95; Juan Carlos Torre, "El rol del sindicalismo en los orígenes del peronismo" (Spanish version; doctoral dissertation, Ecole Pratique des Hautes Etudes, 1983), Ch. 1, pp. 48–49; Doyon, "Organized Labour," 276–77.

21. See Luna, *El 45*; *La Vanguardia*, 23 June 1945.

22. *Federación*, 14 July 1945; *Unión Sindical*, 10 July and 2 Aug 1945; *La Prensa*, 16 June–14 July 1945; *Ritmo*, July 1945; *CGT*, 1 and 16 July 1945; Gay, "El Partido Laborista," 16–18; Luna, *El 45*, 192–93, 225; Torre, "El rol del sindicalismo," Ch.

2, pp. 4–8; Samuel L. Baily, *Labor, Nationalism and Politics in Argentina* (New Brunswick, N.J., 1967), 85–86.

23. *El Obrero en Calzado*, Dec. 1944–Dec. 1945; *CGT*, 16 Aug. and 16 Sept. 1945; *Unión Sindical*, 10 Sept. 1945; *La Vanguardia*, 4 and 11 Sept. 1945.

24. *Leyes obreras de la revolución*, 18–22; "UF, Libros de actas de la Comisión Directiva," 6 (5/7 June 1945), 18–19 (hereafter UF, "Actas"); Torre, "El rol del sindicalismo," Ch. 2, pp. 9, 36–37.

25. Unless otherwise noted, the discussion of 17 October is based on the following: Torre's excellent "El rol del sindicalismo," Ch. 2; *La Prensa*; *Crítica*; Hugo Gambini, *El 17 de octubre de 1945* (Buenos Aires, 1969); Eduardo Colom, *17 de octubre* (Buenos Aires, 1946); and Luna, *El 45*, 319–78.

26. UF, "Actas," 10 (25/26 Oct. 1945), 38; *El Obrero Ferroviario*, 1 Nov. 1945; *La Prensa*, 14 Oct. 1945; Alexander, *The Perón Era*, 37–38.

27. Gay, "El Partido Laborista," 32–35; Cipriano Reyes, *Yo hice el 17 de octubre* (Buenos Aires, 1973), 213–24. The minutes of the CGT central committee meeting are in Elena Susana Pont, *Partido Laborista* (Buenos Aires, 1984), 91–112.

28. Marysa Navarro, "Evita and the Crisis of 17 October 1945," *Journal of Latin American Studies* 12, 1 (May 1980), 127–38.

29. "Reportaje a Jorge Michellón," xi; Daniel James, "17 y 18 de octubre de 1945," *Desarrollo Económico*, no. 107 (Oct./Dec. 1987), 445–61.

30. Gay, "El Partido Laborista," 35–39, 62–65; Torre, "El rol del sindicalismo," Ch. 3; Monzalvo, 200–209.

31. UF, "Actas," 8 (23/24 Aug. 1945), 13. See also *El Obrero Ferroviario*, 1 and 16 Aug. 1945; *El Obrero Municipal*, Aug. 1945; *CGT*, 1 Aug. 1945; *Unión Sindical*, 2 Aug. 1945.

32. Raúl Bustos Fierro, *Desde Perón hasta Onganía* (Buenos Aires, 1969), 39; *El Obrero Ferroviario*, Sept. 1945.

33. Torre, "El rol del sindicalismo," Chs. 3 and 4; Pont, 37–55, 115–56.

34. UF, "Actas," 8–11 (2–28 July 1943); *El Obrero Ferroviario*, 1 July and 16 July/1 Aug. 1943.

35. *El Obrero Ferroviario*, 4 Sept.–1 Nov. 1943, Sept./Oct. 1944, and 1 Sept. 1945; UF, "Actas": 8 (2 July 1943), 15–22; 12 (18/20 Aug. 1943), 5–7; Manuel F. Fernández, *La Unión Ferroviaria a través del tiempo* (Buenos Aires, 1948), 291–300; Torre, "El rol del sindicalismo," Ch. 1, p. 9; *CGT*, 16 Oct. 1943 and 1 Mar. 1946.

36. M. Fernández, 309–10.

37. UF, "Actas," 1 (14 Sept. 1944), 5; *El Obrero Ferroviario*, July 1944; M. Fernández, 303–5; "Historia del peronismo," XI, *Primera Plana*, 24 Aug. 1965, 42–44; Juan Perón, *El pueblo ya sabe de qué se trata* (no publication information), 207; *La Hora*, 4 Sept. 1942. Monzalvo has himself appearing in much too prominent a role (Monzalvo, 55–78).

38. *CGT*, 1 Nov. and 1 Dec. 1943; M. Fernández, 312.

39. *El Obrero Ferroviario*: 1 Nov. and 1 Dec. 1943; Mar., July, and Sept./Oct. 1944; *Unidad Nacional*, second and third issues Dec. 1943, fourth week Mar. and second week Apr. 1944.

40. *CGT*, 31 Dec. 1943 and 16 Jan. 1944; *El Obrero Ferroviario*, Jan.–30 Apr. 1944; Joel Horowitz, "The Impact of Pre-1943 Labor Union Traditions on Peronism," *Journal of Latin American Studies* 15, 1 (May 1983), 115.

41. M. Fernández, 204–8; *El Obrero Ferroviario*: Mar.–July 1944; 1 June and 16 Aug. 1945; Eduardo Rumbo, IDTOHP; UF, "Actas": 1 (2 Feb. 1945), 5–7; 7 (24/25 July 1945), 19; Comisión Ferroviaria Especial, *Los 16 puntos de los ferroviarios argentinos* (Buenos Aires, 1944).

42. *El Obrero Ferroviario*, 1 Dec. 1943, Jan. 1944, and 30 Apr.–Aug. 1944.

43. *El Obrero Ferroviario*, Jan. 1944.

44. *CGT*, 1 May 1944; Matsushita, 269–70; FOEF, *Motivos de su creación* (Buenos Aires, 1939), 45; José Domenech, IDTOHP, 127–28, 177; Comisión Ferroviaria Especial, 7.

45. *El Obrero Ferroviario*, Sept./Oct. 1944. See also 1 Feb. 1945; UF, "Actas": 1 (14 Sept. 1944), 9; 3 (29 Sept. 1944), 12–13; 7 (29 Dec. 1944), 8–9.

46. UF, "Actas," 2 (19 Sept. 1944), 8–9.

47. *Unidad Nacional*, last week Sept. 1944; UF, "Actas," 2 (19 Sept. 1944), 14–18.

48. Circular Conjunta No. 1, UF and La Fraternidad, 31 Oct. 1944; UF, "Actas," 4 (24 Oct. 1944), 3–10; *El Obrero Ferroviario*, Sept./Oct.–16 Nov. 1944; *Unidad Nacional*, last week Nov. 1944; José Beltramé, *La crisis de los ferrocarriles argentinos de propiedad privada* (Buenos Aires, 1946), 113–20.

49. UF, "Actas," 7 (29 Dec. 1944), 9–10. See also the following—"Actas": 3 (21 Mar. 1945), 12–13; 5 (29 Apr. 1945), 18; 11, 18/19 Dec. 1945, 13–17; M. Fernández, 412.

50. *La Vanguardia*, 4 Sept. 1945; see also 27 Mar.–11 Dec. 1945, and *Unidad Nacional*, 3 Aug., fourth week Aug., and first and last weeks Oct. 1944; *Unión Sindical*, 10 Sept.–31 Dec. 1945.

51. *El Obrero Ferroviario*, 1 Jan., 1 June, and 16 Aug.–1 Oct. 1945; UF, "Actas": 6 (15 Dec. 1944), 19–20; 5 (27 Apr. 1945), 9–11; 7 (24 July 1945), 28–29; 3 (13 Feb. 1946), 10–11; 5 (10/11 Apr. 1946), 12–14.

52. UF, "Actas": 2 (7/8 Mar. 1945), 1–3, 15–22; 4, 28 Mar. 1945, 3–6; 5, 27 Apr. 1945, 5–8; *El Obrero Ferroviario*, Apr. and 1 May 1945.

53. *El Obrero Ferroviario*, 1 Feb. and 1 May–1 Sept. 1945; UF, "Actas," 6–8 (5/7 June–23/24 Aug. 1945).

54. Pont, 91–112.

55. *El Obrero Ferroviario*, 1 Nov. 1945–1 Mar. 1946; Silverio Pontieri, *La Confederación General del Trabajo* (Buenos Aires, 1972), 84, 103; Luna, *El 45*, 495–96; Pedro Otero, IDTOHP, 151.

56. *La Vanguardia*, 14 Sept. 1943. See also *Ritmo*, June/July–Oct./Nov. 1943; *El Obrero Municipal*, 16 Sept. and 1 Dec. 1943; *El Empleado* (Córdoba), Dec. 1943; *La Vanguardia*, 19 Nov. 1943.

57. *Ritmo*, Aug./Sept. 1943.

58. Alfredo López, *Historia del movimiento social y la clase obrera argentina* (Buenos Aires, 1971), 400–401.

59. Pedro Otero, IDTOHP, 86; "Historia del peronismo," XI, *Primera Plana*, 24 Aug. 1965, 44.

60. Puiggrós, *El peronismo*, 126. See also Francisco Pérez Leirós, IDTOHP, 127; *Unidad Nacional*, fourth week Mar. 1944; *La Vanguardia*, 21 Nov. 1943; *El Obrero Municipal*, 1 Dec. 1943.

61. *Unidad Nacional*, first week Dec. 1944.

62. *Ritmo*, Aug./Sept. 1943, Dec. 1943/Jan. 1944, and Mar. 1944; *El Empleado de Comercio* (Mendoza), June 1944; *La Prensa*, 28 Jan. 1944.

63. *El Empleado de Comercio* (Mendoza), June 1944; *La Vanguardia*, 7 Apr. 1944; *Crónica mensual de la Secretaría de Trabajo y Previsión*, Nov. 1944, 13.

64. Marrone, 171; *Ritmo*, esp. Sept. 1944–May/June 1945; *La Prensa*, 5 Dec. 1944; Puiggrós, *El peronismo*, 131; Perón, *El pueblo ya sabe*, 21–25; *Crónica mensual de la Secretaría de Trabajo y Previsión*, Dec. 1944, 19–27; *El Empleado* (Córdoba), Mar. 1945; *El Empleado* (Comodoro Rivadavia), Apr.–July 1945.

65. *Unidad Nacional*, first week Dec. 1944 and second week Mar. 1945; "Historia del peronismo," XI, *Primera Plana*, 24 Aug. 1965, 44; *Ritmo*, Jan./Feb.–Mar./Apr. 1945; *El Empleado* (Comodoro Rivadavia), Apr. 1945; *Orientación*, 28 Nov. 1945 and 13 Feb. 1946.

66. *La Vanguardia*, 24 July–2 Oct. 1945; FEC, *Informe del Concejo Administrativo. Asamblea general ordinaria, 26 de agosto de 1930* (Buenos Aires, 1930), 3.

67. *Orientación*, 19 Sept. 1945; *La Vanguardia*, 4 and 11 Sept. 1945; *Ritmo*, Sept. 1945; *El Empleado* (Comodoro Rivadavia), Oct. 1945.

68. Cámara de Diputados, *Diario de sesiones*, XI (1946), 9 Apr. 1947, 510; Torre, "El rol del sindicalismo," Ch. 3, n. 7, and Ch. 4, p. 17; *La Vanguardia*, 23 Oct. 1945; *La Prensa*, 17 and 24 Oct. 1945; *Ritmo*, Nov. 1945.

69. *La Vanguardia*, 6, 13 Nov. and 4 Dec. 1945; *El Empleado* (Comodoro Rivadavia), Jan. and Feb. 1946; *Ritmo*, Dec. 1945/Jan. 1946; Marrone, 159–70; *La Prensa*, 10–13 Jan. 1946; *Leyes obreras de la revolución*, 141–47.

70. Dirección de Estadística Social, *Investigaciones sociales 1943–1945*, 29.

71. *Ritmo*, Mar./Apr.–July/Aug. 1946; CGEC, *Memoria del Concejo Directivo, 1951/1953* (Buenos Aires, 1953), 12; Marrone, 172–73.

72. *El Obrero Municipal*, 16 June, 1 Aug., and 1 Nov. 1943.

73. *El Obrero Municipal*: 16 Aug. and 1 Dec. 1943; 1, 19 Jan. and 16 May 1944.

74. *El Obrero Municipal*: esp. 16 Aug., 1 Sept., and 16 Dec. 1943; 16 Mar. and 16 Apr. 1944; *CGT*, 16 Apr. and 16 Aug. 1937.

75. *El Obrero Municipal*: 16 Aug. and 16 Nov. 1943; 19 Jan., 16 Apr., and 1 May 1944.

76. *El Obrero Municipal*, esp. 1 Aug. 1943, 16 Mar., and 1, 16 May 1944.

77. Francisco Pérez Leirós, IDTOHP, 159–60.

78. *Revista de Trabajo y Previsión*, Apr./June 1944, 414–15.

79. Pedro Otero, IDTOHP, 86–89, 121; *La Nación*, 13 June 1944; *La Prensa*, 13 June 1944; del Campo, 138–39; *El Obrero Ferroviario*, June 1944; *El Obrero Municipal*, esp. 2 Feb., 1 Mar., and 1 July 1944.

80. *El Obrero Municipal*, 1 Oct. 1944. For Ugazio, *CGT*, 1 Dec. 1943; *El Obrero Municipal*, Mar. 1945. For Otero, *El Obrero Municipal*, 1 May 1939; *La Vanguardia*, 18 Mar. 1936.

81. *El Obrero Municipal*, 1 July–1 Sept. 1944 and Aug. 1945.

82. *El Obrero Municipal*, 1 Sept. and 1 Oct. 1944; Perón, *El pueblo quiere saber*, 153–54.

83. *El Obrero Municipal*, 1 Oct. 1944–Jan. 1945; *El Municipal*, Feb. 1939 and May 1941. The number of dues-payers is calculated from figures given at regular intervals in *El Obrero Municipal*.

84. *El Obrero Municipal*: 1 Sept. 1944–Jan. 1945; Apr.–July and Dec. 1945; *La Prensa*, 20 June 1945.

85. *El Obrero Municipal*, Feb.–Aug. 1945; *La Vanguardia*, 14 Aug. 1945.

86. *El Obrero Municipal*, June, July, Sept., and Nov. 1945.

87. *El Obrero Municipal*, esp. Dec. 1944, Feb. and Aug. 1945.

88. *Unidad Nacional*, last week Sept. and first week Oct. 1944; *La Vanguardia*, 24 Apr. and 10 July 1945; *Orientación*, 5 Sept. 1945; *La Prensa*, 16–26 Oct. 1945; Pont, 91; *CGT*, 1 Nov. 1945; *El Obrero Municipal*, Nov. 1945.

89. *Noticiario Obrero Norteamericano*, 15 Mar. 1947; *El Obrero Municipal*, Dec. 1945; *La Vanguardia*, 25 Dec. 1945. For Brennan and Marotta, *El Obrero Municipal*, 1 Dec. 1934, 16 Mar. 1943, and June 1945; *CGT*, 1 Oct. 1943.

90. *El Obrero Textil*, 1 July–Oct./Nov. 1943; *Unidad Nacional*, 29 July and 30 Sept. 1943.

91. *El Obrero Textil*, Oct./Nov. 1943; "Reportaje a Jorge Michellón," ix; *Unidad Nacional*, Mar., 30 Sept., and 7 Oct. 1943.

92. *El Obrero Textil*, September 1944 (two issues).

93. *CGT*, 25 June and 23 July 1943; Lucio Bonilla, IDTOHP, 74–82.

94. *La Vanguardia*, 18, 22 Sept., and 23–30 Oct. 1943; *CGT*, 1 Oct. and 1 Nov. 1943. Also see *La Vanguardia* and *CGT*, Aug.–Dec. 1943.

95. *Crónica mensual de la Secretaría de Trabajo y Previsión*, Nov. 1944, 13; *Revista de Trabajo y Previsión*, Apr./June–Oct./Dec. 1944.

96. *CGT*, 1 Sept.–1 Nov. 1944; Unión Industrial Argentina, Confederación Argentina de Industrias Textiles, *Salarios mínimos en la industria textil* (Buenos Aires, 1946), 21–22, 57–58.

97. *CGT*, 1 Mar. and 1 July–1 Sept. 1945; Unión Industrial Argentina, 26–46, 73–97; *La Prensa*, 30 June–17 July 1945; *La Vanguardia*, 26 June and 3 July 1945; *El Obrero Textil*, Sept. 1945.

98. *La Prensa*: 20–27 Nov. 1944; 26 June and 14, 15 July 1945; *Noticiario Obrero Norteamericano*, 15 Mar. 1947; *CGT*, 16 Nov. 1944 and 16 July 1945; Matsushita, 271–73.

99. Monzalvo, 80; Mariano Tedesco, IDTOHP, 23; *CGT*, 1 Sept. 1944 and 16 May 1945; *El Obrero Textil*, Sept. 1945.

100. *La Vanguardia*, 8 Apr. 1944; *CGT*, 16 Sept. 1945; *El Obrero en Calzado*, Sept. 1945; *Unión Sindical*, 10 Sept. 1945.

101. Lucio Bonilla, IDTOHP, 78. See also Juan C. Juárez, *Los trabajadores en función social* (Buenos Aires, 1947), 77; Doyon, "Organized Labour," 252 (quoting Lucio Bonilla, IDTOHP); *Crónica mensual de la Secretaría de Trabajo y Previsión*, Nov. 1944, 13. For the UOT(SP)'s size relative to other unions, see *CGT*, 1 Aug. 1945.

102. *El Obrero Textil*, Sept. and Nov. 1945; Unión Industrial Argentina, 23–24, 52; *Orientación*: 15 Aug., 5 Sept., and 14 Nov. 1945; 23 Jan. 1946.

103. Dirección de Estadística Social, *Investigaciones sociales 1943–1945*, 28–29. See also *CGT*, 1 July 1944, 16 Dec. 1945, 16 Jan. 1946, and 1 Jan. 1947; *La Vanguardia*, 30 Oct. and 6 Nov. 1945; *Noticiario Obrero Norteamericano*, 15 Mar. 1947; Juárez, 76; *Revista de Trabajo y Previsión*, Jan./Mar. 1946, 118; Mariano Tedesco, IDTOHP, 28–34; "Historia del peronismo," XII, *Primera Plana*, 31 Aug. 1965, 42; Unión Industrial Argentina, 71–72, 98.

104. *Federación*, 31 Aug. and 31 Dec. 1943.

105. *Federación*, 31 Oct.–31 Dec. 1943 and 31 Mar. 1944; *La Vanguardia*, 10 Nov. 1943.

106. Luis Gay: IDTOHP, 53–56; "El Partido Laborista," 24–25; author's interview with Gay, 29 June 1984.

107. *Federación*, May/June–31 Aug. 1944.

108. *Federación*, 28 Oct. 1944; Perón, *El pueblo quiere saber*, 203; *La Prensa*, 29 July and 25 Nov. 1944; *El Obrero Ferroviario*, Dec. 1944; *Unidad Nacional*, first week Dec. 1944.

109. *Depuración*, 2 Aug. 1943–25 Aug. 1944; *Federación*, 31 Dec. 1944 and 11 May 1945.

110. *Federación*, 28 Oct. 1944–14 July 1945, esp. 14 July; *Unión Sindical*, 21 Jan. 1946; *Revista de Trabajo y Previsión*, July/Dec. 1945, 1238–71. For numbers of members, see balances in *Federación*.

111. *Federación*, 11 May, 14 July, and 30 Sept. 1945.

112. *La Prensa*, 17 Oct. 1945; Luis Gay: IDTOHP, 72, and "El Partido Laborista," 32–51; *Unión Sindical*, 5 Nov. 1945 and 21 Jan. 1946; Pontieri, 103–4; *Depuración*, 1 May 1945; *Federación*, 30 Sept. 1945; *La Vanguardia*, 2 Oct. 1945.

Conclusions

1. György Borsányi, "The Great Depression and the Organized Working Class in Hungary (1929–1933)," in *Studies on the History of the Hungarian Trade-Union Movement*, ed. E. Kabos and A. Zsilák, trans. Alex Bandy (Budapest, 1977), 153–81; for an overview of Hungarian politics, Joseph Rothschild, *East Central Europe between the Two World Wars* (Seattle, 1974), 137–99.

2. Julio Godio, *El movimiento obrero venezolano 1850–1944* (Caracas, 1980), 127–58; Steve Ellner, *Los partidos políticos y su disputa por el control del movimiento sindical en Venezuela, 1936–1948* (Caracas, 1980), 83–86; Héctor Lucena, *El movimiento obrero petrolero* (Caracas, 1982), 206–64; Charles Bergquist, *Labor in Latin America* (Stanford; 1986), 227–58.

3. Ricardo Gaudio and Jorge Pilone: "El desarrollo de la negociación colectiva durante la etapa de modernización industrial en la Argentina, 1935–1943," *Desarrollo Económico*, no. 90 (July/Sept. 1983), 255–86, and "Estado y relaciones laborales en el período previo al surgimiento del peronismo, 1935–1943," *Desarrollo Económico*, no. 94 (July/Sept. 1984), 235–73.

4. Rodolfo Puiggrós, *El peronismo* (Buenos Aires, 1969), 126.

5. Nora Gatica Krug, "Entrevista a Luis V. Sommi," *Boletín de Investigación del Movimiento Obrero* (Universidad Autonoma de Puebla), V, 8 (Mar. 1985), 151–52.

6. Joel Horowitz, "Latin American Populism Reconsidered: Peronism as a Test Case"; paper delivered to the New England Council of Latin American Studies, 1987, esp. 6–7.

7. See David Collier, "Choice Points, Historical Legacies, and Trade Union Policies"; paper presented to the 1986 Annual Meeting of the Western Political Science Association.

8. Robert J. Alexander, *The Perón Era* (New York, 1951); Gino Germani, *Política y sociedad en una época de transición*, 5th ed. (Buenos Aires, 1974).

9. See note 4 of the Introduction.

10. Miguel Murmis and Juan Carlos Portantiero, *Estudios sobre los orígenes del peronismo*, I (Buenos Aires, 1971); Hugo del Campo, *Sindicalismo y peronismo* (Buenos Aires, 1983); Hiroschi Matsushita, *Movimiento obrero argentino 1930/1945* (Buenos Aires, 1983); David Tamarin, *The Argentine Labor Movement, 1930–1945* (Albuquerque, N.M., 1985); Gaudio and Pilone: "El desarrollo de la negociación colectiva" and "Estado y relaciones laborales."

11. Joel Horowitz, "The Impact of Pre-1943 Labor Union Traditions on Peronism," *Journal of Latin American Studies* 15, 1 (May 1983), 101–16.

12. Juan Carlos Torre, "El rol del sindicalismo en los orígenes del peronismo" (Spanish version, doctoral dissertation, Ecole Pratique des Hautes Etudes, 1983), Ch. 3, p. 6; Louise M. Doyon, "Organized Labour and Perón (1943–1955)" (Ph.D. dissertation, University of Toronto, 1978), 256–57; Chapter 9 above.

13. For the CD, see Manuel F. Fernández, *La Unión Ferroviaria a través del tiempo* (Buenos Aires, 1948), 149–61. The history of the non-CD members is drawn from

my files, as it is for the other unions. The number active below the executive boards is understated because I made no systematic attempt to collect such data. See also UF: *Acta oficial de la XVIII asamblea general de delegados* (Buenos Aires, 1941), 2, and "Libros de Actas de la Comisión Directiva", 4 (13 Mar. 1946), 1–3 (hereafter UF, "Actas").

14. *Federación*, 15 Apr. 1941, 31 May 1943, and 8 June 1946; *CGT*, 16 July and 16 Nov. 1946; *El Obrero Municipal*, 1 Oct. 1944 and Jan. 1945. The revolving nature of the UOEM advisors makes it difficult to be more specific.

15. See Horowitz, "The Impact of Pre-1945 Labor Union Traditions," 110–15.

16. *El Obrero Municipal*, 16 June 1943 and Dec. 1945; *Federación*, 31 July 1943 and 31 Dec. 1946; UF, "Actas," 8 (4 July 1946), 8.

17. Alexander, 27–28; Torre, "El rol del sindicalismo," Ch. 5, pp. 27–28; *La Prensa*, 27 Nov. 1944.

18. UF, "Actas": 6 (5/7 June 1945), 31–37; 7 (24 July 1945), 33; 12 (28 Dec. 1945), 15–16; 14 (8 Nov. 1946), 2–8; 1 (28 Jan. 1947), 2; 3 (25 Mar. 1947), 7; 9 (11/13 Aug. 1947), 35–37.

19. *Federación*, 8 June–31 Dec. 1946; Silverio Pontieri, *La Confederación General de Trabajo* (Buenos Aires, 1972), 102–3; *CGT*, 16 Mar. and 1 Apr. 1947; Cámara de Diputados, *Diario de sesiones*, XI (1946), 27 Mar. 1947, 140–45, and 9 Apr. 1947, 503–6; Torre, "El rol del sindicalismo," Ch. 5.

20. CGEC, *Memoria del Concejo Directivo 1951/1953* (Buenos Aires, 1953), 12; *CGT*, 16 Oct. 1947; Roberto Marrone, *Apuntes para la historia de un gremio (Empleados de Comercio de Rosario)* (Rosario, 1974), 172–73.

21. *Federación*, 30 Nov. and 31 Dec. 1946; *El Obrero Ferroviario*, 1 Jan. 1947.

22. *Leyes obreras de la revolución* (Buenos Aires: Editorial Primicias, 1947), 59–63. For procedures on appointments, UF, "Actas": 7 (29 Dec. 1944), 8–9, and 4 (28 Mar. 1945), 3–5; *El Obrero Ferroviario*, 1 May 1945.

23. Louise M. Doyon, "Conflictos obreros durante el régimen peronista (1946–1955)," *Desarrollo Económico*, no. 67 (Oct./Dec. 1977), 437–73. For an analysis of the relations between Perón and the unions after the period which is the principal focus of this book, see Torre, "El rol del sindicalismo," Chs. 4–5; Doyon, "Organized Labour," 396–558; Samuel L. Baily, *Labor, Nationalism and Politics in Argentina* (New Brunswick, N.J., 1967), 97–161.

24. Doyon, "Organized Labour," 451, 457–58; for the general purging of unions, see 443–502; Elena Susana Pont, *Partido Laborista* (Buenos Aires, 1984), 70–71.

25. Alexander, 97–99; S. L. Baily, 131–34; Doyon, "Organized Labour," 496–98, 501.

26. CGEC, *Memoria 1951/1953*, 12.

INDEX

Albión House, 84
Alexander, Robert J., 3, 5, 221
Allen, V. L., 153
Almarza, Camilo, 94, 194, 208
Alvear, Marcelo T. de, 11, 14, 19, 21, 59
Anarchists: decline of, 60, 69, 71, 216; dominance of, 56, 57; ideology of, 2; repression of, 13, 58, 68, 133; sectoral base of, 69, 216
Anti-Personalist Radicals, 11, 12, 14, 20, 133, 217
Argaña, José, 200
Armendares, Juan, 172–73
Armour Research Foundation, 34
Arriba Hojas, José, 200
Artela, García y Cía., 135
Asociación Obrera Textil, 211, 221, 227
Asociación Porteña de Trabajadores, 110
Asociación Trabajadores de la Comuna, 64, 100–101, 109–10, 205
Avalos, Eduardo, 24

Bagley, M. S., y Cía., 136
Baily, Samuel L., 5, 227
Barros, Raúl, 176
Basteri, Angel, 159–60
Becerra, Bernardo, 139
Belloni, Alberto, 5
Bergquist, Charles, 4
Bethlen, István, 217
Blanksten, George I., 3
Bonilla, Lucio, 208, 210
Borlenghi, Angel G.: ambitions of, 164, 202; leadership positions of, 80, 166, 225, 227; relations with 1943–45 military regime, 184, 198; relations with Perón, 187, 198–99, 200, 201, 202, 219; relations with Socialist Party, 80, 167, 179; suspicions against, 80, 223
Braden, Spruille, 196

Bramuglia, Juan, 192, 199, 206, 215
Brennan, Juan, 169, 207
Buenos Aires, 26–27; city council of, 44–45, 64, 85, 86, 109, 111, 136–37; municipal government of, 42–45
Bullrich, Eduardo, 129, 130, 131, 132
Buyan, Marcelino, 139n

CA. *See* Comisión Administrativa
Cabona, Andrés, 75
Cabrera, José, 175, 176
Campo, Hugo del, 5, 221
Campo de Mayo, 24, 77
Cárdenas, Lazaro, 220
Carr, Raymond, 182
Carugo, Juan A., 192
Casa Gerino, 145
Casa Gratry, 117, 146
Casa Levy, 93
Casa Pastra, 92
Casa Saltzman, 93, 94
Castillo, Ramón S.: ascendance and rule of, 18–22; relations with unions, 99, 114, 126, 147, 148, 181, 227
Catholic Church, 25
Catholic unions, 96, 110n, 154
Cattáneo, Atilion, 133
CD. *See* Comisión Directiva
Central Argentino, 57, 141, 158, 163
Central Buenos Aires, 143
Central Córdoba, 48, 49
Cerutti, Luis, 156, 209
CGEC (Confederación General de Empleados de Comercio): campaigns of, 82, 106, 107, 199, 200; and CGT splits, 76, 102; FEC dominance of, 7, 82, 167–68; leadership of, 222, 225, 227; membership of, 84, 106–7, 108, 124, 202; relations with 1943–45 military regime, 186, 197–98, 200–201; relations with Perón, 187, 200, 201, 202, 227

CGT (Confederación General del Trabajo): founding of, 61, 74; internal conflicts in, 74–76, 101–2, 160, 164–65; membership of, 7, 74, 182, 187; and October 1945 general strike, 189–90; organizational structure of, 160; relations with Neo-Conservatives, 13, 74–75, 133; relations with 1943–45 military regime, 182–84, 186, 188, 191; relations with Perón, 183, 225, 227; relations with political parties, 74–75, 140, 179; relations with unions, 106, 117, 122, 142, 147, 167, 173; splits in, 97, 102, 161–62
CGT I, 102, 174, 181
CGT II, 102, 179, 181, 202
CGT/Calle Catamarca, 97, 100
CGT/Calle Independencia, 97, 98
Chamber of Department Stores and Subsidiaries, 108
CIO (Congress of Industrial Organizations), 126
Círculo de Armas, 17
Civil Alliance, 14, 15
Class structure, 26–32, 36, 54–55. *See also* Immigrants; Middle class
Cleve, Ernesto, 225
COA (Confederación Obrera Argentina), 60, 61, 74, 156, 160
Colectivos, 34–35
Collective contracts, 48–49, 66, 117–18, 119, 126, 184–85, 209–10
Comisión Administrativa (CA): of FOET, 174–77; of UOEM, 168–70
Comisión Directiva (CD): of FEC, 166; of UF, 155–65; of UOT, 171–72
Comisión Socialista de Información Gremial, 60, 158, 166, 170
Comité Confederal, of CGT, 160
Comité Nacional de Unidad Sindical Clasista, 60, 73
Commerce (industry), 40–42
Commercial code, reform of, 81–83, 105–6, 134, 136
Commission on Socialist Union Information. *See* Comisión Socialista de Información Gremial

Committee for Unity among Municipal Workers, 110
Communists: anti-imperialism of, 99, 122; history in labor movement, 60; and intra-union conflicts, 96, 113–15, 162–65, 167, 170–73, 175–76, 195; relations with CGT, 99, 101, 102; relations with Neo-Conservatives, 13, 20, 68, 71, 99, 146–50; relations with 1943–45 military regime, 23, 24, 182, 183, 185–86, 187, 193, 199, 208; relations with Perón, 195, 215; relations with political parties, 98–99, 121, 148n, 163; relations with unions, 2, 4, 154–55, 179, 216, 219; sectoral base of, 3, 69, 72, 124; tactics of, 72–73, 97, 99, 117, 119, 121, 147, 151; and UOT split, 8, 67, 121; and women workers, 172
Comodoro Rivadavia, petroleum fields of, 69
Compañía General, 142–43
Concentración Obrera, 85, 86, 110, 169–70, 205
Concordancia, 14–17, 19, 20, 85
Conditions in work place, 35, 39, 42, 45, 48–50, 53–54, 86, 93. *See also* Fringe benefits; Pension plans; Wages; Women in work force
Confederación General de Empleados de Comercio. *See* CGEC
Confederación General del Trabajo. *See* CGT
Confederación Obrera Argentina. *See* COA
Confederations of labor. *See* CGEC; CGT; COA; Comité Nacional de Unidad Sindical Clasista; Federación Obrera de Telecomunicaciones de la República Argentina; FORA; Municipal workers' confederation; USA
Confitería Ideal, 108
Confraternidad Ferroviaria, 65–67
Congress of Industrial Organizations. *See* CIO

Conservatives: and fair elections, 10–11; labor and union relations, 15, 110, 139, 219; relations with Socialists, 16; support for presidential contenders, 12, 14, 20, 25
Contractors, 102, 103, 104, 176–77
Conventillas, 34
Corporatism, 12, 16, 69
Creole Monday, 107

Dell'Oro Maini, Atilio, 110
Departamento Nacional del Trabajo. *See* DNT
Depression: effects on economy, 12, 26–28; effects on industries, 17, 38, 40, 46, 50, 87–88; effects on political system, 12, 14; effects on workers, 38, 40, 43, 68, 228
Dimópulos, Basilio, 173
Dickmann, Adolfo, 82
Diskin, David, 202
Di Tella, Torcuato, 34
Dirección General de Ferrocarriles. *See* General Railroad Board
DNT (Departamento Nacional del Trabajo): and labor law enforcement, 35, 69–70, 81; lack of government support for, 35, 127, 134; under Perón, 23, 183, 209; relations with unions, 93, 99, 122, 135, 147–48, 209; scope of, 23, 70, 183; as successful mediator, 71, 117–18, 145–46, 147; as unsuccessful mediator, 70, 93, 118, 119, 128–29, 131
Domenech, José: and intra-union conflicts, 140, 157, 158, 159, 162–64, 191; relations with government, 140, 143, 144, 194; role in CGT, 101, 102, 227
Duarte, Eva, 24, 190, 227
Ducilo, 51, 121, 122, 173
Duhau, Luis, 28
Duró Ameghino, Julio, 163–64, 165, 179

Edo, Carlos, 44
Elena, Reinaldo, 44

Elites, 1, 9, 11, 17, 125, 126, 217
Employment: in commerce, 40–41; effects of depression on, 27, 29; in municipal government, 43, 44; 1929–45 changes in, 29–31; in railroads, 47, 48, 88; in telephone industry, 38, 76; in textiles, 50–52
English Saturday, 81, 107, 134, 135
Entre Ríos Radicals, 133
Escalafón, 44, 86, 105, 185, 212, 2124
Exports, 26, 27, 29

Fabiano, Rafael, 176
Façonniers, 51, 94, 95
Farré, Florencio, 176
Farrell, Edelmiro, 23, 194, 196
Fazio, Ludovico, 166–67
FEC (Federación Empleados de Comercio): campaigns of, 72, 79–80, 81–83, 106, 107–8, 134–36; founding of, 4, 63; ideology of, 7, 63, 80; internal conflicts in, 167, 168, 200; leadership of, 63, 80, 166, 226; membership and dues of, 7, 40, 84, 107, 108, 166; organizational structure of, 165–66; relations with major employers, 40, 108; relations with Neo-Conservatives, 80, 106, 134–36, 197; relations with 1943–45 military regime, 183, 198; relations with Perón, 7, 198–202; relations with political parties, 7, 63, 80, 164, 166–67, 197; relations with unions, 82, 106, 164; strike tactics of, 84, 134
Federación, 177, 225
Federación de Obreros y Empleados Municipales. *See* FOEM
Federación Empleados de Comercio. *See* FEC
Federación Obrera de la Industria Textil. *See* FOIT
Federación Obrera de Telecomunicaciones de la República Argentina, 213
Federación Obrera Ferrocarrilera. *See* FOF

Federación Obrera Ferroviaria, 65n
Federación Obrera Marítima, 57, 59, 63, 71n, 97, 100, 101, 115
Federación Obrera Regional Argentina. *See* FORA
Federación Obreros y Empleados Ferroviarios. *See* FOEF
Federación Obreros y Empleados Telefónicos. *See* FOET
Ferrazzaro, Eracilo, 192
Ferrocarril Oeste. *See* Oeste
Ferrocarril Sud. *See* Sud
Figueiras, Demetrio, 214
Figuerola, José, 182
FOEF (Federación Obreros y Empleados Ferroviarios), 113, 141–44, 150, 162, 226
FOEM (Federación de Obreros y Empleados Municipales), 110, 169, 205
FOET (Federación Obreros y Empleados Telefónicos): campaigns of, 77, 105; founding of, 4, 7, 61; ideology of, 61, 68, 98; internal conflicts in, 103, 104, 175–78; leadership of, 175, 178, 222, 225; membership and dues of, 62, 76, 79, 105, 214, 223; organizational structure of, 174–75; relations with interior, 61–62, 103–4, 213, 224; relations with major employer, 39, 61–62, 76–79, 102–5, 128–32, 152, 175–76, 213–14; relations with Neo-Conservatives, 68, 71, 76–79, 104, 128–34; relations with 1943–45 military regime, 212–14; relations with Perón, 7, 187, 212, 213, 214–15, 225, 227; relations with political parties, 7, 61, 128, 175–76; relations with pre-1930 governments, 59, 61; relations with unions and confederations, 97, 100, 101; strike tactics of, 62, 77–78, 129–30
FOF (Federación Obrera Ferrocarrilera), 65
FOIT (Federación Obrera de la Industria Textil), 8n, 67, 92, 94, 95

FORA (Federación Obrera Regional Argentina), 60, 69
La Fraternidad, 32, 66, 115; and confederations, 76, 97, 102, 115; founding of, 64–65; relations with government, 114, 181, 182, 187; relations with UF, 67, 88, 91n, 142; and wage arbitration, 91, 113
Fraud: under Neo-Conservatives, 9–10, 15, 17, 18, 19, 20, 21; reforms against, 11, 18; in union elections, 156–57
Fresco, Manuel, 18–19, 100, 107, 118, 120, 121–22, 146–47
Fringe benefits: in municipal government, 43, 45, 64, 203; provisions for (1930–45), 35, 106, 199; in railroad industry, 48–49, 66, 193; under reformed commercial code, 81, 108; in telephone industry, 38–39; in textiles, 53, 123. *See also* Social services
Fuerzas vivas, 186–87, 196, 200, 210, 214

Ganza, Marcelino, 139
Gath y Chaves, 40, 63, 107–8
Gaudio, Ricardo, 4, 5, 100, 149, 218, 221
Gay, Luis F.: and intra-FOET conflict, 176–78; leadership positions of, 175, 178, 225; political ideology of, 128; relations with Neo-Conservatives, 129, 132, 134; relations with 1943–45 military regime, 184, 212, 214; relations with Perón, 212–13, 214, 225, 227; relations with UT, 76, 102–3
General Railroad Board, 46, 88, 89, 138, 193
General strike (October 1945), 189–90, 197, 206
Germani, Gino, 3, 27, 221
Godio, Julio, 218
Gómez, Juan Vicente, 218
Gómez, Rufino, 69
González, Luis, 157, 158, 162, 191, 195, 196, 224

GOU (Grupo Obra de Unificación), 22, 23
Grafa, 119
Gratry. See Casa Gratry
Great Britain, 20, 29, 37, 40, 46, 132
Greenstone, J. David, 126
Gregorio, Candido, 208, 210
Grupo Obra de Unificación. See GOU

Harrods, 40
Hermelo, Ricardo, 128
Hitler-Stalin Pact, 99, 121, 163, 171
Horthy, Miklós, 217
Housing for workers, 34–35

Immigrants, 27, 38, 42, 44, 53, 56, 57, 70
Imports, 27–28, 29, 30
Indemnification for workers, 81
Independent Socialists, 12, 14, 16, 60, 80, 133
Industrialization, 17, 26–31, 227
Industria Sérica Argentina, 51
Inflation, 31, 57
Intendente, 44, 86
Internal migration, 3, 221
International Telephone and Telegraph. See ITT
Intervention, 11n, 18, 112, 155, 163, 181–82, 191–92, 194, 203–6, 213, 227
Interventor, 70
"Iron law of oligarchy," 153
ITT (International Telephone and Telegraph), 37, 38

Janín, Ernesto, 167
Jockey Club, 205
Job classification, system of. See *Escalafón*
Juárez Celman, Miguel, 9
Justo, Agustín P.: easing restrictions under, 68, 71, 132-34; import substitution policies of, 28–29; and reform of commercial code, 83; relations with confederations, 73–75, 186; relations with unions, 22, 83, 89, 126, 131–32, 186, 223; rise and rule of, 12–18, 20–21. See also Justo arbitration
Justo, Juan B., 10
Justo arbitration, 91–92, 112–14, 142–44, 162–63, 195

Kenworthy, Eldon, 3
Klan Radical, 11
Kogan, Rafael, 156, 192, 222

Labor laws, 35, 42, 45, 54, 69–70, 77, 81, 107, 123, 135–36, 144–46, 184–85
Largo Caballero, Francisco, 183
Lencinas, Carlos Wáshington, 11–12
Lenhardston, Emilio, 34
Lestelle, Marcos, 102
La Libanesa, 144–45
Leiserson, William M., 152
Little, Walter, 3
López, Alfredo, 198
López, Ceferino, 157
López, Pablo, 224–25, 227
López Contreras, Eleazar, 218
Luna, Telmo, 196
El lunes criolo. See Creole Monday

Maglione, Eduardo F., 69–70, 77, 93, 128–29, 145, 185
Malvestitti, Prospero, 121, 172
Manufactura Algodonera Argentina, 148–49
Marotta, José, 45, 168, 207
Marrone, Roberto, 225
Martínez Zuviría, Gustavo, 22
Mastrolorenzo, Domingo, 169
Matsushita, Hiroschi, 4, 5, 221
Medina Angarita, Isaías, 218
Melani, Antonio, 158n
Mercante, Domingo A., 196, 198, 208, 212, 213; as interventor of UF, 182, 183, 192–94
Mesa Directiva, of UF, 156, 159, 161
Michellón, Jorge, 122, 146, 172, 173, 208, 211
Michels, Robert, 153

Middle class, 10–12, 27, 36, 38, 42, 54, 80, 187–88, 200
Migrant labor, 3, 31
Migration hypothesis, 3, 221
Military regime (1943–45). *See* relations with 1943–45 military regime *under* individual labor leaders, political parties, and unions
Montiel, Alcides, 184, 190
Monzalvo, Luis, 182, 192
Municipal workers' confederation, 109, 206
Muñoz, Sauca y Salzman, 92, 145–46
Murmis, Miguel, 4, 5, 221
Muzio, Agustín, 60

Narciso Muñoz, 74, 93
Nationalism, 5, 20, 21, 22, 38, 46, 88, 128
Navarro, Marysa, 190
Navas, Miguel, 166
Neo-Conservatives: composition of, 9, 14; fraud within, 9, 15, 17–18, 21, 106; regimes of, 21–22; relations with Communists, 13, 20, 68, 71, 99, 146–50; relations with FEC, 80, 106, 134–36, 197; relations with FOET, 68, 71, 76–79, 104, 128–34; relations with Socialists, 13, 16, 20, 96, 127, 133, 140; relations with Syndicalists, 71, 75, 140, 142, 151, 226; relations with UF, 87–92, 112–16, 138–44, 149; relations with unions, 1–2, 6, 107, 125–27, 149–50, 217–19, 222; relations with UOEM, 84–86, 109, 136–37, 149; relations with UOT, 92–93, 117–20, 122–24, 144–50
Nogués, Pablo, 90

El Obrero Ferroviario, 194, 197
October 17, demonstration of, 2, 25, 188–90
Oddone, Jacinto, 179
Oeste, 18, 89, 90, 138, 158–59
Olivera, Juan N., 192
Ordóñez, Manuel V., 140

Orientación, 24n
Orozco, Modesto, 175, 176, 178, 212, 213, 214, 225
Ortiz, Roberto M.: background and rule of, 18–20, 22; and creation of FOEF, 140–41, 142, 144; relations with political parties, 140; relations with railroad industry, 66, 112, 113; relations with telephone industry, 131–32, 134; relations with unions, 99, 126, 223
Otero, Pedro, 168, 170, 204

Pacífico, 90, 142–43, 156, 158, 160
Parallel unions: vs. FOET, 175–76, 178, 213, 214–15; government stand on, 185, 188, 203, 227n; leadership of, 221; organizing for, 102, 164, 200; vs. UF and FEC, 154; vs. UOEM, 64, 109–10, 168–69, 203, 205. *See also* Asociación Obrera Textil; FOEF; FOEM; FOIT; UOT(SP); Unión Obrera Marítima
Pardo, Juan, 208
Partido Demócrata Nacional, 14, 16
Partido Demócrata Progresista. *See* Progressive Democratic Party
Partido Laborista: founding of, 190–91, 197, 223; leadership of, 193, 201, 214, 221, 225; relations with Perón, 25, 191, 226
Partido Socialista Obrero, 19, 119, 166, 172, 219
Patronage, 12, 28, 43–44, 75, 85–86, 224–26
Patrón Costas, Robustiano, 21
Pearl Harbor, 20
Pechini, Ida, 172
Pellet Lastra, Emilio, 148
Penelón, José, 86, 110
Pension board elections, 64, 85, 87, 110, 142–44, 159, 163, 165, 169
Pension plans: campaigns for, 106, 199; provisions for, 35, 38–39, 43, 48, 53. *See also* Fringe benefits
Pérez Leiros, Francisco, 43–44, 184, 198; leadership of, 168, 169–70,

204, 207, 224–25; relations with confederations, 60, 61, 102, 164; relations with municipality, 136; relations with 1943–45 military regime, 185; relations with Perón, 202, 203, 207, 215
Pérez Villar, Pedro, 169
Perón, Eva. *See* Duarte, Eva
Perón, Juan: detractors of, 186–87, 188; government labor policies under, 100, 150, 184–85, 188; relations with FEC/CGEC, 198, 201; relations with FOET, 212–15; relations with interior, 200, 201, 202, 224; relations with political parties, 23, 191, 195, 226; relations with UF, 192, 193, 194–95; relations with unions, 2–3, 23–24, 182–84, 219–20, 226, 228; rise of, 22–25, 188–89. *See also* relations with Perón *under* individual labor leaders, political parties, and unions
Personería jurídica, 57n, 66, 131, 141, 143, 151, 212
Peter, José, 99
Pilone, Jorge, 4, 5, 100, 149, 218, 221
Pinedo, Federico, 18, 28
Pipino, José, 165
Police: stance on union activity, 70–71, 96, 127, 161, 217; union and labor harassment, 57–58, 68, 76, 99, 130, 146, 148, 182
Political spoils. *See* Patronage
Polo, Plácido, 192, 193, 221, 225
Populism, 220
Pomar, Gregorio, 14
Ponce, Angel, 221, 224, 225
Portantiero, Juan Carlos, 4, 5, 221
Potash, Robert A., 16
La Prensa, 142
Primo de Rivera, Miguel, 182–83
Progressive Democratic Party, 10, 15, 16, 83, 133
Prorrateo, 88, 89, 90, 91, 93
Protti, Alejandro, 110
Puiggrós, Rodolfo, 198
Puyol, Raúl J., 192

Radicals: abstention/participation in political process, 10, 14, 17, 96, 105, 106, 109; founding and growth of, 10–14, 17–20, 21; and intra-union conflicts, 101, 115, 142, 163; relations with foreign employers, 61; relations with Perón, 23, 25, 195; relations with political parties, 4, 98, 111, 148n, 163–64; relations with unions and confederations, 56–60, 64, 109–10, 125, 128, 219
Railroad industry, 45–50, 56, 66, 88, 90–91, 112, 195
Ramírez, Pedro, 21–23, 181, 191, 192, 198, 207
Rapoport, Mario, 99
Repression: vs. labor movement, 57, 58, 64, 68–69, 133; under Neo-Conservatives, 13, 14, 20, 21, 132, 147; under 1943–45 military regime, 22, 24, 181–82, 185, 207, 210–11; under Perón, 227, 228
Rhodiaseta, 50–51, 52
Ritmo, 202
Rock, David, 58
Rodríguez, Luis M., 157, 159, 160
Ruggieri, Silvio, 82
Rumbo, Eduardo, 193
Russian Revolution, 57
Russomano, Vicente, 44

Sabattini, Amadeo, 15
Sáenz Peña, Roque, 11, 18
Salvio Morley, 93
Santiago Diz, Domingo, 192
Secretaría de Trabajo y Previsión, 23, 183–85, 187, 188, 194, 199, 208–11, 212–14
Secret ballot, 157, 206
Sector-wide organizing, 94–95, 117–20, 124
Sedalkana, 51
Semiza, Beniamino, 159
Shoemakers' union, 183, 187, 188, 227
Silvetti, Alejandro, 75

Smith, Peter H., 3, 16
Socialists: vs. Communists in UOT, 171–74; ideology of, 10, 74–75, 154–55, 173–74; leadership of, 7, 10; participation in political process, 15–16, 19–20, 74–75, 82, 106, 148, 149, 151; relations with confederations, 59–60, 61, 74–75, 101, 164–65; relations with FEC, 7, 80–82, 166, 167, 197, 200, 202; relations with FOET, 176, 178; relations with Neo-Conservatives, 13, 16, 20, 96, 127, 133, 140; relations with 1943–45 military regime, 22, 185, 187; relations with Perón, 187, 195, 207; relations with political parties, 16, 57, 68, 98–99, 111, 121, 148n, 164; relations with UF, 59, 115, 139, 140, 142, 157–58, 178, 194; relations with unions, 96, 97, 154–55, 179, 216; relations with UOEM, 7, 63–64, 84–86, 110, 168–70, 202–3, 207; relations with UOT, 8, 67, 121, 171–73; sectoral base of, 2, 7; and Socialist unions, 59–60, 68, 121, 210; split in party, 12, 19, 60; vs. Syndicalists in UF, 156–63
Social services: for municipal workers, 64, 85, 87, 153–54, 203, 205; under 1943–45 military regime and Perón, 193, 205, 206, 222, 223; for railroaders, 115–16, 153–54, 193
Sociedad Telefónica de Santa Fe, 103
Sommi Luis, 117
Soto, Florencio, 192
Spagnuolo, Amancio, 77
Spanish Civil War, 98
Standard Electric, 62
Siege, state of, 13, 15, 16, 20, 69, 71, 99
State Railroads, 46, 48, 49–50, 193, 196
Stordeur, René, 185
Strikes: by Anarchists, 69, 133; in commerce, 84; by Communists, 186, 208; general data on (1930–34 and 1935–37), 71–73, 97–98, 100; general strike (October 1945), 189–90; government and union negotiations over, 74, 100, 120, 127, 149; pre-1930, 57–58, 59, 61–62, 63–64, 65, 67; in railroads, 112, 138, 142–43, 227; in telephone industry, 77–78, 127, 129–32, 134; in textiles (1930–35), 92, 93, 95, 145; in textiles (1936–40), 117, 118–19, 120, 121–22, 146, 147; in textiles (1941 and after), 148–49, 209, 210, 227; as union challenges, 127
Substitutes (*suplentes*), 45, 205
Sud, 88, 90, 141, 158
Syndicalists: contemporary definition of, 75n; decline of, 71, 75–76, 159–60, 216; ideology of, 2, 56–57, 74; and intra-union/confederation conflicts, 74–76, 97, 101, 121, 160, 161–62; and railroad industry conflicts, 113, 140–44, 157–63, 192; relations with FOET, 7, 59, 61, 76, 132, 174, 175, 178; relations with Neo-Conservatives, 71, 75, 140, 142, 151, 226; relations with political parties, 2, 56–58, 158; relations with pre-1930 governments, 56–59, 65

Tamarin, David, 5, 221
Telephone industry, 37–39, 58, 70, 83, 102, 103, 104
Testa, Roberto, 194
Textile industry, 50–54, 70, 144–45
Textilia, 51
Tienda San Juan, 84
Torre, Lisandro de la, 10
Tragic Week (1919), 57, 62, 187
Tramonti, Antonio, 90, 139–41, 156–59, 161
Travereso, Clemente, 208
Trolley-car workers' union, 59, 76, 97, 102, 115, 182, 184

UF (Union Ferroviaria): and CGT splits, 76, 97, 100, 101, 102, 160–62, 163–65; and economic conditions in industry, 32, 46–50, 88–90, 162;

founding and growth of, 4, 7, 58–59, 60, 64–67; fraud in, 156–57, 158–59, 163, 164, 165; ideology of, 59, 87, 139, 223; internal conflicts in, 89–91, 112–15, 155–65, 191, 194, 195–96; leadership of, 59, 152, 154, 155–57, 221–22, 224, 227; membership and dues of, 59, 60, 71, 92, 116; organizational structure of, 59, 66, 153, 155–57, 159–60; relations with FOEF, 19, 140–44, 152, 162; relations with Neo-Conservatives, 7, 87–92, 112–16, 138–44, 149; relations with 1943–45 military regime, 181–82, 189, 191–97; relations with Perón, 184, 194, 196–97; relations with political parties, 113–14, 138–39, 154; relations with pre-1930 governments, 58–59, 66–67; relations with unions, 67, 83, 140, 179

Ugazio, Juan B., 169, 170, 204, 206

Unión de Empleados de Comercio, 200

Unión Ferroviaria. *See* UF

Unión Obrera Marítima, 68, 115

Unión Obrera Metalúrgica, 165, 185

Unión Obrera Textil. *See* UOT

Unión Obreros Municipales, 7n

Unión Obreros y Empleados Municipales. *See* UOEM

Union of Maritime Workers. *See* Unión Obrera Marítima

Unions: ad hoc approach of Neo-Conservatives toward, 1–2, 6, 22, 125–27, 149–50, 216–17, 228; changes in after 1944, 220–24; craft-based, 1, 59, 71, 72, 216; dues collection, 153, 188, 205, 223; growth of, 57, 67, 71, 96, 123–24; ideology of, 2, 5, 137n, 154–55, 222, 223; internal conflict in, 2, 6, 59, 99, 151–52, 154, 178; leadership of, 151–54, 178, 221–26; membership and composition of, 32, 36, 57, 96–97, 123–24, 153, 227; organizational structure of, 151–53; relations with Neo-Conservatives, 68–74, 96, 99–100; relations with 1943–45 military regime, 5, 22, 180–85, 189–90; relations with Perón, 1–3, 5–6, 23–25, 180–81, 187, 215, 228; relations with political parties, 2, 16, 60, 67, 98–99, 179, 219, 227; relations with pre-1930 governments, 56–59. *See also* individual unions and confederations; DNT

Union shops, 153n

Unión Sindical Argentina. *See* USA

Unión Telefónica del Río de la Plata. *See* UT

United States, 21, 23, 24, 29

Universities, 24

UOEM (Unión Obreros y Empleados Municipales): and CGT splits, 76, 102, 164, 165, 170, 202; founding of, 4, 7, 61, 63; leadership and organizational structure of, 168–69, 222, 227; membership and revenues of, 64, 85, 87, 111, 205, 223; relations with Neo-Conservatives, 84–86, 109, 136–37, 149; relations with 1943–45 military regime, 183, 185, 203–6; relations with Perón, 202, 206–7; relations with political parties, 63, 64, 84–86, 133, 168–69, 202; relations with pre-1930 governments, 63–64; relations with unions, 109–10, 154, 164, 179; sectoral base of, 63, 64, 224; social programs of, 64, 87, 137–38, 154, 203, 206

UOT (Unión Obrera Textil): and collective contracts, 117–18, 119; and economic conditions in industry, 50–54, 119, 121; founding of, 4, 8, 67; internal conflicts in, 67, 99, 117, 121, 171–74; leadership and organizational structure of, 170–73; membership and dues of, 67, 93–94, 118, 121, 123; relations with CGT, 101, 122, 173; relations with Neo-Conservatives, 92–93, 117–20, 122–24, 144–50; relations with 1943–45 military regime, 207–8;

relations with political parties, 8, 67, 117, 121, 133, 172, 208, 211; relations with unions, 106, 154; sector-wide organizing of, 94–95, 117–20
UOT Entre Ríos, 121n
UOT Independencia, 121n
UOT(SP): membership of, 123, 173; relations with CGT, 174, 187, 210; relations with 1943–45 military regime, 208–12; relations with Perón, 183, 187, 207; relations with political parties, 123, 187, 210; relations with Secretaría, 183, 185, 187, 209–11; split from UOT, 8n, 173
Uriburu, José F., 12–14, 28, 69, 71, 74, 84–85, 126
USA (Unión Sindical Argentina): founding and composition of, 59–60, 100–101; internal conflicts in, 101; relations with 1943–45 military regime, 183, 184, 187, 212; relations with political parties, 59; relations with unions and confederations, 61, 74, 101, 160, 178
UT (Unión Telefónica del Río de la Plata): company unions/mutual aid societies of, 62, 76, 103, 104; effects of foreign ownership, 37–38, 61, 128, 132, 217; founding and growth of, 18, 37–38; nationalization of, 225; relations with FOET, 39, 62, 76–79, 102–5, 128–31, 175–76, 213–14; relations with government, 61, 70, 77–78, 132, 213–14; relations with interior, 61–62, 103–4, 213; work force of, 38

Vacations. See Fringe benefits
La Vanguardia, 13, 22, 82, 99, 166, 206
Varela, Adolfo, 176
Verde, Francisco, 222
Villanuestre, Alejandro, 110

Wages: in commerce, 41–42, 79, 82, 108; by job category and industry, 27, 30–35, 98n; in municipal government, 32, 43, 64, 85, 109, 205; in railroads, 32, 48–50, 66, 89–92, 112, 114–15, 195; real wages, 31–32, 58; in telephone industry, 32, 38–39, 61, 78, 104–5; in textiles, 53–54, 92–93, 118–19, 120, 123, 209–10
Wast, Hugo, 22
Winn, Peter, 5
Women in work force: in commerce, 41–42, 54; Communist support of, 172; in municipal government, 43; relations with unions, 36, 76, 129; in telephone industry, 38, 62, 76, 129; in textiles, 53, 54; and union dues, 62n
Workers: composition in industries of, 38, 43, 44, 48, 50, 53; economic conditions of, 31–35; relations with political parties, 10, 12, 219; societal standing of, 1–2, 189, 227; union membership of, 60, 96–97, 123–24. See also Class structure
Working conditions. See Class structure; Conditions in work place; Fringe benefits; Housing for workers; Wages
Work to regulation, 66, 89
World War II, 19–24, 29–30, 46, 52–53, 124, 147, 173–74

Yrigoyen, Hipólito, 10–12, 28, 56–59, 61, 66, 68, 127–28

Zacarias, Julián, 209
Zugasti, Bernardo, 192

JOEL HOROWITZ is an Assistant Professor of History at Saint Bonaventure University. He has also taught at the University of California, Berkeley, Smith College, and Harvard University. He has published articles on Argentine unions and Peronism in the *Journal of Latin American Studies, Desarrollo Económico,* and *The Americas.*

INTERNATIONAL AND AREA STUDIES
University of California at Berkeley

2223 Fulton Street, 3d floor Berkeley, California 94720

Recent books published by International and Area Studies include:

RESEARCH SERIES

76. *Argentine Unions, the State & the Rise of Perón, 1930–1945.* Joel Horowitz. — $16.95

77. *The New Europe Asserts Itself: A Changing Role in International Relations.* Eds. Beverly Crawford & Peter W. Schulze. — $19.95

78. *The Soviet Sobranie of Laws: Problems of Codification and Non-Publication.* Eds. Richard Buxbaum & Kathryn Hendley. — $16.95

79. *Multilateralism in NATO: Shaping the Postwar Balance of Power, 1945–1961.* Steve Weber. — $9.50

80. *Beyond the Cold War: Conflict & Cooperation in the Third World.* Eds. George W. Breslauer, Harry Kreisler, & Benjamin Ward. — $19.95

81. *Contemporary Catalonia in Spain and Europe.* Ed. Milton M. Azevedo. — $13.50

82. *Liability for Negligence and Judicial Discretion.* 2d ed. Francesco Parisi. — $18.50

83. *The Contradictory Alliance: State-Labor Relations and Regime Change in Mexico.* Ruth Berins Collier. — $14.50

84. *The Future of European Security.* Ed. Beverly Crawford. — $23.50

85. *High Technology and Third World Industrialization: Brazilian Computer Policy in Comparative Perspective.* Eds. Peter B. Evans, Claudio R. Frischtak, & Paulo Bastos Tigre. — $14.95

86. *The New Portugal: Democracy and Europe.* Ed. Richard Herr. — $15.50

87. *Russia and Japan: An Unresolved Dilemma between Distant Neighbors.* Eds. T. Hasegawa, J. Haslam, & A. Kuchins. — $26.50

88. *Political Parties in Russia.* Ed. Alexander Dallin. — $10.95

89. *European Dilemmas after Maastricht.* Eds. Beverly Crawford & Peter W. Schulze. — $22.95

INSTITUTE OF INTERNATIONAL STUDIES
POLICY PAPERS IN INTERNATIONAL AFFAIRS

36. *The Internationalization of Japan's Security Policy: Challenges & Dilemmas for a Reluctant Power.* Michael G. L'Estrange. — $5.95

37. *Why We Need Ideologies in U.S. Foreign Policy: Democratic Politics & World Order.* Edward H. Alden & Franz Schurmann. — $8.50

38. *Vanguard Parties & Revolutionary Change in the Third World: Soviet Perspectives & Their Implications.* David E. Albright. — $9.50

International and Area Studies Publications (continued)

39. *Lessons of the Gulf War: Ascendant Technology and Declining Capability.* Gene I. Rochlin and Chris C. Demchak. — $5.50

40. *Impediments on Environmental Policy-Making and Implementation in Central and Eastern Europe: Tabula Rasa vs. Legacy of the Past.* Peter Hardi. — $6.50

41. *Flying Apart? Japanese-American Negotiations over the FSX Fighter Plane.* Gregory W. Noble. — $7.25

42. *Beware the Slippery Slope: Notes Toward the Definition of Justifiable Intervention.* Ernst B. Haas. — $6.50

INSIGHTS IN INTERNATIONAL AFFAIRS SERIES

1. *Confrontation in the Gulf: University of California Professors Talk about the War.* Ed. Harry Kreisler. — $7.95

2. *Refugees: A Multilateral Response to Humanitarian Crises.* Sadako Ogata. — $5.95

3. *American Intervention after the Cold War.* Robert W. Tucker. — $3.95

4. *Crisis in the Balkans.* Eugene A. Hammel, Irwin M. Wall, & Benjamin N. Ward. — $6.95

CENTERS FOR SOUTH & SOUTHEAST ASIA STUDIES
MONOGRAPH SERIES

32. *Scavengers, Recyclers, & Solutions for Solid Waste Management in Indonesia.* Daniel T. Sicular. — $16.50

33. *Indonesian Transmigrants and Adaptation: An Ecological Anthropological Perspective.* Oekan S. Abdoellah. — $14.95

OCCASIONAL PAPERS SERIES

15. *The Penis Inserts of Southeast Asia: An Annotated Bibliography with an Overview & Comparative Perspective.* Donald E. Brown, J. W. Edwards, & R. P. Moore. — $6.00

16. *Patterns of Migration in Southeast Asia.* Ed. Robert R. Reed. — $19.50

17. *Bridging Worlds: Studies on Women in South Asia.* Ed. Sally J. M. Sutherland. — $17.50

18. *Essays on Southeast Asian Performing Arts: Local Manifestations and Cross-Cultural Implications.* Ed. Kathy Foley. — $14.95

LANGUAGE TEACHING MATERIALS

Devavanipravesika: Introduction to the Sanskrit Language. Robert P. Goldman & Sally J. Sutherland. — $23.50

Teaching Grammar of Thai. William Kuo. — $23.50

Tamil for Beginners, 2 vols. Kausalya Hart. — $12.50 ea.